QUESTIONS FOR THE TWENTY-FIRST CENTURY CHURCH

Russell E.
Richey
William B.
Lawrence
Dennis M.
Campbell

Editors

Abingdon Press
Nashville

UNITED METHODISM AND AMERICAN CULTURE, VOLUME 4
QUESTIONS FOR THE TWENTY-FIRST CENTURY CHURCH

Copyright © 1999 by Abingdon Press

This book is printed on acid-free, recycled paper.

**Library of Congress
Cataloging-in-Publication Data**

Questions for the twenty-first century church / Russell E. Richey, William B. Lawrence, Dennis M. Campbell, editors.
    p. cm. — (United Methodism and American culture) ; vol. 4)
    Includes bibliographical references.
    ISBN 0-687-02146-4 (alk. paper)
    1. United Methodist Church (U.S.)—Forecasting. 2. Twenty-first century—Forecasts. I. Richey, Russell E. II. Lawrence, William Benjamin. III. Campbell, Dennis M., 1945- . IV. Series.
BX8331.2.Q47 1999
287'.6' 0112—dc21   99-17834
                                                                CIP

99 00 01 02 03 04 05 06 07 08 — 10 9 8 7 6 5 4 3 2 1
MANUFACTURED IN THE UNITED STATES OF AMERICA

Contents

PART TWO: What Will United Methodism Need and Expect from Its Leaders?

PART THREE: How Will United Methodism Express Its Connectional Nature?

Preface

United Methodism and American Culture

This volume is one of a series of publications deriving from research, consultations, and conferences undertaken under a major grant from the Lilly Endowment, Inc. This five-year study has been based at the Divinity School of Duke University and directed by Dennis M. Campbell and Russell E. Richey. William B. Lawrence served as Project Associate, and counsel was provided by an Advisory Board composed of Jackson W. Carroll, Director of the Ormond Center, Duke University; Rosemary Skinner Keller, Dean of Union Theological Seminary, New York; Donald G. Mathews, Professor of History, University of North Carolina, Chapel Hill; Cornish R. Rogers, Professor of Pastoral Theology, Claremont School of Theology; and Judith Smith, formerly Associate General Secretary, Office of Interpretation, General Board of Higher Education and Ministry, The United Methodist Church, and now at the United Methodist Publishing House.

The project began under a planning grant that made it possible for the principals to engage in exploratory conversations with a wide array of church members, including board and agency leaders, bishops and district superintendents, clergy and laity, United Methodist faculty, and researchers in other Lilly-sponsored studies. From the counsel received through such exploratory discussions, the project came to pursue three primary objectives:

1. to provide a careful fresh estimate of the history of Methodism in America, with particular attention to its twentieth-century experience;

2. to attempt a portrait of United Methodism at the dawning of a new century; and

3. to explore policy issues, with a view to the church's effective participation in American society and the world in the future.

We pursued those objectives through a variety of means: sponsored research; dialogue with the several internal commissions, committees, and projects studying United Methodism during the 1992–96 quadrennium; and a series of conferences and consultations. In the latter process, approximately seventy-five church leaders, scholars, and researchers participated, each working on a specific aspect, theme, or issue from the comprehensive task.

From their efforts derived three volumes of essays. The first, *Connectionalism: Ecclesiology, Mission, and Identity,* was published in 1997. A second, titled *The People(s) Called Methodist: Forms and Reforms of Their Life,* was published in 1998. Finally, in 1999 *Doctrine and Discipline* will complete the set. These volumes thematically touched on all three of our objectives for the "United Methodism and American Culture" project but focused on the first two.

The third objective is addressed in this policy-oriented volume. It attempts, as the title implies, to pose and address questions facing the church at the dawn of the new century. Policy concerns ran through our conferences and gave rise to a series of *Leadership Letters.* And those in turn gave rise to this volume, an effort augmented by other invited submissions.

Much of the research undertaken as part of this project, we regret, could not be accommodated in these few volumes. Among these results of our work are many pieces that have appeared or will appear in the future in *Quarterly Review, Circuit Rider, Methodist History,* and other media.

From the start of this project, Abingdon committed itself to be the "publisher of record" and to make the results appropriately accessible to United Methodism. As part of that commitment and this project, Abingdon has already published *The Methodist Conference in America* (Richey) and will publish a two-volume collaborative effort (also involving Richey), *The Methodist Experience in America,* one volume of which will be narrative, the other a historical source book. These two volumes and perhaps others are currently slated to appear also in CD-ROM form.

The project will culminate in three synthetic "statements." One of these, like this volume, will address the church's leadership and be most appropriate for clergy and clergy-to-be. A second will be aimed at the adult laity of the denomination. A third, projected in the future, will be in video form and be usable in even a wider set of contexts.

Through these 'publishing' efforts we seek to open conversations about the future of our church and its role locally and globally in the decades and century ahead.

Permissions and Acknowledgments

The essays by Russell Richey, "Is Division a New Threat to the Denomination?" and William Lawrence, "Has Our Theology of Ordained Ministry Changed?" appeared in the Spring 1998 issue of *Quarterly Review,* and that by Dennis Campbell, "Does Methodism Have a Future in American Culture?" in the Spring 1995 issue. All originally bore different titles. They are reprinted here with permission. The essay by Thomas Frank, "What Is the Common Discipline for Local Churches?" drafted for this volume, appeared in *Circuit Rider,* with acknowledgment to this volume.

The editors express appreciation to the staff of Duke University's Ormond Center, John B. James Jr. and Marieta Louise Luna, for their hard work on this collection.

Introduction

Russell E. Richey

This volume of policy essays, not a part of our original publication plan, emerged as a priority in our "United Methodism and American Culture" project only as the sponsored conferences concluded and papers were being submitted. It dawned on the principals in the study:

- that policy questions had been pushed to the fore in most, if not all, of our conference sessions;
- that, however, only a few of our authors had shaped their essays around current issues and policy concerns;
- that much of our commissioned writing, in fact, took longer-range and less pointed views; and
- that we had made no special place in our project publications for policy-oriented research.

To accommodate such policy concerns, we began a series of what we termed *Leadership Letters*. These were short, focused statements on matters that were troubling the United Methodist Church or, in our judgment, should have been. Issued, as their title implies, in letter format and published here at Duke, they were distributed widely from the Ormond Center, our research facility. These seven short essays, typically 3,500 words or so, elicited very interesting responses, not all positive but often intense. The first letter was entitled, "Is There a Better Way to Elect Bishops?" The last, "What Difference Do the Site, Size, and Style of the Annual Conference Make?" Both aroused some ire. The first did so by challenging the politicking, block voting, and conference endorsements that now characterize episcopal elections and by calling explicitly for abolition of jurisdictions. The second occasioned interesting reactions in conferences entertaining the possibility of merger by its questioning of the premises behind such plans, by commenting on the bloating of conferences into aggregations so large as to become crowds rather than communities, by noting the relatively recent character of such growth, and by drawing attention to the quality and style of the annual meeting.

The first *Letter* appeared early in 1995. By the time the last was published in late 1995, we realized that these essays were proving to be among the most engaging results of our overall venture. They had touched, however, scarcely a fraction of the policy questions facing the

1

church. They deserved, we thought, to be supplemented with kindred statements and to be given more widespread circulation. So we proposed to the United Methodist Publishing House to include a volume of essays on policy questions in our publication series. The House accepted our proposal, and the result is the present volume. It includes some of our *Leadership Letters,* now augmented with many other offerings elicited from persons who we thought could put policy issues in provocative fashion before the church. Thus, William Quick, longtime pastor of urban churches, in Durham and then in Detroit, ponders the church's commitment to the city. Roy Sano challenges Methodism to do its theology and to reflect even on the mystery of the Trinity mindful of the particularities of the human condition and the great drama of salvation. Thomas Frank asks whether the church is willing to live by discipline as well as *The Discipline.* Janice Love poses some tough questions about United Methodism's global pretensions. And William B. McClain asks about the church's directions in preaching. The views, in every case, are those of the author and are typically constructively critical. They all serve the volume's purpose, which is to help the church think into its future.

Each essay carries a question as title. Not all authors wrote knowing that their statement would be so prefaced. And the essays tend to be far richer than mere replies to the questions posed. For instance, S T Kimbrough's essay does indeed explore the place of music in our church but frames that exploration in relation to very fundamental questions about mission, cultural sensitivities, and the media of our message. So also Thomas Boomershine puts issues about electronic media in long-term strategic and missional perspective. Garlinda Burton generalizes that same concern to leadership at all levels and calls for the church as a whole to become media savvy. And Kenneth Rowe explores the place of caucuses in our life not as a post-1968 issue but as a long-term expression of diversity and group solidarity.

The question-titles do indicate one of each essay's central emphases and invite the reader to think with us about matters that are complex and perplexing. The statement by Daniel Bell on homosexuality was crafted and submitted long before the Jimmy Creech case forced that issue into such prominence. Inviting us all into some rethinking, Bell probes scriptural and theological traditions on marriage. Similarly, Priscilla Pope-Levison beckons us beyond the contraries of evangelism and social action toward an evangelism that is both holistic and liberationist. And Thomas Langford indicates how our theologizing, driven initially by evangelistic and apologetic interests, has occupied a distinctive niche in the larger Christian tradition, particularly in its philosophizing between gospel and culture.

Recognizing that on such important issues United Methodists will have various opinions, we have not framed these statements in petition format for submission to General Conference or in proto-legislative form for ready decision-making. Our literature is replete with answers, with nostrums, with supposedly simple solutions to complex problems. In our judgment, the church badly needs policy-oriented research that identifies the issues but refrains from superficialities and too easy resolutions. So we offer Sarah Kreutziger's reflections on how lay leadership might look if it reclaimed the resources and integrity of earlier "moral community," specifically that of the deaconess and religious settlement movement. Judith Smith shares visions for the episcopacy drawn from conversations with the bishops. Vision, understanding, and leadership are also needed and *deserved*, Jackson Carroll maintains, in the rural and small-membership church. In several essays, William Lawrence probes recent changes in the ministry as a whole—its social profile, its reward system, and its new, post-1996 configurations. Another set of essays, both within and without the section so entitled, concern Methodism's connectional fabric and its well being. Vivian Bull's statement does so, focusing particularly on finances. Mine do so, examining connectionalism and division, special appointments, corporate structure as a local as well as national phenomenon, and the challenges of localism.

We hope that this offering of policy essays encourages more reflections of the same kind. Certainly we will endeavor through the Ormond Center and with vehicles akin to the *Leadership Letters* to continue such policy-oriented research and communication. We also intend to revisit the questions here posed in our synthetic volume, tentatively entitled *Marks of Methodism: Connection, Theology, and Practice.*

That latter volume will have, as its subtitle indicates, a tripartite theme. We have gathered the essays from our conferences into three volumes around the same broad themes, one entitled *Connectionalism,* another *Doctrines and Discipline,* and a third, though not so explicitly titled, dealt in fact with practice (*The People[s] Called Methodist: Forms and Reforms of their Life*). In these efforts, we have tried to give attention to what we take to be three essential emphases of the Wesleyan movement:

- our practice (or praxis) and mission—what we might have embraced under "piety" in an earlier day;

- our doctrine or theology—including the leadership and media through which it has found "voice"; and
- our connectionalism—including particularly our conference nature.

To this volume we have given the same tripartite structure. Each of these three areas, we know, comprises important issues that we have not covered. The slight (if that is the right term) has occurred for various reasons: because the matter has been dealt with in one of our other volumes, because we intend to treat the concern in our synthetic statement, because persons to whom we turned proved unable to meet our deadline, and because not everything needing attention could be encompassed in one volume. We do not pretend, then, to cover all topics important to the church, but we do intend to offer by this question format a deliberative pattern that we hope will have wider appeal and attract imitations. The approach, we trust, will provoke a wider discussion of the relationship between research and the policies of the church.

On the matters to which we do give attention, we hope to stimulate further research. Each of the essayists brings expertise to the matter at hand—historical, sociological, theological, pastoral—but has been encouraged to keep documentation to a minimum. The essays do not settle the question. Indeed, they do not intend to. Rather, they invite reflection and further research. Hence the title of the overall volume.

Such probing and questioning are by no means new. On topics of concern to the church *Circuit Rider* frequently offers debates or brief exchanges. Letters to the editor, of *CR* or our *Advocates*, pursue the issues raised. And the wholesale decline of "mainline" or "oldline" Protestantism has prompted a spate of books and articles asking what has gone wrong. For the United Methodist versions of these jeremiads one has only to turn to the latest Cokesbury or Abingdon catalog.

Declensions have prompted such introspection, self-criticism, and futuring before. In 1850 Nathan Bangs, for instance, pondered *The Present State, Prospects, and Responsibilities of the Methodist Episcopal Church*.[1] Was his inquiry occasioned by the 1843 or 1844 divisions of episcopal Methodism (the exit of the Wesleyan Methodists or the North–South division)? Not really. Prompting his agonizing were three successive years of membership losses, 31,763 in 1845, 12,343 in 1846, and 12,741 in 1847.[2] More buoyant moods also have elicited such futuring. Our celebrations and centenaries typically elicit statements about the present, past, and future of the church. That of 1884, for instance, produced a great conclave in Baltimore, December 7–17, during which those gathered heard speech after speech on Methodist prospects and challenges.[3] Many of the roughly seventy speeches were

gathered for publication purposes under four thematic heads—Missions, Education, Sunday-Schools, and the Mission of Methodism to the Extremes of Society. In the smallest of these sections, that on Education, seven of the church's academic leaders addressed policy in "educational work." Similarly, leaders in missions explored "Hopeful Signs for Missions," spoke of "Adaptation of the Itinerancy to Missionary Work," or asked "Are Foreign Missions Successful?" The gathering heard other policy statements that did not fit so neatly under the four themes:
"Causes of the Success of Methodism"
"Possible Dangers to Future Methodism"
"Is Methodism Losing its Power over the Masses?"
"The Aim and Character of Methodist Preaching"
"The Doctrinal Unity of Methodism"
"Guards to the Purity of our Teaching"
"The Value of the Press to Methodism"
"The Place and Power of the Lay Element in Methodism"
"What Methodism Owes to Women"
    And through the years such policy-oriented statements have flowed—coming as Episcopal Addresses to or commission recommendations for General Conference; as books from Abingdon Press; as essays in *Quarterly Review;* within theme issues of *Circuit Rider;* as the substance of newsletters, sermons, and letters to the editor; in resolutions at conferences or caucus events; and as study books for United Methodist Women. In speeches, essays, resolutions, addresses, and books we continue to reflect on ourselves and our mission.
    This volume, then, is not what Francis Asbury accused William McKendree of committing when the latter delivered the first episcopal address, namely "a new thing." It is rather a tried and true "thing" to which Methodists have resorted when they thought the whole needed to be looked at afresh.

PART ONE
Where Will United Methodism Find Renewal and Fulfill Its Mission?

Does Methodism Have a Future in American Culture?

Dennis M. Campbell

In order to answer the question that forms the title of this chapter, I first present a brief overview of the historic situation of Methodism in American culture. Then I describe the changing conditions in American society, and especially the changing conditions for mainline Protestantism. I offer a picture of the contemporary shape of religion in the United States, so that the reality in which Methodism finds itself can be understood. Finally, I set forth my own prognosis for Methodism, and the United Methodist Church, in particular, in the United States.

I. An Historical Overview of Methodism and American Culture

Methodism has been a dominant cultural reality in the United States throughout much of the history of the nation. Although Methodism was present before the Revolutionary War, the real strength of Methodism becomes evident in the period after the establishment of the new nation. The development of American Methodism and the development of the new nation coincide. In fact it can be argued that American culture and American Methodism so interrelate that it is difficult to separate them.

Christopher Dawson once observed: "every great civilization that exists in the world today has a great religious tradition associated with it, and it is impossible to understand the culture unless we understand the religion that lies behind it."[1] What we have come to call "mainline Protestantism" is that religious tradition for American culture. Methodism is one major component of that tradition and has been particularly influential in the shaping of American culture. American Methodism and American culture have been inseparably intertwined since their beginnings.

A. Early American Methodism (1784–1816)

Methodism was present in America prior to 1784. Early Methodists from England had developed societies in New York, Philadelphia,

Baltimore, and numerous other cities and towns. The coming of Francis Asbury enhanced the growth of Methodism. But for the purposes of this article, I begin at the Christmas Conference of 1784. The Christmas Conference is important to any understanding of Methodism and American culture because it established several key matters. The conference chose a name for the new church, set a method for selecting leadership, established structure for governance and mission, provided ordained ministers and superintendents for the church, and began a pattern of relationship to American culture.

In England, Wesley had insisted that Methodism was a reform movement within the established Church of England. Whatever we make of his actions, he claimed that he himself and his Methodist movement never broke from the Church of England. He believed that the Church of England, despite its shortcomings, was properly established, and was the best institutional expression of Christianity. He saw his role, and that of his Methodist societies, as seeking renewal of vital holiness within the church.

In America, however, Anglican establishments were a casualty of the revolutionary spirit; much of Anglican leadership left, and the church's survival was in question. Therefore Wesley was free to organize Methodism in America as he saw fit. He sent specific guidelines contained within the *Sunday Service* book with Thomas Coke. In addition to patterns of worship for Sunday, for sacramental services, and for ordinations, the *Sunday Service* set forth a plan of ministry that functioned as a structure for the new church. The plan of ordained ministry included superintendents, elders, and deacons. It can be argued that, although he used the term "superintendent," Wesley envisioned Methodism becoming a church with an episcopal structure, and playing a role in the new American nation somewhat comparable to that of the Church of England in Wesley's native land. I do not mean that Wesley expected Methodism to become an established church, but I do think that the way he thought about church and society was so determined by his own societal setting that he imagined Methodism as a church contributing to the new nation and shaping its cultural values.

The choice of the name of the church is significant. We know from recollections of the Christmas Conference and from the *Discipline* that it created that the delegates understood the shape of the church Wesley proposed in the *Sunday Service* to be episcopal. Although he used the term "superintendent," in reality he was describing an "episcopal" office. The Conference decided, therefore, to name the church The Methodist Episcopal Church. Each word is significant. This was to be a "Methodist" church; it was to take its shape from Wesley and the

Methodist movement in England and America. It was to be an "episcopal" church; the structure proposed by Wesley was clearly episcopal, and thus Methodism would be different from congregational or presbyterian churches. It was to be a "church." I emphasize this because one could imagine early American Methodists choosing to retain the Wesleyan self-understanding and to conceive themselves as a "society" in opposition to a "church." In fact, for years they retained images and language appropriate to an informal religious community. By the choice of the name, however, they also declared themselves a "church," indicating that they were going to play the role of a church in the new nation.

American Methodism was a "new creation." The creation of the Methodist Episcopal Church in December of 1784 signaled the beginning of a Methodism distinct from that of its English predecessor. It was a "church," not a society or movement within a larger church. It was a church with indigenous leadership. Although Wesley specified roles for Coke and Asbury, Asbury's insistence on being elected to the office of superintendent evidenced sensitivity to the American mind, and it signaled that Methodism in America could not, and would not, take its directions from Wesley or any leader in the mother country. The relationship between Methodism and American culture was to be fundamentally different from that characteristic of Methodism and culture in England.

Francis Asbury's episcopacy set a pattern and a standard for the mission and ministry of Methodism in America. The pattern was not one of ecclesial democracy; but it was characterized by aggressive evangelistic endeavor attentive to the unique reality of American development and American mentality. Asbury adapted to the American context and recognized that a traveling ministry was best suited to the frontier. He was willing to adjust church life to the realities of the difficult conditions in the expanding nation. The itinerant ministry, the Wesleyan theology of grace and freedom, the conviction that the believer was responsible for participating in shaping his or her salvation, and the specific populist approach to the common person combined to give Methodism special appeal. Methodism was popular because it met the needs of men and women where they were, and it had the itinerant ministry to reach them. American democratic individualism and Methodist teachings tended to be mutually reinforcing. Methodism enthusiastically embraced its context, even as it sought to make it Christian. Its commitment to "spread scriptural holiness across the land" represented both a critique and an embrace of the society.[2]

B. The Early Period Until the Civil War (1816–1862)

I have chosen 1816 as the beginning of another period of American Methodism because it is the year of Bishop Asbury's death. The leadership of Methodism was now no longer in the hands of men born in England, but of native-born Americans. In the period between 1816 and the Civil War, certain patterns were set that became determinative for the Methodist Episcopal Church. The major point is that the church elected to be inclusive and culture affirming. Two key examples are the reactions to slavery and to the Civil War.

At first, following the leadership of John Wesley himself, Methodism in America was absolutely opposed to slavery. Wesley's famous "Thoughts Upon Slavery" was written in 1784. Asbury indicated his opposition to slavery, and the Christmas Conference specifically forbade it. The *Discipline* of the church was clear. In regard to slavery, Methodists were admonished to recognize ". . . a most bounden duty to . . . extirpate this abomination from among us." By 1808, however, the General Conference authorized the printing of copies of the *Discipline* for South Carolina leaving out reference to slavery. Similar action followed for Georgia and North Carolina. General Conference action in 1816 represented a change of approach. The evil of slavery appeared to be past remedy. Emphasis changed from opposition to attention to the church's mission to the slaves. There followed aggressive evangelization among Blacks, both slave and free. The priority of evangelism necessitated access that required accepting terms set by slave holders.

Methodism grew very rapidly in the early years of the nineteenth century. It was a popular religion embracing large numbers of persons in widely diverse circumstances. The church elected not to be sectarian but to work to figure out ways of including the greatest number of persons as Methodists. There was a definite accommodation to prevailing norms of American society. Methodism did not set itself against the culture but sought to reform from within.

Later, in the social crisis occasioned by slavery, some Methodists insisted on an absolutist position in opposition, some insisted on an absolutist position in favor, and some sought a middle ground. The various positions reflected reactions in the general society. Almost regardless of the section of the country, Methodism and American culture were difficult to distinguish. The church split before the nation divided, and both the Northern church (the Methodist Episcopal Church) and the Southern church (the Methodist Episcopal Church, South) became major advocates of their respective sides in the Civil War. Bishop Matthew Simpson, unofficial chaplain to President

Abraham Lincoln, would talk about "the providence of God as seen in our war."

C. Triumphal Methodism: Post–Civil War to 1924

In the years following the Civil War, American Methodism was increasingly culture affirming. In both the North and the South, Methodism sought to transform and *control* American society. There was tremendous growth in numbers, and significant upward mobility in terms of education, economic strength, and societal influence. Methodists built large and impressive church buildings in the major centers of cities. They wanted their denomination to be represented in the avenues of power, because Methodist laymen increasingly played that role themselves.

There was a particular boom in building at the time of the centennial of American Methodism in 1884. Along with large and impressive "centenary church" buildings came a formalization of worship, the introduction of organs and choirs, longer pastorates, and a more "settled" clergy. Methodist upward mobility included growing wealth, which allowed for the development of church institutions in addition to enhanced facilities for local congregations. These institutions included colleges and universities, schools for ministerial training, orphanages, and hospitals.

The latter part of the nineteenth century and the beginning of the twentieth century may be the key to understanding the struggle in which American Methodism is engaged today. It was in this period that Methodist identity with American culture became fully manifest. Earlier foundations now allowed for the development of significant institutionalization. It is not incorrect to say that the "average" American was a Methodist. In his book *Religion and American Culture,* George Marsden observes, "Methodism during this period was America's largest and most typical Protestant denomination. From 1865 to 1920 the Methodist Episcopal Church (Northern) grew from one million to four million, and its Southern Methodist counterpart grew from half a million to two million."[3] Frederick Norwood calls Methodism the "unofficial national church." "Theodore Roosevelt remarked that he 'would rather address a Methodist audience than any other audience in America,' for 'the Methodists represent the great middle class and in consequence are the most representative church in America.'" In their Episcopal Address to the Methodist Episcopal Church General Conference of 1900, the bishops stated that from 1800 to 1900 the ratio of Methodists to the general population went from one in fourteen to one in five. Membership went from 61,000 to more than 6 million. Everything looked very good. The Methodists were experiencing unbridled growth in ministry, new churches and church properties were being built, church literature was available and widely used, benevolences were booming, mission fields expanding, and philanthropies at an all-time high.

One year later, in a statement to the Third Oecumenical Methodist Conference (forerunner of the World Methodist Council), John F. Goucher reported on American Methodism: "About one-third of all the people in the United States look to Methodism for their religious instruction and Christian ministries." He went on: "While Methodism is in no sense a political organization, its numerical strength and the vital character of its teachings, quickening the perceptions and conscience of its members, purifying morals, diffusing education, determining ideals, and developing character, have made it the most constructive force in our great Republic. The Chief Executive, President McKinley, is a communicant in the Methodist Church; so are many United States Senators and Representatives, the governors of a number of states, and in some states a majority of both houses of Assembly. America and Methodism are two developing world powers so interrelated that to discuss either philosophically requires a discussion of the other." Goucher's virtual equation of Methodism with the national interests of America characterized a great deal of thinking about Methodism and the state.

An overwhelming confidence and optimism characterized the church and its leadership at the turn of the twentieth century. The sociologist E. Digby Baltzell comments, "The new century opened on a note of Anglo-Saxon confidence if not arrogance."[4] The United States was still dominantly Protestant and controlled by persons of European, and especially Northern European, descent. Winthrop Hudson writes, "In 1900 few would have disputed the contention that the United States was a Protestant nation. "[5]

A key example of the way in which Methodism sought to relate to the nation is the movement for the statutory prohibition of beverage alcohol. Methodists were the leaders of the effort to enact laws to prohibit the manufacture and sale of alcohol in the United States. Frances Willard, of the Women's Christian Temperance Union, was a leading Northern Methodist. Bishop James Cannon, a Southern bishop, devoted almost his full time to the political movement that tried to capture the state legislatures so that they would have the votes to ratify a constitutional amendment. The Volstead Act, the Eighteenth Amendment to the Constitution of the United States, was ratified in 1919. That political act, which sought to impose the moral convictions of

Methodists and other mainline Protestants on the general society, suggests the power of the churches and their supposition that they could, and should, control the culture. It is worth pondering the self conception of Methodism that is reflected in these exertions of authority and efforts at social control.

D. Post-1924 to the Present

Historians of Christianity in the United States have observed a "second disestablishment" of Protestant Christian America after 1924. The first disestablishment refers to the rejection of established churches in colonial America at the time of the affirmation of the Constitution, and in the early years of the new nation. The first disestablishment was intended to introduce genuine diversity of religious expression and equality among the several denominations. The dominant religious community, however, was Protestant, and it can be argued that the United States was, in practice, a Protestant nation. The second disestablishment refers to the gradual erosion of Protestant hegemony. This was the result of the infusion of significant numbers of persons who were not Protestants, especially Roman Catholics and Jews from Eastern Europe, and the broadening of older conceptions of what it meant to be an American. While at one time there was a tacit assumption that being an American included being a Protestant, by the 1950s Will Herberg could write a book suggesting that to be an American was to be a Protestant, Catholic, or Jew. In subsequent years even that assumption has had to be broadened to include Muslims, Buddhists, and others, including secularists.

This brief historical overview is not intended to tell the full story of American Methodism. It is intended to suggest that the relationship between Methodism and American culture has been dynamic. In the earliest period, Methodism was marginal, and set over against the dominant and elite culture. Gradually, as the result of extraordinarily rapid growth, and because of related upward mobility, Methodists achieved dramatic social, economic, educational, and even political power. By the end of the nineteenth century, Methodism was a major component of the unofficial Protestant establishment. Methodism and American culture were intertwined. The twentieth century has seen a course reversal. While everything looked wonderful one hundred years ago, some argue that in the course of the twentieth century Methodism has moved, along with other major Protestant bodies, from the mainline to the side line.

II. Changing Conditions for Mainline Protestantism

A great deal has been written in recent years about mainline Protestantism in the United States in the last half of the twentieth century. One can think of such works as William Hutchison's *The Travail of Mainline Protestantism*, Robert Wuthnow's *The Restructuring of American Religion*, William McKinney and Wade Clark Roof's *American Mainline Religion*, Jackson Carroll and Wade Clark Roof's *Beyond Establishment*, James D. Hunter's *Culture Wars*, and the multivolume collection of materials about Presbyterians in America by John M. Mulder, Louis B. Weeks, and Milton J. Coalter.

All of these works document a similar story. Mainline Protestantism is no longer dominant. It has lost cultural power. There has been a significant drop in membership. Its social influence has been eroded. The denominations, especially the national bureaucratic manifestations of the denominations, are experiencing significant financial problems. There is great conflict about theological teaching and doctrine, including debates about biblical authority and interpretation. Wrenching debates about homosexuality, and the recent uproar about the Re-Imagining Conference in Minneapolis, are evidence of the divided character of churches in America, including the United Methodist Church.

Mainline Protestantism is facing difficult readjustments, and there are numerous proposals about what to do. The main point to be made here is that Protestantism in America is confronted by a new awareness of its place in culture as the twentieth century comes to an end. It can no longer think of itself as the only, or even the major, expression of Christianity or of religion in America.

We need to remember, of course, that the loss of "establishment" is not unique to mainline, or liberal, Protestantism in the United States. We are part of a much larger reality across the world. Paul Johnson observes: "During the past half-century there has been a rapid and uninterrupted secularization of the West, which has all but demolished the Augustinian idea of Christianity as a powerful, physical and institutional presence in the world. Of Augustine's city of God on earth, little now remains, except crumbling walls and fallen towers, effete establishments and patriarchies of antiquarian rather than intrinsic interest. But of course Christianity does not depend on a single matrix: hence its durability. The Augustinian idea of public all-embracing Christianity, once so compelling, has served its purpose and retreats—perhaps, one day, to reemerge in different forms."[6]

This larger picture of Christianity throughout the world helps to put the situation of mainline Protestantism into perspective. At the same time, it is important to understand the contemporary realities, and realistic prospects, for Protestantism in the United States.

III. The Contemporary Shape of Religion in the United States

It is useful to consider the shape of religion in the contemporary United States in order to have a sense of the differences between Europe and North America, and it will allow me a context in which to offer some suggestions about the possible future of the United Methodist Church in the U.S., and in the global community.

Let us look first at what statistics show about religious preference. A major recent study commissioned by the Graduate School of the City University of New York suggests that the nation is broadly religious and widely diverse. The great majority of Americans say they are Christians. Six in ten (60.2 percent) are Protestant, and a quarter (26.2 percent) are Roman Catholic. Seven and a half percent indicated no religion, 3.7 percent indicated faiths other than Christian, and 2.3 percent declined to answer. Roman Catholics are now the largest single church group in America. Then come Baptists, Methodists, and Lutherans.

About one in five Americans is a Baptist. One person in ten is a Methodist, compared to 14 percent in 1967. Methodists are represented throughout all regions of the country, with particular strength in the Midwest, Southeast, and South Central regions. Lutherans represent about 5 percent of the population, Presbyterians 4, and Episcopalians 2. Other Protestants are divided into hundreds of smaller church groupings. Surveys show that while Protestantism still claims a majority of Americans, their numbers are declining, and they are becoming increasingly fragmented.

Adherents to living world religions other than Christianity make up a small percentage of the population. Judaism, with 1.8 percent, which equates to 4.3 million people, is the largest non-Christian group. Some estimates put the number of Jews higher, but not above 5.5 million. The difference may be attributable to those who claim religious identity of Judaism and those who claim no religious identity but are identified culturally as Jews. Muslims represent .5 percent, which is 1.4 million people. Of those who identify themselves as Muslims, 40 percent are black. Of the total black population, however, less than two percent is Muslim. There are approximately one million Buddhists, under .5 percent, and half a million Hindus. Significantly, the survey found that most Asian Americans and most Arab Americans are Christian rather than Buddhist, Hindu, or Muslim. The reason for this seems to be that

Christians from Arab and Asian countries are more likely to move to the United States than are non-Christians from those same countries.

Recent studies of religion in America suggest several observable patterns. The most obvious is that Americans remain religious. The growth of Roman Catholicism in the United States is dramatic. Protestantism remains numerically strong, but the percentage of the population that claims to be Protestant is declining. Membership in the old mainline Protestant churches has declined significantly.

The population of the United States is more diverse. White Protestants make up less of the community, African Americans represent about 10 percent of the population, and the Asian-American and Hispanic populations are growing. There is a great deal of talk now about multiculturalism. What exactly does it mean to say that the U.S. is a multicultural nation? Statistics demonstrate that religiously Americans are overwhelmingly Christian. Muslims and Buddhists in fact represent a very small minority, less than .5 percent each. Multiculturalism therefore appears to suggest increasing diversity of countries of origin, of language, and of cultural patterns. A nation once dominated by white, European, Protestant culture is now experiencing extraordinary diversity. But it is important to note that, thus far, this diversity has remained largely within Christianity. Challenges to the churches are great, but these challenges are not primarily in relation to other living world religions. Rather, they are in relation to changing patterns within Christianity.

I do not mean to suggest that Christians in the United States are not faced with issues concerning the other living world religions. We are faced with these issues as we encounter the reality of Islam and Asian religions in the world, and, to a certain extent, in our major cities. We do not know enough about other religions, and we do not know how to think in a sophisticated way about the relationship of Christianity to other religions. But the average American is not encountering a significant presence of persons from other faiths within the United States, at least not yet.

Perhaps the challenging reality for Christianity in America today is not other faith traditions but a growing societal conviction that any religion is tolerable as long as it remains personal and individual and does not make claims on the general social order. While at one time Christianity played a public role in shaping moral values and societal norms, today that role is limited as the result of court cases, legislation, and cultural attitudes. Stephen J. Carter, a professor of law at Yale University, has recently argued in his book *The Culture of Disbelief* that the press, the educational establishment, the government, the courts, and the entertainment media are fostering a negative attitude toward all religion. This may represent the greatest challenge to Christianity, and to other religions as well, in America today. The history of the United States demonstrates that religion has always been a vital, culture-shaping reality. This has been so because it has played a significant role in social institutions and the general society. Currently this continues to be the case. Professor Barry Kosmin writes, "Religion is more important in America than in most industrialized countries. Americans display a greater level of commitment and a greater level of diversity."[7] If claims about growing multiculturalism relegate religion to a purely personal and individual role, then its significance will be diminished. Dramatic changes are now occurring within all expressions of Christianity in America and perhaps especially among mainline Protestants, as the studies cited demonstrate.

IV. The Residual Establishment: The Future of the United Methodist Church

What is to be made of the prospects and realities for the United Methodist Church into the future? We are clearly among the mainline Protestant churches that are experiencing significant change. As our historical overview showed, Methodism was a dominant force in the United States and thought of itself as such. Some Methodists still have not adjusted to new realities, and actions at General Conference seeking to tell the nation what to do participate in old images about the church and its cultural significance. If it could be argued that in the latter part of the nineteenth century and at the turn of the twentieth century Methodism played a dominant cultural role in American society, it can now be argued that Methodism, like all of the once-powerful Protestant denominations, is becoming increasingly marginal. I think such a conclusion both premature and inaccurate. Methodism's enduring strengths are considerable. Perhaps a useful concept to employ is that of a "residual establishment." Images and under-standings of prior strength are no longer workable, but neither is it the case that the United Methodist Church is insignificant. We are a residual establishment in that many of the institutional realities remain. One need only think of hundreds of thousands of congregations, hundreds of colleges and universities, thirteen theological schools, numerous homes for children and for the aged, many hospitals, buildings, boards and agencies, programs, publishing interests, and pension funds. I could mention other examples, including billions of dollars in various endowments to support the varied work of the church and its mission. The United Methodist Church has enormous resources that are both opportunities and problems. On the one hand, there is undeniable evidence of membership decline and of diminished social and cultural influence. On the other, there is continuing vitality in congregations and institutions. These strengths counter the thesis of decline. The real problem is how we are going to think about ourselves. What are we going to do to seize this moment?

There are numerous proposals that have been set forth for renewal of the United Methodist Church. Let me briefly offer my own typology of some these proposals.

1. Try to hang on. I think this has been the position of the General Conference, at least until now. This is the approach that suggests that reorganization and bureaucratic restructuring can provide a future for the church. Even now studies are being done about a restructuring of the whole church, about a new configuration of general boards and agencies. These efforts are not bad in and of themselves, but, perhaps inevitably, they do not go to the heart of the matter. Difficult as it may be, we must at some point admit that the leadership of the church is reluctant to change. We know the problems, and perhaps we even know that we cannot go on as before, but we would prefer that the changes come later rather than sooner and that they involve others rather than ourselves. It is like the prayer of the bad little boy, "Lord, change me if you want, but if not, leave me alone, I'm having a good time."

I worry that some of the arguments for the "global character" of the United Methodist Church fit under this proposal. Some leaders of the church would like to count on other countries around the world to provide growth for United Methodism as it declines in the United States. If we define ourselves as a world church, we might be able to maintain our image as big, powerful, worldwide, growing, and successful. Let me emphasize that not all efforts to deal with the legitimate global dimensions of United Methodism fit this description, but we need to recognize that there is this aspect to talk of our global character. It can be a dangerous new kind of United Methodist triumphalism.

2. Reverse the decline and recover the institution. The previous alternative does not seriously believe that reversal is possible; rather, the attitude is to make the best of the situation. A second alternative proposes to reverse the decline. Much has been a proclaimed and written about ways that mainline Protestantism, and the United Methodist Church in particular, can accomplish such a reversal. Church growth strategies propose all manner of techniques for adjusting to changed cultural circumstances. These include unapologetic efforts to build megachurches, the abandoning of small churches (which are deemed inefficient), calls for less attention to theology, and an increasing focus on management models that answer the self-perceived needs of as many people as possible. Some argue that training for ministry needs to go on in the local church (especially in the megachurches) so that such training can avoid those aspects of theological education thought to be irrelevant to church growth. The conviction of this approach is that decline can be reversed with human effort, and that the institutional church can be revived.

3. Accept our new status, and see it as an honest expression of the true nature of the church. There are those who believe that we should attempt recovery of one aspect of the earliest Wesleyan movement and define ourselves over against the culture. It is clear that for the Methodist movement in England during Wesley's day, and perhaps beyond, one theme was that Methodism stood "over against" the dominant culture, including the Church of England. This same impulse was evident in early American Methodism. On the whole, however, I think that early Methodism, whether in England or America, was not culture denying. It did not seek to withdraw, but to transform and renew. Clearly this was the path taken in American Methodism, as I suggested in my brief historical overview. There are those who propose, however, that the right response to our changed status in contemporary society is unapologetically to reject the dominant culture and to stand as a witness "over against" it. This would result in significant changes in the institutional life of the church and would probably accelerate the decline in membership.

4. Bring about radical change with new leadership. This proposal suggests that renewal of the church requires empowerment of those who have previously not been among the leaders of the church. The thesis is that the future of the church will depend on its ability to serve and include the diverse peoples increasingly characteristic of North American society, especially Asian Americans, Hispanic Americans, African Americans, and other ethnic minority groups. Few would argue against the view that the church must adjust to the changing demographics of the U.S., especially in regard to multicultural issues. The question is whether ethnic-minority leadership can address the realities of mainline Protestantism at the turn of the century any better than any one else. Is a particular kind of leadership the key to renewal in the church?

5. Worry less about the institution and give priority to theology, witness, mission, and ministry. This alternative proposes to relax about the institutional manifestations of the church and to let some of the machinery go. We might neither reject the institution nor maintain it for its own sake. Recognition of the residual establishment allows us to appreciate the incredible gifts that previous generations of believers have given us and challenges us to figure our what to do with these gifts for ministry in our time. This alternative calls for a clear priority of mission and ministry as a result of theological conviction. The real challenges to the church are spiritual, and these challenges are answered by the rebirth of serious worship, sacramental life, and commitment to service.

None of these five alternatives is complete unto itself. Some overlap with others. They are all suggestive. I mention them to demonstrate that serious proposals are being set forth to deal with the situation faced by the United Methodist Church today. Let me suggest several elements that I see as offering possible directions for our future.

Methodism needs clearly to preach the good news of Jesus Christ without regard to attempts at institutional well-being. We were formed by Wesleyan theology, and Wesleyan theology is a positive contribution to world Christianity. We must keep the central aim of gospel proclamation always before us. Wesleyan theology has no particular institutional interest, but the interest of communicating a positive gospel to a hurting world is our abiding interest. The Wesleyan movement was born as a minority movement in a context where there was an established Christianity. It was in the United States where, for unique historical and cultural reasons, that Wesleyan movement became a dominant institutional expression of Christianity. We, in the United States, need to learn from our Wesleyan brothers and sisters in other parts of the world that a dominant institutional expression is not necessarily what we are called to be. Our primary concern should be the positive preaching of the gospel of grace and freedom. We are called to follow Mr. Wesley's dictum: "Offer them Christ."

Methodism needs to emphasize its connectional character throughout the world, but this connection is, in the first place, to be understood theologically, not institutionally. We are in a time when decentralization is the order of the day. The United Methodist Church cannot maintain huge bureaucratic boards and agencies. At the same time, we need dynamic ministries of cooperation throughout the world. This is one of the special possibilities for United Methodism as a global church in mission. What we mean by global church, however, must be carefully and constantly examined. Global realities have to do with sharing and learning in mission together.

Methodism must give up any thought of cultural dominance and see its role as offering an ecumenically significant presence to Christians throughout the world. I think that this is something that

United Methodists in Europe can contribute to the rest of Methodism. The experience of living in countries where Methodism is a minority, where it never was culturally dominant, where there may be established churches, or in settings decidedly hostile to Christianity, has required European Methodists to choose their identity and to live with ambiguity and commitment. I think Methodists in the United States will increasingly be in this situation. For us it will be new and profoundly challenging. To have brothers and sisters elsewhere in the world who have already experienced this reality may be particularly helpful.

Methodists need always to take the long view and trust God's providence. I conclude on a note of optimism and hope. This is not because of any sociological, demographic, or historical factors. I think that "decline" is the wrong word, and that it offers the wrong image. Again I quote Paul Johnson, who toward the end of his *History of Christianity* discusses the decline of Christianity in an institutional, or establishment, sense during the course of the twentieth century. All over the world, by the last quarter of the century, he writes, "Catholicism appeared to have joined Protestantism and Orthodoxy in a posture of decline. Yet it must be asked: is the expression 'decline' appropriate? If the claims of Christianity are true, the number of those who publicly acknowledge them is of small importance; if they are not true, the matter is scarcely worth discussing. In religion, quantitative judgments do not apply. What may, in the future seem far more significant about this period is the new ecumenical spirit, the offspring of the Second Vatican Council."[8]

My hope and optimism come from my conviction that the church of Jesus Christ is of God, and will endure until the end of time. Methodism is one expression of the larger church. Wesleyan theology has particular insights to contribute to the larger church. But what matters ultimately is the gospel of Jesus Christ. Exactly how the future will turn out, we do not know. But we can be certain that God is in our future; and our hope is that God is not finished with us yet. There is still ministry for the people called Methodist as long as we have breath. Our calling is to be faithful in our response.

What Is the Future of Music in United Methodism?

S T Kimbrough Jr.

As we look at the music of United Methodism today, we ask: How has this branch of the Wesleyan movement arrived at its current hymn book, *The United Methodist Hymnal* (1989), its hymnic repertory, and in what ways does this book reflect the nature of the music in United Methodism? And what will the future hold for this denomination and other Protestant denominations that have centered much of their worship life and theology in Christian song?

Origins of Methodist Song

It is a long way from the first hymn book published in America, *A Collection of Hymns and Psalms* (Charlestown, 1737), edited by John Wesley and published in 1737, to *The United Methodist Hymnal* of 1989. It is a long way from John Wesley's three collections of tunes, *The Foundry Collection* (1742), *Select Hymns with Tunes Annext* (1761), and *Sacred Harmony* (1780), to the tunes being sung today and from the hymn book of the Wesley brothers, *A Collection of Hymns for the Use of the People Called Methodists* (1780), to the current hymnal.

Charles Wesley was the troubadour of Methodism who wrote some 9,000 hymns and poems, and Methodist hymnals still carry a substantial Wesley corpus. But hymnals no longer contain anything like the over 700 Wesley texts that were found in the 1876 edition of *A Collection of Hymns for the Use of the People Called Methodists.*

The Reformation laid the foundation for the Wesleys' discovery of the importance of the wedding of music and text as a means of expressing, affirming, and nurturing faith, as well as being a primary motivator for worship and service. Those who find Charles Wesley's language heavily theological, at times flowery or extravagant, and above the heads of the common folk, must remember that it was the Methodist societies of the eighteenth century, filled with coal miners and laborers from many walks of life, that resonated with Wesleyan song, as did the streets and fields of England, Scotland, Wales, Ireland, and, of course, frontier America.

Song called to worship, to sacrament, to conversion, to service, and to the practice of the holy life. And as Methodism spread to the continent of Europe, it was quite natural that a major question for the Wesleyan movement became, how can one of the hallmarks of Wesleyan spirituality, namely, Wesleyan song, be translated into the musical vocabulary and language of other peoples? Hence, a primary task of early missionaries became the translation of Wesleyan texts into indigenous languages.

The Spread of Methodist Song

In large measure the early missionaries simply transplanted the music and texts they knew to other cultures without concerning themselves with the music and texts of indigenous peoples. Of course, the spread of Methodism to the European continent experienced many closely related musical traditions that had grown out of the Reformation; hence, transitions were not so abrupt. And, after all, the Wesleys borrowed much from the continent as they developed Methodist song—John, in his collections of tunes and translations of German, French, and Spanish hymns, and Charles, in his use of well known continental metrical structures in his hymn writing.

Interestingly, Methodism in America took a different turn musically from Methodism in Great Britain and other areas influenced by British Methodism (e.g., the West Indies). Life on the American frontier absorbed and adapted a broad mixture of cultures from Europe and elsewhere. In the early pioneer days there was a scarcity of the printed word, and as Methodism became loosely connected through circuit riders, modeled by Francis Asbury, song often had to be transmitted orally. So practical was John Wesley in structuring *A Collection of Hymns and Psalms* (1737) that he adapted all of the hymns to six meters and so with six tunes in those meters one could sing all of the hymns in the book. On the American frontier simple English, Irish, Scottish, German, and other melodies often were passed on orally with variations. As American and British Methodism grew, somewhat of a common musical base emerged; nevertheless, two distinctively different musical traditions developed, especially for the Wesley hymns. On the continent of Europe yet other music became wedded to some Wesley texts.

This is not the place to dwell on the history of Methodist and Wesleyan hymnody, but these introductory remarks are formative for an understanding of music in Methodism today and in the future. They inform us that from the beginning musical tradition within Methodism has not been unilinear. This is stressed all the more by the emergence of gospel song out of the Great Awakening and the Camp Meeting

movement, both of which greatly influenced the hymnic repertory of
Methodism.

The Impact of the Missionary Movement on Methodist Song

The missionary movement, however, led to a major shift in the
music of Methodism. The Wesleys had been greatly influenced by
hymns from other cultures and languages, namely German, French,
and Spanish, but the early missionary movement in Methodism did not
follow this example and diminished the influence of music and texts
from other cultures in the worship life of the faith community. The use
of music in the missionary movement was based on a number of
principles, whether conscious or unconscious:
1. The missionaries deliver the corpus of songs that Christians sing.
2. Christians sing primarily using the music and rhythms of Europe
    and North America.
3. Christian songs are accompanied in worship by a piano, organ, or
    harmonium, and occasionally by brass instruments.
4. There is no room in Christian song and worship for instruments,
    rhythms, music, and texts that are of "heathen" origin.
One finds, for example, hymn books printed by the Board of Missions
of the Methodist Episcopal Church in the nineteenth century for use in
Native American languages such as Mohawk. The books included only
western hymns translated into that language. Usually not a single
indigenous song was to be found in the books.

One of the significant exceptions to what I have described thus far
in terms of the effect of the spreading of "Christian" hymnody and the
emergence of indigenous song in North America and Europe is the
development of music in the life of African American Methodism. After
most of the African American Methodists were separated from the
Anglo-based Methodist churches, they began to develop their own
music, style, rhythms, and texts, which often had roots in African
culture. The foundations had in some measure already been laid. The
emergence of the slave song, often called the "spiritual," had already
become a distinctive expression of African American life and quite
naturally became a part of, and foundational to, worship life in African
American churches. Freedom was often exercised in adapting the
melodies, rhythms, and texts of hymns received from diverse European
traditions. An Isaac Watts hymn could be "rewritten" as a spiritual and
perhaps even Charles Wesley's famous poem "Come, O thou traveller
unknown" became the spiritual "Wrestlin' Jacob." Even with such
adaptations, African American Methodism remained strongly attached
to Charles Wesley's hymns and sometimes sang the hymns to different

tunes that gave expression to their own identification with Wesley's message, as in the case of "Jesus, lover of my soul."

Reclaiming Indigenous Song

As Methodist missionary churches throughout the world have come of age, however, the commitment to cultural creativity has evoked the reclaiming of indigenous music, texts, rhythms, and instruments as authentic expressions of the praise and worship of God and inspiration for the faith journey with Christ.

Unquestionably, tensions remain. (1) Peoples tend to preserve the songs that have first opened their eyes to faith; hence, a large corpus of western hymnody, be it from the Wesleys, gospel song that grew out of the Great Awakening, or other styles and traditions of music, is claimed enthusiastically by many regions of Methodism worldwide as an authentic way to express faith in song. (2) Nevertheless, creative musicians and poets have emerged within Methodism on almost every continent and are creating authentic songs of faith in the Wesleyan spirit. One might once have said that Methodists are the people who sing Wesley hymns. Today, the hymnic corpus used, for example, in the Methodist churches of Brazil contains little Wesley but reveals an emerging hymnody that is imbued with the spirit of the Wesleys and filled with the kindred emphases of personal and social holiness, and the challenge of the inner journey with Christ that changes life and lives.

Methodists are singing hymns from Latin America written to a bossanova, tango, or samba beat, or to other rhythms once consigned to secular dance. In the Caribbean islands, hymns and spiritual songs resound to calypso and reggae rhythms. African hymns have emerged that are accompanied by authentic drums and other indigenous instruments and rhythms. The vast musical spectrum of music from Asia has introduced a new repertory of instruments, rhythms, styles, and languages into the arena of Christian song and worship.

So there is no simple answer to the question, how and what do Christians sing? Music and poetry come from the soil and soul of a people. They emerge from their language, culture, and ethnicity, and from the rhythms and needs of their lives. Christian song grows out of interfacing these with the mood, spirit, and message of Scripture and Christian tradition.

The United Methodist Hymnal (1989)

The United Methodist Hymnal (1989; henceforth cited as *UMH '89*) was shaped through a most open process to the music and texts of indigenous peoples and to multicultural contexts in the history of Christian hymnody. During the period 1984–88 the Hymnal Revision Committee developed a process that brought together old and new hymnic material from diverse ethnic, racial, and cultural traditions with a view toward local congregations. This required a keen sensitivity to local needs, concerns, and preference for repertory. In addition to bringing together hymnic and liturgical heritages of the Methodist and Evangelical United Brethren Churches, which had united in 1968, the openness to ethnic hymnody uniuquely marked the hymnal that emerged 1989. What is important is not the mere inclusion of a large repertory of African American, Hispanic, Asian, African, and Native-American hymns and songs, but that this hymnal was the direct result of a conscious effort to seek and consider for regular congregational use the songs of people from all around the world. This vital process accompanied an equal enthusiasm for the consideration of hymns by Charles and John Wesley. Careful evaluation was made of Wesley hymns that are of historical and doctrinal importance, those that are a part of worldwide Methodist hymnic "memory," and Wesley hymns that had not been included in an American hymnal of the Methodist tradition before (e.g., "Because thou hast said"; *UMH '89*, 635). Some Wesley hymns were set to different tunes with the hope of giving them new life.

Now, almost ten years after publication, the 1989 hymnal, which presold over two million copies, has sold over five million copies. What does this success story tell us about a United Methodism that would sing its theology into the new millennium? What has been learned from the use of the hymnal?

(1) Where local pastors encourage their use, the ethnic hymns have increased the awareness among local congregations of the global church and of global Methodism. But these hymns and songs require good leadership in introducing rhythms, texts, and musical styles that are unfamiliar to many. Some are easier to sing than others, and singable English translations help tremendously.

There is a definite need for resources that aid local congregations in integrating ethnic song and "new" song into their standard repertory.

(2) The expanded repertory of gospel hymns and African American song has made the hymn book accessible to a broader spectrum of the church constituency. Gospel hymns, spirituals/slave songs, and choruses have been integrated into the theological fabric of

the hymn book with integrity. Thus the hymnody of the church, which provides a commentary on the Christian faith, Scripture, tradition, and the contemporary journey of faith, is experienced holistically without categorizing music and texts in ways that have often prejudiced certain types of song.

(3) Local churches tend *to be* what they sing. In other words, they tend to personify the theology they sing. If they sing only a very limited repertory, their vision will be limited. If they sing primarily hymns with insular hymn texts, ones that turn them inward upon themselves, such as many North American Holy Spirit hymns that emphasize mainly *I/Me* and God, the congregations will tend to be insular, turned inward upon themselves. Many of the new hymn texts of Fred Pratt Green, Natalie Sleeth, Fred Kaan, and Brian Wren, however, tend to have a vision of theology that looks outward toward others.

(4) There is a new art form in this hymn book, namely, the responsorial psalter, which transforms the ancient tradition of the singing, of antiphons, and of short responses that emphasize the message of the psalm, into hymnic responses, many of which come from the hymnic memory of Methodists. This has provided a new avenue for many to sing the psalms again and to experience bringing the full spectrum of their emotions, concerns, and needs, as expressed in the psalm texts, to God in worship through reading and singing.

(5) There is a tendency for many congregations to cling to a familiar repertory of hymns. If they want their vision of the church's mission to be broad enough to include the peoples of the world, wherever they are, they must learn to sing the songs of others as well. Mr. Patrick Matsikenyiri, a distinguished African Christian musician who teaches at Africa University in Mutare, Zimbabwe, has remarked, "I know that Methodists who come to our churches in Zimbabwe feel that they belong when they hear a familiar hymn. I feel that I really belong to the Methodist Church when I sing an African hymn or song in a non-African Methodist church." Those who have ears to hear, let them hear!

(6) There is also a tendency toward "tunnel vision" in many parts of Methodism as regards hymnic and song repertory. While Anglo congregations are often criticized for excluding ethnic song, ethnic congregations sometimes sing their own repertory as though there is no other. Unknowingly, one can create generations of Christians who know only "one" song and "one way" to sing it—and, as far as they are concerned, this is the way Christians sing! But what will happen, when these persons become a part of a global church at gatherings that are becoming increasingly frequent and more inclusive? Whose way of

song will be considered "the right way"? *The* UMH *'89 by its very existence, declares that it matters whether followers of Jesus Christ are committed to include others and their song in the songs they sing.*

(7) Efforts are being made in many congregations to do away with hymnals altogether and to rely on projections and shorter forms of song that supposedly require little memory. All of the "feel good" ecstasy of the present in such practice may not seem to have an immediate and serious impact on the theology of the church, but it will create a church with musical and theological amnesia.

What will be the life of *UMH '89?* If the history of hymnography may be relied on, probably twenty to thirty years. What will it contribute to the life of Methodism in the new millennium? That remains to be seen.

The Role of Music in the Life of Methodism in the Future

Unquestionably the musical life of Methodism is very diverse. We have indicated that it can be insular but that music is a language and an art that ultimately comes from the soil and soul of a people! Does that mean that we have to redefine it in the urban context as something that comes from asphalt, the cement of the people?

It is interesting that as one looks at the plethora of church closings in inner cities, there is often a parallel between the musical repertory and the demise of a congregation. What does that mean? It means that often in urban contexts where traditional Anglo churches have not adjusted their hymnic and song repertory to the changing demographics of their surrounding populations, the churches have not been able to attract others through the sound and rhythms with which they resonate out of their own cultural backgrounds.

Does this mean that there is such a thing as urban music that can save the inner city church? Is there such a thing as asphalt music? If music comes out of the life of the people, that means it emerges from the context in which they find themselves and from which they come. Of course, the radical diversity today among global urban contexts makes matters even more complex.

Urban settings in North America are even diverse. As Methodist churches reach out in mission in their neighborhoods, it is important to ask and explore what resonates among the people where one is! Should it be a composite of the spectrum of sounds of the inner city—rumbling cars, trolleys, subways, honking horns, cable cars, sirens from emergency vehicles and fire engines, the concert of many languages, the whistling of blustering winds whipping between skyscrapers, children playing stickball in the street, and cheers from sports arenas?

The church cannot ignore what resonates in its environment as it creates the sights, sounds, and rhythms of faith! North America is filled with people from all over the world who bring with them their own cultures and heritage. While second and third generations tend to lose linguistic and cultural ties to their past, the church must be sensitive to the need to proclaim a gospel in song that resonates in musical languages and rhythms with which people from diverse backgrounds can identify.

Art gives access to reality and one of the beauties of music and movement, especially jazz and dance, is that they can incorporate the sounds and rhythms of the life of the inner city and countryside and integrate them into their own artistic expression. The African American tap dancer, Savion Glover, can dance the sounds and rhythms of trucks running over a metal plate in the street and bring the whole population in the blocks that hear such sounds throughout the night into his art form. He personalizes their experience. Must not the church do this in its song?

What is the purpose of Christian song in the mission and life of the church? It is to proclaim the gospel, yes, but more; it is to create the pulse of life that beats with the heart of God's loving concern for everyone in creation. It is not merely organized sound. It is for joy, ecstasy, encounter, structure, Christian presence, and bold praise of the Creator. Charles Wesley's vision of music in Christian life and mission is still up-to-date:

> Celebrate th'eternal God
> with harp and psaltery,
> timbrels soft and cymbals loud
> in this high praise agree;
> praise with every tuneful string
> all the reach of heavenly art,
> all the powers of music bring,
> the music of the heart.

What can be more inclusive than this Wesleyan spirit in the church's song? But it must be taken even more seriously than in the past. Here is the hallmark for the role of music in mission in the future. Christians must be willing to "praise with every tuneful string," and to utilize "*all the reach* of heavenly art." When the church willingly brings "*all* the powers of music" to bear upon its life and mission, it will discover that it has indeed brought "the music of the heart" to the people where it is.

There may be many characteristics of music in Methodism, but it is above all "music of the heart." It issues from and speaks to the innermost being of mortals. It links the resonation of words, music, and rhythms with the full spectrum of human emotions and intellect. Hence, in Methodism music is the cohesive matrix of a lyrical theology. Lyrical theology is Methodism's response to the question, "what language shall I borrow to thank thee, dearest friend?" It borrows the language of music, which is both universal and as diverse as the cultures within which it resounds and the languages and rhythms that give it voice. Through a multicolored blanket of sound comes a word about or of God, a *theologos,* and art becomes an avenue of the revelation of God's way with mortals and their way with God. The miracle of lyrical theology is that the word about God, the word of God, can resonate through the unique artistic forms and gifts of all people in creation.

Through music Methodists learn to work, think, and speak for God. Lyrical theology then links "head and heart" through an art form that engages the bodily senses and the sensitivity of head and heart. Lyrical theology is not a passive theology; rather, it is dynamic and experiential. Hence, music in Methodism is a force, a power, a dynamism through which God's word becomes a living word in human experience. This is part of the genius of the evangelical movement launched by the Wesleys in the eighteenth century.

Given the nature of music in Methodism as "music of the heart," what are some of its essential roles in the present and future?

(1) One of the primary roles of music in the future mission of the church is to create a memory that nurtures and sustains people, as they are created, in faith and out of their own experience of God and God's creation. This is not an easy task, for there are those today who want to retain the tradition of the church as a gathered community, but who wish to say that the 2,000 years of its music and liturgical heritage that have come down to the present day are senseless and useless. This is to aver that God's own history with and through the church itself is meaningless.

Unquestionably one must always ask, what will be the nature of our song? If one examines some of the megachurches that have emerged and are emerging, one finds particular styles of music and performance that are the center of attraction: upbeat rhythms, texts that require little investment of personal or corporate examination, ecstatic musical experiences that evoke body movement, clapping, and vocal exclamations. Anyone who would dismiss these musical phenomena as unworthy of true worship, as best expressed by Bach, Pachelbel, Luther, the Wesleys, Bortniansky, and other classical composers and hymn writers, should consider that urban, technological society has produced thousands of people who do not feel good about themselves, who are alienated in body and spirit through broken homes, drug addiction, racism, and a plethora of domestic and societal problems, and that if the church offers them moments of musical joy that make them feel good about themselves, we should rejoice and ask church musicians soulsearchingly how we can find ways for the music and song of Bach, Pachelbel, Luther, the Wesleys, and Bortniansky to do this. Urban settings are filled with broken lives who want to hear that they can "wade in the water" that God troubles and survive. They want to know that "God will be on time," that "God has touched me," and that they are "leaning on the everlasting arms."

Some ask, what is the difference between entertainment and worship? Perhaps it is better to inquire, what will the church's song help the faithful to remember? What will the church's song teach them? The song the church sings creates the memory that can sustain people in the best and worst of times. It is a question of what resonates with the people, but it is not just that! Charles Wesley's challenge to the church is: bring "all the powers of music"—Bach, Pachelbel, Luther, the Wesleys, Ellington, Tindley, jazz, gospel, spirituals/slave songs, black gospel, hip hop gospel, and Asian and African pentatonic-scale songs. Yes, "all the powers of music bring"!

(2) Another role of music in the future of mission in the church is to raise the question, who will sing the songs? Most of the unchurched are among the poor. As the church reaches out, it must know who are the people in the neighborhoods and what resonates with them. This means one must become aware of the needs of the poor, and their language and concerns must be a part of the church's song. It must also know what resonates with persons of means and the very wealthy. The psalmist once asked, "how shall we sing the Lord's song in a strange land?" (Ps. 137:4) The church must always be asking this question, how shall it sing God's song in contexts that are foreign to where the church is? One may claim that God's song should be heard anywhere, but the growth of the global church of Jesus Christ over twenty centuries makes crystal clear that, though the song of the good news may be the same, how people hear it and how people sing it vary greatly from language to language and culture to culture. The content of the song may be the same, but the shape and form of the song have changed radically since the birth of the temple, synagogue, and church.

Who will sing the songs in our neighborhoods, villages, towns, and cities? Who are the singers? Who are the potential singers? If music comes from the soul and soil of a people, the people of God must become intimately acquainted with the sights and sounds, cultures, and backgrounds of the people where they live. This means discovering from house to house, apartment to apartment, who is there. It means learning to hear the pulse of their lives and learning to share in that which resonates with them. This is not easy, for it means constantly encountering the unfamiliar. Nevertheless, we can learn to sing God's song in contexts that are foreign to us.

I hasten to add at this point that though our discussion has centered largely around singing God's song in an urban context, this song also resounds in rural settings, where people live closer to the earth and nature, and where the life of city with its foibles and pressures seems often very far away. In between country life and the city streets lies suburbia, the bedroom communities filled with millions of people who often spend as much or more time during the daily commute to work as they do with their families on weekday evenings. They often hear the voice of radio talk show hosts for longer periods of time than they do the voices of their spouses and their own children. A hymn well known to many Protestant congregations, "Take time to be holy," could take on new meaning as one struggles to find time to survive as an employee/employer, spouse, mother/father, etc. It is not enough to open the hymn book and sing. We must write the songs that touch the hearts of those who need a musical pulse in their lives that puts them in harmony with their Creator God, creation, family, and neighbor.

As one drives up and down the eastern and western seaboards and across the vast North American continent and listens to the radio, it is clear that there is a tremendous listening audience for country western and gospel music. There are only forty-five radio stations, however, that broadcast classical music. Furthermore, few Christian radio stations have a commitment to classical sacred repertory. Is the issue, if you can't fight them, join them? No, the issue is, does the church care enough to explore carefully what music, which texts and rhythms set the tone and pulse for the life of the population? If it does, it will find ways to make a broad spectrum of music a channel of communication for the good news of God's love for all humankind so that those who have never felt the pulse of God's rhythm in their lives will do so. This is why a classically trained artist, Bobby McFerrin, can conduct the best of classical symphonies and tour with his jazz band and never feel a contradiction. He has made the investment of time and study in exploring the sounds to which people from all walks of life will respond.

(3) Yet another role of music in the church of the present and the future is that it must address the full spectrum of human emotion and

intellect. The Psalms, the song book of the temple, synagogue, and church, do precisely that. The music of the church must create the sounds that issue from the ecstasy, disappointment, joy, pain, love, grief, sorrow, reflection, pensiveness, self-examination, anger, loneliness, and alienation of the human spirit. The psalmists provide a timeless principle for the church's song: let the earth resound with all that we are and all that we would be. As important as it is that our songs affirm human reality, personal and corporate, *as it is*, they must not do this in a vacuum. Christian song must link followers of Jesus to God, others, and creation. Christian song may be reflective, but it must reach beyond the self to a broken humankind and world with hope that resonates in every heart and throughout creation. In this way, Christian song will build bridges across the breaches of human relationships and the broken relationship of human beings and creation.

Yes, Christian song is not only for the *human* spirit, for *all* of God's creation is groaning for wholeness. It is easy to sing "Then sings my soul . . . how great thou art." How romantic is the stanza of this hymn that begins, "When through the woods and forest glades I wander / and hear the birds sing sweetly in the trees." Yet, we know that as rain forests are being destroyed by logging and other industries, there are former "woods and forest glades" that are now barren wastes where birds no longer sweetly sing in the trees.

The Scriptures affirm that our song, that yearns for and celebrates God's redemptive and healing Spirit, is not only for humankind and the human condition, but for all creation (Psalm 104). If the church's song of the future does not resound with this linkage of the redemption of human beings and all creation, its music will one day be silenced, like the quiet of a devastated rain forest.

Choirs and Congregational Song

Choirs in Protestantism have become "institutionalized" with professional and amateur conductors, specialized literature, accessories, courses of study, and diverse methods of training. Generations of architects have provided for and accommodated choir space in their designs. Recent years, however, have seen a departure from choir lofts that separate choristers from congregations and that inhibit the maximum use of space in worship.

While liturgical renewal since Vatican II has expanded liturgical participation of choirs in some branches of Protestantism, including Methodism, we have come full circle from Martin Luther's desire to make the entire congregation the choir to the assumption that four-part choral singing is what a select group of Christian people do when they gather to worship. There is a strong tendency in many churches, however, to return song to the people and not make it captive to clergy or a specialized group of singers. The "Praise Song" movement does precisely that.

What will become of the "traditional" choir, anthem, and solo in worship? Will they survive in the future? Saint Augustine wrestled centuries ago in his treatise *On Music* with the tension between the use of music to God's glory in worship and diverse performance practices, as well as music for music's sake. The tension remains, for the "electric church" raises anew the question of how self-aggrandizing performances can be a part of the true worship of God. How does the vessel of praise keep from getting in the way of the praise of God itself?

Choirs, anthems, and solos may survive in some form, but this is not imperative in order for the church to be the church at worship. The electronic age can already imitate the human voice phenomenally well with samplers and modules. Is it possible that technology could provide a more perfect performance than a live group? Could this make organs and organists obsolete as well? The church survived for some ten centuries without this instrument, which has come to dominate western, and particularly Protestant, worship in unimaginable ways.

I shudder to think that the great organ and choral literature of past ages could be lost to technology. One of the commitments of church musicians must be to integrate the classical forms of sacred music with newer, often more popular forms. This cannot be done by being mere champions of antiquarianism or blatantly casting aside all musical inheritance.

It will be difficult, however, for music in United Methodism with its institutionalized "local church" orientation to lead toward the recovery of the evangelical and reforming energy that marked the musical impetus of early Methodism. It must move once again into the streets of the cities and fields of the countryside resounding with the life impulses of people where they are.

As the church becomes more globally conscious, these realities will weigh heavily upon the church and its mission. This author offers one example. Methodism is now emerging in Cambodia, a country whose population is historically about 98 percent Buddhist. Cambodia has a rich musical and artistic heritage, but its music is unlike anything that appears in western church musical traditions. There is no four-part singing. Western scales are not used. Singing is unison and characterized by nasal tone production, slurred and quarter tones, often accompanied by a single- or two-stringed instrument. What singing shall characterize these newly born faith communities of Methodism?

When Cambodian Methodists come to gatherings of other Methodists in the future shall they be expected to sing only western hymns or songs in four-part harmony and to join the mass choirs formed for special events?

One of the exciting aspects of emerging Methodism in Cambodia is that from the beginning the hymnody is growing out of the music and life of the people, as regards music, texts, and rhythms. Perhaps one day soon Methodists in other lands will be singing a Christian hymn/song from Cambodia.

Conclusion

"How shall we sing the Lord's song in a strange land?" remains a gnawing question for churches in the Methodist connection both now and in the future. There is no single answer, except to say, *as God has made us, so shall we sing God's praise! But let us learn to sing in concert with others—with God's global choir!* With this in view, the General Board of Global Ministries of the United Methodist Church has developed a Global Praise program to gather, foster, and disseminate the faith songs of worldwide Methodism and other Christians and peoples of the world.

As we face the future, may we preserve the best of human creative musical gifts and remain ever open to the newness of the song not yet shaped and not yet sung, as well as to long-sung songs that *we* do not know!

What shall we make of the Muslim imam's chanted call to prayer, the Jewish cantor's Kol Nidre or the Buddhist monk's meditative drone? Christians in the Wesleyan tradition cannot ignore the musical sounds to which people of other faiths respond—at least, not if they would follow Charles Wesley's admonition "all the powers of music bring"! Just as dimensions of Gregorian Chant grew out of the music of the synagogue, perhaps, if we are sensitive to the music of others, new ways will emerge to communicate the mystery and meaning of God's redemptive love in Jesus Christ, a love that goes in search of all people at all costs, even death upon a cross.

Is a Holistic Evangelism Possible?[1]

Priscilla Pope-Levison

Effective evangelism for the twenty-first century needs to enlarge and reconceive itself, a transformation pointed to by liberation theologians. This reconception of evangelism was recognized early in the 1980s by Norm Thomas in his pioneering article entitled "Evangelism and Liberation Theology," in which he contended that "support for a holistic concept of evangelization and for creative new approaches based upon it may be the major contribution of liberation theologians to the church's mission in the '80s."[2] Thomas based his conclusions on the fact that liberation theologians have transformed evangelism into a holistic, inclusive concept that seeks to go beyond the boundaries of horizontal/vertical, spiritual/secular, social action/evangelism, personal/social, and individual sin/structural sin that traditional evangelism often advances. Whereas traditional evangelism often gears the message to the individual, liberation evangelism incorporates the individual, the collective, and the structural. Whereas traditional evangelism often concentrates on saving a person out of this world into a heavenly reign of God, liberation evangelism presents God's reign as both now and yet to come and enlists converts for work on behalf of God's reign in this world. In essence, liberation evangelism fuses together that which traditional evangelism frequently separates.

While Thomas noted the creative contributions of Latin American liberation theologies in particular, I envision similar possibilities with feminist liberation theologies.[3] All liberation theologies are striving for liberation across all dimensions of life—social, political, economic, cultural, and religious. Feminist liberation theologies consider these dimensions with particular attention to women, who often represent the doubly oppressed because sexism heightens the effects of poverty. When evangelism is set in dialogue with the holistic perspective on liberation theologies, its vision is enlarged to encompass the fullness of the gospel. As the Roman Catholic bishops declared in the Puebla Document, "Through all these dimensions must flow the transforming treasure of the Gospel" (PD:483).

This chapter on evangelism will explore the holistic perspectives that liberation theologies can bring to evangelism in the next

millennium. The chapter is structured around four means of evangelism: proclamation, denunciation, call to conversion, and witness.

Proclamation

Proclamation of the good news that salvation is available in Jesus'
victory over sin is central, of course, to traditional evangelism. Through
this victory, "all things" are reconciled to God in Christ (Eph 1:10); this
is salvation. "All things" certainly includes salvation for the individual
in his or her reconciliation to God. This has been the emphasis of
traditional evangelism. Liberation evangelism includes this individual
dimension while incorporating additional aspects included in the
phrase, "all things." As one theologians comments, "I don't think that
he [Paul] was speaking in geographical terms. I don't think either that
he was referring exclusively to everyone as individuals. . . . The
reconciling message of the gospel, then, is directed as much to the
individual as to the social structures that form the context of their daily
interaction."[4]

In addition, in liberation evangelism, the proclamation of salvation
in Jesus Christ cannot be separated from the announcement of God's
reign as it was first uttered by Jesus in Mark 1:14-15. Because of this, to
proclaim salvation in Jesus Christ is to declare God's vision for this
earth. To proclaim salvation in Jesus Christ is to declare the coming
reversal of this present order. To proclaim salvation in Jesus Christ is to
predict the replacement of present injustice with justice, present
oppression with liberation, present poverty with plenty, present alienation with community, and present death with life.

Feminist liberation theologians offer a further perspective on
proclamation in evangelism. Of primary concern to many women is not
only the content of proclamation but also the location. Where is the
place of proclamation? Proclamation has traditionally occurred in the
pulpit, and, for women, the pulpit is viewed with ambivalence, for
historically it has been a symbol of exclusion within the church.
Examples of its exclusion are manifold, but one of the more recent ones
is the book *The Evangelistic Preacher* (Nashville: Broadman Press, 1985).
On the cover is a pulpit occupied by a man in a suit and tie. One of his
hands holds an open Bible, and the other hand is poised in a gesture
that resembles a pistol. The book's content further reflects the cover's
imagery; sermon illustration after sermon illustration was taken from
wars. What is a more powerful symbol of the exclusion of women in the
secular sphere than war?

Males in the pulpit and male sermon illustrations coupled with the
traditional strictures against women's preaching have compelled

women to do their proclamation elsewhere than in the pulpit. Women have often circumvented the power centers of evangelism and have evangelized in an informal setting, often around a table. The table as a place for proclamation coincides with the table as an image of God's reign and its concomitant social reintegration.[5] Imagine the impact on proclamation if the table, rather than the pulpit, became the central symbol.

Some will say that this is not evangelism from a liberation perspective because, once again, women are at the table and outside of the power centers. But that is precisely the point! Evangelism from a liberation perspective occurs on the periphery, far from the center of power, but it issues a challenge to those committed to evangelism: will they recognize women's experience of proclamation at the table and allow it to challenge their thinking and practice of evangelism, or will they keep on sharing their war stories?

Denunciation

Denunciation, a second means of evangelism, typically focuses on individual sin. Denunciation has often concentrated condemnation on personal sins, such as the evils of liquor, tobacco, and drugs. However, limiting denunciation to personal evils restrains its powerful potential. Because of this, along with individual sins, denunciation in liberation evangelism encompasses structural evils, such as economic exploitation and inequality, rigid social stratification, false ideologies, unjust institutions, and the individual's own capitulation to these ideologies and institutions. As Latin American Methodist pastor and former bishop, Mortimer Arias, explains, "Part of the task of the Christian messenger is to criticize false gods and false prophets, to unmask the powers and principalities, to confront them, and to denounce anything that is against God's dream, against God's purpose."[6] Denunciation from a liberation perspective does not ignore the reality of individual sin; rather, it considers the larger ramification of that sin and the ideologies and institutions that support it.

In order to adapt denunciation to many women's experiences, evangelists must be careful to consider sin in light of the fact that women are often the oppressed, not the oppressor. The sins of the oppressed, or those who are objects, differ from the sins of the oppressor, or those who are subjects. In her groundbreaking article, "The Human Situation: A Feminine View," written more than thirty years ago, Valerie Saiving argued that the definition of sin in contemporary theology as "pride, will-to-power, exploitation, self-assertiveness, and the treatment of others as objects rather than persons . . ." reflects men's experience and men's sins; yet, sin as pride has been universally applied to men and women.[7] In contrast, Saiving recognizes that "the temptations of woman as woman are not the same as the temptations of man as man." Following from this, she proposes that women's sins are "better suggested by such items as . . . lack of an organizing center or focus; dependence on others for one's own self-definition . . . in short, underdevelopment or negation of the self."[8] Similarly, Anne Carr argues that while women *may* sin as men do, more often "their own 'feminine' formation suggests sins of passive failure to develop a sense of self, a sense of agency and responsibility."[9] These sins are very different from sins of pride! In addition, some feminist theologians have been exploring sin in a more relational sense as breaking relationships with God and other human beings. If this contextual understanding of sin and denunciation has validity, then evangelists cannot continue denouncing sin in generic terms, for generic often equals male.

Call to Conversion

A third means of evangelism, the call to conversion, is most often, in traditional evangelism, the point at which the individual is called to turn away from sin and enter into a personal relationship with Jesus Christ. Liberation theologians have proffered an important critique of any call to conversion that starts there but proceeds no further. In particular, Emilio Castro, a Uruguayan Methodist and former General Secretary of the World Council of Churches, considers inadequate an evangelism that strives to gain a convert's commitment to Jesus first and then afterwards, at some point in time, teaches the convert the importance of loving one's neighbor. In this evangelism, the former, a commitment to Jesus, is essential, while the latter, a commitment to neighbor, is optional. Castro writes, ". . . it appears to me an erroneous theology which teaches that there is . . . a movement of love to God first and a movement of love to neighbor after. . . . (I)n evangelistic preaching we call people to a vertical relationship and afterwards we market Christian education to teach them the horizontal relationship with the neighbor."[10]

The evangelist from a liberation perspective recognizes that the call to conversion is holistic in two ways: 1) Conversion entails a turning away and a turning toward, and 2) Conversion is for the individual and the collective. First, conversion requires a person to turn away from sin, both individual sins and structural sins. Involvement in sinful structures is difficult to discern, but these sins must be included in a full conversion. Coinciding with a turning away from sin is a turning toward God and neighbor. The convert turns toward God and neighbor and establishes changed relationships on the divine and human level. Because conversion occurs within a sociohistorical context, even the interior, individual change has a collective, societal impact for at the very least, conversion should create new relationships. "Positively viewed, conversion is the implementation of altered relationships at every level of personal and social reality. These altered relationships will express concrete forms of liberation and anticipate the kingdom of God."[11]

Second, conversion affects both the individual and the collective. Individuals receive salvation and enter the reign of God; yet, they now have a responsibility to the work of God's reign on earth. Persons who have entered the reign of God through conversion are subsequently enlisted to help in furthering the reign of God. In this way, conversion benefits more than just the individual; the collective profits as well. Castro contends, "Conversion always implies the question of the apostle Paul, 'Lord, what do you want me to do?' And the evangelist should not be hesitant to indicate what in his/her knowledge is implied in a concrete manifestation of the living Christ, calling us to join him in the struggles of the world and in the struggles of his kingdom."[12]

To draw out these implications a bit further: if the reign of God has as its center a vision for social reintegration around the table, and if conversion is a commitment to Jesus and a commitment to neighbor, then the call to conversion might be understood as an invitation to join Jesus and those gathered with him at the table. Jesus himself issued invitations to feast with him to those who would not be scandalized by his controversial table habits. These habits had gained him a reputation that must have been common knowledge, for he quoted it of himself in Luke 7:34: "The Son of man has come eating and drinking; and you say, 'Behold, a drunkard, a friend of tax collectors and sinners.'" Many were put off by Jesus' actions at the table, but others responded to his invitation. Who are those who accepted Jesus' invitation? Luke does not keep us in suspense. Three verses later, after Jesus calls himself a friend of tax collectors and sinners, we read of the first one who comes to Jesus at the table. She was a woman of the city, a sinner, who crashed an all-male dinner party to attend to Jesus' feet with her tears, her hair, her kisses, and her oil.

The life of Jesus provides a further refinement of the call to conversion from a liberation perspective. Jesus, himself, made different demands on different groups of people in different contexts. While some of what he said, such as, "The kingdom of God has come near; repent" (Mark 1:15), applied to all people, the concrete nature of the conversion he required actually varied. Jesus called the poor to believe that God could ameliorate their apparently hopeless situation. The poor must be converted from despair to hope in the recognition that the reign of God is theirs (Luke 6:20). In other words, the poor must be converted "so that they may believe in the good news, precisely because it is so good, so seemingly incredible and so different from their accustomed situation."[13] In contrast, Jesus called the wealthy to evaluate critically their contribution to oppressive institutions, the very institutions that prevent them from being a neighbor to the poor. The Pharisees, for instance, by means of their interpretation of Torah, provided religious rationale for regarding poverty as the effect of sinfulness. In this way, they helped to produce a class of people who were perceived to be socially inferior, economically insignificant, and religiously devalued. Consequently, Jesus challenged the Pharisees to a conversion that entailed a move "from the oppressive security of the letter of the law to the liberating insecurity of having to opt for the poor, even in the face of God's very word."[14]

Thus, the evangelist operating within a liberation perspective must develop and practice a critical awareness of the context as he or she calls to conversion. For instance, the call to conversion at the table of a businessman's lunch in a downtown Hilton will be different from the call to conversion at the coffee break table of housekeepers who clean the downtown Hilton. Their sins may not be the same, and they certainly will have different life experiences. Therefore, the invitation to the table with Jesus and those gathered with him must reflect the context that includes the intersection of such factors as class, race, and gender.

Witness

Witness, a fourth means of evangelism, traditionally has been understood as speaking about and doing deeds that show forth one's personal faith. Integral to witness is the evangelist's lifestyle. For instance, the proclamation is greatly hindered by an evangelist who, by a sinful lifestyle, is understood as committing personal sin. However, as might be expected, liberation theologians have expanded the notion of witness to include not only the individual evangelist's lifestyle but also the community whose corporate witness can have an impact on oppressive structures and ideologies. Witness, in this broader sense, "implies that it is impossible to bring good news of salvation . . . if one is allied to structures that disregard life and perpetuate injustice. . . . It would mean sharing the liberating message of the gospel with one hand and justifying domination and exploitation with the other."[15]

To adapt this to the experience of many women, if conversion is accepting the invitation to the feast, then witness involves bringing the feast to persons on the margins, especially to the doubly oppressed. Jesus told a story about such a witness: "When you give a luncheon or a dinner, do not invite your friends or your brothers or your relatives or rich neighbors, in case they may invite you in return, and you would be repaid. But when you give a banquet, invite the poor, the crippled, the lame, and the blind. And you will be blessed, because they cannot repay you . . ." (Luke 14:12-14).

Edwina Gateley was well acquainted with witness to the marginalized. In 1969 she founded the Volunteer Missionary Movement, a missionary movement of lay people within the Roman Catholic Church. Then in the early 1980s, during a nine-month retreat, she sensed that God was calling her to another witness. Her response was to move into one of the poorest areas of Chicago and "to walk the streets and work towards establishing relationships of trust and friendship with the rejects of the streets." In particular, her friendships with prostitutes led her to found Genesis House, a place of hospitality and nurture for women involved in prostitution. In her own words she testifies to the reciprocity of witness.

> I have come to know and love many prostitutes and to gain insights into their life-styles, their suffering and their experience of God. This continues to enrich my own spirituality and to stretch my awareness of God's amazing grace. I am grateful that God has filled my life with many guides and teachers; the prostitutes and the street-people being amongst the most significant.[16]

Conclusion

The fourfold approach to traditional evangelism, proclamation-denunciation-call to conversion-witness, serves here also as the basis for a holistic evangelism based on liberation perspectives. Each of the categories has been expanded and redirected beyond traditional understandings. I hope that, as the next century dawns, a holistic evangelism will enliven the whole church from the centers of power to the margins. At the very least, may this chapter on evangelism from a liberation perspective begin to uncover blindspots, unmask biases, and most important, unleash the potential of unused resources in the unusual invitation to join with Jesus and those at table with him in the reign of God.

What Is the Character of Methodist Theology?

Thomas A. Langford

John Wesley set a fundamental dialectic in his first conference. Two of the questions to be addressed were: what to teach? and how to teach?

What to teach: How is the Christian gospel to be best understood? Can we hear what the gospel says? And can we say it more adequately or authentically? That is, can we listen to the gospel and let it form our understanding of Christian faith?

How to teach: How may the gospel be effectively preached? What are our hearers able to hear, and can they appropriate the Christian message? That is, can we help listeners to hear the gospel, to understand so that they can respond? Wesley's annual conferences were a time for a theological discussion as well as a time for business. These ongoing explorations were a distinctive characteristic of his revival movement. He persistently asked: How do we understand the gospel? How do we present the gospel?

Wesley was more consciously engaged in analyzing the received Christian message than in analyzing his cultural setting. It was theological opponents whom he most directly challenged and by whom he was challenged. It was more by instinct, by developed sensitivity, and simply through engaging ordinary people that he developed his awareness of his audience.

Wesley stood astride the border of listening and speaking and kept the issues of what and how to teach bound together. This balancing begun with Wesley was significant, but the counterpoising was difficult to maintain. Successors, beginning with Richard Watson, tended to loosen the strong connection and to stress one side over the other; and, increasingly, the side emphasized was that of the receiving listeners, the persons to whom the message was presented. The trend, once begun, became increasingly strong as the nineteenth century stressed heavily the task of how to teach.

The impulse to move to the audience's side was understandable for a preaching/revival movement, a movement that wanted to present the gospel in persuasive and engaging ways. More and more, it was assumed that the gospel was adequately known; what was more problematic was how the understood gospel could be conveyed to contemporary hearers. It was no accident that Methodist clergy were exclusively called "preacher" until mid-twentieth century. Proclamation was the task. Persuasive presentation was the goal.

For the purposes of this short chapter, we shall quickly survey the ways in which this interest in speaking effectively has taken particular forms in North American Methodism.

Proclamation and Philosophy

In American Methodism, a pervasive concern has been to understand the mind of the time so as to meet it with the Christian message. Most often, this has been an effort to locate the contemporary intellectual ethos, to determine its pulsations, and both to criticize and use the resources it affords. Principally this has meant an analysis of regnant philosophical understanding. With achieved clarity about who is listening, the received gospel is creatively brought into conversation with those who are so encultured.

A friend asked why so many American Methodist theologians were *philosophical* theologians, a characteristic he thought distinctive of Methodist thinkers. It may be; and, if so, it is in part due to the evangelistic interest of speaking to the mind of the time. If so, it arose out of a desire to understand one's audience correctly and to meet its convictions with Christian truth.

Boston Personalism, in the first quarter of the twentieth century, represented the most vital effort among Methodists to assess the philosophical climate and respond in a theologically viable way. Idealism, Absolute and Personalistic, was the reigning philosophy of the time in Germany (with the outworking of Hegel), in Great Britain, both Scotland and England (with the clustering of the Cairds, Pringle-Pattison, and F. H. Bradley, among many others), and in the United States (with the St. Louis School and Josiah Royce). The varieties of Idealism were legion, and many were striving to make the differences more readily apparent. But the main trunk of Idealism was its character as a philosophy of religion. Especially in its personalistic forms, it was a sustained effort to understand both God and human beings in relation to one another.

Borden Parker Bowne breathed this air; he saw it as a fight against materialism (he taught a seminar on Herbert Spencer each year) and as an affirmation of God in language that spiritually serious people could appropriate.

This attention to cultural norms always ran the danger that contemporary—and always changing—thought forms would recolor, reshape, or reinterpret the gospel in their own images. But the danger could be recognized, and serious effort could be made to preserve the authentic character of the gospel.

Bowne and successors, such as Albert Knudson, intended to be loyal to the received message. But their primary interest was in speaking to their age and interpreting the gospel in ways agreeable to the affirmed philosophical position. Their chief concern was how to teach. With vigor, they explored the vital intellectuality of contemporaries and wanted to speak a clear and challenging word from a Christian position. Idealism was not necessarily Christian, so a theological task was to sculpt the materials in such a way as to make sense from a Christian perspective.

The effort was apologetic. That is, they intended to explore and defend the faith in the arena of the dominating intellectual ethos. Dogmatic theology would have been more focused on received doctrine, on New Testament theology or on creedal formation—that is, on what to teach. How is what is preached formed by the gospel?

Boston Personalism was interested in underwriting preaching and in finding the points of contact within their intellectual culture so as to make the gospel relevant. Relevance often dominated. For theologians who remained devout and pious, who continue to worship (and attend midweek prayer meetings, as many in this movement did), the core of the gospel seemed clear, the great challenge was to speak with convincing clarity to their contemporary hearers.

Apologetic theology continued to characterize Methodist theology, but there were sporadic protests. Edwin Lewis, for instance, represented an effort to turn around and freshly emphasize the other pole: what to teach? Having been a personalistic theologian, he made an effort to return to biblical and creedal roots, to hear again what the gospel said. Consequently he stressed Christology, the sinfulness of human beings and the meaning of human redemption. Later, he stressed a position adjacent to the received gospel, namely a cosmic struggle of good and evil, and allowed this philosophical perspective to shape his interpretation of God.[1]

Apologetic theology continued with strength as the century developed. For instance, Carl Michalson used existentialism as the philosophical context for interpreting the Christian faith. Existentialism was a European phenomenon. It was expressed both theistically (Kierkegaard) and atheistically (Sartre). Michalson creatively came into this discussion and utilized existentialism not only to define the problems but also as a vehicle for expressing Christian faith. Again, the question of how to teach received more attention than what to teach.

To put if differently, proclaiming the gospel was given priority over listening to the gospel.

Balance between receiving and offering is very fragile; appropriate tension is hard to achieve and maintain. Most theologians understood themselves to be attending to both dimensions but appropriate weighting is a constant challenge. The issue is often, where does one stand? If you stand on one side in order to view the other, can distortion be avoided? How can theology do justice to both tasks?

A counterpoint to the apologetic effort can be found in the undertaking to produce a definitive text of John Wesley's works. One intention guiding that endeavor was the conviction that much reading of Wesley was refracted through contemporary persuasions; interpreters were viewing John Wesley through their own eyes; they remade Wesley to suit their tastes and times. The Wesley Works project would counter such immediatism and produce a text as nearly original as possible. Can Wesley be appropriated, first in terms of his own time and then in terms of how he should be interpreted for each changing time? Once again, the interrelation of past and present demands extremely sensitive, nuanced interpretation. Under the leadership of Albert Outler, Robert Cushman, and William Cannon, there was an effort to reset the balance by doing a critical historical study of both Wesley and the subsequent interpretations of Wesley. This effort continues in the Wesley Works project.

Philosophical interests persisted among Methodist thinkers in mid-century, although philosophical convictions were changing. In the middle decades, process thought became a matter of serious intellectual interest. Initially of English origin (Alfred North Whitehead), process theology built upon this foundation as a distinctively American concern. Major process thinkers, such as Methodists John B. Cobb Jr. (who found his primary influence in Whitehead) and Schubert Ogden (who was shaped more by the work of Charles Hartshorne), were intent on reinterpreting the doctrine of God in ways congenial to this dynamic philosophy. Cobb and Ogden made sustained efforts to meet a pressing challenge. The issues that faced Christian faith, especially in the decade of the sixties, were the expanding cosmos, the exploration of space, and the theological climate that claimed, God is Dead! How is God to be understood in this newly discovered world? How can contemporaries understand the reality of God? The intertwining of message received and presented was thoroughgoing and impossible to disentangle. But the particular intellectual context tended to predominate.

Gospel and Culture

It needs to be noted that what has been true of Methodist theology has also been true of Methodist preaching. Preachers also have focused on their hearers, on what the congregation can understand, appreciate, value, and respond to.

Preaching has, for Methodists, been an apologetic effort. Even those who quote Barth often preach like Tillich. One way is not more Christian than the other. Apologetic theology need be no less a faithful Christian understanding than doctrinal theology. The necessary thing is to recognize what one is doing, to place one's mode of working under careful scrutiny and to stand with the gospel in one hand and cultural expression in the other. Adroitness is required in order to achieve this balance.

The claim made here is that Methodist theology has been culturally sensitive and that its sensitivity is both a great strength and a contribution to Protestant theology as a whole. Methodism has been responsive to the claims of its time. This sensitivity to cultural formations continues in black theology (James Cone), feminist theology (Rebecca Chopp), liberation theology (José Míguez Bonino, Theodore Jennings), and in developments of tradition, such as the philosophy of A. MacIntyre (Stanley Hauerwas). Again, all of these persons are attempting to keep the tension alive, with each placing her or his own emphasis.

To say that one is culturally sensitive does not have to mean that one endorses the status quo. It can mean that one also finds a point of leverage from which a particular character can be criticized. (In economic and social ethics, Methodism has traditionally been more countercultural than it has been in philosophical commitment.) The sharpness of sensitivity is to be applauded, even as there remains a responsibility for self-criticism that assesses how thought is affected by cultural context.

Part of the current struggle among Methodists over their theological statement is a debate over what role current experience (such as cultural formations) should play. Experience rooted in general philosophical convictions has given way to particular experiences of oppression (race, gender, poverty, and political disenfranchisement). Those who want to stress that Scripture is primary and must take precedence over experience consider themselves as moving back into consideration of what to teach. Both sides have value, and both possess danger. Their value is in recognizing the tradition that has been striving to bring text together with context; gospel and culture are both recognized. The danger is in allowing one to dominate, in such a way as to distort, the other.

The relation between gospel and culture is dynamic, and everyone who is aware of both areas struggles to find an acceptable way of relating the two. An illustration of the issues may be found in the structure of a classical symphony. The symphony is organized around a theme. The theme may be identified and then recognized as that which provides unity for the entire symphony. Nevertheless, the theme is more thoroughly known as it is developed and as variations are produced. The symphony would not be distinct except for the theme. The symphony would not be distinct without the variations and developments of the theme. Each may be known in isolation from the other, but each cannot be as fully known or as richly known except in relation to the other. The sum is more than its parts.

So it is with the gospel and its cultural enfoldments. The gospel of God in Jesus Christ is the theme. It organizes the whole and sets its possibilities. The developments and variations are the cultural context. Through these expressions the theme is enriched. Only as the two are held together can the full richness of the Christian message be presented.

Methodist theology in the twentieth century has lived on this border. It has been primarily characterized, however, by attending to its listeners. While this awareness of context should continue, listening to the gospel has tended to be subordinated. What would bring Methodism more in line with John Wesley and its originating questions would be to address the tension between the two. To establish and maintain this balance is a challenge for contemporary Methodist thinking and preaching.

Can United Methodist Theology
Be Contextual?
Roy I. Sano

The emphases John Wesley gave to the Methodist movement in Britain were clearly in response to the ecclesial, spiritual, and economic contexts of the day. In this chapter, I offer a glimpse into the world I inhabit as an Asian North American church leader at the turn of a very different century, and suggest how, as a United Methodist, my theology is shaped by this context or world.

The Context: I am an Asian North American bishop responsible for overseeing the Los Angeles Area of The United Methodist Church.[1] The four hundred churches and their 110,000 members in the area cover Southern California, Hawaii, Guam, and Saipan. This area is part of the Pacific Basin, where the weight of U.S. trade shifted from the North Atlantic in 1978, followed by world trade in 1980. Amidst the major changes in the post–Cold War era, nations in Asia, in the Pacific, as well as in North, Central, and South America have rushed to secure a place for their interests in this region. The scramble has intensified economic rivalries, raised serious justice issues, escalated massive movements of people, and promoted fascinating and promising cultural exchanges. The U.S. seeks to maintain dominance by controlling the region's airways, ocean routes, and underwater areas with sophisticated surveillance, counterinsurgency networks, and redeployment of armed forces.

In recent years, longtime residents of this vast area, but particularly in Southern California, have been traumatized by transitions in the economy. Despite stoic denials and sly evasions, many of these residents are reeling from the dizzying diversity of newcomers and their cultures.[2] Pent-up frustrations over failure to protect their familiar worlds recently erupted from the ballot box in attacks on immigrants and affirmative action. For their part, recent arrivals consistently come from homogeneous societies and are therefore less prepared to relate to strangers around them. Their inability to obtain acceptance or find gainful employment spawns gang violence and explodes in fury such

51

as that of the 1992 urban uprising in Los Angeles. Social tensions have been further exacerbated by a quick succession of record-breaking natural disasters, including typhoons and hurricanes, landslides and fires, droughts, and the costliest earthquake in U.S. history. A measure of hospitality is fortunately rising in some neighborhoods, but a pervasive alienation increasingly drives people back to their own familiar cultural enclaves for work, housing, and socializing.

In light of demographic and cultural shifts and economic and ecological disruptions, we United Methodists face enormous challenges as we both seek to make the body of Christ an inclusive community and strive to promote that sense of community in the body politic that is necessary to be human.

Contextualizing. Such demographic and cultural shifts and their attendant repercussions make it particularly appropriate to explore theological issues of community and power. Understandings of the triune God are particularly pertinent in this task of contextualizing our beliefs. We give meaning to our experiences of struggle, setbacks, sufferings, injustice, and hope as we process them through the cultural and religious traditions we have received. Critical reflection on these traditions uncovers the crucial stories and scripts, symbols, and rituals that are actually at work. It can also lead to a reformulation of traditions so they will process experiences more adequately and offer better guidance to promote the divine reign and realm (Matt. 6:33). The Bible has consistently provided promising options. ·

As United Methodists, we do this contextualizing work through the lens of the so-called Wesleyan quadrilateral. And we do this intellectual work with the practical desire of faithfully promoting the ministries of the *ethnē* (understood as marginalized people, or *minjung* in Korean) in mission with the triune God.

The beautiful picture of the divine community portrayed in the "immanent trinity" can seduce us into sublime euphoria and distract us from involvement in the nitty gritty work of God's mission in the world. While we need a glow of hope in our arduous sojourn, it is the *economic trinity* that directs us more sharply to the good news of the triune God's unrelenting involvement in the divine mission. This vision braces us for participation in the grand drama of the mission through repentance and faith.

God as Creator

1. *God creates us out of nothing and says we are good.*

An openness toward the strangers rises like tender shoots in some quarters. At the same time, both longtime residents and recent immigrants feel a loss of their distinctive identity and question their worth. Defensive reliance on a narrow strand in our theological heritage dismisses these concerns. We have learned from the global ferment for human dignity over the last half century that faith directly addresses matters of identity and worth.

The God who creates *ex nihilo* offers hope to us when we seem to fall into oblivion and become nobodies. The Creator broods over the "formless void and darkness (obscurity) covering the face of the deep" (Gen. 1:2). This God calls us forth and gives us a distinct identity that is not just "good," but "very good" (Gen. 1:4, 10, 12, 18, 21, 25, 31). We who were no people become the people of God (1 Pet. 2:10).

Excesses in affirming or recovering our distinct identity and worth can, however, degenerate into a quest for ethnic cleansing and a zeal for an exclusive religious orthodoxy. This applies to all people, regardless of their race or gender, age or station, religion or culture. Ezra broke up racially mixed marriages (Ezra 9:1-4; 10:6-22), and Nehemiah excluded Gentiles from the temple (Neh. 10:28-31; 12:44-47). Other legalisms in the same vein moved leaders to prohibit crossbreeding animals, sowing two kinds of seed in the same field, and wearing garments made from two different materials (Lev. 19:19). We obviously need other stories to correct these excesses. While God separates creatures from one another (Gen. 1), this does not justify segregation or ideologies of racial superiority.

2. *The Creator continues to diversify human families.*

Celebrating diversity offers one corrective. Many who were indifferent to the previous point are troubled by diversity that threatens their familiar landscape. "From many one" (*e pluribus unum*) is, after all, the creative and hallowed dream, according to the motto that launched the U.S. Republic, 1789.

The Bible challenges the dis-ease with diversity. The Creator acting as Providential Caretaker diversifies the descendants of key figures like Adam and Eve, Noah and his family, Abraham and Sarah (Gen. 5; 10; 17:3-6). Hence, the apostle Paul says in Athens, "From one ancestor, (God as the Source) made all nations to inhabit the whole earth" (Acts 17:26). "From one many" is a hallowed part of the biblical story of creation.

3. The Creator mixes creatures.

A further corrective to the idolatry of our identity being the unique and only acceptable one lies in affirming mixture in our heritage. Mixing of cultures, and most particularly, religious traditions, is generally resisted. For example, many in my episcopal area oppose immigrants because they see in them waves of barbarians bursting the frontier barriers and contaminating holy places in neighborhoods, schools, and churches. The immigrants themselves also resist mixed marriages and combining cultures in their own households and churches.

It has therefore become important to recognize God the Caretaker mixing distinct identities of people and using persons with mixtures of ancestries and cultures. The most telling instance appears in Jesus himself (Matt. 1:1-17). His ancestors include three Gentiles, namely, Tamar, a harlot of Canaanite descent (Gen. 38:13); Rahab, a Gentile prostitute in Jericho (Josh. 6:25); and Ruth, a Moabite widow, who married Boaz, a Jew (Ruth 1:4; 4;13-22). Jesus Christ, our Savior and Sovereign, is therefore a descendant from precisely such racially mixed marriages as Ezra opposed. Similarly, the apostle Paul, the great missionary figure in early Christianity, was himself a bicultural person, a Jew heavily shaped by Hellenism. The work of the Providential Caretaker, who cultivates the ancestry of Jesus and oversees the upbringing of Paul, invites us to welcome persons who come from mixed marriages and cultures. They can be agents in God's mission.

Though our intention is to demonstrate the creative and providential care of this God, we introduce sin and evils at all points. God in Christ leads us to rectify what has gone awry.

God in Christ

1. Christ transforms us while affirming our distinct identities.

We are deeply indebted at some point in our sojourn to missionary efforts that transformed us and our ancestors. In the midst of the resurgence of repressed historic cultures in the human family, we see Christians in those cultures and lifestyles naming limits to those changes. As people incarnate their faith in new cultural expressions, some persons reject these expressions as misguided instances of syncretism, a return to paganism, and even an abomination.

A vivid example of such a negative response appeared in the outcry against Chung Hyun Kyung after she delivered her keynote speech at the Seventh Assembly of the World Council of Churches in Canberra, 1991. She subsequently faced threats on her life. Professor Chung contextualized her Christian faith with Shamanism from her Korean cultural heritage. Many of us who applauded her efforts did so because we had seen instances of cultural imperialism in missions. It is not too much to say that some converts were expected to commit cultural suicide when they accepted Christ. "Become like us and we will like you," is what some of us heard.

Our conversion involved dying to our sins and rising to newness of life expressed with a unique cultural slant. This recalls the historic decision of the early church concerning Gentile converts. They were not subjected to circumcision because Gentiles were not required to become Jews before they became Christians. However much the Savior transforms us, the Savior does not contradict or violate the work of the Source who creates and cultivates our distinct identities, including the cultures that shape us. Similarly, while there is diversity of "persons" with unique attributes and actions, the triune God of three persons or aspects is nonetheless one, as we learned from Judaism.

2. The order of salvation belongs in the history of salvation.

We have learned from the struggles of people in the last half of the twentieth century that a lot more is required for community than a sense of worth and personal salvation. First, we learned the need for liberation from the broader systemic, ideological, and environmental domination and exploitation. People fought and continue to fight for freedom from European colonialism, from the neocolonialism based in the East and West, and from persisting instances of internal colonialism in racism, sexism, classism, and in policies that threatened indigenous people. The struggle is now directed against U.S.-based domination in the post–Cold War era. Second, these efforts tried to reunite people whose communities were destroyed by colonizing policies and practices. Third, these movements struggled to create livable space by rebuilding neighborhoods, nations, and the natural environment.

Despite the moral ambiguities and flaws of these movements, many of us sensed a divine presence in them and therefore supported them. Others dismissed them as secular and claimed they diverted us from the good news in Jesus Christ. Persistence in supporting these movements through our denominational boards of mission and social action eventually heightened the objections, which turned into acrimonious attacks from well-financed, self-styled "biblical caucuses" of Wesleyans. What had priority among the critics was the Wesleyan *ordo salutis* 'order of salvation' (justification–sanctification–glorification; the Latin titles *ordo salutis* and *via salutis* give the doctrine a sacrosanct status). The conflict deepened in North America and was exported globally.

In examining the Bible, we cannot minimize the importance of the order of salvation in the work of the Savior. We see its importance in tragic instances of justice advocates and liberators who fail to attend to their own personal sins. What the critics overlook, however, is the biblical approach of subsuming the *ordo salutis* under the history of salvation.

The prophets Jeremiah and Ezekiel offer the paradigm by placing the *ordo salutis* (Jer. 31:33-34; Ezek. 36:25-27) within a wider drama in the history of salvation (Jer. 31:31-32; Ezek. 36:24). The history of salvation that interprets recent movements first appeared in (1) the Exodus from Egypt, (2) covenant at Sinai, and (3) sojourn to create a new home. The story was updated in the face of the Babylonian captivity, as well as Persian and Hellenistic domination. Space will not permit illustrations of the same twofold story of salvation integral to Gospels, the Pauline epistles, and the Apocalypse under Roman occupation and persecution.[3]

When the Sixth Oxford Institute dealt with liberation in 1977, it located liberation in sanctification.[4] The move was a clear case of cultural imperialism based on a Wesleyan bias. The rich contributions from liberation theologians who had burst on the theological scene at that point could hardly be subsumed under sanctification in the *ordo salutis*. The tradition of the elders that made a fetish of the *ordo salutis* nullified the Word of God (Matt. 15:8-9; Mark 7:7-8). Attentive examination of the Bible would have urged us to subsume the *ordo salutis,* including sanctification, under the history of salvation, which begins with liberation. With more than a century of studying histories of salvation in the Bible and after recent scholarship on centuries of resistance and revolutionary movements influenced by the Reformed traditions, no systematic treatment of salvation, evangelism, and holiness is defendable today that does not incorporate the *ordo* or *via salutis* in the larger sweep of the work of Jesus Christ as Savior and Sovereign in the history of salvation or redemption.[5]

God as the Consummator

1. *Community in the consummation of God's realm*

Economic and political injustices, as well as social and cultural exclusion, destroy communities.[6] A case in point is the subtle exclusion of the Asian North American middle class in the church and society. Studies in political economics indicate that middle-class Asian North

Americans may live "above the poverty line," but they remain "below the power line." A preoccupation with economic status has led us to overlook this political reality. The issue is that the distinct needs of Asian North Americans are thereby excluded from the issues that white middle-class progressives address. Furthermore, white middle-class progressives name the contributions of Asian Americans.

What is sad is the false consciousness that affects these progressives. They miss the fact that they are caught in the same political reality and are therefore marginalized. Although they are not manipulated, progressives are effectively managed. Although they are not oppressed, progressives are consistently outmaneuvered by principalities and powers operating through key individuals and institutions that are driven domestically, regionally, and globally by ideological forces and sanction. However much their efforts may mitigate evil, the activism of white middle-class progressives basically amounts to little more than the flaying of a "kept" people. The mainline denomination they represent is now largely sidelined. It has become increasingly difficult to continue supporting their politically correct causes without confessing the charade in those noble efforts (Isa. 6:5).

Such a false consciousness is a function of a powerful cultural force, a force that can effectively turn a St. George into an icon. In many representations, St. George rides high on a white horse, dressed in shining armor. From this vantage points, St. George is slaying a dark dragon on the ground below him. He does this to rescue a fair, distressed damsel in the background pleading on her knees for help. We find here all the trappings for sexism, racism, and condescension (paternalism and materialism) that discredit noble crusades and corrode community. We struggle to find anything redeeming in this prevailing cultural understanding that energizes evangelicals to save benighted and lost souls and rallies liberals to rescue poor and powerless victims.

Similarly, in the Asian North American context, reflection on the biblical stories about the Jewish sojourn in the depths and heights of an alien society is revealing. People prominent in any rehearsal of Jewish history, like Joseph, Moses, Esther, and Daniel, suggest illuminating options. Whether they were desperately deprived or whether they found fulfillment in high, if precarious, places, these models bear witness to God's actions and to the responsibilities we have for ourselves, our people, and others.

The biblical stories therefore offer us correctives. First, God empowers "victims" to tackle their situations before rescuers arrive on the scene. No St. George was required. Second, if we eventually make our way into the power structure and even help existing structures function beneficially in some measure, we still remain aliens and guests. No St. George roams unhampered and triumphant. Third, acknowledging our marginality and seeing we still have far to go ironically becomes an opportunity for God to act through us (Heb. 11:13-16). When we, therefore, walk humbly in faith with our God, we can love mercy and do justice (Mic. 6:8; Matt. 23:23*b*). The racial ethic minority middle-class and white progressives who have accepted these realities for themselves begin addressing their sexism and racism, as well as their paternalism and materialism. We thereby increase solidarity in mission with integrity and build in the church and society eschatological signs of hope for genuine community.

We long for the fulfillment of that eschatological vision of a truly inclusive community where we all have a place with our distinct identities. One vision appears in Revelation 7, where great numbers of people from the tribes of Israel will be gathered around the throne of God. In addition, there will be innumerable Gentiles from every *ethnos*, language, and dialect (Rev. 7:1-10). The inclusive vision reappears in Revelation 21, where the new Jerusalem will have twelve gates named after the tribes of Israel and the twelve foundations are named after the apostles. Judaism represents the entry points from all directions and the apostolic outreach to all people represents the foundations of the new City of Shalom. Finally we read that the gates will not be closed to the *ethnē* and their rulers. Together they will bring their glory and honor to the new community (Rev. 21:25-27). This community in the divine realm is multiethnic, multilingual, and multireligious. Praise God!

2. Fruit and gifts of the Sanctifier

Working for an inclusive community in missional efforts has reminded us of the crucial role that personal and spiritual qualities play. We have therefore appreciated the witness of our forebears who said the Sanctifier nurtures those qualities. The Sanctifier does indeed cultivate the fruit of the Spirit in individuals (Gal. 5:22-23; Rom. 5:1-5; 12:9-21; 2 Pet. 1:5-11), and gifts for service come through the same Spirit (Rom. 12:6-8; 1 Cor. 12:4-11; Eph. 4:11-13). These qualitative changes restore the divine image in us and therefore make us more humane toward one another. They offer tangible signs that God will be all in all (Eph. 1:23; 4:6, 10) and will dwell in fullness in creation (Rev. 21). Because they are signs and not solutions, we look for more.

3. Empowerment for mission in the world

Critical reflections on our efforts to promote an inclusive, life-inducing community have brought to our attention additional actions of the Sanctifier and Consummator, especially in the baptism of Jesus. (1) We hear from John the Baptist how God had given Jesus a distinct identity (Mark 1:7). Immediately after he was (2) baptized by water, (3) the Holy Spirit descended on him with a witness. Jesus was a "son" or child, and the "Beloved," with whom God was well pleased (Mark 1:10). The same witness is heard again in the Transfiguration (Mark 9:7).

Students generally understand that each title functioned as a clue word to specific biblical passages. Although the symbol system is quite offensive, it is nevertheless summarized here to track the substance of the witness before it is restated in what I hope are more accessible terms. First, "son" recalls Pss. 2:7-10 and 110:1. These passages work with the male-dominated law of primogenitor in that cultural setting. A son therefore implies an heir. In a royal court, the heir who is next in line to reign is seated to the right of the one who is presently reigning. To the extent that the son is seated and not standing, it suggests the heir is reigning in some sense. When the early church used this symbol system, they confessed that the risen Christ had become a Sovereign and Savior (*kyrios*, or Lord). At the same time the early church cried out, "Come, Sovereign Savior" (*maranatha*). "Seated at the right hand" thus symbolized the "already and not yet," of the "time between the times." The heir still had a task to accomplish in the interim. The task is to overcome the enemies of the righteous, just, and holy Sovereign with frightfully violent means (Pss. 2:7-9, 110:5-6). Thus, while a child of God already prevails over the forces of evil, work remains to permeate the new creation with the divine presence.

Second, the "Beloved" refers to a chosen servant who is to undertake the task in less problematic terms. It is generally understood that "Beloved" recalls Isa. 42:1-4, one of the servant songs. It announces a commissioning to practice mercy, foster righteousness, and implement justice. The passage is explicitly cited in Matthew to explain that Jesus was anointed by the Holy Spirit, rather than by the unholy spirits as his opponents claimed, when be broke the taboos of his day (Matt. 12:18-21). The anointing of the Holy Spirit also called Jesus to accomplish liberation in the Jubilee (Luke 4:18-19, from Isa. 61:1-4, 58:6).[7]

Early Christians similarly (1) heard God creating them good with their distinct identities. They saw themselves (2) entering into the death and resurrection of Jesus Christ when, in faith, they were baptized in water (Rom. 6–7). (3) When the Holy Spirit descended upon them, they too heard a witness of the Spirit that they are children of God, and if children then heirs, and heirs with Christ in the glory he experienced, so long as they suffer as he did in service (Rom. 8:16-17). Furthermore, the servant is (be-)loved despite all the suffering that service entails (Rom. 8:28-39). Read therefore in the light of the baptism of Jesus, (1) a child of God who has (2) died to sin and is raised to newness of life is (3) anointed by the Spirit to become an heir with a task of creating the realm of God. In place of sin, evil, and death permeating the created order, the holiness, love, and life of God will reign (Ps. 2:7-8; 110:5-6). Through repentance and faith the trinitarian drama in baptism incorporates all Christians into God's mission. The ecumenical consensus also reminds us to look and work for God's reign and realm.

The Apocalypse recounts the arduous and costly spirals of creation/salvation into which the *ethnē* are anointed to participate (Rev. 4–11). The people of God are also promised periodic interludes of Sabbath rest en route (Rev. 4, 7, and 8). The overall flow of the story moves toward the final spiral in the history of salvation to a new creation. First, principalities and power are decisively overturned (Rev. 12–14; 17–18) and secured in their place (Rev. 20), as the Exodus led to the drowning of Pharaoh's legions. Second, there will be unity among people, and most especially between God and the created order (Rev. 19 and 21), as it occurred in the covenant at Sinai. Third, the drama of the divine mission is consummated in creating a new livable space where a river flows with the water of life and trees abound for the healing of nations (Rev. 21–22), as the children of Israel journeyed toward and reached the promised land. In the new heaven and a new earth, where God dwells in fullness, sin and death are no more. In the Apocalypse, we see the *ethnē* participating in the divine mission that creates an inclusive new community in a life-flourishing ecology. Hallelujah!

Conclusions

Critical reflections on our experiences have led us to contextualize our theology for the *ethnē* in mission with the triune God. The Bible has led us to reformulate our cultural and theological traditions. First, while contextualizing theology calls us to reaffirm the crucial role of the *ordo* and *via salutis,* it equally locates our distinct Wesleyan contribution within the broader sweep of the history of salvation in the work of the Christ, our Sovereign and Savior. If we fail do this, we allow antiquarian interests in the tradition of our elders to nullify the Word of God (Matt. 15:8-9; Mark 7:7-8). Second, contextualizing in turn locates salvation in an even broader trinitarian economy of the divine mission. On the one hand, contextualizing draws us into the distinct work of Creator/Caretaker who continues creating and cultivating new creatures apart from the divine salvific activities. On the other hand, critical reflection leads us to recover our participation in the unique work of the Consummator who combines a new creation with a definitive salvation. What begins in the Source and takes a decisive turn through the Savior is now consummated in the Sanctifier. Third, and finally, we are drawn into the names (attributes and actions) of the triune God through the trinitarian shape of sacramental faith and spirituality in baptism, just as the trinitarian drama in the Eucharist guides and rejuvenates us in the mission of the triune God. Thanks be to our gracious God for this hope-filled identity and calling. Amen.

Will the City Lose the Church?

William K. Quick

Someone has well said that "The very things that make the Church most needed in the city, are the things that make it hardest for the Church to survive there."

*The **city** means the throng and pressure of multitudinous life; the easily indulged extravagances of wealth, and the close standing economies of poverty; the crowd of people, and the lonesome lack of fellowship; the ever alert plans and attractive dress of designing vice, and the oft timid retiring attitude of virtue; life in all its various tempers and expressions and all at top speed; in all these things and many more grown familiar to us today, the Church in the city finds the challenge of its liability and its opportunity.[1]*

For thirty years the preacher at Metropolitan Methodist Church in Detroit, Dr. Merton S. Rice provides in these words a descriptive and insightful appraisal of the church in the city—an appraisal that is as true at the close of the twentieth century as it was sixty years earlier. A city is a racial and ethnic kaleidoscope, replete with customs, languages, costumes, skin colors, music, and food that those who live there are privileged to experience.

Early Christianity was a religion centered in cities and towns; it quickly became urban, not rural. It spread from city to city, from province to province, along the highways of commerce and trade, by land and sea. The transition of Christianity from a religion of rural, Galilean peasants, as it was in the time of Jesus, to what it became in the time of Paul, is clear in the New Testament. From early on, Christianity was a religion of the city.

The church is a part of all that the modern city is. It is important to find ways to express that, to give visible form to our incarnational theology, not simply accommodating ourselves to the city and its values, but affirming with joy and commitment that the city is a particularly intense and critical part of the creation God loves. Enormous and significant cultural changes have occurred in our cities, and our churches have suffered a decline numerically as well as in terms of public influence. The traditional churches are in trouble throughout our nation and yet the American people are asking religious questions—questions of value, meaning, purpose, and hope—in droves. Does the mainline church understand the importance of this renewed quest for spirituality and authentic faith?

Statistics

Statistics from cities across the Northeast and the Midwest are very discouraging. In 1965 there were 66 United Methodist churches in Detroit. In 1997 there are 19, many surviving only because of the city mission society (United Methodist Union) and annual conference support. Philadelphia in 1965 had more than 100 Methodist churches; by 1996 only 37 survived. Tindley Temple, the city's largest Methodist congregation, reported 5,500 members in 1965 and 971 in 1995.

Ohio, Indiana, and Illinois have been called "the heartland of Methodism." As the circuit riders traveled westward from Maryland, Methodism experienced phenomenal growth. Three decades ago over 1.5 million Methodists lived in that heartland, but by 1996 the membership in those three states had dropped below one million members. In 1965 the largest Methodist church in Indiana was Anderson: First Methodist, with 3,258 members. In 1996 its membership was 1,288. Broadway Church in Indianapolis reported 3,218 members in 1965 and 436 in 1995. The largest United Methodist church in Indiana and the North Central Jurisdiction at present is St. Luke's in the extreme northern section of Indianapolis; it claims 3,754 members.

Ohio Methodism's largest congregation in 1965 was North Broadway in Columbus with 4,483 members; in 1995 its membership was at 2,032. In Cleveland of 1965 the Lakewood Church reported 4,294 members; thirty years later it had 943 on the rolls. In Minnesota, the Hennepin Avenue Church in Minneapolis was the state's largest, with 4,400 members; three decades later its membership had dropped to 2,251.

In 1965 Michigan Methodists exceeded 300,000; within thirty years they had shown a 125,000 membership decline. There were once 980 churches in the state, 56 with a membership exceeding 1,000, and 14 with membership exceeding 2,000. In 1997 only three churches in the state have a membership exceeding 2,000.

In 1913, when Merton S. Rice was appointed to Detroit's Metropolitan Church, the congregation had a membership of 1,200. At the time of his death in March of 1943, that church had grown to 7,304 members and had become the largest church in World Methodism. Two major emigrations, the first after the Second World War and the second following the riots of the '60s, saw the membership take a downward plunge. Upon my arrival, in 1974, Metropolitan United Methodist Church reported a membership in excess of 2,000. However, the members for whom the church could find current addresses numbered 1,285. In 1998 the church's membership is 1,566—no phenomenal growth but a reversal of the national trend.

Dramatic losses in membership during the past three decades were experienced in Detroit's largest African American United Methodist Church, Scott Memorial, whose reported membership dropped from 3,152 in 1965 to 322 in 1995. The Strathmore Church, with 2,513 members in 1965, was merged in the late '70s with St. James Church, which had a peak membership of 1,800 members, to form the St. Timothy congregation, which now has a membership of 331—half African American, half Caucasian.

Why the instability of many city churches? Do they see their main mission as preserving the past? Do they see reform as a threat? Why the rigidity and fear of innovation?

Core city congregations are finding neither simple formulas nor new missionary spirit for survival. United Methodism is a denomination with a 94 percent white membership, predominantly middle-class, suburban, and rural in location, and having difficulty finding a strategy or a vision for the twenty-first-century city church. Complicating the plight is a growing realization that neither the council of bishops nor the General Council on Ministries and its program boards have articulated an agenda for our cities or given visionary leadership for the urban church.

Urban life increasingly influences American culture, and corresponding options to expand vital and meaningful ministries in the city continue to diminish. Without discounting some scattered, vibrant urban parishes that dot the city landscape, my investigation tends to reinforce myths of urban decay or confusion regarding urban ministry. Caught up in the confusion, city congregations languish because of poor deployment of pastors, dispirited lay leadership, lack of support for multicultural, multiracial churches, and a reluctance among many pastors to locate their families in high crime neighborhoods and poor city educational systems.

The Death of American Cities?

In the 1970s we were told that the cities were dead. New York City was in bankruptcy. Large companies fled the urban jungle. They headed for the serenity of New York's Westchester County, escaped to quiet Connecticut dells, or moved from mid-Manhattan to places like Alexandria and Arlington, Virginia, separated from Washington, D.C. by the Potomac River, pushed onward to the Carolinas, where life could be lived more quietly, handy to leisure-time pleasures, and even established themselves in the exurban reaches of California.

In the 1950s the cities represented crowds, traffic, noise, pollution and crime: muggings, rapes, and being "ripped-off." The green fringes promised trees, space, good schools, and breathable air . . . all on a half-acre of heaven. In 1974 the United States Senate authorized the expenditure of $750,000 for an urban study and reported its findings to the Senate in three brief words, *"Cities are dying."*

Change in the city was not only brought about by the movement to the suburbs but also by the deterioration of central city public school systems, the fear of crime, the closing of downtown department stores, the malling of America, the decline of public transportation, and the erosion of inherited institutional loyalties. We watched the flight to the suburbs for the tract house, lawn, and garden, followed by the relocation of the great department stores that provided the keystone for enormous shopping malls covering suburban greenery with asphalt and tar to allow parking space for Detroit-made automobiles. Grafted onto suburban life were the very things those fleeing the concrete jungle had sought to escape.

Then, more suddenly than it had begun, the emigration slowed. Some people began to turn back to the cities. So did some large corporations. One of the largest companies left New York City in 1972, relocating in a southern town of 100,000 population. In 1979, they closed shop and moved back to New York. Midtown apartment buildings and lofts are being renovated in the cities—some in even grander style. Americans are learning what Parisians and Londoners have known all along—that it is both convenient and entertaining to live in a midcity that remains alive around the clock.

Huge amounts of money are being invested in city after city. New and rakish towers soar out of vacant lots. Millions are being spent in New York, Baltimore, Pittsburgh, and Kansas City, to reincarnate (in grand luxury) great old hotels. In 1978 Henry Ford II spearheaded the Detroit development of Renaissance Center with the construction of the then tallest hotel in the world.

In city after city, retail, entertainment, hotel, office, and even residential business is being turned back toward the center city. What has caused this monumental renaissance that has given new life to cities like Minneapolis, Birmingham, Cincinnati, Hartford, Atlanta, and a dozen others?

The reasons are manifold and often complicated, differing from city to city. But the underlying reasons can be traced both to people's disenchantment with the suburbs, which began a massive diaspora from urban centers to the country in the years following World War II and the racial riots of the 1960s, and to the large corporations that followed them there. Turn around is due not only to disenchantment but also to the realization that the marketplace action is not in the suburban green fields, but in the inner cities. Convention business is up, as is city tourism. By 1997 New York had become a magnet for retirees. Along with economic changes came the social comprehension that marketplaces are symbolic of peoples' need to congregate. High taxes in the suburbs and the increased toll of travel time are factors as well.

What we are witnessing is the result of disillusionment along with a growing sense of nostalgia and a renewed sense of history. Therefore, we are beginning to experience a counter movement, a reverse gravitation—back to the city. There is a burgeoning sense of a need to be together, to rub shoulders in a crowd, and to rediscover historic identity; there is a revulsion against regimentation; and there is an ultimate realization of the values that exist in the preservation of one's task.

There are no hard data on the movement from city to suburb or the return from suburb to city, according to the Census Bureau. But there is a real movement, particularly by young singles, the recently married, or the unmarried living together. They have returned, not only because of the excitement and challenge of urban life, not only because of the proximity to the arts, but also because of the escalation in the cost of housing everywhere. Housing in many cities costs less than in the suburbs. In apartments and lofts there are no huge heating bills to pay, no homeowner's insurance premiums, no repairs to leaking roofs. Cities are attracting a different generation of empty-nesters and young adults. In practically every instance, couples both work; having children is not uppermost in the young adult mind. Two people, without children, both working, don't care to commute and they conclude, "Let's live downtown where we can enjoy life and get the best out of a city."

Reclaiming the Church's Urban Mission

What has also been rediscovered is that we cannot truly escape the human need for other people. Across the nation, suburban exiles are coming home. Yet in their return to the city, their church—particularly mainline Protestant, and in many instances, Roman Catholic—may not be found. Yes, those returning will find churches, but not the type (or names) of churches that were in the city when they or their parents left it thirty years ago. Between 300 and 400 Protestant churches in Detroit have closed, merged, or moved to the suburbs since 1946. Edmund

Cardinal Szoka, in the greatest mass closing of churches in the history of Catholicism, closed thirty churches in Detroit—*in "one fell-swoop"*—and declared sixteen other city parishes *"questionably viable."* The second wave of closings in a major city occurred in Chicago and a third in Pittsburgh, where thirty-six Roman Catholic churches were closed between 1992 and 1995.

Whenever a church closes, the quality of life in the neighborhood is diminished. A church closing creates a vacuum, and anything and everything rushes in to fill the vacuum. Churches serve the city by their presence, by providing community, by reaching out and serving the needs of persons. Any organization, including the church, over time may stray from its basic reason for being. With the passing of years it will tend to devote its energy and resources to its own survival and not to the purpose for which it was established in the first place. The U.S. Post Office, at regular intervals, must find a way to remind itself and postal employees that its purpose is to deliver the mail; the school system, to teach children; and Chrysler, Ford, or General Motors to manufacture automobiles and trucks that people want to purchase. Likewise, the church—at regular intervals—needs to remind itself of its purpose for being—to do the work of Jesus Christ and to carry out his mission in the world.

Churches lose sight of the fact that they are communities of pastoral care for their members and places for worship, nurture, and Christian education. But, if the church is not engaged in a missional outreach to the community and to the world, a vital dimension of the church as an institution and the body of Christ, is missing. *"God so loved the world that He gave his only begotten Son that whosoever believes in Him should not perish but have everlasting life"* (John 3:16). To be the church is to be in the world. Authentic being means serving and giving away something of its life.

Unfortunately, reaching urban people is difficult. Many inner-city churches simply are not up to the task of evangelizing huge, increasingly diverse, and rapidly growing populations. A city church with an aged congregation, whose members are tired and whose finances are limited or unable to accept a changing community, begins to die.

Trends in Urban Life

Our world has become an urban world. We are faced with unbelievable growth of the world's existing cities and human problems of a magnitude that no previous generation has had to face. Few trends in twentieth-century America have been more dramatic than the mass movement of the population from the country to the city. In 1790 less than 5 percent of the American people lived in cities and the percentage began falling as pioneers moved westward. Ninety percent of Americans lived in rural areas at the turn of the century; today 50 percent live in 39 cities with populations of one million or more. The migration from farm or village to city or metropolis has been a central phenomenon in American history since the end of the nineteenth century.

New immigration laws have resulted in what TIME magazine calls the "browning of America." Fully 87 percent of the newcomers in our cities are people of color. Although the ethnic mix continues to change, what never changes is the human need for the message and hope of the gospel. People crowding into our cities need the church every bit as much as the earlier immigrant groups.

As we face a new millennium, the majority of people will be living in cities worldwide. The world will be more urban than rural for the first time in its history. It is estimated that by the end of the twenty-first century, 94 percent of the U.S. population will be city dwellers. Whereas in 1950 only seven cities in the world had a population of more than 5,000,000, by 1985 the number of such giant cities had become thirty-four. By the year 2020 it is estimated that the "Third World" will include 80 of the 93 cities in the world with populations in excess of 5,000,000.[2]

The cities of America are chiefly populated by ethnic, vulnerable elderly and fragile people who are economically locked into life in the city center. Most city churches are reminders of that time in history when communities were formed on the basis of ethnicity, language, and religion. But a revolution has happened in our cities and the old order has passed away. As each immigrant wave achieved prosperity and moved to the suburbs, or as neighborhoods changed and white flight ensued, church buildings were left behind that had to be supported by smaller congregations most likely experiencing change in both economic and ethnic makeup.

Knowing that the city centers are typically home to marginalized, poor, powerless persons, many mainline denominations have shifted their focus to the suburbs, where ambitious goals for future church growth seems the most promising. There is a gnawing sense that the immense problems of the city and the needs of its inhabitants are too massive for the church to tackle. Today, city congregations face increasingly violent street gangs, crack cocaine use, high teen pregnancy and infant mortality rates, deplorable housing, extremely inadequate schools, neighborhood blight, and in general, urban decay.

An example of this shift from rural to urban poor is the large numbers of Appalachian poor who left their small highland farmsteads and abandoned coal camps, migrating to the industrial cities of the Great Lakes before and during World War II, settling first in Detroit, Dayton, and Columbus. Similarly, in the years following World War II the Whites in the U.S. migrated to the suburbs while African Americans and Hispanics migrated from the rural South and Southwest to the central cities. Black city churches became institutions of urban socialization—humanizing the impersonal—and, as white congregations relocated to the suburbs, church buildings were purchased by black denominations or former storefront church communities while others were sold to businesses or to house restaurants. But the transformation of even the church buildings deepens the story.

Buildings: Shrines or Missions?

Most American city churches remain standing where they were built, but the names on the majority of them are different from the name their denomination originally carved on the cornerstone or the front entry. Along Detroit's main artery, Woodward Avenue (labeled by older local citizens as Piety Row), the First United Methodist Church in Highland Park is now Soul Harvest Ministries; Trinity Methodist Episcopal is The New Mt. Moriah Baptist; Central Woodward Christian (Disciples of Christ) is Historic Little Rock Baptist; Temple Beth El is renamed Lighthouse Cathedral (its bulletin board sports a United Methodist cross and flame symbol); First Baptist is St. John's Christian Methodist Episcopal; North Woodward Congregational is The People's Community Church. The Bethel Evangelical Church on Grand Boulevard (which Reinhold Niebuhr served before going to Union Seminary in New York) is today The Sweet Home Baptist Church.

In cities across the country thousands of venerable religious and architectural treasures have fallen into disrepair or become financial burdens rather than sources of inspiration and home to thriving congregations. Locked doors remind one more of a fortress than a place of fellowship. Victims of deferred maintenance and shrinking congregations, many of these city church buildings are liabilities instead of assets. Large and cavernous, they drain enormous amounts of money from church budgets and endowments and face abandonment or demolition. Among those that have been demolished are two historic and once-vital churches in Los Angeles—First United Methodist and Trinity United Methodist. As United Methodism merged churches or fled to the now-troubled suburbs, dwindling congregations became marginalized—with some surviving on endowments, thanks to the generous benefactors and philanthropy of past generations. Others struggle to remain open by a strategy of deferred building maintenance, low salaries, part-time employees, or worker-priests.

Buildings have become shrines or monuments instead of mission stations. Those built at the beginning of the twentieth century tend not to be user friendly today, and although many are aesthetically pleasing to architectural buffs, they are not functional for worship or contemporary church life.

Perhaps the day of the downtown church is over. It may be an endangered species, destined to be as extinct in the twenty-first century as the Kresge or Woolworth dime stores are today. Other churches in downtown areas across America are either moving to more promising locations, slipping in their effectiveness, or changing their ministry profiles altogether. Speaking of institutional forms of religion rather than of statistics, Paul Tillich remarked sixty years ago that Protestantism is at "the end of an era." A generation later, Gibson Winter predicted a "Protestant Deformation" for North America. The religious practices of Protestants in the large city have changed due in part to a high rate of mobility and rapidly changing moral and social values. And often this change in religious practices has not kept pace with changing urban life. The church suffers from "culture lag." People comment that it is "the caboose instead of the engine."

So what are we to do? Will the church be content with providing shrines or committed to mission in the cities? Will mainline Protestants rediscover the city and invest in building creative and healthy parishes with a strategy for congregational life and worship suited to the aforementioned realities of ministry to city dwellers? Will the church embrace the new poor who face cross-ethnic and interracial strife, poor-on-poor crime, and the destruction of low-income and blighted neighborhoods? A new pastoral presence in the city can serve only if the church is willing to identify with this new context. Urban pastors must be *community* pastors trained in *community* building. Imperative upon urban pastors is the call to embody and impart a vision of what can be, despite pain-filled lives. Congregations and pastors need to be living in the city and walking in faith toward what "should be" while living in the "not yet." Christian faith does not allow the luxury of believing *without* putting faith to work.

The Wesleyan Urban Legacy

As we look to rebuilding vital church life in the cities, let us recall that Methodism took root among the poor, the forgotten, the disenchanted of the city in Wesley's day. While it is true that John

Wesley found an extraordinary receptivity in rural Cornwall, it was in the population centers of London, Bristol, Newcastle and in the urban ghettoes of England's Industrial Revolution that the Methodist Societies flourished.

Wesley, in his early years, had been confused and sanctimonious, a failure as a missionary to the Native Americans in the newly founded colony of Georgia, uncertain of his own faith. In his midthirties, following a "heartwarming and life-changing experience" on May 24, 1738, his preaching became so threatening to the established church that he was banned from their pulpits.

He began to draw crowds of five or ten thousand in the open air: coal miners from Bristol and poor women from the back streets of Newcastle. In many cases their lives were entirely changed by hearing him preach the gospel, and by submitting to his "methodist" discipline of regular meetings and "bands."

Therefore, we need to remind ourselves that the original setting of historic Methodism was twofold: (1) in the religious experience of John Wesley and, (2) in the vast spiritual destitution of eighteenth-century England. English society was in the midst of an agricultural and industrial revolution that drew men, women, and children from the countryside into the factories, mines, and mills, where they worked under conditions of indescribable cruelty. The factory system was the new moneymaking, death-dealing Moloch to whom the poor people of eighteenth-century England were thrown. A new moneyed class arose, imbued with a greedy materialism. This hard-ruling class, dedicated to material success, lived in luxury; the submerged mass, uprooted by the new industries, lived miserably, many out of work, while many labored in dehumanizing smokestack factories, finding no satisfaction in their work and only the squalor and loneliness of the city.

The suffering and misery of the poorer classes herded into factory towns caused them, in the pain of hopelessness, to seek "temporary release" in the new cheap tipples, rum and gin. Every sixth house in London was a saloon, and drunkenness became so universal through-out Britain that the very nature of the citizenry was changed. The upper classes set an example of profligacy that was generally followed by politicians and clergy. Crime was rampant among all classes and so common were murder and robbery that no one thought of stirring out of their house at night without being armed. At no period in all the history of the English people had morals sunk to such a low ebb.

And what was the religious situation in England at this time? The depth, apathy, and shame to which organized religion in eighteenth-century England had sunk begs description. In 1731 Montesquieu reported, after a visit to England, that the people had no religion, and no more than four or five members of the House of Commons attended church. The Church of England, from the Archbishop of Canterbury down, was riddled with indifference and complacency. Many of the clergy spent their time in gambling, fox hunting, and drinking and made little pretense of caring for the spiritual well-being of their parish.

The urban crisis in our American cities parallels, in many ways, the immense problems Wesley found in the cities of his own day. The problems facing the church—then and now—bear remarkable similarities: immense drug problems (crack cocaine today, gin then), family disintegration, social disorder, and violence. Wesley encountered thousands left to fend for themselves in harrowing conditions—a new dependent, self-destructive "underclass."

"The streets were dark with something more than night" perfectly catches the feel of eighteenth-century London as well as twentieth-century Detroit, Los Angeles, and Washington. The streets of London were blanketed with fear and stalked by "footpads" and "highwayman" (today, we call them "carjackers" and "criminals"). Perhaps what saved London was Wesley, an innovative, bold, and resourceful religious and social leader who addressed the "demoralization" of his day with a message that empowered the poor to lead their own crusade in fighting social injustice, economic exploitation, and spiritual impoverishment.

The Methodist societies became distribution centers for food, clothing, money, and medicine for the poor. They also became job-training centers, housing-finders, lending banks, and providers of legal aid. Wesley started history's first people's medical clinic and led the struggles for child labor laws, prison reform, and the abolition of slavery. He believed, "The Gospel of Christ knows of no religion but social; no holiness but social holiness. This commandment we have from Christ that he who loves God loves his brother also."

An Effective Urban Church

We have briefly glimpsed what Wesley and the Methodist church innovated and achieved in his day. But what describes an effective city church today? What factors are related to *urban* church effectiveness? What insight is relevant as the church comes to grips with urban problems? What sort of strategy ought to be developed? Can churches cope and survive the problems of urban community? If mainline Protestantism is to be a part of the survival, it must learn to minister in the twenty-first-century city. The urgency—the necessity—is apparent.

Effective city churches are no longer in the grip of tradition. They are sensitive to changing needs and opportunities to witness to the gospel day-to-day. A church community is redeemed and transformed as it directs its emphases and adapts its programs to meet the city's changing needs. Unless a church witnesses responsibly to the community, it cannot reach and minister effectively to individuals and families—members or not.

Mainline Protestantism, including Methodism, is being forced to face pressing institutional problems as well as sociopolitical issues. These include:

- the lack of an urban strategy by the denomination
- controversy over methods of doing theology in an urban society
- the failure of theological seminaries to provide a curriculum in formation for effective urban ministry
- the dysfunctional way annual conferences and national church bodies prioritize support to nurture local mission effort
- difficulties in sustaining funding for innovative ministries
- confusion and default (sometimes even failure) of city church pastors and lay leadership to relate to the political and economic power base in the city, especially as regards education, housing, and health care

Most cities in the United States are seeing an increase in fundamentalist, independent, and nondenominational churches that have a passion for saving souls but lack the vision and impetus for urban mission. In Detroit and southeast Michigan, there are 2,016 Protestant, Catholic, and Orthodox congregations and at last count 2,000 storefront and/or independent churches in the city of Detroit. In this postmodern age we are witnessing a growing number of people attracted to "eclectic beliefs": New Age, the Occult, Mysticism, Fundamentalism, Far Eastern Religions, even Satanism. Furthermore, we are seeing a growth pattern among such conservative groups as the Church of the Nazarene, Seventh-Day Adventists, Assemblies of God, Pentecostals, Mormons, and Southern Baptists while the mainline churches continue to decline.

The church has an unprecedented opportunity to reach out to people who are searching for a new vision of life. This opportunity will pass unless the church makes some fundamental attempts to relate and become more accessible to the rank-and-file and to make its message more understandable to contemporary society. Life is shifting in some directions that we cannot clearly judge. Something is being born. We are in a phase where one age is succeeding another. There remain two basic forces in human nature: one that aims at suppressing the spiritual in a human being, and another that seeks to enrich and give greater expression to the Spirit.

The Urban Ministry Movement

The urban ministry movement of mainline Protestantism grew out of a resistance to the suburban abandonment of the city. For more than two decades, from the mid-1950s to the mid-1970s, church-based action training centers mushroomed. Twenty-seven were set up in twenty-two cities, one of them training 4,000 people in a hundred programs in five years. The better known were in Chicago and New York. They flourished and withered in just fifteen years.

Unfortunately, some urban leaders seem convinced that the situation facing us in the late 1990s is no different from that of the 1960s and 1970s. To the contrary, the need today is for well-designed programs that will retrain and retool urban church leadership to deal with unprecedented dangers, risks, and opportunities faced by our city churches.

In many Protestant communions during the 1990s, the large city or megachurches have turned away from seminary or denominational boards of education to develop their own in-service or management training institutes. This new approach to clergy training for urban pastors is at times based on group dynamics, action training, and a pastoral theology that in some instances may be more secular than Christian and in other instances, more fundamentalist than mainstream. We have begun to witness major difficulties faced by many of the pastors trained in these ecumenical or conservative in-service institutes in their effort to overcome lethargy and tradition. Following training events many pastors return to a city parish to face a rigidity and inflexibility on the part of their lay leaders unwilling to accept the change being introduced in their local congregations. Pastors are stonewalled where such entrenched lay leadership dominates and they face a reinforcement of the status quo, not to mention renewed resistance to new visions requiring change and innovation.

The Need for Pastors and Prophets

Dedicated laity within the city church cry out for a "good pastor" and for clergy who understand their role as both pastoral and prophetic. A truly pastoral and prophetic role is paramount in a downtown or inner-city ministry. Regrettably, many pastors fail to hear the cry of the laity for a caring shepherd. The English word "pastor" derives from the Latin and means "shepherd." The pastor, in the etymological sense of the word, is one who ". . . knows my sheep and my sheep know me." The late Bishop Gerald Kennedy often said, "No minister can be a prophet who has not first been a priest (pastor)."

A pastor needs to have a basic concern for all persons, a sound theological undergirding for his or her work, and such a sufficiently mature faith that s/he neither strikes out in futile anger nor withdraws in hopeless despair in the face of opposition or lethargy. Crossing cultural lines and assimilating persons of different ethnic backgrounds into the fellowship of a city church cannot be accomplished unless the pastor is a shepherd who has a love for all of God's sheep. A shepherd has the ability to win the support of followers and the wisdom not to confuse fans with followers.

The pastor remains in many respects the central figure in the life of the church, the leader in defining identity and role. A pastor wears many hats and performs ministry as a visionary, creative, and future-oriented leader. Less obvious may be the symbolic nature of the pastoral role. In a special sense the pastor stands as one apart—a representation or symbol of the divine. Yet, the pastor is expected to have organizational abilities, bound by and responsible to a bureaucracy whose traditions are rooted in denominational history and polity. Each aspect of the pastor's role has implications for who one is, how one performs, and the authority exercised.

A multifaceted role, the burden of responsibility for the success or failure of a church consequently is often seen to fall primarily on the pastor called to lead and equip the laity for the ministry. One must be a preacher and a shepherd, administrator and organizer, counselor and educator as well as fund-raiser. This poses a number of problems: how does one acquire competence to perform, how does one judge the *important* over against the *relative,* dividing one's time accordingly, and how does one resolve the pressures when there is more to be done daily than can be done effectively? The caring, effective pastor is ever conscious of this multidimensional role and sees the importance of sharing ministry tasks with the laity.

Effective urban ministry includes a personal relationship of the pastor and congregants with people in the community as well as institutions of power. Thriving inner-city churches collaborate with and draw upon a wealth of corporate and community resources as well as denominational assistance. Effective city churches have a positive effect upon the neighborhood. The church and community leaders work together to relate to the neighborhood, to make it safe, decent, and attractive for everyone living there.

Nowhere is the cry of the heart more urgently heard than in the lives of the children and youth in urban communities. The church is called to address the need for attractive and life-giving alternatives to the many dead ends that are present in their lives: drugs, suicide, AIDS, malnutrition. Our concern for the city has been shaken by the mindless violence of its youth and undermined by the cold indifference of institutional mayhem. Fifty-three teens (aged 15 to 19) were murdered in Detroit in 1996. They died not from illness or car accidents. They were murdered—many by gang members, and many as innocent bystanders caught in the cross-fire. There are neighborhoods where nobody walks home from school any more; where metal detectors are at school doors; and where nearly every student has a gun or knows where to get one. Youths take a bullet from kids they don't even know or over arguments that nobody can even remember.[3] Thirty-nine percent of all Detroit's children live below the poverty level. The issue in urban ministry is systemic and embraces us all. The contradictions go to the heart of our national life: the gross disparity of rich and poor, the alienation of city and suburb, the enduring divisions and conflicts of race.

Thriving city churches help those who are in need. They welcome and minister to all people regardless of their economic, racial, or cultural circumstances. They teach, tutor, and encourage the children, many of them from single-parent homes.

Urban ministry is carried out by the church that *feels* and *acts with* the people and not *for* the people. The church provides fellowship and refuge while working to bring about a more just society. The strangers in our neighborhoods need to know they matter to the church and are loved by God. They best understand this when the people in God's church are merciful, just, and kind. Those of us who care about the church, who pray and work for the renewal of the church, must help the church in the demanding task of responding faithfully. Sometimes the church can lead; sometimes the church should follow. We have a word to say, a love to share, and a saving gospel to live out.

The task of urban ministry cannot be clergy dominated but is successful when the laity are empowered, nurtured, and set free to articulate the faith and implement God's mission. So for example, inter-generational ministries could be a vital solution, with young adults bringing energy and new ideas, and older adults bringing organiza-tional experience and financial backing. A healthier, more inclusive church may be the outcome.

There is a fundamental dilemma in defining the church's task in contemporary American society. The church is confronted with the complexities of a postmodern culture. In that confrontation traditional answers stated in abstract terms will no longer suffice. The church has to say explicitly what its objectives are and what values it is dedicated to in ways that are meaningful, not only in principle, but also in practice, as the twenty-first century dawns. Neither naive optimism nor grand-sounding platitudes will suffice.

The mainline church is adept at making prophetic pronouncements and sponsoring well-meaning church resolutions. Is it not hypocritical for us to pass noble resolutions in our conferences and conventions about the importance of the church's urban mission when we are not serious about training clergy and laity for urban ministry? I am convinced that we cannot fundamentally better the future of poor city dwellers unless we live in the city. We need to address the carpetbagger suburban Christian who moves from the safe suburbs into the city core—shuttling back and forth two or three times a week to salve a social conscience. That will not suffice in today's world. Lest the city lose the church, we are compelled to choose whether our major priority for church growth is in new, affluent, suburban communities or if we are going to be faithful to our mission to reestablish the church's presence in the city's slums we have deserted over the past 40 years. Unless we are willing to put our funding and personnel into rebuilding the city church, it is futile to hope that our talk about it will accomplish the task. This is a serious call for the church to address not only its opportunity but the needs of the city.

Urban ministry is more than soup kitchens, clothes closets, and shelters—as important as these may be for the daily lives of thousands. In the long run, ministry in the city calls for bold visions that move us beyond a food pantry or temporary housing. As the twentieth century breathes its last and the new millennium begins, we are called to rethink our priorities and our mission in the computer-driven, high speed, supercharged world culture that has broken in upon us. How do we choose to respond to the new things God is doing in our cities and the new demands the Holy Spirit places upon our heads, hearts, and pocketbooks? Will we look to create something new rather than simply preserve the old, will we be involved rather than disengaged, will we worship rather than merely ritualize?

At the very time in 1916 that Merton S. Rice was planning to build what would become in 1935 Methodism's largest church, George Santayana was writing words that seem to be coming true in the late 1990s: "Romantic Christendom—picturesque, passionate, unhappy episode—may be coming to an end. Such a catastrophe would be no reason to despair. Nothing lasts forever. . . ."

Perhaps the real question is not, "will the city lose the church?" but *"will the church lose the city?"* Any vital future means being true to the biblical mandates that gave us identity and purpose. To discern and claim God's vision is to implement that vision in the world. God calls and empowers the church for mission.

Paul put the challenge to Christians of his century and ours: "Don't let the world around you squeeze you into its own mold, but let God remold your minds from within, so that you may prove in practice that the plan of God for you is good, meets all God's demands, and moves toward the goal of true maturity" (Rom. 12:2 Phillips).

Does United Methodism Have a Future in an Electronic Culture?

Thomas E. Boomershine

When described from the perspective of communication systems and culture, the United Methodist Church now uses an oral/print system of communication designed for the communication of the gospel in print culture. The basis of its oral communication network is the system of local churches. The congregations are led by a cadre of ordained ministers most of whom have earned an M.Div. degree at the church's seminaries by demonstrating that they have mastered print communication in the writing of a series of papers. The church is also a network of annual conferences who communicate with their constituencies both by oral contacts of various sorts and in conference newspapers and programmatic documents. The church is a conglomerate of general church boards, all of whom in different ways carry out their mission by the production of a series of written documents. The whole of the connection is served by the United Methodist Publishing House, which prints thousands of documents for the church: books, curricula, magazines, pamphlets, journals, and other documents of an almost infinite variety. All of these institutions operate within the same basic interpretive system. That system is the interpretive framework of the Enlightenment, the interaction of science and theology that formed the modern mind. The United Methodist Church is, then, an organization structured by and for the systems and cultures of print.

That system has been highly effective in the communication of the gospel in the American print cultures of the nineteenth and early- to mid-twentieth centuries. The problem of the church is, however, that the culture in which it seeks to embody and communicate the gospel now is predominantly an electronic culture. The United Methodist Church is a print-structured church that is seeking to communicate in a postmodern, postliterate culture in which the most pervasive and powerful means of cultural communication are electronic rather than written. For the children of the electronic age, walking into a typical United Methodist church means stepping back into an earlier culture in which there are only static images, books read out loud, organ music, and the cultural atmosphere and hymns of the nineteenth century. The steady declines in membership and the growing percentages of elderly persons within the membership since the 1960s are clear indications that the United Methodist Church is not communicating to the generations that grew up with TV. Bishop Richard Wilke noted in 1986 that average attendance in the church school programs of the United Methodist Church had declined from 4.2 million in 1960 to 2.1 million in 1984.[1] On the basis of present patterns, it appears probable that the United Methodist Church will continue to decline at an accelerated rate as the elderly majority of the church dies over the next two decades.

The purpose of this essay is to reflect on the future of the United Methodist Church in the electronic cultures of the twenty-first century and to outline in broad strokes a reformation of the church for ministry and mission in that culture. The present communication network of the church will be evaluated by a comparison with the systems the church developed in the nineteenth century, and a system for the future will be outlined that would be in greater continuity with that history. When seen within the larger framework of United Methodist history, it is relatively easy to envision the broad outlines of a future church that would effectively embody and communicate the gospel in the electronic cultures of the twenty-first century.

The Communication Network of the "Connection" in Twenty-First Century Print Culture

Seen from the perspective of communication and culture, connectionalism in the early decades of the Methodist Episcopal Church was an immensely dense system of oral and written communication. Russell Richey's description of the church in the introductory essay to this series describes some of the major elements of the oral system:

> Preaching mediated a Wesleyan reading of scripture, hymns instilled our doctrines, class meetings translated promise into practice, love feasts expressed the joy that young and old, rich and poor, white and black, English and German had *heard* and *experienced*. Methodist connectionalism *voiced* itself and measured its effectiveness by the quality, intensity and volume of its utterance.[2]

The richness of the preaching, singing, testimonies, and prayers in the classes, worship, quarterly meetings, and annual conferences of early Methodism is evident in every description of the life of the "connection." Methodists spoke and heard a common Arminian gospel and they welcomed persons into a network of oral communication.

From the beginning of the establishment of the Methodist Episcopal Church, however, the printed page was an integral part of the communication system of the "connection." In the years of the American Revolution that led up to the establishment of the Methodist Episcopal Church in 1784, Asbury and his associates were dependent on books from England. John Dickens, who proposed the new church's name, established the Book Concern with money provided by his 25-year-old wife, Betsy, who, on May 22, 1783, sold her share of her father's 1300-acre plantation to her brother-in-law, Thomas Crawford. Some ministers of the Baltimore Conference later recalled what happened:

> Feeling an anxious desire to promote to the utmost of his ability the welfare of the connexion, John Dickens devoted three hundred pounds (the part proceeds of the sale of a small tract of Land obtained by marriage to his present widow) to the publication & circulation of Books designed for the service of the Connexion. Thus originated our book concern, and Br. Dickens was appointed our first Book Agent. . . ."[3]

A month later, Dickens was appointed as pastor of the John Street parish in New York City, the second most important appointment in the church. As a result, Dickens's ministry at John Street and the formation of the Book Concern were totally interconnected. The literary character of Methodist culture is further reflected in Dickens's role in the establishment of a school, Cokesbury College, in New York. They probably began publishing in 1787 but in 1789 the Methodist Episcopal Church officially entered the publishing business.[4] The first periodical publication was *The Arminian Magazine.*

The position of the book agent became a central role in the missionary outreach of the church as well as in the management of the agency itself. Joshua Soule, who was made book agent in 1816, was also the first treasurer of the Missionary Society of the church. This pattern of the head of the book business also serving as treasurer of the Missionary Society continued until the Civil War. He in turn was, as Pilkington puts it, "the first of a long line of book agents and editors to become a bishop."[5] Soule and especially his successor, Nathan Bangs, made the Book Concern a major enterprise that became one of the nation's largest publishers and the most innovative and connecting force in Methodist life. *The Methodist Magazine,* the successor to the short-lived *Arminian Magazine* (1818), and the *Christian Advocate* (1826) became the central means of unifying the various far-flung enterprises of the church and provided both nurture for the pastors and members of the church and outreach to those who were not yet Methodists. And as the production capabilities of the church increased, the itinerants provided a highly effective system of distribution. As Richey observes, "Every itinerant peddled for the Book Concern."[6]

The Book Concern published a wide range of books and periodicals needed for a growing church. The book list included hymnals, devotional books, biblical commentaries, theological treatises as well as Greek and Hebrew grammars, Wesley's *Primitive Physic,* and school books such as Tytler's *History,* Dymock's *Caesar,* and Adam's *Latin Grammar* (1823).[7] Thus, the Book Concern published materials that were of a more general cultural interest as well as specifically religious books. Other Methodist publishing ventures followed. The Methodist Episcopal Tract Society was established in 1817 and became the foundation for the Sunday School Union by publishing a wide range of tracts, and the Methodist Episcopal Bible Society was formed in 1828. When one considers that at the time of the fire that destroyed the Book Concern in 1836,[8] it was second in size only to Harper and Brothers among the publishing companies in New York, the combination of various Methodist publishing ventures placed it among the largest, if not the largest, coordinated publishing system in the country.

The Methodist Episcopal Church in the nineteenth century was, therefore, a highly complex and progressive force in the appropriation of mass printing and distribution. The Methodists mastered the most advanced technological developments in mass communication of their time and used that technology for the building of the church. In a recent essay, Mark Noll has characterized the goal of Protestants during the evangelical Enlightenment as being to Christianize and evangelize the new country, and to a large measure they succeeded. As he states:

> Success in spreading that message is indicated by the fact that in 1859, something like one-third of America's church adherents were Methodists, another one-third were Baptist or Presbyterians, and a further one-sixth belonged to some other variety of mostly evangelical Protestantism.[9]

Noll concludes from a study of the period:

> It is hard to think of a better way of accounting for that success than . . . that the triumph of Christianity in antebellum America was due to Protestant mastery of the culture's most powerful means of communication and its most compelling interpretive system.[10]

That is, the mastery of the technological and the conceptual systems were integrally related to one other.

From the perspective of an electronic age, a striking fact about the Protestant churches in this period is that their technological powers were yoked together with their intellectual powers. In the same essay, Mark Noll shows the way in which the evangelical churches mastered the communications system of mass publication and distribution and the conceptual languages of what he calls "theistic Enlightenment science." The character of that science is reflected in a statement from John Miley's *Systematic Theology*, an 1892 publication of the Methodist Book Concern:

> A system of theology is a combination of doctrines in scientific accord. . . . [T]hrough a careful study of the facts of geology the doctrines of the science are reached and verified, while in turn they illuminate the facts. . . . So must systematic theology study the elements of doctrinal truth, whether furnished in the book of nature or the book of revelation, and in a scientific mode combine them in doctrines.[11]

This system of interpretation was developed in the network of seminaries that was formed by the church in the nineteenth century. Miley was a professor at Drew, and the publication of his book was a resource for seminary students across the country. This pattern has continued throughout the history of the United Methodist Publishing House and Abingdon Press.

Thus, when seen in its cultural context, the Methodist communication system in the nineteenth century had quite distinct characteristics:
1. a mastery of the communications technology of the age and a fully integral use of its productions in every part of the connection,
2. a combination of oral and written communication of the Methodist tradition, and
3. the yoking of the intellectual and technological resources of the age to produce an interpretation of the gospel that was both intellectually tenable and technologically viable.

The Methodist Episcopal Church was a vertically integrated network of institutions for creation, production, and distribution of oral and printed communication of the gospel. It succeeded to a remarkable degree in its evangelism, congregational formation, and ministries of care, service, and social action. Its oral network was culturally advanced and grounded in knowledge of the Christian tradition and the oral gifts of preaching and teaching. That oral network was in turn empowered by the church's own highly advanced print communication system.

The church mastered the communications technology of the age and developed a commercially viable production and distribution system that produced all forms of printed material. The brightest and most creative persons of the community were enlisted as directors and producers for the production company. They had, in turn, mastered the most powerful interpretive system of the age and made the gospel meaningful in the intellectual systems of theistic Enlightenment science. The materials they produced served as resources for every part of the connection: classes, worship services, Sunday schools, seminary training of pastors and teachers, missions, evangelism, and social action. Every itinerant was part of the distribution system, and every local charge used the products of the publishing house as an integral part of its life and ministry.

The Methodist communication system was among the most creative and effective integral systems of communication in the culture. This position lent credibility and power to the message and work of the connection in the culture. The Methodist Church was among the most progressive institutions of the country in making the resources of the most technologically advanced communications system of the age available to common people. The businesses and other cultural institutions of the age learned from the churches and their satellite organizations such as American Tract Society and the American Bible Society how to implement printing and distribution in a mass media culture.[12] The Methodist connection was a vertically and horizontally integrated system for the communication of the gospel both to those who did not yet believe and to those who had received the gift of faith and were on the way to perfection.

The Communication Network of the "Connection" in Twentieth-Century Electronic Culture

The development of electronic communication systems in the twentieth century has been the most extensive revolution in communication technology, at least since the invention of the printing press and probably since the mass implementation of writing in the Hellenistic culture of antiquity. In this century, radio, television, films, and computers have replaced mass printing as the dominant systems of communication. The systems of business, political, and military power have been transformed by the appropriation of these systems of communication.

The history of electronic communications technology in the United Methodist Church has been quite different. The Methodist Church and its then-sister churches that later formed the United Methodist Church were far behind the other institutions of the culture in the appropriation of electronic communication systems. The institutionalization of electronic media in the Methodist Church began in 1940 with the establishment of Methodist Information under the leadership of Rev. Ralph W. Stoody. He opened an office at 150 Fifth Avenue in New York with a budget of $25,000. One day at lunch an advertising friend asked about his annual budget. As Ed Maynard reports, "When Stoody said $25,000, his friend protested, "No, no I didn't mean your salary, I meant your budget."[13]

Methodist Information was a news bureau and public relations agency for the church whose goal was getting stories in newspapers and magazines and placing personalities on radio. Some work was also done in promotional campaigns. According to the 1940 *Discipline,* the stated purpose of the Commission on Public Information, which governed Methodist information, was: "to gather news of public interest concerning Methodist activities and opinion and disseminate it through the secular press, the religious press, the radio, and other legitimate media of public information."[14] This role for electronic communication of publicity agent for the church would prove to be determinative for its future.

The Radio and Film Commission (RAFCO) was established in 1948 and in 1956 added television to its name and became TRAFCO (Television, Radio, and Film Commission). Even this issue of the name was indicative of the attitude of the church toward electronic communication. The founders wanted to include television in the name in 1948, but it was deemed impolitic because of the controversies around television. The General Conference of 1948 established the new agency *with no money and no staff* (my italics). It was to be staffed and financed by whatever the church's various boards would be willing to contribute. Its mandate was "to unify and co-ordinate the audiovisual programs of all Methodist agencies dealing with projected pictures, recordings, transcriptions, radio and television programs, and other audiovisual materials."[15] Thus, its mission was to serve as a publicity agent in radio and TV for the work of the general boards and agencies of the church. As a result, electronic communications was strictly subordinated to the needs of the already-existing boards and agencies. This purpose was also determinative in the location of the offices in Nashville, where it could serve the agencies, rather than New York, where it could relate to the world of broadcasting, filmmaking, and communication peers in other churches.

A unified agency for electronic communications was not established until 1972. The General Commission on Communication was established in 1972. UMCom brought together the three functions of news, public relations and promotion, and mass communication that had previously existed in separate agencies. An enabling Mass Communications fund was established in 1976 and was promoted by the now UMCom Division of Program and Benevolence Interpretation, which was established in 1952 as a separate agency. This fund was to enable broadcasting and the placing of United Methodist stories in all media. Television dramas were produced in the early years of TRAFCO. In the '60s the first national phone-in radio program in the communications industry was produced, *Night Call* (how I wish we had *Night Call* rather than Rush Limbaugh and G. Gordon Liddy!). In the '80s, UMCom produced *Catch the Spirit*, a cable television series directed to United Methodists about United Methodist ministries. These programs were distributed via broadcast or cable to a general audience and had minimal use within the connectional system. The one "multimedia" program of video/print produced by UMCom and the publishing house that has been widely used within the connection is *Disciple*, a Bible-study program developed by Bishop Richard Wilke and the Publishing House.

Throughout the fifty-eight years since the establishment of Methodist Information, there has been extensive discussion within the church about the church's position in relation to electronic communication systems. Just as the Book Concern was a perpetual topic at General Conference in the nineteenth century, so also in the twentieth have TRAFCO and UMCom been frequent subjects of argument. But the structural decisions by the church have been radically different. In 1983, for example, there was a major initiative to raise a relatively small amount of money for a then-eight-or-so-million-member church to buy a television station. The total goal of $25 million would have been raised easily with an average contribution of $5 per member. This initiative to move aggressively into the electronic communication system of the culture was rejected decisively by the general church.

This same pattern is reflected in the seminaries of the church. The production and distribution of written resources and the training of persons who can interpret the tradition in oral speech and writing in the interpretive systems of the Enlightenment has continued to be the defined task of the seminaries. But, apart from pioneering efforts at United Theological Seminary, there has been virtually no attention to training persons for production and distribution of electronic communications resources or for the interpretation of the Methodist tradition in electronic culture. Nor has there any significant effort on the part of the communication agencies of the church to relate to the work of the seminaries. As Maynard's history reflects, efforts to organize on-going collaborative thinking about electronic communications between the theological communities of the church and UMCom have failed.[16]

In essence, UMCom and its predecessor agencies have been marginal agencies whose primary role has been publicity for the church in the broader culture and for the boards and agencies of the church within the connection. This in turn reflects the marginal role that electronic communications has had within the connection. Radio, television, and computers have been alien technologies and electronic culture an alien culture to the institutions of the United Methodist Church that were formed for the culture and technology of nineteenth century literate culture. As a result, the dominant systems of communication and interpretation of the tradition within the connection are essentially the same at the end of the twentieth century as they were at the end of the nineteenth. While electronic communication agencies have been created in this century, they are structurally and theoretically marginalized in the connection and are used as instrumental means to do the work of the existing institutions and agencies of the church. Instead of being fully integral to the connection as was the Book Concern, UMCom supplies the electronic "techies" of the church.

An Alternative Future for the United Methodist Church in the Twenty-First Century

When seen within the broader perspectives of history, it is clear that the United Methodist Church tradition made a major turn in the twentieth century. In the nineteenth century, the Methodist Church was characterized by:

1. a mastery of the communications technology of the age and a fully integral use of its productions in every part of the connection,
2. a well-integrated combination of oral and written communication systems in the institutions of the church from the local church and class meeting to the Book Concern/Publishing House, and
3. the full interweaving of the theological and technological resources of the church to produce an interpretation of the gospel that was both intellectually tenable and technologically viable.

In the twentieth century, the Methodist and United Methodist churches have been characterized by:

1. a minimal use of the communications technology of the age and the marginalization of the agencies of the church that have been created to implement the technology within the connection,
2. virtually no coordination or combination of electronic communications with the oral and written electronic communication systems of the church and the utter absence of an overall strategy for the communication and embodiment of the gospel in electronic culture, and
3. minimal attention within the intellectual and communication communities of the church to the development of an intellectually tenable interpretation of the gospel that is viable in electronic media and culture.

This difference is illuminating because the precipitous decline in the membership of the church precisely corresponds with the period in which electronic communications became the dominant communication technology and the TV generation came of age, namely, the '60s.

The pattern is clear from earlier major transitions in the history of communications technology and the church. The Roman Catholic Church at the time of the development of the printing press implemented the same policies in relation to the communication revolution of the fourteenth and fifteenth century as the United Methodist Church has in relation to the communication revolution of the twentieth. It resisted major aspects of the new communications technology and its culture militantly from the invention of the press (1450s) until the Council of Trent (1545–63). At that monumental eighteen-year meeting, the church developed a new policy in relation to print culture. That policy included the establishment of seminaries, the empowerment of the Jesuits who vigorously established new print-centered institutions around the world, and a new interpretive system that was more congruent with the age of the Renaissance. In general, therefore, established churches tend to equate faithfulness with maintaining the systems of the past rather than with the ongoing reformation of the church for the faithful communication of the gospel in the changing communication systems and cultures of the human community.

From the perspective of communication history, therefore, the ongoing decline of the United Methodist Church and its mission is inevitable unless there is a radical change in attitude and policy toward electronic communication and culture. The United Methodist Church needs a Council of Trent to reorient the church and its institutions to the realities of mission and ministry in postliterate, electronic culture. The present posture of the church as a whole is to maintain the communication system of the past and to reject electronic communication and its modes of thought as an integral part of its life. The United Methodist Church in the late-twentieth century needs to regain the progressive posture of the Methodist Church in the late eighteenth and nineteenth centuries in relation to communication systems.

The outlines of a church structured for mission and ministry in an electronic culture are relatively easy to identify. There are the following foundations to such a reorganization:

1. There are essentially two communication systems that need to be integrated in the electronic age: oral and digital. The oral communication system of the church is its network of face-to-face

communities that extends from the local churches through the conferences, educational institutions, and general boards of the church. The digital system is all nonoral communication: print, audio, video, graphics, television, films, and multimedia. The digital system needs to be vertically integrated rather than dispersed in a series of independent print and electronic communication agencies.

2. The creation, production, and distribution of digital resources needs to be fully integral to the oral communication system of the church at all levels: local parishes, educational institutions, general boards and agencies. These two systems—oral and digital—need to be vertically integrated so that creation, production, and distribution of oral and digital communication at all levels support and strengthen the other elements of the connection.

3. An interpretive system needs to be developed that will make it possible to communicate the distinctive traditions of the Methodist tradition faithfully and credibly in digital forms. The intellectual, educational, and artistic communities of the church need to be empowered to work at this interpretive task in a manner that contributes to the overall mission.

These overall foundations will require the restructuring of the church's institutions at every level. The local parishes of the connection organized for worship and nurture need to be reoriented to ministry in electronic culture. Every local church can be thoroughly equipped for the utilization of all aspects of electronic communication—video, audio, computers—in its worship, education, evangelism, and ministries of care and action. And each local church can be electronically connected with churches around the country and the world as well as with the resources developed by the general church. These technological changes can be the basis for enabling the interpretation of the gospel in new forms of proclamation and education.

The conferences also need to be restructured for ministry in the redefined national and global geography of twenty-first-century electronic communication systems rather than the horseback systems of the nineteenth century. The conferences and jurisdictions of the church need to place people across the connection in relation to the needs of parishes and agencies. This would include the development of a national data base of needs and personnel.

The communication system of the general boards and agencies of the church needs to be restructured for digital communication in all parts of the connection. A first step is to unify the production of resources in a fully coordinated digital communications agency. Print, audio, video, CD-ROM, and graphics production and delivery systems need to be integrated in a system that can generate and distribute materials more efficiently and in a coordinated manner.

The seminaries, colleges, and universities of the church need to be reoriented to the interpretation and teaching of the Christian tradition in the interpretive systems of electronic culture rather than the systems of high literate culture. This means that they need to be the masters in the implementation of electronic communication technology for the interpretation of the Christian tradition in postliterate culture. And they need to train future clergy and laity of the church for this interpretive task in all its dimensions. Just as graduates now have mastered the technology of writing for the interpretation of the religion, so also in the future graduates need to master the technologies of video, audio, and multimedia for the interpretation of the religion.

These steps would continue the tradition of the American Methodist connection in the future. Of course, the church will need to maintain its ministries to persons who live in the literate cultures that were formed in the past. At this point, however, the needs of those relatively small and aging parts of the culture are commanding virtually all of the church's personal, intellectual, and financial resources. In order for the church to accomplish its mission in the future, those resources need to be redirected to the electronic communication system and cultures of the future rather than the literate cultures of the past.

Is it possible for the United Methodist Church to make such a radical turn of direction for the sake of the communication of the gospel in a radically new cultural environment? By the grace of God, of course.

Why Can't United Methodists Use Media?

M. Garlinda Burton

What would a media-literate, media-friendly, media-minded church look like? It would not look like what is currently the United Methodist Church, mainly because such a media-literate church would:

- **train** bishops, superintendents, seminary faculty, pastors, and prominent laity to be bold spokespersons through the media on behalf of the church, with an emphasis on including the voices of women, people of color, clergy, laypeople, and representatives of the church beyond the United States;
- **initiate** a news and commentary magazine—and corresponding computer online version with an editorial slant—that reflects mainstream Christendom and is geared toward grass-roots United Methodists and, perhaps, members of other, like-minded Protestant denominations (perhaps in cooperation with the National Council of Churches);
- **unite** with other denominations to lobby for—and give funding to—prime-time programming on mainstream TV networks (CNN, C-SPAN, etc.) that reflects Judeo-Christian interests and concerns;
- **strengthen** the current Disciplinary "open-meeting" laws to include deliberations by the council of bishops, the university senate, the judicial council, and other parties who currently use the closed-meeting provisions in an effort to control media coverage;
- **release** regional and general-church media from the slavery of church programs and bureaucracy, and empower them to provide news, commentary, critiques, reviews, and stories about people that reflect and inform the thoughts, actions, and civic involvement of grass-roots United Methodists; and
- **create** a churchwide computer-and-fax network (with at least one station in every district or three in each conference) for exchange of membership, attendance, and confirmation statistics; service bulletins (including current disaster and emergency information from UMCOR or its antecedent); and churchwide and ecumenical news. Included also would be various "chat lines" and vehicles for informal polling of United Methodist opinion.

Another Brick in the Wall of Church Decline?

Nearly three decades of membership decline in the United States and increasingly brutal schisms in the denomination between "conservative-liberal" theologies and ideologies have taken their toll on the United Methodist Church. As with other mainline denominations, enthusiasm, influence, and identity seem to be waning.

In the midst of falling membership, theological confusion, and evangelistic malaise, I would add another "crisis" or reason for our lukewarm state; namely, that *our denomination is becoming increasingly invisible and irrelevant to society, in part because we refuse to commit time, energy, and financial and human resources to interpretation of our ministry and mission through church and public media.*

Despite our denomination's collection of more than 50 monthly, weekly, or semiweekly conference newspapers in the United States, at least five churchwide magazines, the oldest and best denominational press service (United Methodist News Service) of any mainstream denomination, and a variety of television ventures (from the now-defunct "Catch the Spirit" program to participation in the Faith and Values cable TV channel), the major impact of the denomination's message on both its membership and society at large is often lost because our denomination refuses to become media-literate, media-friendly, and media-minded.

Why the Church Won't Harness the Media—and Vice Versa

A few years ago a now-retired bishop recalled in an interview that when he was first elected and assigned as a bishop 25 years ago, a local television station—a major network affiliate—had offered him, as spokesperson for United Methodism in that area, 30 minutes a week of airtime to do some programming about the church. The bishop and church leaders had carte blanche, and could use the half-hour for worship, a talk show, a call-in show, or whatever they could conceive.

The bishop declined the offer.

"Can you believe I did that?" he asked. "But I just couldn't conceive of what to do with that time. Do you know how much it would be worth now? But no one had prepared me to be a media spokesperson for the church, and I had no idea what a gold mine that was," he said.

Ignorance about the purpose and power of media is pandemic among leaders in the United Methodist Church. And because media are bombarded with requests from other institutions and entities that are more than willing to harness media power and tell their stories, the church has become virtually invisible in media. Why should a reporter chase down a bishop who refuses to return calls about a squabble over homosexuality, when the local teachers' union is clamoring for air time to talk about low salaries and lack of safe teaching environments for children? Why turn to the mainline church for a sane voice on the abortion debate—and be passed around to seven different offices—when Operation Rescue folks use their media literacy to such an extent that their brand of "pro-life" rhetoric has become erroneously synonymous with the "Christian" point of view?

To be sure, the leadership of United Methodist and other Christian churches do not shoulder all the blame for the communications gap between public media and religion. A 1993 study of religion and the news media, conducted by the Freedom Forum/First Amendment Center at Vanderbilt University in Nashville, Tenn., found several disturbing trends in the gulf between religious institutions and public media, among them:

- An "unhealthy," often unreasonable mistrust—even fear—exists between religious leaders and journalists.
- Many church leaders, particularly clergy, believe the news coverage of religion is "biased, unfairly negative, and too sensational."
- Although "overt anti-religious sentiments are rare," reporters are often intellectually lazy about getting their facts straight when assigned to cover religion. Indeed, if a reporter assigned to cover the White House were as ignorant about the players, polity, and history of the federal government as many religion reporters are about the institution they cover, those government reporters would lose their jobs.
- Many church leaders and journalists agree that the news media should be more aggressive in their reporting about religious leaders and that publicity-seeking clergy and Christian organizations receive too much press.

The report also offered recommendations to both public media and church leaders, based on interviews with leaders in both camps. For the purposes of this paper, we will concern ourselves only with the recommendations to religious leaders, namely:

- that church leaders should learn more about the journalistic process, understand what is considered newsworthy, and learn to communicate religious actions and events that fit those journalistic definitions;
- that the church needs to work harder—and faster—to provide media with access to those who can articulate the church's "informed viewpoint";

- that the church should commit greater financial resources to effective communications offices within church institutions; and
- that rather than dismissing the media as incompetent or conspiratorial when they make an error in religious reporting, church leaders should take responsibility for correcting misinformation and help journalists find the "wise persons" in their areas who can give accurate information.

Media Know-How: The Church's Weak Link

Our society is indeed in the midst of an information and communications boom. Like it or not, today's public is media-driven, and people often join organizations, support causes, vote, and make life-changing decisions based on what they see and hear in the media.

Following natural disasters such as Hurricane Andrew in 1992 and heart-breaking acts of human destruction such as the spring 1995 bombing in Oklahoma City, medicine, money, emergency housing, and food came pouring in within hours of the time news of these disasters hit the airwaves.

People with no connection to any church organization sent money, clothing, and toys for traumatized children. Because the United Methodist Church has developed such a strong internal network for disaster aid, church people also rallied. But, the majority of church people probably heard of the disaster and were ready to act days—perhaps even a week or more—before United Methodist media were able to disseminate the information. For, although our denomination has a top-notch plan for mobilizing disaster-relief teams and getting resources to places where they are needed, that network breaks down when it comes to getting information out quickly and efficiently to church and public media, and through them to the rank and file.

As director of the Nashville, Tenn., office of United Methodist News Service for 11 years, I can recall making numerous phone calls over several days to get *any information* on United Methodist disaster response that I could report to the church and public at large. Sometimes it would take more than a week to reach a spokesperson, and then another few days to get the information necessary to disseminate to the network of annual conference and district news outlets.

One long-standing major complaint that comes from rank-and-file United Methodists after a disaster is, "We didn't see anything about our church on the news!" Denominational leadership, the people receiving aid, and some churches in the affected area know we've been there. But the reality of modern society is that if it doesn't happen in the public media, it virtually doesn't happen at all for the vast majority of people in general, including United Methodists.

The lack of disaster-relief information from the United Methodist Committee on Relief, the General Board of Global Ministries, and United Methodist Communications created such frustration among regional editors of church publications after the summer 1993 U.S. Midwest floods that the United Methodist Association of Communicators in November of that year drafted a formal petition asserting the need for a comprehensive communications plan in the event of a disaster. The 150-member group asked United Methodist Communications, the Board of Global Ministries, and the United Methodist Committee on Relief to develop a comprehensive media plan for reporting news in the event of a disaster. That plan is still being discussed by the three agencies.

A media plan may seem a secondary consideration in the effort to relieve human suffering. However, when the TV cameras roll at a disaster, and when they pan to fully outfitted response trucks emblazoned with the logos of the Southern Baptist Church and Catholic Relief Services, those scenes communicate immediately—to an international audience—that those denominations care about human suffering. Those media images also tell even an unchurched, uninitiated person that he or she can give money to a Baptist church or Catholic church for disaster relief. The images communicate, more effectively than an altar call in a sanctuary where an unchurched person may never come, what that denomination is all about, and such communicated information may encourage someone to take a second look and consider becoming a part of the church.

Are "They" Hiding Something from "Us"?

Along with complaints about our invisibility in media, grass-roots United Methodists and other watchers are also struck by what appears to be a lack a credibility among leaders in the church, a seeming reluctance to provide forthright information to grass-roots United Methodists about "controversial" issues, and the absence of vehicles for rank-and-file members' influence.

Church leaders fuel this suspicion among rank-and-file members, the media, and the general public by their strong reactions to media scrutiny and "too much" media coverage. As lead reporter for the United Methodist News Service during the 1985–88 revision of *The United Methodist Hymnal*, I—along with our city's award-winning religion editor of *The Tennessean* newspaper—was roundly criticized by denominational brass for my extensive coverage of the 25-member revision panel's deliberations.

After the committee voted to delete "Onward, Christian Soldiers" because of its so-called "militant" language—and received 20,000 calls and letters of protest, leading them to reinstate the hymn—I was accused by two general secretaries, three bishops, and several annual conference councils on ministries of "creating controversy." The criticism continued throughout my coverage of the four-year revision, as I reported on the committee's debate over inclusive language versus traditionally "male" images for God and the struggle to represent the racial-ethnic diversity of the United Methodist Church. My reporting—along with secular media reports—generated lively and sometimes painful debate at all levels of the church, particularly among grass-roots members. Leaders were upset that media had "stirred up a fuss" and "upset the people in the pew."

However, my supporters—among them the editor of the hymnal and some members of the revision panel—credit the process with giving grass-roots members a renewed sense that their opinions mattered to someone in leadership. With the reinstatement of "Onward, Christian Soldiers," people who had long been suspicious that church bureaucrats never listened to anybody felt that at least one general-church-level group was concerned about their preferences. The editor, the Rev. Carlton "Sam" Young, also insists that debate over the hymnal was minimal at the 1988 General Conference because grass-roots members had been kept well-informed about the revision process through church and public media. There were few surprises for voting delegates of the church's highest legislative body, who approved the hymnal overwhelmingly.

Other episodes in recent years have not ended as positively. Pressure continues from some agency heads and episcopal leaders to keep controversy and "negative" information out of the hands of the church and public media—and, therefore, away from the rank and file. The church continues to lose credibility with each attempt to control and withhold information.

The result of "circling the wagons" is invariably more negative than positive. Consider these recent examples of media disasters in the United Methodist Church.

The 1983 Resignation of Bishop James Armstrong: In the late 1970s and early 1980s, James Armstrong, Indiana Area resident bishop was hailed by national church and public media as one of the most powerful and influential men in Christendom. As president of the National Council of Churches, he led the ecumenical agency in strong and stunning pronouncements on some of society's most pressing social, moral, and theological issues. Within the United Methodist council of bishops, he was instrumental in convincing episcopal leaders to be more forthright as the moral and spiritual voice of a denomination with the potential to improve the climate of global social justice.

Armstrong's influence came crashing down in November 1983, when he resigned, citing personal reasons. In closed sessions at the council of bishops' meeting, Armstrong disclosed the personal problems and decided—against the advice of some colleagues—to step down.

To this day, most grass-roots United Methodists do not know exactly what happened. They only intuit that this was a devastating blow, a vaguely shameful episode in modern church history. No United Methodist-related publication or other church media outlet ever disclosed the full Armstrong story, from allegations of sexual misconduct with a former parishioner to hints of alcohol abuse. Most of the information that came out in the next two or three years was unearthed by probing secular media.

In hindsight, this decision by church leaders and church media to withhold information had a devastating effect on the credibility of the church bureaucracy among both grass-roots members and the public. While leadership figured that withholding information would protect rank-and-file members from disillusionment and shield the church from harsh scrutiny from the outside, what actually happened was:

- *The truth was never presented in a coherent, compassionate, and straightforward manner; therefore rank-and-file members were left to draw their own conclusions, many based on erroneous accounts and secondhand speculation in the public media.* The result for the church was devastating in terms of trust. People who were already cynical about corruption in high places in the church had their worst suspicions confirmed. Others, who clung to the hope that the public-media coverage of the Armstrong issue was just another example of the big, bad secular press out to "disgrace" the church, were denied a needed reality check, namely, that church leaders can be fallible and that the church can withstand public scrutiny and still survive.

- *By their silence, church leaders left the impression that although they were more than willing to criticize governmental and other leaders, they were not willing to confront tough issues within their ranks.* It seemed a hypocritical "circling of the wagons" to protect one of "our own."

- *Internally, church leaders missed an opportunity to educate themselves and grass-roots United Methodists about the need for more support, counseling, and accountability for clergy, bishops, and others in high-pressure positions in the church.* Some of the allegations against Armstrong were long-standing, and had been ignored or dealt with perfunctorily in the years before his resignation.

By the 1988 and 1992 General Conferences, the issue of clergy sexual misconduct had become such a concern that new legislation was drafted, and annual conferences have been working ever since to develop a plan for dealing with complaints. Since the Armstrong resignations, several other high-profile clerics have left their positions in disgrace—including Texans Barry Bailey and Walker Railey. The denomination has been subjected recently to numerous lawsuits related to alleged sexual misconduct by clerics in high places. Perhaps, if church leaders had dealt forthrightly with—that is, reported, discussed, and answered grass-roots queries about—Armstrong and the broader issue of clergy misconduct in 1983, we would have a better handle on the issue and its media implications today.

The 1987 Death of Bishop Finis Crutchfield: The issue of homosexuality, the ordained ministry, and the church has been a highly publicized, painful front-burner issue for United Methodists since at least the early 1970s. Current church law prohibits ordination of "self-avowed practicing" homosexual persons, but it is widely known that gay men and lesbians do serve as pastors—many of them highly regarded—at all levels of United Methodist life. In fact, in July 1995, the Rev. Jeanne Audrey Powers, associate general secretary of the denomination's Commission on Christian Unity and Interreligious Concerns, revealed publicly that she has been lesbian all her life, including her 37 years of ordained ministry in the United Methodist Church. Some would point to cases like Powers's as an example of the futility, hypocrisy, and wrongheadedness of the denomination's ban on homosexual pastors.

In 1987, Texas Bishop Finis Crutchfield died of complications from AIDS. Immediately, speculation arose about Crutchfield, who was married, had one son, and was well-known for his conservative stances on issues, including gay ordination.

Although United Methodist-related media reported the cause of death and briefly probed Crutchfield's family on how the bishop—who had not had a blood transfusion—had contracted AIDS, no discussion of rumors about his sexuality ever surfaced in United Methodist media. A family member offered the absurd speculation that Crutchfield may have contracted AIDS while visiting with or helping clean the apartments of people who had died from AIDS.

Some months later, *Texas Monthly* magazine published an article about the so-called "double life" of the bishop, with eyewitness testimonies by gay men with whom he allegedly had relationships. No response was ever made to the article by church leaders, and no official church media ever did a similar investigation.

What would have been the point? Is it is the role of church media and church leaders to pour salt into a wound such as the death of Crutchfield? All compassionate Christians would answer "no." But the point of more church and church media scrutiny and discourse is not to inflame, shame, or degrade. Instead, an honest inquiry by United Methodist media and honest revelations about Crutchfield's life and death might have netted at least one positive result. We might have put a more human face on one aspect of the torturous debate about homosexuality in the church, namely that every gay man and lesbian is someone's child, someone's brother or sister, someone's spouse or friend, and—in more cases than we want to admit—someone's pastor or bishop.

While it may have been impossible to prove that Crutchfield engaged in homosexual behavior (and that, if true, it is beside the point), an honest discussion might have been opened about the appropriateness of using sexual orientation as a criteria for ordination, when such a revered church leader obviously served with distinction.

The November 1993 Re-Imagining Conference in Minneapolis: Perhaps the most damaging media misstep of the United Methodist Church in recent years was our handling of the November 1993 Re-Imagining Conference, an ecumenical theological conference for women in which United Methodist women—some supported by the Women's Division of the Board of Global Ministries—participated. The now infamous allegations of "heretical" teachings and practices at the conference—including suggestions that the women were urged to worship "Sophia" (the Greek word meaning wisdom, used by some as a metaphor for God)—have provided fodder for naysayers of denominational leadership for years since.

As a staff member of United Methodist News Service at that time, I must assume some responsibility for not covering the event. At one point in our staff planning I was schedule to attend but our staff decided, based on a review of the agenda, that "re-imagining" was something that could be covered after the fact with a brief news release featuring interviews of key leaders. We were wrong.

Of course, most of us now realize that much of the hoopla about "re-imagining" was whipped up by certain conservative factions trying to make a name for themselves by fanning flames of misogyny, xenophobia, homophobia, and idolatry of so-called orthodoxy and church tradition. However, the leaders of the conference, the United

Methodist women involved and other leaders in the denomination certainly erred in several media-related ways.

First, the initial reaction to criticism was one that continues to put distance between the bureaucracy and the grass-roots membership: leaders dismissed critics as hysterical, ignorant, and theologically illiterate. At first glance, some leaders of the conference took the high-handed tactic of ignoring legitimate concerns about the most inflammatory aspects of the Re-Imagining Conference (namely, discussion of feminine attributes for God).

The first round of responses by conference leaders seemed to suggest, in essence, that anyone who didn't understand the language and purpose of re-imagining was just a reactionary, sexist, misogynist naysayer. In fact, wisdom literature and other such concepts are, for the average Christian, obscure. This attitude drove a wedge between the elitist church leadership and the rank-and-file church members who lack a seminary education and for whom "wisdom" literature is not cocktail conversation. It also put the church leadership in the position of seeming out-of-touch with the average member, and put the conservative Good News caucus (and its magazine by the same name) in the position of speaking to and on behalf of the average, uninitiated church member.

After realizing that the Re-Imagining Conference and the response to it were not going away, however, leadership was still sluggish in offering explanations, points for study and clarification, and answers to critics' claims head-on. One Women's Division response was, to paraphrase loosely, that "our women are big girls and can decide for themselves what is appropriate," but it neglected to admit that the church gave money and support for this event, the controversial nature and content of which had, in reality, caught them off guard.

The conference has been somewhat vindicated, nearly a year later, when the United Methodist council of bishops released a cogent, straightforward, and welcome paper discussing the biblical and theological legitimacy of wisdom literature. However, among the rank and file, the damage control continues to be too little too late. The church and the public would have been better served if church leaders had:

• released a statement immediately after the controversy began, explaining, from their point of view, wisdom literature and biblical support for "feminine" attributes of God. It might also have been helpful to include some recent history by respected women theologians about the gender politics in the church (ordination of women, debates of the Inclusive Language Lectionary, the hymnal revision process and inclusive language, etc.).

- provided a follow-up story in *Interpreter*, now the most widely circulated official publication of the denomination. (As it was, *Good News* magazine, being quick to react, became the voice of the rank-and-file church, despite its right-of-center rhetoric.)
- positioned spokespersons to appear on local and regional TV talk shows, give radio interviews, etc., in order to diffuse churchwide concern about the "re-imagining" event

Seven Possible First Steps

1. Make a conference-level public-media relations position Disciplinary. In the early 1980s, United Methodist Communications offered incentive grants to annual conferences for media relations. These grants, according to former UMCom executive Roger Burgess, were specifically designed to encourage the hiring of professional, trained journalists and media personnel whose primary tasks would be:

- to train the bishop and other church leaders to be informed, articulate local media spokespersons on behalf of the United Methodist Church;
- to orient regional church leaders on developing a media-relations plan (including crisis management);
- to develop relationships with local newspaper reporters and editors, broadcast station managers, and news personnel, and to facilitate placement of United Methodist-related stories and news makers in local media.

The UMCom proposal was an ambitious one, and a number of conferences took the money and started newspaper and media offices. However, the success of their enterprises has been marred by a number of factors, many of them financial.

As conferences have experienced the reality of shrinking memberships and budgets, communications positions and offices are high on the list of expendable expenses. Conference publications are seldom self-supporting (that is, by individual subscriptions and advertisements); therefore, many are supplemented by conference apportionments or pledged subscriptions by local churches. However, as postal and publishing rates continue to drive costs up, and falling membership and dollars drive demand down, the feasibility of many papers is continually questioned.

More important, the media-relations proposal has been blighted by a general misunderstanding of, and lack of commitment to, the view of the public media as a tool for interpretation and mission. Journalism and media relations have been seen as jobs that "anybody could do" rather than as tasks requiring dedicated professional skills. In many cases, the bishop or conference council director has rewritten media-relations jobs, adding unrelated tasks as divergent as being the conference camping director. While this was a cost-cutting measure in many cases, more often it was a blatant attempt to create a position for an ordained minister for whom there was no acceptable ministerial appointment. The conventional wisdom was that tacking communications onto spiritual-formation director or executive secretary for evangelism was a way to tailor a position for a hard-to-place clergy person, give a nod to communications, and save money.

I would add that the media positions could be at least half-time (although I prefer full time), and that the persons hired should have some background in journalism. I have no biases against an ordained person who is media literate, but the job will not be done well if it becomes a dumping position for an ineffective cleric.

2. Create media offices—complete with fax, computer, and modem—in the Central Conferences, and hire indigenous media professionals to staff them. Although we give lip service to being a global church, most of our communications—along with other services—are done on a national (U.S.) level. At present, most "churchwide" publications and programs are not circulated among, and do not receive first-hand input from, United Methodist bodies outside the United States. This makes consistent and smooth exchange of ideas nearly impossible, especially with regard to the church in the Southern Hemisphere.

I would propose that the church investigate creating a computer, e-mail, and fax network, with stations in every episcopal area outside the United States, for exchange of news, information, membership and attendance statistics, etc. In addition, the Board of Global Ministries and United Methodist Communications should have at least one satellite office each in Africa (a location at Africa University would be ideal), the Philippines, and Europe.

3. Make churchwide computerization—including online resources and news, and grass-roots-friendly opinion and chat lines—a programmatic and administrative priority.

4. Work ecumenically to increase mainline church presence in public media. The Consultation on Church Union and the National and World Councils of Churches notwithstanding, the United Methodist Church and other mainline denominations are wasting valuable resources by trying to reinvent the wheel instead of working together on media presence. One reason that media are reluctant to engage mainline Christian spokespersons and issues is that there is such a clamor for "my" denomination to be the voice of authority—as opposed to someone else's—that untrained and uninitiated media sometimes chose the slickest, best organized, and most simplistic Christian spokespersons.

While Presbyterian, United Church of Christ, Episcopalian, and Disciples of Christ leaders clamor about who will talk, afraid to speak out of turn on behalf of mainline Christians, members of the Christian Coalition and Pat Robertson take center stage, unabashedly proclaiming their dogma in the name of Christians everywhere.

Mainline denominations need to unite their efforts to increase awareness and presence in public media. The National Council of Churches has become so gun-shy in the wake of the late 1980s "exposes" by *Reader's Digest* and "60 Minutes"—and its budgets have suffered so much from restructure—that one seldom hears a word from the council on issues that really matter.

We, as leaders among mainline denominations, must begin to develop a thick skin and patience to deal with public media who may not understand much of our jargon, personalities, and territorialism. We must become more knowledgeable about how media work. We must understand that the public media are not "public relations" agents for the church, but that a reputation as an honorable, forthright, efficient, straightforward voice will make us a valuable tool for interpretation of another Christian viewpoint, and that kind of presence increasingly will become the best public relations, far more effective than sugar-coating our problems and pushing our evangelism festivals to hide our misconduct trials.

5. "Test drive" a populist news and feature magazine. I'm not talking about a rehashing of *Together* or *Today*. While those magazines served a valuable purpose, a general-readership, feel-good publication like those would not work anymore. However, Christians who live with divorce and step-families, demanding bosses, confusion over sexuality, cousins killed in drive-by shootings—and many more people who have a Christian ethos, but who are not part of a church—are hungry for a media tool that sees the world, offers commentary, and addresses social, personal, moral, and political issues from a mainline Christian (as opposed to a conservative fundamentalist) point of view.

There are many ways to do it that may not involve reinventing the wheel. For one, *Interpreter*—currently a program magazine for general church agencies—could be expanded and merged with such publications as *New World Outlook* (missions) and *Christian Social Action* to present a multifaceted publication with enough human interest stories and news about the international church to keep rank-and-file members abreast of bureaucratic happenings. However, I would suggest expanding coverage of social, political, moral, and theological issues by reporting them through the eyes of local church folks for whom such issues as poverty, theological discourse, spiritual malaise, war in Rwanda, and battles over homosexuality, racism, and sexism are real.

We have to stop letting narrowly focused, special-interest groups with the loudest voices and (the largest budgets) become the only conscience and voice of the church.

6. Strengthen the United Methodist News Service, allow it to be more of a link to secular media, increase its electronic-news presence, and give it more autonomy, including a separate advisory board.

7. Make media literacy a criterion for employing church leaders, and require every bishop, general secretary, college and seminary president, and superintendent to be trained as a media spokesperson and required to take continuing education in news media and technology. Our leaders must become a catalyst for change in the denomination with regard to our relationship with news media. We must see media relations as an integral part of our mission initiative. Without a better sense of media, the good works, prophetic statements, social and moral stances, and the cutting-edge theological and pastoral impact of United Methodists remain virtually unknown and unfelt beyond the walls of our denomination.

Is Division a New Threat to the Denomination?

Russell E. Richey

Conventional Wisdom

Conventional wisdom[1] today holds:

- that denominational loyalty, at least among mainline denominations,[2] has weakened, decidedly;
- that the once-prominent "establishment" denominations[3] as institutions are fading;
- that individuals, congregations, and regional judicatories are staging "Boston Tea Parties" protesting decisions, priorities, inefficiencies, waste, monetary claims, and the onerous, oppressive burden of the bureaucratic board and agency structure that seems to be the cohesive principle in denominations today;
- that caucuses and struggle groups have balkanized denominations, turning conventions, assemblies, and conferences into contentious and demoralizing rather than unifying and galvanizing experiences;
- that many of these struggle groups and caucuses align themselves into two broad coalitions, liberal and conservative;
- that these coalitions transcend denominational, indeed religious, boundaries; and
- that liberal and conservative,[4] or liberal and evangelical,[5] identities threaten now to divide, perhaps even destroy, denominations.[6]

The range of such problems, including especially the divisions within denominations, spell, some would suggest, the end to denominationalism.[7] At the very least they portend, as a United Methodist bishop and a seminary president both prophesied in the aftermath of the 1996 General Conference and as many proclaimed after the Jimmy Creech trial,[8] the clean division of such mainline denominations into new conservative and liberal entities and the end to United Methodism as we know it.

Denominationalism as Division?

This paper endeavors to show that division does not constitute a new threat at all but is a reality that has haunted denominations and denominationalism rather continuously throughout American history. Indeed, were theology rather than history and sociology to be the metier of this book, one might affirm with H. Richard Niebuhr that division is the essence of denominationalism:

> For the denominations, churches, sects, are sociological groups whose principle of differentiation is to be sought in their conformity to the order of social classes and castes. . . . They are emblems, therefore, of the victory of the world over the church, of the secularization of Christianity, of the church's sanction of that divisiveness which the church's gospel condemns.[9]

Even on historical grounds, one might view division as a characteristic of denominations. Divisions and/or near divisions constitute the story of virtually any denomination or denominational family, a fact readily discernible in the annual *Yearbook of American & Canadian Churches*[10] or any other effort at the full mapping of American religion. And the larger pattern of denominations or denominationalism evidences periods of intense fracturing and fragmenting—periods when existing bodies experience internal strain, when some denominations do split and when new denominations emerge, often with commentary on the prior denominational order as constitutive of their purpose and self-understanding.

The "great awakenings" of the eighteenth and early nineteenth centuries represent such periods of fracturing and fragmenting. So also do the slavery and sectional crisis of the middle-nineteenth century and the late-nineteenth, early-twentieth-century time of centralizing, professionalizing, corporate restructuring, and cultural realignment. The latter period, with its great pentecostal effervescence, has sometimes been portrayed as one of cultural crisis or as though the new denominations sprang up ex nihilo. Recent scholarship suggests that Pentecostalism has stronger ties to Methodist and other existing traditions than has sometimes been supposed and that those as well as the Holiness and Fundamentalist movements ought to be seen as developments from, if not divisions out of, earlier denominational stock. At any rate, the Holiness, Pentecostal and Fundamentalist eras represent times, if not a time, of serious denominational sifting and shifting. And, so, too, does this period from the 1970s to the present. Division within the denominational house may be, to adapt an image from Robert Handy, the religious counterpart to economic depression.[11]

Certainly all denominational divisions do not occur in these periods of fracturing and fragmenting. Some movements, as this chapter will indicate with respect to the Methodists, have shown a genius for dividing every decade. And yet we should not lose sight of these larger patterns in the history of denominational division. Individual denominational divisions have coincided sufficiently with these larger processes of restructuring for one to suspect that denominationalism, in effect, renews and reconstitutes itself (that is reshapes the denominational form) through divisions and severe tension.[12] The Presbyterians perhaps best represent in their own saga the larger pattern of tension, division, and reunion. They took their rise amidst the Puritan crisis within and without the Church of England, divided new side and old in the First Awakening, suffered significant losses from the Cumberlands and to the Christian (Disciple) movements in the Second Awakening, split New School and Old over issues that would ultimately divide the nation, and narrowly escaped a major division during the fundamentalist controversy. Current turmoil within Presbyterianism, paralleled across mainstream Protestantism, suggests that once again individual denominations and the larger pattern of denominationalism is in a period of transformation.

Constitutive Division: The Methodist Story

Division is not only part of the fabric of denominationalism. It is also woven into the life of individual denominations. Such a history of division is well illustrated, perhaps fittingly illustrated, by the Methodists. Methodism began, of course, as a reform movement within the Church of England, pledged in deference to, if not always in agreement with, the Wesleys, John and particularly Charles, who insisted that Methodism did not and would not separate from the Church. To that pledge British Methodism remained committed through and beyond John's life. And yet, as Richard Heitzenrater has demonstrated, even under Wesley, Methodism increasingly structured and conducted itself in ways that pointed toward separation.[13]

The inertial pressures toward separation from the Church of England that the Wesleys resisted were, if anything, more intense in the colonies. Methodists immigrating from Ireland or England and persons here who developed Methodist or Methodist-like sympathies found it more difficult to structure Methodist life within an Anglican parish, for that system was not everywhere established, and even where established, it was not always well led or maintained. The parish system deteriorated dramatically during the Revolution when Anglicans—clergy and laity—fled to Canada or to Britain (as did all the preachers Wesley had sent over, save Francis Asbury). The first division occurred during this period, even before Methodism officially separated from the Church of England in 1784. The movement split badly.

In 1779, during wartime hostilities, the regularly called conference, meeting in Fluvanna County, Virginia, proceeded to establish American Methodism as a church through autonomous act and presbyterial ordinations. They asked,

> Q. 14. What are our reasons for taking up the administration of the ordinances [sacraments] among us?
> A. Because the Episcopal Establishment is now dissolved and therefore in almost all our circuits the members are without the ordinances, we believe it to be our duty.
> Q. 19. What forms of ordination shall be observed, to authorize any preacher to administer?
> A. By that of a Presbytery.
> Q. 20. How shall the Presbytery be appointed?
> A. By a majority of the preachers.
> Q. 22. What power is vested in the Presbytery by this choice?
> A. 1st. To administer the ordinances themselves. 2d. To authorize any other preacher or preachers approved of by them, by the form of laying on of hands and of prayer.[14]

This declaration of independence had been anticipated and countered by an "irregular" conference held the prior month in Delaware to accommodate Francis Asbury, then in hiding, and clearly to contravene the anticipated separation.[15] This conference, almost exactly the same size as the later "regular" body, queried:

> Quest. 10. *Shall we guard against a separation from the church, directly or indirectly?*
> Ans. By all Means.[16]

And the following year, this Chesapeake group queried:

> Quest. 12. *Shall we continue in close connexion with the church, and press our people to a closer communion with her?*
> Ans. Yes
> Quest. 20. *Does this whole conference disapprove the step our brethren have taken in Virginia?*
> Ans. Yes.
> Quest. 21. *Do we look upon them no longer as Methodists in connexion with Mr. Wesley and us till they come back?*
> Ans. Agreed.[17]

This latter group, which insisted on awaiting John Wesley's provision for ecclesial order, eventually won out and the schism was healed.

Continuous Divisions?

I have dwelt at more length on this particular separation than I can on subsequent ones to make two points: (1) that American Methodism was already dividing internally before it officially 'divided' itself from the Anglicans and established itself as a distinct denomination, and (2) that the formal separation in 1784 actually involved a threefold disengagement—(a) from the Church of England, (b) from the North American Anglicans among whom the Methodists had labored, who were then also being reconstituted as an independent church and among whom were kindred spirits, chief of them, perhaps, Devereux Jarrett, who were deeply offended by the Methodist departure, and (c) eventually from Mr. Wesley and British Wesleyanism. The latter also was to be an occasion for offense, for in their first *Discipline*, the Americans pledged:

> During the Life of the Rev. Mr. Wesley, we acknowledge ourselves his Sons in the Gospel, ready in Matters belonging to Church-Government, to obey his Commands. And we do engage after his Death, to do every Thing that we judge consistent with the Cause of Religion in *America* and the political Interests of these States, to preserve and promote our Union with the Methodists in *Europe*.[18]

This pledge and unity, too, American Methodists found impossible to honor when Wesley sought to exercise church government. In 1787 Wesley ordered the convening of a general conference and the election of specific persons as bishops. The Americans resisted these commands and stripped the above pledge from the *Discipline*. So American Methodism began in a complex division, though one it has consistently celebrated, rather than bemoaned.

To 1787 is often traced yet another division, namely the beginnings of the African Episcopal Church, traditionally associated with Richard Allen's walkout from St. George's. Full separation took a number of other provocations. In 1816 several African American churches formed in similar reaction to Methodism's racial policies covenanted to establish the denomination. From these small beginnings and those of the African Union Church and the African Methodist Episcopal Zion Church, much of Methodism's significant black membership was drained off.[19]

The losses were gradual, and the actual break between black and white Methodists more gradual and more gradually recognized on both sides than we have sometime been led to believe. These were divisions caused by white racism and unfortunately rather ignored because of racism. By contrast another division, largely among whites, registered itself immediately and traumatically. It came in 1792, when Methodists from the Virginia-North Carolina area, followed James O'Kelly, an erratic but prominent leader, in demanding "democratic" rights for preachers, protesting monarchical behavior by the bishops, and especially Asbury, and witnessing against slavery. The break came over a proposal made to the General Conference of that year that would have given preachers a right of appeal over their appointment, a popular initiative that seemed destined to pass.[20] When the legislation failed, O'Kelly's supporters, later called "Republican Methodists," walked out.

Their departure, from the vantage of the late twentieth century, looks like a minor one, primarily because the "Republicans" proved stronger in protest than they did in subsequent organization and evangelizing. Their "schism" was not minimized in the 1790s. Then it seemed a major "culture war," a battle over the soul of the movement, a question as to whether Methodism would be a Wesleyan or an American cause, a denomination shaped primarily by the culture, practices, beliefs, style, and ethos of the inherited Wesleyanism or of the republicanism of the new nation. The latter had tremendous appeal and seemed to capture essential elements of what both the New Testament and pietism envisioned for the Christian life. Republican Christianity, as O'Kelly articulated it, offered a vision of equality, fraternity, justice, and human rights. And it made sense to persons, particularly the preachers, who experienced any arbitrariness in the appointive powers, the bishops. A new church for a new nation, a democratic church for a democratic nation, so urged O'Kelly. Was the choice, as he presented it, between Wesleyanism and Americanism? To move beyond that dilemma and contain the schism took a decade of concerted effort on the part of Asbury and his supporters.

In appreciating the significance of this division and several of the subsequent Methodist schisms, we might well keep in mind the close divisions in the presidential contests within the Southern Baptist Convention in those years when moderates still mounted resistance to its conservative drift. A number of those votes were extremely close, suggesting an SBC that was deeply divided. Such proportions do not register, however, in the much smaller numbers of churches and clergy now formally affiliated with the moderate southern Baptist organizations. The depth and extent of a fault line and the size of the parties divided thereby do not always correspond with, nor are they accurately measured by, the size of a party that departs. This was clearly the case for the Republican Methodists and would prove to be the case in the subsequent nineteenth-century divisions. Similar, major "cultural" and social issues surfaced—in virtually every decade of the nineteenth century—to split Methodism again and again.

Divisions: Minor and Major

To be sure, not all the cleavages within the Methodist family can be traced to a decisive moment and a legislative contest, and not all produced such serious trauma. The separate organization of the German movements, the United Brethren and Evangelical Association, reflects their distinct origins in the broader evangelical movement and the specific leaven of Reformed, Mennonite, and Lutheran pietism. Still the first conference of the former in 1789 and its formal organization in 1800 and the first conference of the latter in 1803 and its formal organization in 1807 represented failures (on both sides) to carry through on the looser comity they had enjoyed with the Methodists. Unification was revisited in the next decade and repeatedly thereafter until the two movements, united in 1946, joined with the Methodist Church in 1968. Early Methodism experimented with intercultural, bilingual community but found differences along language lines difficult to bridge.

Three protests of the early nineteenth century had regional or local effect. William Hammett, ordained by Wesley, settled eventually in Charleston. He built a strong following, resisted the authority of Asbury and Coke, and led a schism of Primitive Methodists (there and in North Carolina) that began around 1792 and largely dissipated after his death in 1803. At the northern reaches of the movement, a group of "Reformed Methodists," led by Pliny Brett, who had itinerated from 1805 to 1812, sought church government and local authority more akin to that appreciated in New England. They protested episcopacy, emphasized the attainability of entire sanctification, and repudiated war and slavery. Formally organized in 1814 at a convention in Vermont, they drew several thousand adherents across New England, New York, and Canada. By the Civil War, most of the Reformed movement had affiliated with the Methodist Protestants.

In the second decade of the century, the African Methodist Episcopal (1816) and the African Union (1813) Churches organized. Their centers were and remained in Philadelphia and Wilmington respectively. The organization of the African Methodist Episcopal Zion Church in 1820 was closely related to a separation among white Methodists also in New York led by Samuel Stillwell, a trustee at the flagship John Street Church, and his nephew, William Stillwell, a preacher then in charge of two of the African American congregations. At issue in both divisions was ownership of church property and control over ministry. The Stillwellites grew to some 2,000 members in the New York, New Jersey, and Connecticut areas, continuing until the younger Stillwell's death in 1851. Another separate Methodist body, also with the name Primitive Methodists, developed around the figure of Lorenzo Dow, the export of American-style camp meeting revivalism to Britain after 1805, and import-of-the-export as a distinct denomination, beginning in 1829. The Primitives developed strength in Pennsylvania and especially in Canada.[21]

The democratic themes associated with these several movements came to focus in the reform efforts of the 1820s—to permit election of the episcopal lieutenants or surrogates known as presiding elders, to allow some conference role and representation to the two-thirds of the Methodist ministry functioning as local rather than itinerant preachers, and to permit laity a say in the governing annual and general conferences. Here, as with the Republican Methodists, a set of legislative proposals gave focus to concerns, practices, and styles that went far deeper and presented the church again with the question as to how its internal life would draw on the best aspects of democratic society. Here, too, the reformers initially carried the day. They passed (decisively, 61 to 25) legislation at the 1820 General Conference providing for election of presiding elders, a proposal surfaced early in Methodist history and repeatedly urged up to the present, but vehemently resisted by the bishops, by William McKendree in his opening episcopal address to that conference and by bishop-elect, Joshua Soule, the architect of Methodist constitutional order. Soule pronounced the change unconstitutional and insisted that he could not "superintend under the rules this day made." Soule's resignation prompted the conference to suspend the new legislation.

A decade of intense, bitter, recriminating politics followed; new media emerged to carry the campaign to the populace; popular conventions met to broaden the reform agenda; bishops and conferences suppressed dissent and excommunicated dissenters. This movement found support from some of the strongest of Methodist leaders and its following at the heart of the Methodist movement, namely in the upper south and middle states. In 1830 a new denomination, the Methodist Protestant Church came into being to consolidate the reforms. And here, too, the rather modest size of the new denomination scarcely registers the deep division and cultural war through which Methodism had passed.

Slavery, Region, Race

Each division produced not only losses—of persons, of richness and diversity, of leadership, of principle—but also countermeasures that sometimes paralleled, sometimes negated the points of the reformers. Losses and reactive countermeasures certainly attended the divisions of the 1840s and 1850s, the exiting of abolitionists to form the Wesleyan Methodist Church in 1842, the north–south split of the Methodist Episcopals in 1844, and the emergence of the Free Methodists in the late 1850s (formally organizing in 1860). In each of these divisions, high principle on one side produced compensating efforts on the other. The MEC, particularly in New England and the burned-over district, became more receptive to abolition in the face of competition from the Wesleyans. The MECS intensified its mission to the slaves in the wake of the division of 1844. And New York Methodists contended with the witness of reformers who criticized elite control of the annual conference, the use of pew rents, slippage in the church's teaching on sanctification, and irresolution on slavery. "Freedom" emblemed their several pronged attack on Methodism's bourgeoisification and compromise with society's practices and their call for a return to primitive Methodism.[22]

The division of 1844 produced differing ecclesiologies and notions of the relation of church to the civil order, north and south, and both churches have, at times, read the division as though it primarily concerned notions of the power of General Conference, the authority of bishops, the limits of social witness. Underneath these theological and polity concerns, of course, lurked slavery and the differing sectional attitudes thereunto. Sectional division of the churches produced intense moral warfare, principled posturing, undergirded by fears and hopes about slavery. The several church splits anticipated and aggravated, if they did not "cause," the growing division of the nation.[23] 1844, creating a Methodist Episcopal Church and a Methodist Episcopal Church, South, left scars that continue to this day and fault lines that now vibrate over abortion and homosexuality rather than slavery. If these current issues constitute banners in a larger and deeper culture war, so might we also portray the contest between slave and free civilizations of the 1840s and 1850s.

The 1860s saw massive population shifts among black Methodists and one major new African American denomination, the Colored Methodist Episcopal Church. The latter, formalized in 1870, represented the culmination of MECS efforts to minister to slaves and then freed persons under strict racist guidelines and can be read as either extrusion of or exodus by African Americans.[24] One stimulus to MECS cooperation in the establishment of the CME was the success enjoyed by the MEC (the northern church) with the ex-slaves and the even greater and politically more radical advances of the AME and AMEZ.[25] All these population shifts, and not just the emergence of the CME, ought to be seen as important divisions. Also of a divisive quality was the decision by the MEC in 1864 to authorize the creation of separate black annual conferences, a segregating gesture "perfected" in the north before it was spread across the south. This de jure separation of black and white proved as complete as, and longer-lived than, the division of the MEC and MECS.

Language, Gender, Class

Some internal divisions look benign in hindsight, but they raised then, as they raise today, questions about the character and unity of the church. I refer to the establishment of distinct language conferences, an issue that has resurfaced as highly controversial when requested by Korean Americans. The year 1864 saw the authorization of German annual conferences by the MEC. German mission conferences had been established in 1844, as also had a mission conference for Native Americans. Swedish, Norwegian, Danish, Spanish, Japanese, and Chinese conferences would emerge later.

Episcopal Methodism granted laity rights in General Conference only gradually (in 1866 and 1872 in the MECS and MEC respectively) and had even greater difficulty with overtures to include women as laity or to ordain them. But Methodism did sanction women-run voluntary societies that functioned like conferences, notably the Woman's Christian Temperance Union (1874), interdenominational but always heavily Methodist, the Woman's Foreign Missionary Society (1869), the corresponding entities for the MECS (1878) and MPC (1879), and the Ladies' and Pastors' Union (1872). There was no threat of division along gender lines, but the internal structural differentiation deserves notice.

Class differences were not so easily contained. From the 1860s on, the holiness cause increasingly took on aspects of class war. Church leaders who initially embraced their fervent piety increasingly reacted to sustained holiness criticisms and freelance itineration with a heavy, disciplining hand. Schisms proved inevitable. The Free Methodists had, we noted, already exited in 1860. The National Camp Meeting for the Promotion of Holiness of 1867 led to the formation of a National Camp Meeting Association. Holiness camp meetings and itinerating holiness preachers called Methodism to return to its primitive practices. They recalled a pre-war and pre-1844 Methodism of entrepreneurial circuit riders, of outdoor quarterly meetings conjoined with camp meetings, of shouting preachers and demonstrative religiosity, of discipline through class meetings, and of side-street preaching houses. Many felt ill at ease in the grand, uptown gothic cathedrals, lavishly appointed and funded with pew rents; unnourished by worship centered in the Sunday service rather than the camp; ill-equipped to function in the increasingly nationalized and centralized program of the church and in the corporate board and agency structure authorized in 1872; and unsatisfied by a view of the Christian life as nurtured by home and Sunday school and provisioned through John Vincent's uniform lesson plan, teacher institutes, and Chautauquas. The holiness camp meetings represented one side in a culture war that pitted the anxious bench and class meeting against the Sunday service and the Sunday school. The prophetic spirit became, in places and at times, a come-outer spirit. And so in the 1880s and 1890s, regional and state holiness associations and conventions gradually transformed themselves into new denominations, the Church of God (Anderson), Church of God (Holiness), the Holiness Church, and the Church of the Nazarene. The later separate organizations make it hard to recall and envision the broader war within Methodism in which they had campaigned. The same, with important qualifications, might be said of the Pentecostal movements.

Coda

The twentieth century, of course, represents something of a different story. Its agenda was reunion, the ending of denominational divisions, ecumenism, and Christian unity. Methodism experienced several major reunions—the MEC, MECS, and MPC uniting in 1939 to form the Methodist Church; the EA and UB uniting in 1946 to form the Evangelical United Brethren Church; the two new bodies uniting in 1968 to form the United Methodist Church. And a century of reunions has not yet ended. The most recent General Conference gave authorization for Methodists to proceed with COCU and to explore rapprochement with the AMEs, the AMEZs and the CMEs.

Yet unifications, as well, have proved immensely divisive in ways that need to be recalled if one wishes to understand internal and trans-denominational coalitions today. For instance, the prospect of unification of the MEC and the MECS caused near division in the South (the MECS), with race as the major concern. And when unification came, it did so with an accommodation to the South that built a radical division into the very fabric of the denomination—namely the segregation of African Americans nationally into a Central Jurisdiction.

And the ending of that scandal coincided with the birth within Methodism of the caucuses and special interest groups.

Division and culture wars have been a rather constant feature of Methodist denominational life and, if not an every-decade affair for others, at least very common. Conventional wisdom has a short memory.

PART TWO
What Will United Methodism Need and Expect from Its Leaders?

Is There a New Role for Lay Leadership?

Sarah Kreutziger

This chapter[1] offers a model of compelling leadership given to us by our spiritual foremothers. In an era familiar to ours in terms of social and theological unrest, a group of nineteenth-century women emerged from the confines of hearth and home to call the churches to accountability and service. Overcoming formidable odds, they pried opened a place in the denominational hierarchy that allowed their voices to be heard on behalf of other women and children. By basing their authority on Christ-led servanthood instead of traditional notions of temporal power, they forced the church to hear again the marginalized voices of its disenfranchised members and the disinherited community. By "going where the spirit led" into the inner cities and less-hospitable rural areas, they allowed local needs, not the church hierarchy, to determine their actions. By understanding the Wesleyan tie between public mission and personal renewal, they maintained the delicate balance necessary for successful outreach. In the process, they forged a vibrant organization of committed women, using the Methodist connection, whose legacy lives on in the lives and activities of hundreds of individuals who serve the common good through our social institutions and missions. These women were the leaders and workers in the Methodist Religious Settlement Movement. Their example of laity-led moral community as seedbed for spiritual renewal offers a promising harvest for a contemporary church seeking new alignments in power and structure and clearer visions to follow.

Methodist Women in Motion

The world we face at the end of the twentieth century is remarkably similar to the world at the turn of the last century. On the positive side, late-nineteenth-century America was a time of relative calm and prosperity when military powers were scaled back, trade was growing, and democracy was spreading.[2] Less positive were the side effects of that prosperity. The massive industrialization of the United States brought millions of immigrants to fuel its labor force and created devastating social problems. Many of the newcomers lived in squalid conditions in crowded slums where substance abuse was rampant, domestic violence common, and law and order had broken down. African Americans and other minorities faced major obstacles to full citizenship with little recourse from the government or other social institutions besides their own churches. Women not working as domestic servants or in factories were relegated to "the women's sphere" of the home. Child labor was expected and education ignored. Local political leaders cared more about their authority and position than they did about the poor.

Yet, out of the shadows of social and spiritual despair, a significant and successful movement for social reform led by church women, emerged to reclaim the land "for Jesus' sake." Using the argument that as Protestant women, they were free to "go where the spirit led," they maximized the limited powers of their lower social status by claiming allegiance to the higher calling of the spirit and utilizing the female "internal networkers"[3] of church communities to successfully meet the challenges of the day.

This Religious Settlement Movement, a long-neglected part of the very public and lionized Social Settlement Movement, financed and run primarily by lay women, developed programs to reach the poorest inhabitants of the inner cities and rural areas. These Methodist women founded Sunday schools, hospitals, orphanages, kindergartens, nursing homes, bathhouses, dispensaries, loan banks, and job bureaus, while developing industrial education, children's clubs, reading rooms, and legal services as part of a well-organized outreach to the nation's dispossessed. Rooted in the early tract societies and city missions, the movement came into full flower as deaconesses and city missionaries, backed by the women's foreign and home missionary societies, created a community of committed volunteers under the auspices of the church. Their work laid the foundation for much of community work done in the United Methodist Church today and helped pave the way for women to enter professions such as social work, medicine, and religion.

Their driving vision was Wesleyan in origin. Their goal was no less than to "reform the American continent and spread Scriptural holiness throughout the land." They wanted a sanctified America composed of sanctified homes created by sanctified women working on behalf of other women. Deaconesses, who lived together in a "motherhouse" supervised by a "housemother," were especially motivated by this vision. Their aim was to create a worldwide "household of faith" inspired by "the Mother Heart," the practical, feminine side of a caring God. Their strength came, they said, from the model of "ideal home life"[4] that deaconess residences created. The result, as Rosemary

Radford Ruether and Rosemary Skinner Keller[5] point out, was a blending of outreach and retreat that served to energize and nurture their ever-widening sense of mission.

Their global objective, the building of the kingdom of God on earth, utilized the ideology of the social gospel, the motivating drive of Wesleyan perfectionism, and the structure of the Methodist church for its success. This satisfactory blending of cause and function enabled the movement to enlist thousands of other women and men in their purpose and to create a network of volunteers willing to work on behalf of the poor and needy in the name of the church. As such, they were a major drive in the burst of evangelical energy that built many of the social institutions of the Methodist Episcopal Churches, North and South, and created a place for women inside and outside of the church hierarchy.

One of the major strengths of that effort was Methodist connectionalism. Leaders of the Religious Settlement Movement were able to overcome the limitations imposed on females by custom and male authority by using the combined strength of women joined together in prayer and mission through the local women's voluntary groups. Women too timid to face the ire of societal censorship alone could do so in the company of other committed and respectable Christian sisters. These local groups in turn were strengthened by forging bonds with other missionary societies in the connection. In time, these ever-widening spheres of influence enabled women to move from local church leadership to national prominence, learning administrative skills that moved them on to positions of influence and responsibility. This was especially true for those trained in the deaconess and missionary schools set up for that purpose.

In a similar fashion, the leaders of the movement were able to reach many others through church communications. Books, missionary and deaconesses journals, pamphlets, and tracts had a ready made audience of eager Methodist readers. As deaconesses and home missionaries were sent out through the church structure to replicate the training they had in the local churches and communities they served, these channels were strengthened by personal contact. The grassroots support, in dynamic fashion, further enhanced the work of the general church.

In summary, community and connectionalism, grounded in Christian compassion and commitment, were the empowering forces that liberated others as it set the settlers free. Their lives and activities offer the church a model of leadership development that emerges from feminist images of mutuality and association combined with the strength of authentic belief.

Developing Leaders through Moral Community

Moral leadership is created when belief in the rightness of one's cause is stronger than one's fear of failure. The religious settlers had the uncompromising view that discipleship was a response to the call of a suffering community. There were several reasons for their steadfastness. While leaders such as Lucy Rider Meyer, Jane Bancroft, and Belle Harris Bennett were influenced by the same cultural currents that spawned the social gospel, they were also moved to action by prayer, preaching, the example of foreign missionaries, and their distress over scriptural illiteracy.[6] Strict adherence to "means of grace" such as regular worship, daily devotions, fasting, and serious Bible study further reinforced their call. They heard the biblical injunctions to "go forth and preach the gospel" (Mark 16:15) and obeyed.

Yet, there was another, directly personal reason that serving the oppressed was important to them. Settlers were sensitized to injustice because of their own experiences. Denied opportunities for advancement outside of the home and ridiculed as "hen preachers"[7] because of their claim to ministry, the moral crusaders had to fight for their place in a world hostile to highly educated women. In claiming their intelligence and the responsibility for their own development, as Carol Gilligan says, they "began to address issues of responsibility in social relationships."[8] Despite their work on behalf of inner-city residents and other marginalized groups, they were often perceived even by those whom they sought to serve as representatives of incomprehensible values and alien beliefs.[9] Nevertheless, they fought on. The settlers succeeded because their vision of where they were called to go was strong enough to trust God to lead them there.

That vision was tied to their identity as nineteenth-century Christian women. The settlers accepted the cloak of submission, claimed that role as their authority, tied that authority to the power of Scripture through the deaconess Phoebe (Rom. 16:1), and moved forward in the confidence of their "sphere." As historian Carolyn DeSwarte Gifford notes, "rather than creating a totally new role for women within the church, the diaconessate was an official recognition by the church of women's traditional societal functions as nurturers, teachers, servants, nurses of the sick and dying—caregivers for the poor, the young, and the elderly."[10] Since it was a traditional role that settlement leaders were asking to expand under the guidance of the Spirit, it was difficult for the church's patriarchy to argue with their call.

Settlers succeeded because they understood that God could use them where they were; that their "weakness," as Paul says (1 Cor. 1:25), was God's strength; and that servanthood, under spiritual guidance, is transformed into power. In other words, moral leadership, as Carol Becker proclaims, means "be[ing] ourselves boldly."[11]

Leaders also lead. By definition, they bind others to them by their personal characteristics or the passion of their causes, creating or enhancing the community around them.[12] But this action is reciprocal; leaders are created by the community as well. This is especially true in the emergence of female leadership. Many researchers point out, for example, that emotional development of women is the product of "relational growth" and mutuality. "The girl's sense of self worth," as Jean Baker Miller puts it, "is based in feeling that she is a part of relationships and is taking care of those relationships."[13] The "woman's voice" of nurture and responsibility for others, undervalued in western culture because of the ascendancy of male identity as autonomous power and authority,[14] is nevertheless pivotal for the growth of women. The web of caring relationships undergirded the settlers' sense of self worth and strengthened their courage to move forward in their mission. This was especially true for the deaconesses.

Deaconesses were woven by and into the community in every aspect of their lives. As members of the "Protestant sisterhood," they lived and worked together within egalitarian notions of mutual understanding and service. Their model of home life under the management of a caring, older sister allowed them to develop what Janet Surrey describes as "an experience of emotional and cognitive *intersubjectivity*: the ongoing, intrinsic inner awareness and responsiveness to the continuous existence of the others . . . [and] the capacity to identify with a unit larger than the single self and a sense of motivation to care for this new unit."[15] These communal living arrangements gave them the inspiration to venture into the larger landscape with the model of a worldwide family as an overriding metaphor of their work. So positively reinforcing was their association with each other that settlers continued their communal living and working arrangements even as the rest of the church was adopting the individualistic administrative and managerial habits of business and industry. As late as the mid-1960s, deaconesses continued to live in the neighborhoods and organizations that they served.

Practical divinity was the function of settler cause. The city missionaries and deaconesses began their ministry with preconceived notions of what they would find among the nation's dispossessed. These notions were embedded in a viewpoint that saw poverty as the result of deficient moral character and influence. After they walked, worked, and wept with the poor, however, the settlers realigned their thinking to include a larger vision of cause and effect that took into consideration the daily barriers and hardships that their neighbors faced. As a spirit-led community, settlers were "frantic learners," the kind of servant leaders who made things happen because they were so attuned to the environment around them.[16] Such visible successes enlarged the scope of their vision and brought recognition to the church as a caring organization.

At a time when northern Methodism was retreating from the cities in the wake of the "foreign" invasion of millions of immigrants, the deaconesses and city missionaries expanded their mission to those left behind. In the Methodist Episcopal Church, South, their ministry was to former slaves, disadvantaged mill workers, and impoverished farmers. Each of the groups benefitted from being at the table.

Another benefit of communal inclusiveness that sustained settlement drive and activity was the supportive networks with other women and men that the Methodist settlers forged throughout the church. To succeed in their home missionary work they needed the help of others who could not make the same sacrifices of time and service as they had, but who could offer funding and other resources. The deaconesses and city missionaries, therefore, linked the missionary societies and other agencies to their work in a mutually supportive relationship by sharing their story. Their communications focused on the people they served, the conditions of their work place, and the faith that sustained their mission.

Their audience were the thousands of women who belonged to the missionary societies who funded, supported, and, in many cases, oversaw their work. Lay women in the pews identified with the vivid stories of rescue and redemption that religious settlers wrote about in their publications and books and lectured about in church meetings. Local societies studied their activities in mission courses with great interest and responded with volunteer help, energy, and advocacy for home missionary outreach within the national and local structures of the church. A major part of that network included much-needed support for missionary training schools.

Shut out by the theological seminaries that discouraged women from entering ordained ministry, deaconess and missionary society leaders built their own system of training and education, taught the courses themselves, and developed the administrative skills needed to direct their national and international work. Time and time again, they appealed to the local churches for help after repeated rebuffs from a general church that underestimated their influence and mission. In doing so, they helped to equalize the power differential in an intransigent, hierarchical system by mobilizing grassroots support. This paved the way for female leadership, including ordination, within the church. Each small victory, however, created more work. After the General Conference of the Methodist Episcopal Church, South passed the vote for laity rights in 1918 following twelve hard years of struggle, friends rushed to Belle Harris Bennett, the resolution's most ardent supporter. "When congratulations were showered upon her, she raised her hands and said: 'Don't women! Don't! We are not so foolish as to count the battle won. This matter must be remanded to the Conferences, where the great struggle must begin!'"[17] Even when she lay dying four years later, she talked of the service that awaited her in Heaven.[18] She and the others never stopped working.

One last word needs to be added about moral communities as spiritual energizers. Liberating systems, structures, and relationships for greater mutuality and sharing is a fearful thing to do because freedom often encourages "speaking the truth in love" (Eph. 4:15) even when such discussion may not seem very loving. Although the religious settlers shared common vision and purpose in their work, there was much disagreement both inside and out of the community. Deaconess and missionary leaders disagreed on who would control the diaconate and how the lines of authority were to be established.[19] There was criticism and conflict between the church's emphasis on evangelism for church growth and the settlers' differing perspective of the greater need for systematic societal transformation.[20] And the deaconesses incurred the wrath of male church leaders who saw "Methodist sisterhood" as "leading the church straight back into the fold of Rome," while they hinted darkly about the inefficiency of unsalaried labor and "its unhallowed effects upon salaries in general."[21] These divisions brought much pain to the settlers and their supporters, but also bonded tighter to their cause, clarifying their vision, and sending them to their Maker in earnest prayer. As a result, the movement grew rapidly for fifty years until the peak of their influence merged into the success of their accomplishments. In one sense they did their work too well. The doors that they had opened for others led Methodist women into different paths of ministry and service that more and more bypassed religious settlement work as a calling.

Implications for Policy: A New Old Way

Still, the Religious Settlement Movement has much to teach us since visions for the future come out of an organization's past history.[22]

Looking back is a way of looking forward in a rapidly changing culture yearning for places to anchor its values and beliefs. The settlers teach us much about establishing such anchors. The cultural climate of the religious settlers' was similar to the apostolic paradigm, described by Loren Mead[23] as the society early Christians faced. Our church fathers and mothers, he says, were the "ekklesia," or outsider community, who were sent out in the name of Christ to a world that was hostile, foreign, or indifferent to their faith. The settlers created a successful ministry under just such conditions.

Today's secularized society offers similar conditions and circumstances. Effective evangelization will require, just as it has in the past, religious commitment from laity spiritually formed in the small groups of Wesley's organizing genius. Such modern-day missionaries will have to confront the restless meaninglessness of an uprooted world by "bringing the stranger into life-giving relationship to the Gospel and to a nurturing community."[24] That was the call that our foreparents answered just as it is the call we must answer today. The church needs to be a nurturing community that sends forth and welcomes back its members and the newcomers they bring with them. A major objective for our church is to strengthen that moral community for the work that it has been called to do. Some of the ways we can meet that objective are outlined in the next two sections.

Strengthening the Moral Community Within

Moral communities are developed and sustained within by:

1. Taking a stand. Spiritual formation cannot begin unless it is molded around life-changing beliefs and practices. United Methodism must boldly reclaim its mission to the dispossessed in the name of a Savior who was very clear about where the heart of the church should be. Reaching out to a broken community "for Jesus' sake," affirms our Wesleyan conviction that we have been transformed by the grace of God and are ready to share God's grace with others. As Willimon proclaims, "our people are as hungry for order, adventure, and meaning in their lives as were the Bristol coal miners who heard Wesley."[25] Individuals who share their inheritance with others acknowledge their connection as brothers and sisters in Christ.

2. Telling the story. We initiate and reclaim community when we repeat the metaphors and narratives that inform our lives and weave them into "the master stories" of our faith.[26] Singing, dancing and acting out the joy we have found in our covenantal relationship with God teaches others about who we are and how the gospel is played out personally in our lives and in the lives of our foreparents. We can honor our story tellers and support their work by writing plays, songs, and skits to help them in their mission. We can make them our present-day circuit riders by hiring them for Sunday schools, Vacation Bible Schools, conferences, and meetings during portions of the year. We can train church leaders, especially church historians, to transform archives into programs for Administrative Board meetings, Charge Conferences, and other assemblies. That will make it easier to repeat the stories in the work places, the market places, the Internet, and wherever else people gather.

3. *Re-imaging contemporary Christian identity.* Honoring the roles of "servant" and "nurturer," while recognizing the difference between chosen service and servitude, is a major part in forming moral community. These images have become less popular in recent years because of their link to the subjugation of women and minorities and because they clash with the currently fashionable emphasis on the em-powered, autonomous self. As a result, servant leaders in our churches, particularly those who live and work in marginalized communities, are often not recognized or honored. Yet, servanthood properly linked to the example of Jesus is the cornerstone of Christian discipleship and evangelism.[27] Our churches must be intentional about looking for the servant leaders in our midst and asking them to share their experiences and wisdom with others. We will find them in such places as inner-city missions, the kitchens of church buildings, the corridors of hospitals, the twelve-step programs, and the foreign mission fields.

4. *Paying more attention to symbols and rituals.* Part of the collective memory that informs our vision of who we are and sets us apart for our spiritual journey comes out of shared rites and ceremonies. As Thomas Moore reminds us, "ritual[s] maintain the world's holiness."[28] They connect everyday life to the sacred and feed the impoverishment of our souls. Methodists understand that connection. Our church provides satisfying rituals for worship services and other forms of devotion, but we often neglect the informal rites and habits that bind us just as closely. Greeting each other on Easter with "He is Risen!" wearing red or white flowers on Mothers' Day, or having ice-cream socials on the Fourth of July are examples of informal rituals that add richness to church life and trigger memories that invite her prodigal children back. Churches can be intentional about claiming or creating their rituals and maintaining their use. Church agencies that offer worship and planning resources can also help by incorporating ideas and suggestions in the materials they send to church workers.

5. *Setting an open table.* The church can no longer tolerate constraints, either institutional or individualistic, that keep us from

enjoying the hospitality of each other. Without inclusiveness, there can be no moral community. Besides eliminating structural barriers with crosscultural appointments and the creation of interracial congregations, we can be more intentional about bringing people together to celebrate the contributions of the different cultural and ethnic groups that make up our communion. Such activities as church festivals that tell the stories of each group in word, song, or dance; rituals that emphasize the blending of different cultures or backgrounds; and outreach projects that require the joint participation of all groups facilitate that process as they add life to our experiences.

6. *Establishing centers of refuge.* The importance of having a space for retrenchment is both visceral and emotional. God gave us the Sabbath for just such a reason. We can heed the Creator's example by offering "Sabbath rest" to our members. Sabbath rest is time away, under the sponsorship of the church, for spiritual renewal. It can last from three days to a year, depending on available funding and the needs of the individual. The time away can be spent in monastic silence, in focused study, or in activities at Conference Centers or other retreats that offer restful reflection. Scholarships open to clergy and laity can be drawn from a general fund pledged to by boards, committees, and individuals who want to reward the hard work of their church leaders. Sabbath rests are not limited to individuals. They can also be used by annual conferences, districts, or local churches that need to take time off for prayer and discernment. One of Lucy Rider Meyer's top priorities was to build a "home for worn-out deaconesses." That needs to be our priority as well.

7. *Keeping the focus on the sacred.* Prayer and other means of grace connect us to Christ and remind us of the sacredness of our time together. Too much busywork detracts from that purpose and deflects our focus. Churches, in keeping with the spirit of Sabbath rest, can help us unclutter our lives by scaling back routine meetings and eliminating most committee work during the seasons of Advent and Lent. Meetings that do occur should be seen as additional avenues for worship and structured accordingly. The extra time could be spent in small groups organized for spiritual formation, such as directed Bible study, house churches, covenantal clusters, and Sunday schools. God's handprint should be on everything we do.

Strengthening the Moral Community for Outreach

Moral communities are developed by looking outward as well as looking inward. We can further mobilize our church for outreach by:

1. *Spotlighting the Permanent Deacon.* The General Conference of 1996 created a new Order of Deacon that opened and expanded its role. This decision offers both opportunity and challenge for the church. On one hand, the order reenforces further professionalism of ministry at a time when there is a emphasis on enhancing lay authority based solely on baptism into the universal priesthood. The creation of the office flies in the face of that emphasis by incorporating those currently serving the church as lay people into the clergy circle. Additionally, care must be taken to make sure that the role of the Permanent Deacon does not become a lower-order position in the expansion of an ordained hierarchy. Another potential trap is to view the office merely as a renamed and ordained form of the diaconal ministry and continue as before without opening up other opportunities for the position in the spirit for which it was intended. One of the ways to avoid that trap is to envision one of its possible functions as the building of a sectarian Peace Corps. Members of the "Methodist Corps" would elect to work and/or live among people in our country too overburdened to respond to the gospel. Deacons could be asked to serve in the corps for a period of one year or more as part of their "primary appointment of service."[29] Social and community workers officially or unofficially connected to the church could be asked to design the program and to generate ideas for its support and enhancement.

2. *Rethinking the role of Deaconess.* Not to be overlooked is a place for those who want to remain among the ranks of the laity and validate their role with official connection to the church. The current office of deaconess offers such an opportunity, despite its somewhat invisible status in the church. While there needs to be some consideration of a name change in the spirit of inclusiveness, the office carries the seeds of a model for leadership that more appropriately fits the lifestyles of the majority of church members who do not feel the call to ordained ministry but want to heed "the daily practice of serving the needs of people [as] the more visible symbol of the link between the church and the world."[30]

Facilitating the growth of the office will require an intentional reacquaintance of the public with deaconess work by telling their story in a updated call to work with society's dispossessed. Making the educational requirements "user friendly" by using electronic models of distance learning and incorporating it into other training avenues such as the United Methodist Women's School for Missions or lay academies may also be helpful. At the very least the office should be made visible to the church and have a voice in any discussion and development of lay ministry.

3. Training the laity. In like manner, laity who want to serve more effectively in any capacity need to be trained in substantive ways rather than the "watered-down theology" that Mead rightly deplores.[31] Such training has to be tolerant of time constraints that lay persons face and must be cognizant of the vast knowledge and life experiences that lay people already possess. A solution allows lay people to collaborate with theologians and other clergy leaders in the creation of the curricula. In a reciprocal manner, laity can offer their services to seminaries as "missionary" consultants. Seminaries can also take advantage of many of their second-career students for this help.

4. Aligning with other institutions. Seeking shared ministry with schools of social work, law, and medicine will provide cross-fertilization for effective community service. In the field of social work, for example, the renewed interest in spirituality might make such theological discussion attractive. Distance learning and other avenues to connect educational endeavors that are not in the same cities would increase opportunities for such partnerships.

5. Creating mutuality in Annual Conferences. The annual conferences should be realigned to reflect greater mutuality and association among all those called into ministry. Conference journals, for example, are centered around clergy communication networks, making it difficult to contact the laity. Meetings are often held at times when working church members cannot attend. Clergy and laity are differentially represented in many conferences on the Board of Ordained Ministry and the Board of the Laity. And conference funding is skewed to finance clergy travel and learning enrichment at the expense of the laity. Conference Councils on Ministries can be charged to examine these and other inequities and offer suggestions for solutions.

6. Celebrating community work. On the local and district church levels, celebrating the community work of laity and clergy could become a larger priority. Churches could sponsor "community days" or "community fairs" that highlight the activities of individual and congregational outreach. Other recognition could be in the form of a fall festival (combined or not with Laity Sunday) that invites volunteers to bring the "fruits" of their discipleship to the altar in symbolic form.

7. Planting missions with small groups. Developing sites for missions calls for creativity and practicality. Homes, work sites, inner-cities, playgrounds, housing projects, and jails are logical places where the laity see themselves as the church in the larger world. Greater use of part-time local pastors, deaconesses, deacons, and specially trained lay volunteers could set up small groups for prayer, Bible discussion, or social causes if they were backed by a plan that was intentional in design for this outreach. The plan could include curricula, mentors, and "scouts" who check out the sites and do the necessary preparation.

In summary, we must: (1) continue to open up church processes, procedures, and structures by utilizing alternative ways of understanding that focus on mutual association and relationships rather than the hierarchical systems of a less inclusive age; (2) allow our sacred cause to determine what the structure of the organization will be, even if it means discontinuing or downsizing existing programs and procedures; (3) bring the laity into full partnership with the clergy and make church and community service more "user friendly" in terms of scheduling and uncluttering the structure from unnecessary busywork; (4) mobilize and encourage the laity to serve the church and community in a renewed call to the world's dispossessed; and (5) most of all, not underestimate the power of the Holy Spirit to manifest itself when we least expect it. God touches the church in unexpected ways and blows winds of change even through tightly held places. What God needs are moral leaders willing to work for the kingdom.

Clergy Leaders: Who Will They Be? How Will They Emerge? To What Will They Lead Us?

William B. Lawrence

Among the collection of "Blessings for Persons" in *The United Methodist Book of Worship* is one for "Leaders." Its words ask God, who has "anointed leaders and called prophets of old," to bless us so that we can "recognize our true representatives and authentic leaders." The prayer goes on to invoke the fire of the Holy Spirit, in order that the Lord might have emboldened and commissioned leaders to "transform our political system, to serve [God's] people, and to bring real glory to [God's] name."[1]

It is not all that common among us to petition for leaders in such eschatological prose.

Most often, our language is merely scatological. Complaints about leaders are commonplace: laity who volunteer to lead in local churches are vulnerable; anyone, ordained or lay, who holds a program or administrative staff position is a potential target. But clergy, who occupy most of the official leadership positions in United Methodism, are the most exposed; in fact, they often direct their scorn at one another. Pastors deplore both the lack of leadership by their bishops and the lack of direction by their district superintendents. Bishops and their cabinets fret about the ineffectiveness of pastors in leading their congregations. During a continuing education event focused on the pastor as local church leader, a district superintendent was heard to say that "Leadership is like pornography. It's impossible to describe in the abstract, but I know it when I see it. And right now I'm not seeing much of it!"

We have shown a greater capacity for cursing leaders than for blessing them. We have also demonstrated a high degree of cynicism about leadership and about training people to lead.

Trusting and Training Leaders

To some extent, Americans (not excluding United Methodists) are inveterate cynics when it comes to leaders. In part, that attitude derives from the way we associate leadership with power. The notion that "all power corrupts" has committed us to the principle that powers must be balanced against each other to protect humanity from its own corruption. Thus, anyone who holds a position of leadership is presumed to have some degree of power and therefore, by definition, to be corrupted. Questions about that person's judgment, competence, integrity, spirituality, or ethics become the devices for balancing the power that such a person is thought to hold.

There is also considerable doubt that leaders can be trained. "Leadership is an art to be cultivated and developed," wrote Harry Levinson, but it "cannot be learned by prescription or content."[2] Even Lovett Weems, who has focused his energies on training leaders for the church, echoes the sentiments of the superintendent cited earlier, though more aesthetically. "Leadership is like beauty," Weems wrote. "It is hard to define, but you know it when you see it."[3]

So there appears to be skepticism that leadership can be trusted or taught. Yet there is also a consensus that leadership can be recognized, observed, and described. An abundance of work in recent years has been dedicated to these tasks. Some of it draws upon secular, corporate leadership techniques, but all of it[4] is intended to show laity and clergy what it means to lead. Within the programmatic structure of United Methodism, a cottage industry is developing, as the denomination tries to turn the descriptive task into prescriptive activities for training leaders. Notable among such efforts are the conferences on "The Primary Task of the Church," scheduled by the General Board of Discipleship.

Even these efforts at observation are treated with some suspicion. Do the described forms of leadership embody such a white, male, western view of authority that they are spiritually compromised? Can the techniques of leadership ever be imparted to those who lack the gifts to lead? Or, to put it another way, can one ever do enough refining, trimming, shaping, grinding, and cutting to teach a stone to swim?

In our current situation, cabinets and boards of ordained ministry in the annual conferences know that a prevailing concern among laity is their frustration and disappointment with the quality of clergy leadership. Theological educators know that their visits across the church evoke questions like, "what are you people teaching these preachers in seminary nowadays?" One such faculty member, visiting a congregation, had been introduced to a small group when someone in the gathering inquired about the subject that the professor taught. "Homiletics," he answered. The questioner responded immediately: "Oh, so you're the one who has been teaching our ministers how *not* to preach!" By implication, the laity may be wondering if seminaries are teaching, annual conferences are approving, and bishops are ordaining people who know how *not* to lead.

Therefore, amid the doubts that leaders can be trusted or trained, there is a desire for effective pastoral leadership. And this raises questions concerning clergy leaders: who will they be; how will they emerge; where will they lead us?

Thinking Theologically

First of all, to answer those questions United Methodists will have to do something that we have rarely troubled ourselves to do—namely, *think theologically about leadership.* Typically, our interest in clergy leaders is centered upon matters of management and morality. We give attention to the administrative offices for which clergy might be selected: a prestigious pulpit; the chair of a major conference board; membership on, or executive staff service with, a general agency; institutional placement, such as in higher education or in health and welfare ministries; the episcopacy. We also give plenty of attention to the moral behavior of clergy: whether they smoke, drink, gamble, have sexual encounters outside of marriage, or have sexual interests within their own gender group. Our polity is ordered to address such things.[5] But we leap to these secondary matters without pausing to focus upon the primary one—that leaders in general and clergy leaders in particular have their identity not in the offices they hold or the ways they behave but in the gracious gift of God.

There shall be leaders for the church because God has willed it! Leaders exist not because of personal charm (though they may have it), or because of eloquence (though they may employ it), or because they administer efficiently (though they may do so). Leaders exist because God has willed that the church have in its midst persons with certain specific gifts for leading. Conferences, cabinets, boards of ordained ministry, and committees on pastor-parish relations must include in their consultations and interviews the following question: *"with what capacity for leadership has God blessed you?"*

In our boldness to be faithful to the Scriptures by emphasizing that we are an egalitarian church,[6] we have to be similarly bold and faithful to the Scriptures by emphasizing the distinctive gifts of the Holy Spirit to individuals in the church.[7] Among those gifts is "leadership," which translates the Greek term *kybernēsis*. Literally, the word means the "pilot" of a craft, or "one who steers." From the earliest days of Christianity, the church was envisioned as a ship, and Christian tradition developed the notion that Christ was its pilot. But 1 Corinthians 12 clearly shows that the first-century church understood piloting or leading the ship to be a charism given to one or more members who had the helm.

Some persons have the capacity to lead, direct, steer, guide, drive, orient, pilot, control, and serve at the helm of the community of faith, for the well-being of the whole church. To pilot a ship is to have responsibility for everyone aboard, and God has willed that such persons exist in the church. It has been our practice to set them apart for specific ministries, by such acts as ordination. But persons may not exist in every annual conference with the constellation of other gifts needed for particular ministries in that conference. Therefore bishops should solicit from their clergy the names and special leadership gifts of ordained ministers in their conferences; they should share those lists with episcopal colleagues, mindful that an institutional or pastoral or educational ministry in another area could be served by someone appointed across conference lines; they could use such means as electronic billboards both to describe unusual appointment needs and gifted leaders who might meet unusual needs. Such strategies are rooted in a theological conviction that God has provided the leadership that the church needs. All we have to do is recognize these leaders and place them.

Two specific changes could be made in *The Book of Discipline.*

Paragraph 430.2 encourages appointments across conference lines, using the jurisdictional committee on ordained ministry as an agency to facilitate that. But why should such moves be limited to jurisdictional regions? Is it not possible that a pastor in Memphis with gifts for leadership in urban ministry might be uniquely suited to start a new urban congregation in Trenton? The current language of this provision could be replaced by the following: "As general superintendents of the church, bishops shall develop methods for communicating with one another about the gifts of clergy leaders and the needs of specific ministries."

Paragraph 432 includes two groups beyond the cabinet for consultation in appointment-making: "congregations" and "pastors." Absent is any reference to the whole "connection." A third sub-paragraph could be added, to make it clear that clergy leaders can be recognized and appointed to ministries in education, health and welfare, cooperative parishes, institutions, and other settings for the benefit of the church rather than just for congregations and pastors. To think theologically about leadership is to think comprehensively about the wholeness of the church. To serve God faithfully is humbly to accept that God has provided leaders, and to set them free for leading.

Thinking Ideologically

Second, to answer the questions about coming clergy leaders, we have to move from theology to ideology. As Edwin Freedman indicates,[8] there are two models of leadership with which we tend to function. One is called the "charismatic" type—a powerful individual personality with such prodigious talents and enormous personal presence that he or she dominates any group. Such a person leads by force of character, rather than by institutional process. Any organization that such a person leads probably does not endure more than a generation beyond her or his passing. The other type functions by "consensus," deriving her or his leadership from the authority of the group. Such a person may emerge from a segment of the church, for instance, and lead by expressing the will of the group. The organization or institution that the consensus leader represents will endure well beyond any particular individual, but it will not likely have a vision or sense of purpose other than managing its continuing existence.

Freedman proposes a third model, which he calls "leadership by self-differentiation." In this mode, a leader functions by caring first for his or her own self-understanding. One leads by clarifying a sense of one's own place in the group and one's own vision for the community. Thus does a leader catch a vision that sees beyond the immediate circumstances and pilots the group to a promised shore.

Clergy leaders will not be those who depend on a secularized personal charisma, except by the shortest-term measurement of effective leadership. Likewise, clergy leaders will not be those who manage coalitions while waiting for a consensus to form. Rather, clergy leaders remain part of the group that has set them apart for the benefit of the whole group: to glimpse a vision that the community did not see; to articulate a hope that the community did not know it could claim.

Cabinets and committees on pastor-parish relations can hold clergy accountable for the courage to lead. They can organize church and charge conferences not on the basis of reports for the year just concluded, but on the basis of a pastor's declarations of the objectives to be met in the year just beginning. They could even change the way a pastor's compensation is set—not as a fixed amount to be paid in the coming twelve months, but as a base "support" amount to be paid, with full compensation to be determined in terms of the goals achieved. They could change the length of appointments from one year to an agreeable longer term.[9] Why not allow the consultative process to set appointments for three or five or seven years, with renewal periods of two or four years following? Itinerancy does not require frequent mobility!

Thinking Inclusively

Third, we know that our clergy leaders will increasingly be female. It has been little more than four decades since women were explicitly given full clergy rights by the General Conference. Though women are the majority of United Methodists, they remain a minority among clergy. Their numbers are growing, yet they serve in a small fraction of leadership positions. And while it may be true that most conferences can claim to have the same proportion of women in the superintendency as they have in the ordained ministry, relatively few women have been appointed as senior pastors of larger-membership churches.

That is changing. In the future, the rate of change will increase. With theological school enrollment now counting women as nearly one-half of the student population, the gender mix of ordinand classes will shift. Unless women exit from the ordained ministry at an alarmingly rapid rate, they will become a growing leadership pool for the church.

But more than statistics will be altered. Women tend to exercise leadership differently from men. They are more relational than hierarchical, and they generally stress intimacy over efficiency.[10] Large-membership churches with women as senior pastors, and those with more than one woman on the pastoral staff, will experience new patterns of clergy interaction with each other and with laity. Small-membership churches, which are stereotypically thought to be more resistant to women in the pulpit (but have been more likely to receive an appointed clergywoman than larger congregations have), tend to function with a greater sense of relational intimacy and community; thus they may help larger churches learn some things about openness to women's style of leading. Furthermore, women tend to preach differently, using imagery that is more creative and that draws more frequently upon acts and symbols. An increase in sacramental observance and a decrease in didactic preaching may result. Cabinets will operate differently when the bishop and half of the superintendents are female. The day will come when paragraph 353.6 (maternity leave for bishops and superintendents) is invoked.

Thinking Connectionally

Fourth, our clergy leaders will be persons with a narrower range of experience in ministry than has been customary in the past. Several factors contribute to this.

One is the prevalence of persons who have had other life and career experiences before entering the ordained ministry. The rising average age of seminarians points to this. The styles of leading that they developed in former roles will shape their patterns of clergy leadership, but there will not be time for them to "pay their dues" to the system before they step into leadership positions. Informal procedures that assume that leaders will rise through the ranks will have to be displaced by the acknowledgment that one's gifts for leading may have matured before one was ordained.

Another is the trend toward longer pastorates. Persons who emerge as leaders after fifteen years in pastoral ministry may have served in only two appointments, whereas a generation ago they may have served twice as many. The typical pastor, with a ministerial career in fewer settings, will have been exposed to fewer kinds of communities and fewer types of churches.

Still another factor results from the necessity for consultation about an appointment prior to its being announced. There are explicit requirements in *The Book of Discipline*[11] that clergy family concerns (including, in practice, the spouse's career) be taken into consideration. One consequence of this will be that clergy may tend to move within a more limited geographical range inside the bounds of an annual conference, while a spouse's career develops. This will tend to restrict the clergy member's exposure to the broader conference environment.

One additional factor may arise as appointments across conference boundaries become more common. It is entirely possible that increasing numbers of United Methodist clergy will serve four appointments in three different annual conferences. This would broaden their personal experiences and expand the connectional life of the church. Yet it will severely limit their sense of investment in the conferences where they serve. They may very well exercise leadership, but it would tend to be leading based on a specific skill rather than upon broad experience in the conference.

Given these factors, the "connection" will have to devise new strategies for identifying and placing clergy leaders. It will become increasingly important for bishops and district superintendents to create situations for a conference to connect as a community. Such devices as clergy gatherings at midyear with working groups on theological and pastoral issues will be vital, to allow clergy leaders to emerge.

Though individual clergy may have backgrounds that are limited in focus, it is still possible to foster connections that transcend geographical, ethnic, racial, and cultural boundaries.

New strategies are essential because our current situation in United Methodism might be described as one of "segmentation." It is manifest in various patterns. There is localism, which tends to show in clergy commitment to congregation and community above conference. There are the segments shaped by cultural, ethnic, and language identities.

Leaders emerge within each segment and link with others of like mind. Thus, evangelicals establish a forum for themselves, ethnic groups use caucuses, and program specialists form associations. They seek and acquire political strength within the church by cultivating coalitions that are internal to their segment. Often their leaders are the persons who seem best at identifying the agony of one constituency segment. They may be able in a most compelling way to articulate the grievances and hopes of that segment. But can they lead the denomination beyond its segmentation?

Thinking Pragmatically

Whether or not leaders can lead us beyond our segmentation will depend, finally, on the ways they institutionalize their leading. It will not so much be determined by bishops, superintendents, or legislative actions by the General Conference as by the clergy leaders themselves. They may choose to lead on a local or constituency-based level, as pastors of local churches, directors of caucus groups, contributors to ideological forums, or in some other segment of the church. Or they may glimpse a greater vision, and pursue a broader promise. Wesley chose to lead by organizing a renewal movement within the Church of England. Phoebe Palmer chose to lead by preaching at camp meetings and conducting midweek Bible studies. Ralph Sockman chose to lead by remaining for forty-four years as pastor of one local congregation and cultivating his pulpit as a national voice. The future of the United Methodist Church will be shaped by the institutional choices that clergy leaders make.

Those who will be our clergy leaders will discern the gifts that God has granted them for the well-being of the church, will have the courage to use those gifts for the sake of the whole church rather than just some segment of it, and will subordinate their personalities not to the will of the people but to the will of God for the sake of God's people. They will be blessed.

Leading Small Congregations: Persistence or Change?

Jackson W. Carroll

My theme is leadership in small congregations. Rather than focusing on patterns and structures of leadership, I treat leadership as an activity essential for small-membership churches if they are to serve their members and their changing communities in ways that are faithful to the gospel and effective in terms of their size, resources, and location.

In an important new book on congregations,[1] Nancy Ammerman examines a number of congregations across the country located in changing communities. Although most are in urban or suburban settings and not all are small, much of what she learned about how these congregations are responding to community changes is applicable to small congregations regardless of location. Moreover, what she learned is especially important for congregational leadership.

Ammerman groups the congregations into three categories, depending on their response to community change. One group of congregations have mainly "hunkered down" in the face of change and either continued to decline with diminished resources or relocated to avoid changing. A second group of congregations have become "niche" congregations. A niche identity doesn't depend on serving a particular neighborhood but instead serves a particular "market" whose members drive to it from around the region. A third group of congregations have found ways of adapting to the changes in their communities, which in most cases has meant opening their fellowship to newcomers in the community. Some have been able to adapt with minimal change to their existing ways of doing things. Most, however, have had to make significant changes in their culture, programs, and organizational patterns. Some have even undergone a complete change of identity as older members have left or died and a new constituency has emerged.

There is no way that I can do justice to the richness of Ammerman's findings; rather I will concentrate on what she learned about leadership dynamics in the first and third of her congregational types, namely, those that declined or relocated and those that adapted in some way to their changing communities. These two types, especially, seem applicable to small congregations. For example, in a recent study of small congregations (75 or fewer average attenders at worship) in the two United Methodist annual conferences in North Carolina, I found that most were located in areas undergoing change—in some cases demographic, in others economic. These congregations represented both of Ammerman's types in response to community change. Most would be in her status quo category. Approximately 60 percent had lost members from 1983 to 1993 (the period covered by our study); less than three percent had remained stable. At the same time, however, 30 percent give signs of having adapted to change over the decade, especially if growth in membership and attendance can be taken as signs of adaptation. Growth is clearly not the only criterion for judging either congregational adaptation to change or the quality of a congregation's life and ministry, nor do I wish to imply that all of the congregations that lost members resisted trying to adapt. Yet, membership growth, or at least remaining stable, is important and cannot be ignored for long.

If Ammerman's categories are applicable to small congregations, then what she says about differences between status quo and adapting congregations is important. Leadership, especially clergy leadership, was one of the primary differences between the two types of congregations.

Regarding congregations that adapted to changes in their communities in constructive ways, Ammerman says, "Someone has to see the connections between the congregation as it now exists and the congregation as it might someday exist. Someone has to imagine that [the congregation] might remain spiritually and socially rewarding for its participants." In short, change has to be "imagined and planned for."[2] This, she says, is the task of leadership, and it was a primary characteristic of the congregations that adapted.

In contrast, in status quo or declining congregations, leaders took a different approach:

> Pastors tended not to introduce new ideas and programs. Most provided excellent care of the people in their congregations and performed well the duties expected of them. Most fit nicely with their parishioners, working hard to maintain the pattern of church life all of them expected. If they perceived any need for change, they were often unwilling or unable to undertake the difficult (and often conflictual) work of dislodging old routines. A few expressed . . . their sense that their leadership skills were simply not up to the challenges they knew the congregation faced. Others simply pastored the best they knew how.[3]

I suspect that many small congregations have had leaders mostly of this second type. At best, they have provided excellent care for their members and performed well the duties expected of them. They've led worship, preached, and given pastoral care. They have not, however, tended to introduce new ideas and programs, since they assume that longtime members have a strong desire to maintain the status quo. These pastors are aware of the likely conflict that proposals for change would precipitate, especially among the longtime lay leaders. One of my students described the patriarch of his small Baptist congregation: His motto, the student said, was "slow and steady," and his favorite question when anything new was suggested was, "What have we done in the past?" Also, since small church pastors realize that they are not likely to stay in the congregation for long—the average tenure of the pastors in our North Carolina study was 2.7 years—many are tempted to say, "Why work for change? Why rock the boat? Why risk the pain of conflict? Why not, instead, just do the best I can to help the congregation stay afloat in its current state?" Lay leaders too are aware of the short tenure of their pastors, so they ask, "Why should we make the effort to make these difficult, costly changes when our pastor probably won't be here long enough to see them through, and a new pastor will want to do something different? So let's just 'hunker down' and hope that we can survive."

I do not wish to devalue the desire or capacity for small congregations simply to survive. Many keep going in the face of considerable difficulties. At the same time, however, is it possible to do more than just keep the congregation going? Most, including members of small churches, would like to do more. Most would like to be like Ammerman's adapting congregations, imagining new possibilities and finding the resources to respond creatively to the changes taking place around them.

So let us come back to the issue of leadership as a central activity in the life of small congregations. In particular, what kind of leadership is required if congregations are to adapt to their changing communities in ways that are both faithful to the gospel and effective in their setting? Or, to put it differently, what kind of adaptive work is necessary on the part of leaders if they are to help their small congregations respond constructively to change rather than be overwhelmed by it?[4]

Leaders who help their congregations do the necessary adaptive work are ones, as Ammerman put it, who help them imagine new possibilities and plan for change. They see connections between the congregation as it now exists and what it might someday become. They also help present participants continue to find their congregation spiritually and socially rewarding even as it adapts to change. Adaptive work is not merely passive acceptance of what comes or merely surviving but helping members discover what it might mean to faithful to Jesus Christ under the new circumstances; and it means helping them learn the new attitudes and new behaviors that the new circumstances require. Let me make several points about what the adaptive work of leaders in small congregations entails.

Understanding the Culture

First of all, *to help a congregation do its adaptive work, a leader must take the time and make the effort to understand and appreciate the culture of small churches generally and the particular congregation or congregations that he or she is serving.* Here I'm speaking especially of pastors.

Small churches *are* different, as Lyle Schaller emphasizes in the title of one of his books. They are not simply miniature versions of large churches. They value different things. For example, they value relationships over efficiency, people over programs and procedures. They operate on a different rhythm—people time rather than clock time. They value competence in their leaders, but even more, they value caring. Carl Dudley described the effective small church pastor as a "lover."[5] One might want to avoid that particular image in today's cultural and political climate, but the instincts of the image are exactly right! Pastors with strong organizational and management skills who know how to get things done, who have energy and drive, and who are gifted preachers can still fail miserably as pastors of small congregations. They can also succeed, but to do so, they must have strong people skills and learn to value the rhythms and relationships that make most small congregations so attractive to their members. They also have to understand that because of these valued characteristics, change is threatening. Members fear losing what they so highly prize!

Furthermore, each congregation is itself different. Each has its own culture—its own story, its distinctive way of embodying the gospel in its beliefs and practices, its own norms about "how we do things around here"; and each will have its own set of matriarchs and patriarchs who are the guardians of the congregation's heritage. Leaders need to learn and value these stories and understand how the congregations does things before jumping in with proposals for change. A recent graduate wrote to one of our faculty members with the following advice for students who are graduating and accepting pastoral appointments:

Learn to read the church. Enthusiastic pastors sometimes rush too fast to make changes, begin programs, and force issues that some churches are not ready for. Pastors should spend their first year studying that church. Besides, once a pastor has been able to develop a relationship with a church, change will come easier and there will be more support for new programs. Moreover, the personality of a church and its history need to be taken into consideration before any new programs [are] attempted or any changes made.

I suspect that his reason for writing the letter was not only to give advice to graduating students, but also to serve as a not-so-subtle reminder that we had not prepared him well to do this important adaptive work of understanding and appreciating the unique culture and dynamics of the church he was serving.

Understanding Community Dynamics

Understanding the culture of the congregation is not the only leadership task for effective adaptive work. *The leader must also understand (and help other congregational leaders understand) what is happening in the community around them.* Leaders, lay and clergy, need a clear and realistic picture of their community and how it is changing if they are to adapt creatively rather than simply "hunkering down" in a survival mode.

In one of his poems, the American poet Wallace Stevens suggests that we live in the description of a place and not in the place itself. By this, he means that our understanding of the reality is always filtered through some description, construction, or mental model of what that reality is. Often our descriptions of the community around us don't fit the reality of the situation. This was illustrated in our study of small United Methodist congregations in North Carolina. In the pastor's questionnaire, we listed a number of social, demographic, and economic changes that may be taking place in the community around their church. We asked pastors whether these changes were occurring in their community, and if so what has been their effect on the congregation? A significant number of pastors agreed that their community was experiencing some of the changes we listed. Often they viewed the changes negatively, even when the data for the congregation's ZIP code area suggested that the changes were likely to be positive for the community and congregation alike! For example, in areas where the population had grown over the decade, many pastors perceived it to have declined. Where there was population growth among youth and young adults, some complained that the aging of their community was having a negative effect on their congregation.

Why such misreading? Is it because we have been conditioned to think that rural and small town America is in decline? Is it because the newcomers to the community aren't "our kind of people" and thus remain invisible? Is it perhaps also the result of a conscious or unconscious fear of the changes that congregational growth might bring? Or, as Ammerman suggests, is it because of the pastor's fear of what might be required if he or she tries to lead the congregation to adapt to its changing community? I suspect that all of these factors affect the pastors' "descriptions" of the place in which they live.

If, however, congregational leaders and members are to do the kind of adaptive work that is needed to help the congregation respond to the changes taking place about them, then leaders must describe as accurately as possible the place in which God calls them to serve.

Using One's Authority to Lead

A third characteristic of leaders who help congregations do adaptive work is that they *use their authority to help the congregation face the changes it needs to make.*

Many leaders, especially pastors, don't like the word authority. They identify it with authoritarianism. We've all seen the bumper sticker that says, "Question Authority." So pastors resist thinking of themselves as authorities or claiming any special status or expertise that is implied by claiming authority as leaders.

When pastors do this, they not only shortchange themselves; they also shortchange their congregations. Please don't get me wrong: I am not encouraging those who lead congregations to be authoritarian in their leadership style. I am not encouraging them to violate the high premium that small congregations—and indeed the gospel itself—places on caring and sharing and mutuality in relationships. So what do I mean by claiming and using one's authority as pastors or lay leaders to help congregations do their adaptive work?

I mean by authority the right to exercise leadership based upon a combination of the formal position that one holds and the qualities, characteristics, or expertise that one demonstrates as a leader. For pastors and lay leaders, authority is the right to lead in the church

Actually, many leaders have two kinds of authority, whether as pastors or lay leaders. Let me stick for a minute with pastors, but much of what I will suggest applies also to those who hold other church positions. The two kinds are what I call *office* authority and *personal* authority. Another way of thinking of them is as *formal* and *informal* authority. Office or formal authority is what pastors receive in their ordination as the church authorizes them to fulfill certain important tasks: proclaiming the Word, celebrating the sacraments, and ordering the life of the church. Personal or informal authority is that authority that one earns by virtue of personal qualities that lead people to trust one's ability to lead. Personal authority also comes through a kind of ordination—a "second ordination" or time when a congregation really accepts the leader because she or he has won their respect and trust by virtue of loving, supporting, and caring for them as persons.

Both kinds of authority are important. Office authority signifies that the church has recognized a person as having the necessary gifts and graces to lead in the church. In the case of pastors, it gives them initial entrée into the life of the congregation. On arrival at a new pastoral assignment or call, one is received primarily on the basis of authority of office. In contrast, personal authority must be earned. It is based on trust that the leader has the best interests of the congregation at heart, that he or she is not there for self-promotion, that he or she will not take advantage of people's trust.

Such trust that exists between pastor and people functions as what Ronald Heifetz calls a "holding environment";[6] that is, it is a relationship that allows the leader and the congregation to do the hard, adaptive work when there are no easy answers to the problems the church faces. In this "holding environment" the leader has the authority to raise difficult questions and to propose new ways of thinking and acting.

A student who served as pastor of a small congregation while he was in seminary came to talk with me. He was at his wits' end. Try as he would, he could not get the leaders of his congregation to change their ways or face up to several important issues confronting the congregation—despite the fact that the congregation's average weekly worship attendance was sixteen persons and declining. But attendance decline was not the only issue. The building also was in bad need of repair. When he would call meetings of the church council to discuss these issues, members would agree to attend but then fail to show up—a kind of passive-aggressive behavior. He was in near despair and questioning his call to ministry. Clearly, a substantial part of the blame for this unhappy situation lay with the members themselves, but the student also was part of the problem. For whatever reason, he had failed to earn the kind of personal authority that is essential for establishing a "holding environment" to help the congregation members do their necessary adaptive work. Encountering their negativism made him negative too, which in turn only reinforced their own. It had become a kind of "catch-22," a no-win situation for him and the congregation.

What, more specifically, does it mean to use one's authority, especially one's personal authority, to help congregations do their adaptive work? Let me make several points about this process all of which suggest that teaching is a major task of pastoral leadership.

First, the leader must *help the congregation understand or frame the situation that it faces so that members can see both the challenge and opportunities that confront them in realistic terms.* In some instances, it may mean accepting that their community is in decline, that their congregation is not likely to survive, but that there are positives in their past and present that they can celebrate even as they accept and prepare for their eventual closing or merger. Having a good death, celebrating God's grace through the years of the congregations life, is for some a way of adapting to change.

But it also may mean helping the congregation, especially key leaders, to imagine new possibilities for being faithful to the gospel. My experience has been that those who emerge as leaders in this change process may not be the longtime members but often come from those who have joined the church more recently—and I don't necessarily mean young members. In our study of North Carolina congregations, there was a positive correlation between church growth and the percentage of members who had transferred from other churches. While this may be the result of an openness of the congregation to newcomers, it also suggests that these new members brought fresh perspectives. They were able to see possibilities for the congregation that old-timers could not. Whatever the case, it is important for the leader to use his or her holding environment to help members to frame and describe the congregation and its community in new and different ways, to imagine new possibilities and means for achieving them.

The leader needs also to *use her or his authority to help members surface the beliefs and values that are guiding their present attitudes and behavior, and examine them in light of their understanding of the gospel.* This kind of reflective process is often painful, and it can lead to anxiety and conflict. In fact, without exception, every congregation that Ammerman classified as having adapted to change had experienced some degree of conflict because of the changes proposed. In contrast, most declining or status-quo congregations were distinguished by an absence of conflict. This is simply to say that change is not easy! If one wants to help a congregation adapt to its changing circumstances, one should be prepared for a fight!

Consider the example of a small congregation whose community includes newcomers from socioeconomic, racial, or ethnic groups who are different from the congregation's members. The leader suggests to them that their future lies in welcoming the newcomers else the congregation will eventually cease to exist. But she or he also helps them to surface their own feelings and beliefs about this option. It is likely to be painful for them to have to face the prejudices that block them from reaching out to the new residents. Some will deny any prejudice and express anger at the leader for suggesting it. An effective leader, however, will contain his or her anxiety over the anger and conflict, as painful as it may be, so that they can confront and begin to own the feelings and beliefs.

Those familiar with the late Rabbi Edwin Friedman's work on family systems will know that he calls this "maintaining a non-anxious presence." Many of us dislike conflict. Our proclivities are to step in and try to rescue the situation like well-meaning parents. But the effective leader will learn, as someone put it, "to bite his tongue until it bleeds." As Friedman once said, the leader must pull back and let "things fall apart a bit, so others can pick up more responsibility. The leader has to contain his or her own anxiety, because the change will take awhile."[7]

The previous example of a congregation in a changing community is not the only situation where beliefs and values need to be surfaced, faced, and clarified while the leader maintains "a non-anxious presence." Instead, conflict may erupt around values and beliefs about money or whether to allow an AA group to use the church building, or any number of other small or large adaptive challenges that a congregation needs to address.

The comment from Friedman touches on a third point about leading congregations to do adaptive work: *the leader must be willing to share authority in such a way that congregations can develop their own theological and behavioral resources to imagine new possibilities and make necessary changes.* The pastor does not need to be the "boss" telling people what they should think or do. Instead, he or she will encourage and elicit the ideas and opinions of members of the congregation even as the leader puts forth his or her own. The aim is to help the congregation's members develop the capacity to respond to what is confronting them.

A simple story illustrates the point. A small congregation had the practice of celebrating communion once a month on the first Sunday. Once when Easter fell on the first Sunday of April, a board member asked the pastor whether communion would still be celebrated on Easter. She reminded him that there would be a full church, several baptisms, and three anthems by the choir.

The pastor replied, "Why shouldn't we? It's the first Sunday, and Easter is a very appropriate time for communion."

"But," the woman continued, "we will have just celebrated communion on Maundy Thursday. Besides there will be visitors present who might feel uncomfortable taking communion, and it will add close to an hour to the service."

The pastor, feeling that he was in a win/lose situation, exerted his authority: "We'll have communion on Easter Sunday."

"Why?" the woman persisted.

"Because I'm pastor, and worship is my responsibility."

As the one who told the story said, that ended the discussion; it ended all communication; and the woman and her family were not present.[8]

What would have happened, instead, if the pastor had turned to the board and said, "Well, what should we do?" As it was, the board had sat quietly, aghast at the exchange. Had he asked the board's opinion, he would have empowered them to consider the issue; he could have helped them clarify their beliefs about what was at stake and arrive at a responsible decision that best served the church. That would have been a sharing of authority that helped members develop their own resources rather than turning responsibility over to him.

Does this mean that a pastor should not express his or her own convictions? Certainly not; but he or she can do so in such a way that invites others to express their convictions instead of sealing off all discussion. To do this is to help members claim their own authority for exercising the ministry given them in their baptism.

Staying Long Enough for Change to Happen

Let me make one final point about using one's authority to help a congregation do its adaptive work. *Change takes time, especially in small congregations. Integrating change into the congregation's life so that it lasts may take even longer.* This argues not only for patience on the part of pastors but, more important, it argues for longer pastorates. Patience and time are required to develop the trust necessary for leadership and to help a congregation visualize the change, plan for it to happen, and move through the change process. Clearly the 2.7-year average pastoral tenure is much too short! Lengthening tenure raises important issues of compensation and support for those who chose to serve small congregations for long haul. It also raises questions about alternatives to full-time pastoral leadership. Both of these are complex issues that I cannot treat here. Rather, I simply reiterate: change takes time, and leading a congregation through the adaptive process demands patience and long-term commitment to small church ministry that denominational leaders need to learn to honor and support.

To sum up: My purpose in this chapter has been to consider aspects of the work of leadership that are needed if small congregations are to face and adapt to their changing communities instead of "hunkering down" in defense of the status quo. I suggested first that, before a leader jumps in to "save a small congregation," he or she would be well-advised to come to appreciate the unique culture and characteristics of small-membership churches generally, but especially of the one that she or he is attempting to lead. Second, I discussed the use of one's authority—especially one's personal authority—to help congregations learn to do their own adaptive work. This includes helping them frame and reframe the issues facing them, clarify their theological convictions and values about the issue so that they can imagine new possibilities, and develop the resources and capacity to take responsibility for their own congregational life and ministry. And I suggested that such change takes time and calls for longer pastorates than are currently the norm.

Has Our Theology of Ordained Ministry Changed?

William B. Lawrence

A. Introduction

Was the 1996 General Conference of the United Methodist Church "the most radical" legislative session of the denomination in two centuries?[1] Did it make any specific changes that alter our tradition at its roots? Did it shake our forms of ministry to their foundations?[2] Did it take action to revise the theology of ordained ministry in United Methodism?

All of these questions are pertinent. But the last of them points toward the real problem facing the denomination as it reflects upon and implements a new ordering of ministry. Does the United Methodist Church understand the ordained ministry theologically? Did the decisions in Denver reshape the theological basis of the ordained ministry for the church?

As I have pondered such matters, two pictures have begun to form in my imagination.

1. Scene One: A Bishop Prepares for Annual Conference

The first is an image of a bishop preparing to preside at a session of annual conference. In the midst of this process, it occurs to the bishop that it may be necessary to plan for—and preside at—seven different liturgical events for persons who are being given authorization to conduct the ministries of the church.

Liturgical event number one could be a service to ordain elders to ministries of word, order, sacrament, and service. These are persons who will have already been elected full clergy members of the annual conference. Their ordination would grant to them a permanent authorization for ministry, which could only be removed by their voluntary surrender of credentials or some judicial proceeding. Otherwise, until their deaths, the authorizations granted by their ordination would remain.

Liturgical event number two could be a service to ordain deacons to ministries of word and service. These are persons who also will have been elected full clergy members of the annual conference. Prior to the actions of the 1996 General Conference, they may have been candidates for diaconal ministry, but they have sought and received the affirmation of the church as candidates for ordination, in terms of the way the 1996 *Discipline* defines the office of deacon. Their authorizations are for a lifetime. However, the authorizations are semi-permanent, in that they remain valid only so long as these deacons find positions to which the bishop will appoint them, or request leaves of absence for any period when they are not appointed.

Liturgical event number three could be a service to ordain deacons to ministries of word, service, and sacrament, under the provisions of the 1992 *Discipline*. These are persons who will have been elected to probationary membership in the annual conference and who expectat that they may also be ordained elder some years hence. Their authorizations are permanent in time, lasting until death, unless judicially or voluntarily removed. However, their sacramental authorizations are limited in space to the place where they are appointed by the bishop.

Liturgical event number four could be the ordination of deacons to ministries of word, sacrament, and service, under the provisions of the 1992 *Discipline*, for persons who will have been elected to associate membership. These individuals have completed the course of study, have served four years as a local pastor, have met some educational requirements, and are at least thirty-five years old. Their authorizations are permanent in time (unless voluntarily or judicially removed), but limited in space to the places of their appointment by the bishop. Further, they have no expectation that they could be ordained elders at any point in the future.[3]

Liturgical event number five could be a service of consecration for diaconal ministers. These are persons who were candidates for that office before 1997 and who wish to continue on that track toward lay membership in the annual conference. They are not interested in ordained ministry. Their authorization as consecrated diaconal ministers is permanent, but they are not consecrated to forms of ministry; rather, they are consecrated to a relationship with the annual conference.

Liturgical event number six could be a service of commissioning for persons who are to be appointed either to pastoral ministries in local churches or to ministries of service. Those individuals who are commissioned will have been elected to probationary membership and they "shall" receive an appointment from the bishop—to ministries of "service" (if they intend to seek ordination as deacon) or to ministries of "service, word, sacrament, and order" (if they intend to seek ordination as elder). The authorizations granted by this commissioning are limited in time to the period of one's probationary membership[4] and apply only to the form of ministry for which one is seeking eventually to be ordained. This commissioning service is supposed to include the laying-on of hands by the bishop, according to paragraph 316 of the *Discipline*. But it is not ordination and should not be construed as, or confused with, ordination!

Liturgical event number seven could be a service for licensing local pastors, all of whom are to be appointed to local churches for ministries of word, order, sacrament, and service. Many different types of persons might be licensed in such a liturgical event: some will be currently enrolled in the local pastors' course of study; some will have completed the course of study; some will have completed a theological degree but will *not* have been elected to probationary membership or commissioned; some will have completed a theological degree *and* will have been elected to probationary membership *and* will have been commissioned; and some will have been ordained deacons (in the sense of liturgical event number two above) *and* elected to full clergy membership in the conference *but* because of unusual circumstances are going to be appointed as pastors. In fact, anyone who will be appointed as a pastor and who is not an ordained elder must have a license, according to paragraph 341. The authorizations granted by this license are limited in time and space: they must be renewed annually, and they only apply to the places where these persons are appointed.

In my imagination, I see a bishop exhausted by all these possibilities even before the gavel falls calling the annual conference to order. Shall some of these liturgical events be combined? Which ones? How will the distinct and confusing authorizations be communicated to the variously ordained, commissioned, consecrated, and licensed persons, to say nothing of the persons who otherwise participate in the service?

2. Scene Two: A Local Church Meets the Ministers Appointed to the Charge

A second picture has begun to develop in my mind. This is an image of a Sunday morning in a local church where several persons are appointed to various ministries. In other words, it is a congregation with a multiple staff. It is the practice both of this congregation and of this annual conference that, on the first Sunday of a new appointment year, the chair of the staff-parish relations committee formally introduces to the worshipers all those who have been appointed by the bishop for the ensuing year. I imagine that the chairperson could have all five of the appointees stand in a line facing the congregation and introduce them in the following manner.

"I am pleased to announce to you that the bishop has appointed these persons to us, and I have the honor of introducing them to you. Beginning with the individual standing next to me and moving down the line, I will identify them by name and by the nature of the ministry to which each has been appointed.

"First is Chris, who is an ordained elder and therefore is authorized to preach, to administer the sacraments of baptism and Holy Communion, to serve the community, and to order the life of the church. Chris can celebrate marriages and perform all other acts of ministry that we might expect of a pastor. I might add further that Chris is an ordained minister and may be addressed as 'Reverend.'

"Next is Jan, who is an ordained deacon and who, because of the specific nature of that ordination, is authorized to preach and to administer the sacraments. Jan can also celebrate marriages and perform all other acts of pastoral ministry, but is authorized only to do them here, within the bounds of this appointment. I might add as well that Jan, as an ordained minister, may be addressed as 'Reverend.'

"Next is Lin, who is also an ordained deacon. However, because of the specific nature of that ordination, Lin is authorized to preach and to engage in ministries of service, but is not authorized to baptize or celebrate Holy Communion. Lin can do weddings, but not if the couple wishes to include the sacrament of Holy Communion in the wedding ceremony. I might add, nevertheless, that as an ordained minister, Lin may be addressed as 'Reverend.'

"Next is Pat, who is a consecrated diaconal minister. Pat is consecrated to ministries of service and is authorized to preach as well as serve. However, Pat cannot conduct services of marriage or baptize or celebrate Holy Communion. Finally, since Pat is not an ordained minister, I would suggest that we not address Pat as 'Reverend' but as—well—Pat.

"Finally, there is Lee, who is a licensed local pastor. With that authorization, Lee can preach, baptize, celebrate Holy Communion, and do weddings. But as a local pastor, Lee can only do those things here in this appointment. Lee is not an ordained minister, but Lee is not really a lay person either since in the annual conference Lee is counted as clergy. Therefore, I will leave it to you and to Lee to decide whether or not Lee may be addressed as 'Reverend.'

"Last of all, it may be important to note that all five of these persons have the same educational background. All hold undergraduate degrees from four-year colleges, and all hold master of divinity degrees—in fact, they all graduated from the same seminary."

3. Epilogue: The Theologian's Dilemma

It is bewildering to describe the perplexities of the consecrated, ordained, licensed, commissioned, and otherwise authorized forms of ministry in the United Methodist Church. Obviously, some of the confusion exists because we are in a time of transition, adapting to the major changes adopted by the 1996 General Conference. Yet this period of transition will last to at least the end of the year 2000. And it could last as long as the year 2009 if persons who entered some form of candidacy prior to 1997 wish to continue their pursuit of the ministry to which they feel called even though the church no longer receives new candidates for that option.

Moreover, between now and 2009 we will have at least three sessions of the General Conference. What happens if the legislation changes again? One of the results of the radical decisions in Denver was the elimination of diaconal ministry. Approved in 1976, it was revoked in 1996. Apparently, after twenty years, the denomination decided that it was not working. Who knows what will happen twenty years hence, when the General Conference of 2016 will mark the two hundredth anniversary of the death of Francis Asbury? Who knows what will happen twelve years hence, at the General Conference of 2008, which will mark the two hundredth anniversary of the adoption of our first constitution?

Since all of these changes are merely legislative enactments, any of them can be altered by subsequent legislation. And all it will require is a simple majority of the General Conference delegates to do so.

We have been studying ministry for at least half a century. Perhaps the changes wrought in 1996 will be left alone for a while. Surely, some of the disarray will settle down with each passing year.[5] Nevertheless, persons who were granted authorizations under a former *Discipline* cannot lose those authorizations by some retroactive legislation. So the potential exists for a very long time that chairs of staff-parish relations committees may be facing unenviable tasks on the Sundays when the bishops' appointments are shared with the church. And bishops who preside at liturgical events in annual conferences will face many interesting decisions about how to distinguish ordinations, consecrations, commissionings, and licensings from one another and about whether episcopal and other hands should be laid on persons in each particular group.

But the *real problem* is cloaked within those visible—whether real or imagined—words and deeds. *Polity,* manifest in ecclesiastical actions that grant authorizations for ministry, *is an expression of theology.* The real problem facing United Methodists is not trying to describe who is authorized to do what. Rather, the real problem is to understand the whole situation theologically.

B. Toward a Theology of Ministry

Some might argue that we have arrived at this current set of circumstances because we lack a theology of ministry in the United Methodist Church. I would demur. It is not that we lack a theology of ministry, but that we have a plethora of theologies of ministry. Some of them are congenial with one another. Some are in conflict with one another. And right now we have no mechanism for exploring them, reconciling them, or deciding which ones among them to reject.

The General Conference, where all of this occurred, is a "legislative" body[6] not a theological seminar. The only way it knows how to handle church doctrine is to turn it into church law. It is constitutionally prohibited from altering our doctrines. But the only process for determining whether it acts in violation of this constitutional principle is to appeal to the judicial council, and that council has ruled repeatedly that it decides matters of law, not matters of theology.[7] So the General Conference, which is not established to do theological work, makes theological decisions by getting advice only from within itself (or from the commissions, task forces, or agencies it chooses to create) then turns those theological decisions into legislation. Sometimes, it creates legislation, then leaves itself and others wondering what the church law is saying theologically.

Amid this confusion, I think it is still possible to identify two general principles that have had a major impact on the theology of ministry in the United Methodist Church. *First,* our sources and guidelines for doing theology are multivalent; that is, they are expansive rather than restrictive in meaning, they lead to different interpretations, and they encourage rather than inhibit diversity. *Second,* our theology of ministry has been built upon foundations that are boldly ecumenical yet distinctly Wesleyan.

1. Our Sources and Guidelines for Doing Theology Are Multivalent.

The legislative enactment that appears as paragraph 63 in *The Book of Discipline* under the title "Our Theological Task" lists the famous four sources and guidelines for doing theology: Scripture, tradition, experience, and reason. Scripture is identified as primary.

But Scripture does not offer a single, clear, unambiguous pattern for ordering the ministry of the church. As David Bartlett has said, "the various writings of the New Testament provide evidence for a variety of forms of ministry in the first century church."[8] One can point to the New Testament and recognize there the concept of apostolic ministry. One can find there the offices of bishop, elder, and deacon. But one cannot find in the New Testament a uniform code for those three offices. Neither can one find any consistent witness that authority to preside at sacraments was limited to certain persons or offices.

In other words, the whole Bible is the proclamation of God's good news—in the words of Paul Scherer, "a place to meet God." It is not a textbook on polity, nor is it a legislative manual.

Therefore, our primary theological source and guideline is not definitive about ordained ministry. We must read it through our other sources in an attempt to arrive at defining theological positions. We must read it from the perspective of tradition, with the insight of reason, through the lens of human experience. And we must do all of that within a denomination that does not have an entity whose focus is on theological work.

Of course, tradition, experience, and reason are also multivalent. As presently constituted, our denomination is heir to multiple theological traditions about ministry.

We inherited the threefold pattern of ordained ministry—bishops, elders or presbyters, and deacons—from the broader Catholic tradition and specifically from the Church of England, in which John Wesley was a priest. We inherited that threefold pattern, however, with an important modification from Mr. Wesley. His decision in 1784 to ordain persons in England and to authorize the ordinations in America was based on the principle that as an elder he was equal to a bishop—a "scriptural *episkopos*," he said. This shifted the authority to ordain from the episcopal to the presbyterial office.

Within the Methodist Protestant aspect of our tradition, that theological principle became a matter of polity: as people in "the church without a bishop for a country without a king," Methodist Protestants valued ordination, but they vested the authority to ordain in the hands of "a thousand bishops." In referring to what he called "the paradox that truly expresses the polity of the Methodist Protestant Church in relation to her ministers," Lyman Edwyn Davis wrote: "It is an elementary principle of our denomination that there is but one order in the ministry; that all elders of the Church of God are equal; and Christian ministers are forbidden to be lords over God's heritage."[9]

Besides the Catholic-Anglican-Tory ordering of ministry and the Democratic-Jacksonian ordering of ministry, we have inherited (and, at various times, explicitly embraced) an element of Reformed theology in our understanding of ministry. Is one ordained to word and sacrament? Or is one ordained to ministries of word, sacrament, and order? The Reformed tradition tended to emphasize the latter, and in fact since 1968 United Methodists have done the same.

We are also heir to a development in Wesleyan Methodism that distinguished the authorizations required for different types of ministerial practice. Wesley permitted lay preaching, but he did not permit the lay administration of sacraments. Ordination was not required to proclaim the word, in Wesleyan practice, but it was required to preside at the font and at the table.

Furthermore, our multiple traditions have expressed various forms of ministry within our theology of ordained ministry. The United Brethren (like the Methodist Protestants) had only one order of ministry, the elder. The Evangelical Association apparently ordained persons as both deacons and elders, but perhaps in something closer to Asbury's experience of consecutive ordinations on consecutive days. Evangelical Association attitudes toward the episcopacy also varied: officially, they had bishops; but in the mid-nineteenth century they went decades without bothering to elect one to fill a vacancy.

So we bring many theological traditions to our ordering of ministry. We also bring varieties of experience.

There is the cultural diversity that United Methodists experience in different regions and different homelands. To be a United Methodist in the southeastern United States, where Southern Baptists are dominant, is very different from the experience of United Methodists in regions where Roman Catholics or Congregationalists or Lutherans dominate.

There is the ethnic diversity that characterizes the denomination. Black United Methodists in the ordained ministry, tragically, have found that they are far more likely to be welcomed in African American churches outside the Wesleyan fold than they are in white United Methodist congregations. Korean United Methodists are more likely to feel at home in a congregation of the Korean Methodist Church than in a United Methodist congregation of the dominant culture. Native American United Methodists value their freedom to draw upon the cultural heritage of their many nations quite beyond the narrow confines of Anglo Wesleyanism.

To impose any one experience upon others as normative is to violate the integrity of their experience.

And reason does not lead us to discover some central truth that lies at the heart of all traditions or experiences. Some might wish to argue that there is a rational structure to doctrine in general, and to a theology of ministry in particular, which we United Methodists once accepted and to which we should again aspire. That, however, has never been true, and it is not true today. Moderate and liberal advocates of social justice emphases in ministry, like moderate and conservative advocates of individual conversion emphases in ministry, wonder how each other can claim the right to be called "evangelical." Systematic theologians construct their systems while facing attacks from deconstructionists. Modernists are assailed by postmodernists. Arminian theologians wonder how the human will can be brought into accord with God's will. Process theologians wonder if it is even possible to say that God has a will.

Every one of these well-reasoned theological approaches has something to say about the ordained ministry. And all of them can be found in the United Methodist Church.

So the first general principle about our theology of ministry is this: our sources and guidelines for theological reflection are multivalent; they have many meanings and many values. Our theology of ministry has no single source. We are a much more complex people than that.

2. We Have Taken Some Clear Theological Stands in Our Views of Ministry.

In our evolving theological perspective on ordained ministry, we have taken some clear stands. Briefly, I shall list and illustrate a number of them.

One involves our commitment to an emerging ecumenical consensus. There is a sacrament that authorizes persons for the ministry of the church, and it is baptism. We affirm "the ministry of all Christians," and we do it not simply with rhetoric but with the way we have institutionalized candidacy for ordained ministry. No one can become a "candidate" without receiving overwhelming support from a community of faith. A congregation in its church (charge) conference, or multiple congregations in their charge conference, must endorse an individual by a super majority (two-thirds) vote. No pastor, no ordained minister, and no bishop can simply bestow an authorization for ministry upon someone. A local, nonordained body of the *laos* ('people'/'laity') must first offer its confirmation to an individual's sense of call. This is a converging ecumenical insight. It also embodies an aspect of connectionalism in the theological tradition of Wesley.

Moreover, we continue to find ways to enlarge the participation of the *laos* in that activity. Now the lay members of the Board of Ordained Ministry will vote on the character and qualifications of persons to be ordained when those ordinands are presented to the clergy session for approval (par. 605.6). And the hands of the nonordained, as well as of ordained non-United Methodists, may be imposed upon the ordinands when the prayers are said at the time of ordination.

A second theological stance taken by United Methodists is that, because this ministry is a ministry of the church, it is part of the mystery of salvation. Paragraph 101 of the 1996 *Discipline* (whose present form dates back to 1976) speaks of God's saving work through covenants. It then celebrates "the new covenant in Christ" as "another community of hope" through which God acts to save God's people.

God is free to save us in whatever way God mercifully wills to do so. But one way God saves is through the church. So the church's ordained ministry is a ministry of salvation.

A third, and related, theological stance is one that we have continuously affirmed since the days of Mr. Wesley: the ministry of salvation is both social and personal. There is no holiness without social holiness. As Ralph Sockman, in his own sexist way, reminded his elite congregation of executive leaders in the depths of the Depression, no businessman could claim personal holiness for not having committed adultery if he paid a wage to his secretary that forced her to violate the seventh commandment in order to survive.

Racism, sexism, economic exploitation, and other sinful social systems are as much in need of God's saving, transforming grace as any individual thief hanging on a cross.

This commitment to social holiness has been institutionalized in the ordained ministry of the United Methodist Church by the way we have historically understood the office of deacon. Since the 1784 ordinations in England and America, the broadest streams in our multivalent tradition expected that ordained ministers would enter the offices and orders of both deacon and elder. The ministry of deacon is the ministry of social transformation, and it has been theologically as well as liturgically imbedded in our practice of ministry.

Until the 1996 General Conference, that is. We still have the office, and now we have a new and legislatively separate order, of deacon. We now say that elders are ordained to ministries of service, as well as to word, sacrament, and order. But we have separated the ministry of deacon from the ministry of elder. It happened, in part, because of a confusion of language. Some United Methodists began casually to talk about the new form of the diaconate as a "permanent deacon," without realizing that everyone in the broadest Wesleyan/Methodist tradition who was ordained since 1784 was also a "permanent deacon." One's ordination as deacon was not surrendered or removed when one was ordained elder. Rather, the authorizations to ministries of word and sacrament (and order) were added to the institutionalized and theologically sound authorization given to a deacon to serve.

By our act of liturgical and institutional separation in 1996, we have lost something vital and theologically profound.

A fourth theological stance we have taken is our continuing commitment to the call to ordained ministry as "inward" and "outward." This is neither new nor uniquely Wesleyan, of course. But it remains essential to our understanding of ordained ministry that there is no self-authenticating call, just as there is no objective imposition of the authority to minister without the faithful commitment of an individual to serve. From the initial action by the supermajority vote of a charge conference, to the annual renewal of candidacy by that same body, to the annual actions of district committees on ordained ministry, to the recommendations of the annual conference board of ordained ministry, and to the decision of the conference itself, the "inward" and "outward" call will have been repeatedly tested.

A fifth theological stance involves some recent choices of language. Back in 1976, the *Discipline* began to use the phrase "representative ministry" to describe the lay diaconal ministry and the ordained ministry. Linked to the sense of call as inward and outward, this concept of representative ministry offered a significant way to think theologically about the (ordained or consecrated lay) ministry as:

- representing the church to God (in liturgy, prayer, and pastoral presence),
- representing Christ to the church (in presiding at the table, in a model as servant), and
- representing Christ to the world (in witness, service, love, and sacrifice).

As a theological concept, "representative ministry" had a broad ecumenical value and was widely valued across the church—even among Christians whose specific views of the ordained ministry differed from ours.

With the 1996 *Discipline*, the phrase "representative ministry" has all but disappeared from our legislation. Its echo seems to appear in only one place, namely paragraph 303.2, where we assert that "the Church's ministry of service is a primary representation of God's love." Theologically, it sounds like the bland serving the bland.

What has gained prominence in the current legislation is the concept of "servant leadership." While from one side the phrase may look unobjectionable, from another it lacks the richness and subtle nuance of the now absent "representative ministry." For one thing, "servant leadership" does not seem to have the transcendent character of representing the people to God, or Christ to the people and to the world. Rather, it is limited to the perspective of immanence: the human Jesus, the despised suffering servant, or the successful business or political leader. This is a democratization or leveling of theology that risks robbing our doctrine of its mystery, and hence of its power.

C. Implications

With all of the changes that the 1996 General Conference adopted in reference to ministry, many will be apparent at the time that subsequent annual conferences actually convene. Voting patterns will shift, places will change, the color of name tags will be suddenly altered, and the number of members will rise.

About 4,500 part-time local pastors across the connection have now become voting clergy members of the annual conferences. Though their voting rights will be limited, they certainly could have a significant impact on the organization, operation, financing, programming, and social witness of a conference. Further, their presence as clergy members will require that an equal number of lay members be added. To be sure, this will be more significant in some conferences than in others, but the addition of a sizable number of new voters will be an interesting phenomenon to observe. It will also add to the cost of an annual conference session, where increased numbers of lay and clergy members have to be housed, fed, and provided with printed documents. Will it shrink intimacy as it enlarges franchised participation? Will it reduce the number of hours that the conference is in session. Will it lead to more worship or less, more business debate or less, more theological reflection or less?

Similar questions arise with reference to the decisions facing the 1,400 diaconal ministers in the United Methodist Church. If all of them are eligible for, and choose to seek, full clergy membership in the annual conferences and ordination as deacons, that will have an enormous impact on several areas of church life. That will not only add a great number of new clergy members but also reduce (by the same number) the lay membership. Hence, to meet the equalization requirement, an impressively large number of new lay members may have to be added to the annual conference.

Besides these numerical considerations and all of the social as well as financial considerations attached thereto, a political matter looms on the horizon next year. The diaconal ministers who (in 1995) sought election to the General and Jurisdictional Conferences as lay delegates may (in 1999) be full clergy members with deacons' orders seeking election as clergy delegates. While this may seem like a purely political matter, the decisions of the 1996 General Conference have potentially invested such issues with theological significance. The Denver meeting created the concept not merely of two separate and distinguishable ordinations as deacon and elder, but of two "orders" of ministry in the order of deacon and the order of elder.[10] These are to be "covenant" communities, whose purposes are fulfilled in regular gatherings "separately or together" for study, for "mutual support and trust," and for accountability.

Theologically, this appears to offer the potential for a further fragmenting of the larger (and more historic) covenant as "conference." Persons who are ordained to, and invested in, the diaconate will have a separate house from those ordained to, and invested in, the presbyterate. This could further separate a servant ministry from a sacramental ministry. The invitation to font and table could, by the very nature of the ways we have chosen to order and ordain our ministry, be unfortunately distinguished from the sending forth to serve.

Each order will have its own officers and its own representative on the executive committee of the board of ordained ministry. The risk that their common calling will be subsumed under separate political agendas is great indeed.

Finally, it is the separation of ordination from authorization for ministry that raises the greatest theological issue for understanding the ordained ministry in the United Methodist Church.

The problem can be illustrated in two particulars.

One involves the authorization we deny to deacons in their ordination but expect them to fulfill as full clergy members of the annual conference. Ordained to ministries of word and service, these deacons still participate in one of the fundamental acts by which we *order* the church—determining the character and qualifications of persons for ordained ministry. Deacons, as full clergy members, will vote on whether persons become local pastors, deacons, or elders. Deacons will participate in deciding whether all the clergy are blameless in their life and official administration. But they will do so in an office that has not been ordained by the church to exercise such ministries.

Theologically, the question is not whether they should have such authorization. It is whether granting such "ordering" authority to people not ordained to it eliminates any meaning from ordination to order. If people who are not ordained to ministries of order participate in ordering the church in the same way that people who are ordained to ministries of order do, then ordination is irrelevant. Do we really want to say that, theologically, ordination is irrelevant?

The second particular that illustrates the point is a decision in which the General Conference has sundered the relationship between ordination and the authorization to conduct the acts of ministry.

It was Mr. Wesley's vision to separate the authority to preach from the authority to preside at sacraments. He allowed laity to preach, but not to administer baptism or Eucharist. The sacramental authorization, he believed, was solely granted in ordination.

Theologically in the broad Methodist tradition, that same principle has been maintained. Even when exceptions were granted, such as by allowing nonordained local pastors to administer sacraments in the bounds of their pastoral charges, these practices were very clearly understood as exceptions for the higher purpose of providing pastoral care that included baptism and Holy Communion.

With the 1996 General Conference, however, the basic principle has changed. Now the fundamental standard for the exercise of all ministry will be a minimum of three years serving in an appointment appropriate to one's calling before any ordination occurs. All persons who serve as pastors to congregations will serve as local pastors for three years. These will not be exceptions. They will be normative. In effect, the General Conference has sundered the relationship between authorizing the exercise of sacramental ministry and ordination to that ministry. It is a major theological shift, with potentially great ecumenical implications.

We are at a point in our developing theology of ordained ministry where we have no entity in the church claiming responsibility for theological reflection while we turn issues of doctrine into mere legislation. The cost to us for this kind of theological indifference is already great.

And the cost is being incurred at a time when we are committed to extensive ecumenical endeavors. With what theology of ordained ministry will United Methodists approach such conversation partners as the African Methodist Episcopal, the African Methodist Episcopal Zion, and the Christian Methodist Episcopal churches? With what theology of ministry will we pursue covenant union toward a Church of Christ Uniting? And from what theological perspective on the ordained ministry will we continue the work expressed in the World Council of Churches' document *Baptism, Eucharist, and Ministry?* Have we radically altered our understanding of the relationship between deacon and elder, between ordination and the exercise of pastoral ministry?

Who, on behalf of United Methodism, is wrestling with those questions?

There may only be one existing body in the church that is constitutionally equipped to claim theological competence for the denomination. The General Conference cannot. The judicial council will not. That leaves the council of bishops. Can they? Will they?

D. Conclusions

Was the 1996 General Conference the most radical such meeting in two hundred years regarding ministry? Did it shake our forms of ministry to their foundations? Did it revise our theology of the ordained ministry?

"Yes." "Yes." And, perhaps unintentionally, "Yes."

In my view, from a theological perspective, these radical changes have been more chaotic than creative. I assert that on the basis of the following conclusions.

First, we have altered the theological understanding of vocation, or call, to ministry. The twofold sense of call as inward and outward has been shifted to emphasize call as inward, with some outward monitoring by church. Candidates for ordained ministry will now have to articulate the form of ministry to which they feel called. Those who feel called to the diaconate will have to initiate their own placement: they will not itinerate; and if they do not find a venue to which the bishop will appoint them, they can lose their orders. This imposes all of the vocational authority upon the inward call of the individual who feels summoned to a ministry of service. It makes ministry even more a profession than a calling.

Second, we have severed the relationship between ordination and the acts of ministry. Every United Methodist who is a candidate for ordained ministry will exercise the office of deacon or the office of elder before she or he is ordained to it. Every elder will be ordained to ministries of service (as well as word, sacrament, and order) without having been ordained deacon. By legislative fiat, that strips the diaconate of its unique, historical, biblical foundation and transfers it to elders' orders. (To argue than baptism is authorization to engage in ministries of service does not help. For that would make the ordination of deacons irrelevant, also.) The ordering of the church's ministry thus has no relationship to ordination. Ordination ceases to be a symbol that the ministry of Christ's church is represented in a minister of Christ's church.

Third, we have sent confusing theological messages to the ecumenical community and to the candidates who might be appropriately gifted for specific ministries. One form of servant ministry is the chaplaincy—hospital, nursing home, child care residency, and military. Presumably, someone who is ordained to the servant ministry would properly fill such a position. However, we have said that deacons are not authorized to administer the sacraments. For the church to ordain persons to servant ministries but deny them the authorizations to carry out those ministries is bewildering, at best. How could one be a hospital chaplain but not administer Holy Communion as part of the ministry? How could an ordained deacon be expected to find a position in prison chaplaincy, when the institution will likely judge the deacon to be less than fully ordained?

Fourth, this chaos invites arbitrary or ill-considered actions. A board of ordained ministry may choose to affirm a policy that would simply "license" all deacons and thus enable the cabinet to create a virtual appointment to a pastoral charge near the place of a deacon's service, authorizing the deacon to administer the sacraments within the bounds of her or his appointment. Theologically, this both invalidates the integrity of a servant ministry and destroys any pretense of a connection linking ordination to the exercise of ministry. Or a future General Conference may decide to add sacramental authorizations to the office of deacon. Theologically, this would effectively end our self-understanding as a connectional church with an itinerant ministry, since nonitinerants would be authorized to do everything that itinerants are ordained to do.

Fifth, even this much theological confusion is consistent with our history. What is not new about this crisis is that we are facing it. Within the Wesleyan tradition and the Methodist connnection, we have been able to discern in our theological heritage a theological hope. We must do it again. In Asbury's time, it was through discerning the relationship between our connectional life and our itinerant ministry. In the nineteenth century, it was through discerning the relationship between sanctification and social holiness, between social holiness and social institutions. In the twenty-first century, it may be through discerning the relationship between a servant ministry and a sent ministry.

But someone will have to claim the spiritual and theological competence to exercise such discernment.

We are at a curious point in Methodist history. There is a confrontation, of sorts, occurring between the General Conference and the annual conferences. And it is being played out within our connectional theology as it is articulated in our theology of ministry.

The General Conference turns theology into legislative regulations. It writes educational standards, creates regulatory boards to administer its policies, and adopts laws such as those that exclude homosexuals from candidacy, appointment, and ordination.

Each annual conference turns that legislation back into a living connectional covenant. It decides who meets those standards. It decides whether preference will be given to graduates of United Methodist seminaries or other schools. It decides whether a local pastor, trained through the course of study, is as well-trained for ministry as seminary graduate with a Master of Divinity degree. It decides what constitutes "practice" and self-avowal with regard to sexuality. It decides whom to include in the ordained ministry and whom to exclude.

Some body in the church has to provide the theological discernment and leadership to guide us through this confrontation, to define our theology of ministry, and to keep it connectional. Only the council of bishops has the constitutional freedom, the theological responsibility, the corporate identity, and the general oversight of the church to accomplish this. Bishops cannot vote either in the General Conference or the annual conferences. But they can be servant leaders to the whole connection if they will find their theological voice and guide the church to inspect its shaken foundations of ministry.

Has United Methodist Preaching Changed?
William B. McClain

For almost twenty years, I have taught the preaching course for the second-year students in the summer course of study school at Wesley Theological Seminary in Washington, D.C. The course of study school is a program designed to help lay pastors more effectively serve local churches by offering seminary-like courses in the major area of theology, including preaching and worship. The students in that program tell a somewhat humorous story about an incident that happened in my preaching class that I don't remember happening quite as they tell it. But sometimes feelings become facts, especially when they convey a plethora of attitudes about changes that affect long and deeply held beliefs and practices. The transformation of feelings to facts is even more serious when it is involves the task that pastors and congregations know is their primary calling: *to preach the gospel.*

As they tell it, one of the students delivered a sermon in the preaching practicum, and afterwards, during the critique by the professor, I asked, "what season are you preaching in?" to which the student replied: "I don't have a season." And those who tell this story say I quipped rather sharply, "you'd better *get* a season!" They go on to advise every new and unsuspecting student that "you have to have a *season* if you are preaching in McClain's class!"

What this story illustrates (albeit somewhat edited by the story-tellers) is a feeling of fear and suspicion, something like what has been observed by Professor Thomas Langford of Duke University: that Methodism, which started out "as a preaching movement," "has become a liturgical church." Or, at least that is the perception of many.

A Preaching Movement or a Liturgical Church?

I would not go nearly that far. In these days of a market economy, surveys pass as research and seem to count (and cost) so much. In every survey exploring what congregations want in a pastor, "*a good preacher,*" places on top, or near the top, of the list. That finding holds true even in this age of postmodernism, the ubiquitous television and videos, the information technology revolution, and cyberspace.

Although I would probably not define "liturgical" in the sense intended by Langford, I think I understand what he meant. And I try to understand the history of Methodism in the United States and the concomitant changes in its preaching practices as it has feverishly and fervently tried to be "the church of the people." But the Methodist tradition has been a twofold one with reference to forms of worship, as Nolan Harmon pointed out more than fifty years ago, when he said,

> It has been both liturgical and non-liturgical—liturgical in the fixed, recurrent services of the church as these have been embodied in ritual and formal orders of worship; and non-liturgical, that is, free in the spontaneity of its many services, its use of extempore prayer, and its insistence on perfect liberty for every worshiper.[1]

I must confess, however, that I am sorely disappointed that there is no written history of preaching in the Methodist tradition! There has been no true effort to place side by side, or even chronologically, the preaching of such powerful preachers as the early Methodists, e.g., Freeborn Garrettson, Edward Dromgoole, William Phoebus and the circuit riders; pathfinders like Jesse Lee, John Major, John Smith, and Jeremiah Lambert; midcentury giants like Matthew Simpson and John Price Durkin; and subsequently the social gospel and prophetic preachers Ernest Fremont Tittle and Henry Hitt Crane; the evangelical preachers like E. Stanley Jones and Charles Albert Tindley; the popular pulpit and radio preachers Ralph Sockman, Gerald Kennedy, and Halford Luccock; and the social change and civil rights-era preachers Joseph Echols Lowery, Dan Whitsett, and James M. Lawson—to name but a few categories. This is a task that needs to be assumed by some energetic and insightful homiletician(s) for the good of the whole enterprise of preaching in general, and the United Methodist Church and the other Wesleyan bodies in particular.[2]

The United Methodist Church and preaching today are becoming more and more aware that Christian worship (and ipso facto, preaching) is about "keeping time" and preaching the seasons of the gospel. Sunday morning worship can and ought to be more than the preachers' personal choice of topic or subject; more than the reading of a few verses of Scripture with commentary and accompanying scolding to make the congregation feel sorry in order to make amends; and more than an individual responsibility to "think up" an interesting idea, create an engaging story, entertain the congregation, and hang out personal history that is best left in the preacher's private closet. Such a Sunday morning experience can simply lead to a nebulous assortment of people of good will but without any real identity.

The Lectionary as Wesleyan

We are gradually growing into a realization that using a lectionary and paying attention to the Christian calendar is not necessarily or even commonly "high church" or "high brow," and it certainly does not mean becoming *Roman* Catholic. To relive in our Sunday morning worship and preaching schedule the experiences of Israel, the life of Jesus, and the history of the church in an orderly way is simply to continue to be "Method-ists"—to follow a pattern of doing things. To use a common lectionary—shared by many other organized Christian bodies—as a guide for planning worship and preaching, in no way violates the calling to preach the gospel! In fact, it can enhance the Sunday morning preaching occasion and help all of us who preach to bring the gospel to bear on human needs—the raison d'être for standing and saying "I have a word from the Lord!" in the first place. In our recovery of the centrality of Scripture to worship and preaching we can have new wings!

Part of what is happening in preaching in the United Methodist Church, as also in many other Christian denominations, is a recovery of our roots, a re-cognition of Scripture as the central repository of our corporate memories and the source of our self-identity. It is fundamental to worship and preaching to hear and respond to God's action toward us in God's word in both covenants (Old and New Testaments)—a word that is mediated and expressed in human speech. This means that we are also recovering and rediscovering what the Reformers intended in that ancient collect based on Rom. 15:4: ". . . Thou hast caused all holy Scriptures to be written for our learning."

That many United Methodists are beginning to take somewhat seriously what Pius Parsh called "the church's year of grace"[3] is evident in the numbers of churches and pastors who use the lectionary (even if only occasionally, in some cases). Sunday morning bulletins in local United Methodist Churches across the connection (including churches outside of the USA) often tell us in what *season* of the church year we are worshiping. This practice is reinforced by numerous ecumenical "aids for preaching," the lectionary in various professional journals and magazines, and many other such "helps" for preaching Sunday after Sunday the biblical texts based on the Common Lectionary published by organs of the United Methodist Church itself.

If there is loud protest from those who would insist that we must be more *Wesleyan*, we counter with the fact that John Wesley, the founder of Methodism, over and over again in his *Journals* tells us the day and the season that he preached. There is no "seasonal" day more prominent in his entries than when he preached on All Saints' Day. But as James White points out, "John Wesley, always the pragmatist, abolished 'most of the holy-days as at present answering no valuable end.'"[4] Mr. Wesley kept several other days, such as the Sundays of Advent, Christmas Day, Whitsunday, Trinity Sunday, and so on, but these were soon lost to American Methodism as it moved closer to the Free Church and the influence of the Reformed tradition with emphasis on the preached word and its involvement in revivalism.

American Revivalism

Methodism's emphasis on spirited congregational hymn-singing, along with its other trademarks of extempore preaching and prayer, were to become part of what accounted for its vast expansion and growth throughout the United States. Starting in the wooded hills of Frederick County, Maryland, at Sam's Creek, and on up to the bustling ports of New York and Philadelphia, and down to the seaport town of Savannah, Georgia, and as far north as Boston and Maine, these evangelical preachers made their preaching excursions proclaiming that God's free grace was available to all. They urged people to repent and receive God's grace. These itinerating horsemen of grace [there were no women circuit riders that I know of] organized societies to facilitate the growth and durability of Methodism and the people who joined it.

The evangelistic preaching of these early Methodists was purposefully designed to yield souls to Christ through a conscious conversion experience. And its harvest was great. So much so that, in 1773, it was estimated that one in 2,050 colonial Americans was Methodist. But by 1830 phenomenal growth showed one in 20 Americans was a Methodist. Churches established by these traveling evangelists were soon viewed as "preaching stations" where the sermon became the center of the worship. Fiery and enthusiastic lay preachers continued the work the traveling preachers had started. Many of these recently converted souls were soon to become exuberant exhorters and local preachers for these "station churches."

Recoveries

According to Nolan B. Harmon Jr., these preaching stations with the pulpit at the center, not just in architecture but in worship practice, were to continue until about the 1920s, when "there came a sort of resurgence of interest in liturgy. . . . Up to that point the pulpit had been central."[5] But the change had really begun in Methodism with the adoption of a common hymnal in 1905 and the placing of a formal order of service in the front of the hymnal. This caused a storm among many Methodists, with some asking what the church was coming to with this kind of formalism. If they thought it smelled like formality, they were right. For here we see Methodism influenced by the American-based Protestant Episcopal Church [as distinguished from the Anglican Church] and other Protestant churches such that the worship began to look alike in the major Protestant bodies. But the order soon became firmly planted and almost universally practiced across the denomination. And in the ensuing years we have continued to become a church where liturgy and the "book" have played an increasing role in the shape and form where preaching takes place.

As my worship colleague, James F. White, a fellow-United Methodist, keeps reminding us in a number of places, but especially in *Introduction to Christian Worship:*

> Through the reading and exposition of scripture, the Christian recovers and appropriates for his or her life the experiences of Israel and the early church: escape from slavery, conquest, captivity, hope for a Messiah, incarnation, crucifixion, resurrection, and mission.[6]

Implications

What does this mean for next Sunday's sermon? What does this say about how preaching in the United Methodist Church is changing? What does it suggest about the future for preaching in the United Methodist Church? What does this offer for preaching in a new century and even a new millennium? Does this mean that preaching in the United Methodist Church must become less evangelical and more pastoral?

For starters, it means that preaching must become more tied to the liturgy, and liturgy needs to be more tied to the lectionary. It does *not,* however, involve some "high falutin'" notion about what liturgy is—"high church" or "high brow" worship. The root meaning of the word from which "liturgy" derives, *leitourgia,* is simply "the work of the people." Every zealous, hard-working, over-taxed pastor ought to welcome that! Every congregation ought to welcome that, too! Any pastor ought to understand that his or her work becomes easier when the worship is the work shared by the whole congregation.

Thus, the preaching act becomes more than a solo act, more than a single-person "performance," more than the preacher's production, but instead, the work of the people of God who gather around the word and the sacrament. It means more congregational participation. It means that the sermon becomes more than the preacher coming up to divine worship to offer up his or her "masterpiece" that was constructed in the study to please an "audience," but rather the whole church preaching! As I like to say sometimes, preaching becomes *a cooperative act between the pulpit and the pew*. It becomes more dialogical. Here we can take a page from the book of the African American preaching tradition as a help.

I have told the story often of my first church after seminary. I had just obtained what I thought was the best theological degree available. In Haven Chapel Methodist Church in Anniston, Alabama, there was a lady named Aunt Bea who must have been at least eighty years old. A faithful and devout soul she was, attending worship every Sunday. But as I strained and struggled to make the gospel clear, preaching with all of the power and passion and persuasion I could muster, Aunt Bea strained and struggled with me. When I was in the throes of a point and trying to get it across, I could hear Aunt Bea, once in a while, in a clear and audible voice say: "Jes' hep' him, Jesus!" She was always with me, a part of the cooperative act of preaching. She was preaching along with me. She knew that preaching was a matter of cooperation between the pulpit and the pew. While I am not suggesting that there must be audible call and response—although I certainly have nothing against it—I am suggesting that preaching must be dialogical and a matter of the congregation actively participating in the sermon as they do in other parts of the liturgy.

Such participation can be facilitated and enabled by the use of the lectionary and an orderly plan of preaching where the members of the congregation do not come to be entertained or amused, but rather can prepare to participate by reading the lections ahead of time. My colleague and good friend, Zan Holmes, the pastor of St. Luke Community United Methodist Church in Dallas, Texas, endorses this notion with active groups of persons in the church who meet each week to work on the lectionary readings—Bible study groups, if you will. Each week Holmes meets with one or two of the groups as they work on the lections for next Sunday and help to discern God's message from the texts. And each week after the sermon has been preached, he meets with one or two groups to review the sermon and the texts. What a marvelous cooperative effort between the pulpit and the pew. Is he less evangelical? Is this simply pastoral? It would seem that this is both, since St. Luke Church has grown from fewer than a hundred members in a downtown church to more than five thousand in a few years. Holmes credits most of the growth to the cooperative act of preaching. This would seem to be more than growth in numbers, but growth in faith and the discernment of God's will and way in the lives of the people and the life of the church. Often, he tells me, new ministries, projects, programs, actions, and recommendations to the council on ministries and to the staff come from these lectionary groups as they work on the texts/sermon. This suggests to me a reclaiming of our roots in putting Scripture back at the center of worship and preaching. But it also suggests to me a reclaiming of some Wesleyan roots, too, that Methodism could well use now and in the time to come. These are wings to fly!

Conclusion

I am not suggesting the observance of the Christian year and the use of the lectionary for preaching as some kind of formalism or slavish commitment. Nor am I calling for a mechanical formalism that John Wesley described as "painted fire." To follow anything slavishly would be to make it your master, and even worse, your idol. To become mechanical and formalistic in liturgy and preaching would be to perpetuate a body that has no soul.

I believe that exciting, creative, enthusiastic liturgical preaching can help renew the church—especially if the pastor plans to stay long (and we are now staying longer in the same pulpits). I believe that United Methodists can be as good preachers as anybody else. And I *know* that every church wants good preaching. We can be a *liturgical church,* observing the Christian year, using the lectionary, and celebrating communion often in praise for a risen Christ, *and* we can be a *preaching church,* where the guilty prophet of God declares the judgment of God upon guilty ones, but a love, mercy, and grace that are wider and kinder than any judgment—and we can do it all at the same service! These are the wings we need to mount up like eagles.

Are Extension Ministries an Opportunity to Reclaim a Wesleyan Understanding of Mission?

Russell E. Richey

Appointments to Extension Ministries

334. Appointments Extending the Ministry of The United Methodist Church—1. Elders in effective relationship may be appointed to serve in ministry settings beyond the local United Methodist Church in the witness and service of Christ's love and justice. Persons in these appointments remain within the itineracy and shall be accountable to the annual conference.[1]

A Query

With the notion of "extension ministries," the General Conference has made some real progress in rethinking what it previously termed "appointments beyond the local church" and even earlier "special appointments." As it has found more apt ways of understanding such ministries, capturing their relation to the connection and providing for more regular accountability, has the General Conference exposed something of the poverty in its/our conception of the regular or non-extension ministry? To put the matter bluntly one might ask, has the General Conference ascribed to those in "special appointments" what Wesley expected of himself and his itinerants and ascribed to those in regular appointments what he knew to be the task of the parish clergy of the Church of England? Was not extension the mandate of Wesley's itinerants? And was not "beyond the local church" where they were charged to position their work? And were not he and they special, providentially given rescuers of a stagnant parish system?

Introduction

This essay attempts three things. *First,* it explores the ambiguity of connectional appointments, showing the church's indecision—from the start—about how to handle tasks that lay beyond the normal circuit assignments. The essay makes a case, *second,* for the special appointments as indeed continuations of roles played by Mr. Wesley, for their

175

exercise amid the appointments held by "fellow" itinerants, for their connectionalism as genuinely conference in character, and for an appropriate oversight of such special appointments by annual conferences. All that changed in the latter part of the nineteenth century as connectionalism increasingly restructured its operations in corporate boards and such centralization eroded the close ties between the special appointees and their conferences. *Third* and finally, the essay suggests that those of us in such "special appointments," "appointments beyond the local church," or "extension ministries" have responsibility for defining and enhancing our place within Methodist connectionalism that we—or I should say I—have not been always very eager to exercise. Ought we not to be helping the church envision how our special assignments serve the connection as a whole? Underlying the presentation and each of these points is the conviction that our connectionalism is at risk and that we, United Methodists generally, and the church at large have much to lose from selfish localism.

The Ambiguity of Connectional Appointments

The *Minutes* for 1799 answered the standard query "Where are the Preachers stationed this year?" as follows:

> Jesse Lee travels with Bishop Asbury.
> Ezekiel Cooper, Editor and General Book Steward.

And for 1801 the answer was:

> Thomas Coke, by consent of the general conference is in Europe.
> Nicholas Snethen travels with Bishop Asbury.
> S. Hutchinson travels with Bishop Whatcoat.
> Ezekiel Cooper superintends the printing and book business.[2]

The provision for a traveling companion for the bishops was not new. Nor was the arrangement for a book steward new.[3] New was the organizational or conceptual treatment of the special appointment for Ezekiel Cooper. The *Minutes* that year made provision for what we now term "extension ministries" or "appointments beyond the local church" and visualized Cooper's appointment as not just "within the connectional structures" but also in relation to the connection as a whole. Specifically, the *Minutes* isolated Cooper, as book agent, along with the episcopal companions, as in service of the connection, though continuing in the traveling relation and serving under appointment. The 1799 and also the 1801 *Minutes* lodged that assignment first, right after the question and before the long list of other appointments.

The next year, in 1802, the *Minutes* buried that connectional assignment in the list of appointments, listing it as one of the assignments on the Philadelphia District: "Ezekiel Cooper, superintendent of the Printing and Book-Concern."[4]

The following year, in 1803, the *Minutes* struggled with another special assignment that it nevertheless located within the conference listings. That year four persons carried the designation "missionary" after their names, Shadrach Bostwick on the Deerfield circuit of the Pittsburgh District, and Samuel Merwin, Elijah Chichester, and Laban Clark on the Montreal and St. John's and Soreille circuits of the Pittsfield District.[5]

By 1804, the church arrived at something like the present arrangement. That year the *Minutes* listed Ezekiel Cooper and John Wilson as editor and general book-steward and assistant respectively and listed them in New York along with the others assigned there—N. Snethen, M. Coate, and S. Merwin.[6] By 1809, the *Minutes* struck something of a compromise, listing the book agents in relation to the conference (New York) and above the districts. The *Minutes* privileged that special appointment above others. It listed the missionaries and the person traveling with the bishop (Henry Boehm for that year) in relation to a specific district, though without a circuit or station designation.[7]

Accountability

Very early, then, the church recognized (1) that it had duties, tasks, roles of a connectional nature—in service to the entire connection—and that those needed staffing; (2) that the exercise of such responsibilities belonged to or were appropriately undertaken by the traveling ministry; and (3) that the persons under such appointment had to be made accountable to the connection.

What was unclear then and has remained unclear to this day, is how best substantively and structurally to care for that connectional accountability. How were and how are those of us in "special" appointments to exercise those in truly connectional fashion? How should they and we be connected, and where should we report—on the most general level, primarily to the annual conference, or most directly to local Methodism?

In 1799 and 1801, the church achieved and represented the accountability as to the connection as a whole by depicting Cooper with the bishops and those traveling with the bishops. In 1802, the *Minutes* displayed the accountability to the conference as primary by lodging Cooper immediately behind the presiding elder on the Philadelphia district. In 1804, the *Minutes* accented local accountability by visualizing the book agents as on the circuit. In 1809, the *Minutes* again isolated the placement of the agents, but in relation to the New York Conference as a whole.[8]

In each of these depictions the church, we would have to concede, understood such persons in special appointments—the book agents, the missionaries, those traveling with the bishops—to be accountable at every Methodist level. But where would that primary accountability lie—to the general church, to the conference, to local Methodism?

Early Methodism struggled to achieve a multilayered accountability with respect to the book concern. Always the bishops and especially Asbury took a hand in its operations. So also did the short-lived council and later the General Conference. But such general oversight had, perforce, to be episodic and epistolary. Some local body was designated to work along with the book agent or book agents. And then in 1796 the General Conference[9] assigned oversight to the Philadelphia Conference, and that body delegated the responsibility to the presiding elders and elders of Philadelphia, a body of seven in 1797.

The *Minutes* specified that new agency:

> *Quest. 14. What regulations have been made in respect to the Printing-Business, and the publication of books?*
> Ans. The Philadelphia conference, in whom the management of these affairs was invested by the general conference, and who have not time during their annual sittings to complete this business, have, by the advice and consent of Bishop Asbury, unanimously appointed the following persons to be a standing committee, viz.
>
> Ezekiel Cooper, *Chairman*
> Thomas Ware ⎫
> John M'Claskey ⎬ Presiding Elders
> Christopher Spry ⎭
> William M'Lenahan ⎫
> Richard Swain   ⎬ Elders
> Solomon Sharp   ⎪
> Charles Cavender ⎭
>
> . . . [T]he general book-steward shall lay before the committee, all manuscripts, books, and pamphlets, which are designed for publication, except such as the general conference has authorized him to publish.[10]

When the book concern was moved to New York, the same provision applied. The New York Conference assumed oversight and "voted that the stationed preachers in New York and Brooklyn be a committee on the Book Concern."[11] Thus the church set a pattern of conference oversight of special ventures. Missions, colleges, theological schools, hospitals, and a variety other ventures would be handled similarly. Individual conferences or several conferences together would oversee efforts that served the connectional common good and would oversee those *specially* appointed to serve in these efforts.

Special Appointments: Heirs to Wesley

That American Methodism would struggle to find ways of structuring these connectional roles should not surprise. The roles, after all, had inhered in an office that American Methodism had never fully replicated, namely that of John Wesley. Although both Thomas Coke and Francis Asbury aspired to his mantle, the American conferences proved unwilling to countenance such benevolent autocracy. Wesley had personified the connection. He served as publisher (as well as author). He directed the mission of the movement. He served as its primary fund-raiser. He directed the organizational life of Methodism. He constituted the faculty for the preachers, though delegating that role for lower schools to others. He was chaplain.

These were the roles to which, over the course of the nineteenth century, American Methodists gave "special" status:

publisher

missionary and director of that cause

fund-raiser for colleges

secretary of Methodist and interdenominational Bible

tract, Sunday school and missionary societies

faculty in Methodist schools

chaplains (prison or Army)

The "special appointments" in American Methodism really institutionalized and divided offices held by Wesley. So several points:

first, special appointments structured as connectional offices or roles that Wesley played;

second, the century saw the gradual expansion of the number and character of these;

third, the church increasingly struggled to find ways to centralize such offices; and

fourth, Methodists recognized these offices as essentially connective for Methodism as a whole.

Both the array of such offices and the continuing oversight played by conferences for the connection as a whole can be exhibited by the Philadelphia Conference. By 1862 that conference enjoyed the special responsibility of appointing and reviewing the character of the Corresponding Secretary of the Missionary Society (the nineteenth century counterpart to general secretary), John P. Durbin. He was accountable to the North Philadelphia District. Three other persons joined him below the regular appointments: A. Manship, Agent of Philadelphia Conference Tract Society; S. Higgins, Sunday School Agent; and J. Y. Ashton, Agent of Home Mission and Sunday School Society. South Philadelphia listed two faculty members from Dickinson College. Reading, Easton, and Snow Hill Districts had none in such special connectional roles. Wilmington carried two faculty members of Wesleyan Female College.[12] By 1865 the conference listed more such appointments, the additions primarily as chaplains in the United States Army—one for N. Philadelphia, six for S. Philadelphia, one for Reading, three for Wilmington, one for Easton, two for Snow Hill.[13] Four special appointments per district continued to be a common pattern, as also their role, mainly to carry out and represent the work of the conference itself. For instance, by 1886 Northwest Philadelphia still carried four special appointments:

James Neill, Financial Agent of the Methodist Episcopal Church Hospital;

J. B. McCulough, Editor of the *Philadelphia Methodist;*

T. A. Fernley, Corresponding Secretary of the Philadelphia Sabbath Association; and

E. I. D. Pepper, Editor of the *Christian Standard and Home.*[14]

By this point, as my other essays in this volume indicate, Methodism had restructured and reincorporated its boards as corporate bodies accountable to and appointed by the General Conference. A new kind of connectionalism eventually emerged out of these special appointments—namely a connectionalism defined by boards and agencies, anchored on the national level and establishing corporate power centers that would serve but also compete with General Conference and the episcopacy.

This new corporate structure, eventually but only gradually bureaucratized, had several implications for special appointments. In the first place, it necessitated ever more of them.

Second, and perhaps more important, by centralizing and nationalizing denominational decision making, program development and staff leadership, and by making accountability primarily to the General Conference, the boards eviscerated the reporting and accountability that special appointments had had to annual conferences. The John Durbins of the twentieth century remained theoretically in "effective relation" to the annual conference, but that relation did not register the connectional value of the appointment as it once did. The connectional meaning of the "special" appointments— often clear intrinsically in what such persons did for Methodism and typically registered in some national fashion—lost its salience and visibility within the annual conference. And so ministers serving in circuits and stations gradually and naturally came to think of those taking special appointments as "leaving the ministry."

Conference Connectionalism

The loss of conference-level meaning to special appointments or extension ministries has something to do with the loss of the connectional and missional value to conference itself. In early American Methodism, conferences served as the primary agent of all that the movement attempted. Conference was the spiritual home of the itinerants, their class or band. Conference was also spiritually alive. Conferences featured testimony, relation of experiences, preaching, counsel, prayer. Their spiritual vitality drew lay observers, and conferences often had a revivalistic quality. That quality Richard Whatcoat captured in entries for conferences over which he presided. First, for 1800:

> On the 1st of June we held a Conference at Duck Creek Cross Roads, in the state of Delaware. This was a glorious time; such a spirit of faith, prayer, and zeal, rested on the preachers and people, that I think it exceeded any thing of the kind I ever saw before. O, the strong cries, groans, and agonies of the mourners! Enough to pierce the hardest heart; but when the Deliverer set their souls at liberty, their ecstasies of joy were inexpressibly great, so that the high praises of the Redeemer's name sounded through the town, until solemnity appeared on every countenance: the effect of which was, that on the Thursday following, one hundred and fifteen persons joined the society in that town, while the divine flame spread greatly through the adjacent societies.[15]

For an 1802 Virginia conference he reported:

> Our Conference began at Salem, March 1st, and closed the 4th. I ordained seven travelling, and five local preachers to the Deacon's office; it was thought that ten or twelve were converted during the sitting of our Conference . . . .[16]

And for a conference of 1804 in March at Edward Droomgoole's, he noted:

> I ordained five travelling, and four local preachers to the Deacon's, and three to the Elder's office; Sabbath-day was a great day: after the love-feast the public service continued from 11 o'clock, until 9 at night, in the woods: it was thought twenty, if not thirty were converted.[17]

To facilitate their own revivalistic endeavor for a time, particularly in the midwest, conferences actually appointed a camp meeting to sit concurrently during their sessions.

Conferences were revivalistic in themselves and clearly also in their outreach. The ministry was sent out from and returned a year later to conference to be sent again. Conferences expanded their circuits to encompass newly settled or unmissionized territory and then divided when growth made further effective strategizing and missionizing difficult. Methodism quite literally conferenced the frontier and conferenced the nation.[18] Ministry was missionary, and conference was the agency, framework, resource for mission. That is what Stevens meant when he said:

> Though American Methodism was many years without a distinct missionary organization, it was owing to the fact that its whole organization was essentially a missionary scheme. It was, in fine, the great Home Mission enterprise of the north American continent . . . .[19]

Methodism was indeed a "missionary scheme," and conferences were the working element of the scheme. Only when conferences and the church as a whole began to confront missionary situations that demanded more than elaboration of new circuits—as for instance the challenging work with the Wyandots or sending a person to work with the French in the Louisiana Purchase or commissioning evangelists for Liberia—did Methodism create a Missionary Society (and the women their counterpart).

But even those persons, if in full connection, remained accountable to conferences. And conferences exercised the supervisory, report-receiving, monitoring roles with great effectiveness through much of the nineteenth century and over the myriad of activities and institutions represented by special appointments. In particular, conferences oversaw Methodism's colleges and later her theological schools. They did so with visiting committees, through institutional reports, by close connection, with presence on boards, by sending students, and by episcopal appointment and oversight. Conferences also commanded a peculiar kind of oversight, a sinew of connectionalism, that made conference work as a agency of accountability, and conference's special appointments as genuinely conferenced, connectional endeavor. It was called the review of character. Today that is a routine, largely ritual gesture, with the district superintendents, saying with a straight face "nothing against the preachers on the Raleigh district." In early Methodism, each preacher's name was called individually and his character reviewed.

Early Methodism functioned like a series of classes or at least like a series of conferences, each the size of a class. In reviewing the character of the preachers, the conference did for its members what the class did for its. The review of character was a class-like, a covenant-discipleship-like exercise. Through the annual review conferences exercised theological, ministerial, ethical, familial accountability. And when they found deviance, they conducted enquiries and trials, meting out judgments as the case demanded. The process held Methodism's institutions accountable by holding its people in special relation accountable. To illustrate, Methodism worried from the start about theological education and whether it would serve Methodism's purposes well. Among its worries was the issue of theological accountability. In a remarkably insightful statement in 1872, William F. Warren noted a variety of checks on the then three northern theological schools (Boston, Garrett, Drew). Key among them was the following:

> At the Annual Conference examination of character, every professor—save one who chances to be a layman—is each year liable to arrest if even a rumor of heterodoxy is abroad against him.[20]

With the review of character, as well as through its various offices and activities, conferences kept in touch with and in oversight of those in special appointments and were, in turn, enriched and informed by those extension ministries. So conferences kept as their own the various roles or offices that had belonged to Wesley.

Change

Over the course of the twentieth century the conferences' structures of accountability have eroded or been delegated to boards of ordained ministry or committees or special offices. And the special ministries have, until recently gravitated out of conference life. The forces making for both changes are many and diverse. They include:
- the sheer growth of annual conferences,
- the admission (for other than Methodist Protestants) into confer-ences of laity in equal numbers,
- professionalization of the ministry and particularly of special ministries,
- the routinization of review of character,
- further centralization of the program and initiative-taking activities of the denomination,
- the jurisdictioning of the connection,
- drift of special appointments into accountability to other institutions,
- explosion of numbers of those in such special situations,

- the apotheosis of the local church, and
- the consequent gravitation toward understanding "real" ministry as within a local church and everything else as "beyond the local church."

The last General Conference indeed improved our understanding, and the last several have clearly worked at the relation of those in extension ministries to the conference. We still have not recovered structures and processes that once claimed special ministries, those once exercised by Wesley, as belonging to conference and as intimately connected with all ministry. And the reports, special meetings, and attendance at annual conference seem to be less significant, substantive accountability than acts of compliance.

Our Responsibility

To this point, those of us in extension ministries, or ABLC, or special appointment seem to have waited for General Conference to discern and remedy the problem we present to the appointive process and for connectionalism. What if we were to exercise some responsibility in raising the issue and proposing solutions? To that end some queries, intended to work at connection and connectivity:

1. Would the *Discipline* be more faithful to our Wesleyan heritage if it more consistently employed the new rubrics "appointments extending the ministry of The United Methodist Church" or "appointments within or appointments beyond the connectional structures" and removed entirely the remaining, repeatedly used, and clearly congregationalist or parish notion of "appointments beyond the local church"?

2. Should offices wholly within present conference structures and determined by episcopal appointment, as for instance the district superintendents or conference staff posts, be removed from this category and recognized as they should be—as genuinely itinerant appointments?

3. Might the notion of "location" be reclaimed to serve, as it once did, for persons who would remain "deacon" or "elder" but who elect not to itinerate; whose job or vocation involves them in service but not in word, sacrament, and order; and/or whose exercise of such ministerial roles will be through their membership in Methodist bodies rather than through their job? Alternatively might the church provide for some transfer of elders into the new permanent diaconate when their roles come more to approximate that order than the one to which they have been ordained?

4. Should new conference structures be elaborated into which those within the connectional structure and those beyond the connectional structure would be appointed?

Might the structure of "central" connectional units again be utilized or some similar rubric generated?

Might some appointments be made within annual conferences but in central districts—when the ministry in question has a translocal but not transconference range and have a strong nexus with district superintendents?

Might others be made within new central conferences—when the ministry has a transconference range and have a strong nexus with one or more bishops?

And might truly national or transdenominational ones be made within a central jurisdiction? Might such central bodies have rights of representation in the higher regular conference structure (district within the annual conference; annual within a jurisdiction; jurisdiction within the General Conference)?

Should the point of such central bodies be not the segregation of those in such special appointments but rather the creation of structures of mission and accountability appropriate to the range and character of their ministerial service? (Indeed, the primary utility of such conferences for persons in special appointments would be to recreate something like the review of character, something that would give those conferences a covenant discipleship dimension.)

Should persons located or appointed within or beyond the connectional structure and within such a central (or similar) conference surrender guarantees of appointment they might have had in their former conference? (They might be expected to affiliate also with their former or a contiguous conference but would enjoy voice not vote therein.)

5. And whatever might be done in relation to points 1–4, should those of us currently included in the extension, ABLC, or special category and however continued under the new rubrics be zealous in making the Disciplinary accountabilities and affiliations work?

Is There a Better Way to Elect Bishops?

Dennis M. Campbell

Leadership is one of the most crucial issues facing all movements and organizations today. Christian churches confront the question of leadership at every level. One of the complexities of church organizations is that they specifically require, and therefore seek to call forth, leadership from a wide variety of persons including lay volunteers in congregations, professional lay persons in both local and wider settings, and clergy in many roles. While senior clergy leadership is only one aspect of the total picture, most Christians would probably agree that those persons who are elected or appointed to serve the church in senior leadership roles are of enormous importance to the present state and future shape of the church. In the United Methodist Church, the office of bishop is the key senior leadership position.

The Role of the Bishops

United Methodist bishops are called upon to exercise enormous spiritual, theological, presidential, executive, juridical, managerial, financial, and trusteeship responsibilities. They are elected for life and even after retirement are called upon to serve the church in many ways through their continued role in the council of bishops. Appointed to episcopal areas over which they have direct superintending responsibilities, they also are charged with general superintendency for the entire United Methodist Church. While there is a president of the council of bishops elected annually for a one-year term, and a secretary of the council, who carries responsibilities for the work of the council between its meetings, neither of these offices is full-time. All of the bishops hold direct residential responsibilities in an episcopal area, and all are equal. The importance of the office cannot be overemphasized, and its complexity has grown with the years.

Bishops are called upon to perform numerous diverse roles. They are preachers of the word of God, ministers of the sacraments, teachers of the Bible. They pass on the Christian tradition and vital Christian faith to clergy and laity; they are presidents of the annual conference; juridical officers interpreting the *Discipline,* executive officers of the conference; senior personnel managers determining the appointments

186

of hundreds of clergy; financial administrators in the annual conference as well as at the general church level; and trustees for multiple organizations such as colleges, universities, hospitals, homes, boards, and agencies. They are also called upon to be fund-raisers, public relations experts, interpreters of the life and work of the church both to the church and to the larger society, and volunteer leaders in regional and national organizations not specifically related to the church. They have heavy travel schedules within the episcopal area as well as in the wider world. The importance of the office is acknowledged by most United Methodists; the enormous complexity is understood by some, but serious reflection on the way in which persons are called to the office is seldom a part of church thinking. It is not likely that the range or nature of the office will be simplified. If anything, the office has become far more difficult with the increased institutionalization that has characterized Methodism in the twentieth century. The church faces the urgent questions of what kind of episcopal leadership it needs and how it is going to get such leadership appropriate for the new century.

Currently, in the United Methodist Church in the United States bishops are elected in meetings of jurisdictional conferences. The five jurisdictional conferences (Northeastern, Southeastern, North Central, South Central, Western) were created at the time of the merger of the Methodist Episcopal Church, the Methodist Episcopal Church, South, and the Methodist Protestant Church in 1939. A Central Jurisdiction of black Methodists also functioned from 1939 until 1968. A major reason for the establishment of the jurisdictions and the jurisdictional conferences was to guarantee that bishops would be elected from across the connection. Previously, in episcopal Methodism before the split over slavery in 1844, and after that in both the northern and southern churches, bishops were elected at the General Conference. Their role as general superintendents was thus symbolized by their election at the general church level and practiced by their active leadership across the connection.

Election in jurisdictional conferences, in July following the quadrennial meeting of the General Conference in May, has been the pattern since 1939. Bishops are appointed to serve in the jurisdictions in which they are elected. It is possible for a bishop to be assigned to another jurisdiction, but it has never been done. Any ordained elder in the church is eligible for election in any of the jurisdictions, but only in three instances has a jurisdictional conference elected a bishop from outside its own boundaries. Elected delegates to the jurisdictional conference each have one vote, and there are no formal nominations.

Each delegate writes a prescribed number of names on the ballot, and the process continues until an elder receives the requisite number of votes.

A Politicized Process

The formal disciplinary procedure for election of bishops has actually functioned in a variety of ways, and even the several jurisdictions have carried on the elections with slightly varying processes. In recent years, however, notable changes have occurred, and increased anxiety on the part of many United Methodists is raising the question as to whether there is not a better way to elect bishops in order to assure the nature and quality of leadership the church must have as it moves forward.

Perhaps the most notable change in episcopal elections has been the provision for the nomination by an annual conference of what amounts to an "endorsed candidate." What usually happens is that the General Conference delegation, which is elected by the annual conference the year prior to General Conference, will bring a recommendation to the subsequent meeting of the annual conference that a particular person be "endorsed." This may be the elder elected first in the General Conference delegation, but it may also be another elder who has garnered enough support to be so recognized in the annual conference. The formal "endorsement" does not preclude other elders in that annual conference from being candidates, but it has had a profound effect on the dynamics of the election process.

It is worth observing that more attention should probably be given by annual conferences to the implications for the election of bishops *at the time of the election of their General and jurisdictional conference delegations.* It is these delegations that shape nominations and ultimately elect episcopal leadership.

Once an annual conference has "endorsed" one of its members for the episcopal office, it becomes a matter of pride for the annual conference to try to assure the election. The significance of this reality is very great. Enormous pressure is often exerted on delegates from the given annual conference to support the candidate "for the sake of the annual conference," even if the nominee was not (or is not) a delegate's preferred candidate. Furthermore, some delegations designate a "campaign manager" and demand the right to control the votes of the delegation. This allows the "campaign manager" to trade votes with other annual conference "campaign managers." The process tends to emphasize the power of an annual conference organization and the sheer size of the voting delegation.

In an effort to offer alternative candidates to those officially endorsed by annual conferences, a variety of interest groups in the church are putting forth candidates, some formally and some informally. These persons seek to appeal to jurisdictional conference delegates on the basis of gender, ethnic identity, theological position, or political position (or some combination of these). The process has become increasingly politicized, with active campaigns being waged on behalf of specific individuals. These campaigns seek to cut across conference lines, but vote trading and "deals" are nevertheless part of the process. Since a new bishop will not be assigned to the annual conference in which he or she is a member at the time of election, often deals involve the placement of current and new bishops after the election. This "trading" on the part of jurisdictional power brokers on behalf of annual conferences or interest groups can produce great unhappiness as certain conferences declare their willingness or lack of willingness to receive certain bishops or candidates.

Implications

There are positive aspects of these recent developments. It can be argued that the process is more "open." There has always been politicking in episcopal elections, but it went on "under the table." Now, it can be argued, the political reality is "out in the open." Also, most of the jurisdictional conferences have developed ways for the delegates (generally in annual conference delegation groupings) to meet "endorsed" candidates. Sometimes in the past, delegates would complain that they were asked to cast ballots for persons they did not know, and in some cases had never even seen. The older system tended to limit election to prominent persons well-known across the church for their preaching or executive abilities.

Having noted these things, there are also negative aspects of the current system. Perhaps the most negative is the annual conference endorsement procedure. United Methodism has experienced increased tendency on the part of annual conferences (and the jurisdictions) to view themselves chauvinistically. High walls have been built both symbolically and practically around annual conferences. It is difficult for elders to transfer across conference bounds. Some annual conference boards of ordained ministry even expect transfer candidates to, in effect, start the whole process anew with "probation." Annual conferences operate benefit programs that sharply distinguish them from others. Practices and procedures vary greatly. The United Methodist Church is too large and complex for all annual conferences to conform to the same general pattern. Nevertheless, the theology and language of the church emphasize "connection." No place does the chauvinism of the annual conference become more apparent than in the election and assignment of episcopal leadership.

Large annual conferences, with high numbers of delegates to the jurisdictional conference, exercise great power. A few large conferences can control elections if their "campaign managers" can in fact control the votes. Why is it that few, if any, delegates ask hard questions, such as:

- Why should it be the case that annual conference pride plays such a large role in the election of a bishop?
- Why is it always the case that our endorsed candidate is better than a candidate from another annual conference?
- Why should annual conference identity or affiliation have anything to do with whether a person would be a good episcopal leader for the church?
- Why should jurisdictional conference delegates be expected to give their vote to a campaign manager?
- Since a new bishop will not be appointed within the annual conference in which he or she holds membership, why should that annual conference have such a large role in determining episcopal suitability?

The same kinds of questions can be asked about candidates "endorsed" by interest groups:

- On what grounds do appeals to special constituencies have validity in the election of bishops for either annual conference leadership or leadership throughout the connection?
- Does the conflict between roles and expectations for annual conference residential leadership and general church leadership mean that the church has a fundamental problem with its understanding of the episcopal office?

Is the episcopal office primarily symbolic, or do the expectations we have of a bishop really require proven experience in doing the kinds of things a bishop must do for the good of the whole people of God?

Suggested Remedies

The need for outstanding episcopal leadership, coupled with the problems that now exist in the methods of election, suggests that steps should be taken to improve the process. The following possibilities, or some combination or modification of them, might improve the way in which bishops are elected and thus offer hope for the church as it seeks leadership for its future.

1. Abolish the jurisdictions and elect bishops at the General Conference.

The jurisdictions really exist to elect bishops. If a jurisdictional conference has few or no bishops to elect, it really has no business. Inevitably, perhaps, some of the jurisdictions, notably the Southeast and South Central, have developed elaborate jurisdictional programming agencies. It is not clear that these are essential, and they certainly perpetuate and encourage a regionalism in the church that can be as chauvinistic as that of the annual conferences. Abolishing the jurisdictions would eliminate one layer of bureaucracy and simplify the church. Abolition of jurisdictional conference meetings would save significant amount of money and eliminate a major additional meeting for the General Conference delegates, thus ensuring that a greater diversity of persons would be able to serve. The regional jurisdictions have outlived their usefulness.

2. Alternatively, or as a first step, have jurisdictional conferences meet only at the site and at the time of the General Conference to elect bishops.

General Conference should be shortened, anyway. Much time is wasted on promotion and unessential presentations. Great saving of time and money should be achieved by attaching jurisdictional meetings to the General Conference. Symbolically this would emphasize the role of the bishop as general superintendent. All new bishops could be consecrated together in a great festival service, and the general church would have a renewed sense of its shared ministry through the episcopal office.

3. Assign bishops on the basis of missional need without regard to the regional origin of the bishop.

If bishops are truly general superintendents, they should be placed where they can best serve the needs of the church. This pattern, actually a recovery of tradition in Methodism, would serve to lessen regionalism and allow the church to make better use of its episcopal resources.

4. Recover a sense of the theological meaning of superintendency.

The election of bishops will be improved if the church remembers that what it is doing is electing persons to serve it by overseeing its life, work, and ministry. Too often the images brought forth in episcopal elections are borrowed from secular institutions that emphasize power and privilege. The episcopal office should not be thought of as a prize, as a reward for outstanding service, or as the ultimate career advancement, but as an opportunity to fulfill the obligation to serve the church. Indeed, the church might well beware of persons who too actively seek the office. Stories from the whole history of Christianity can be told of bishops who were reluctant but who were persuaded to serve for the sake of the church. The question for the church is, whom do we want to serve us as general superintendent?

5. Eliminate official annual conference endorsements.

This political process can have very negative consequences within the annual conference, and it creates a kind of competition among annual conferences that is destructive. The church needs to recognize that in a given quadrennial period, an annual conference may not have a really outstanding person for episcopal office. At the same time another annual conference may have more than one. This should be recognized and celebrated. A prospective bishop's annual conference affiliation should make no difference. What matters are a person's spiritual gifts, knowledge of the Bible and Christian faith, experience in the church, abilities, sensitivities, and commitments.

6. Prohibit block voting.

Delegates are elected because lay or clergy colleagues believe they will be effective participants in the life and work of the general church. The Holy Spirit works through the assembled delegates as they pray, worship, share ideas, and work together. In the election of bishops, we should trust the Spirit to work with delegates in the total community of the conference, not only in annual conference delegations or interest groups. The process is demeaned by the overt political aggressiveness of a system that brings out the worst competitive instincts of some. Consideration might be given to seating all delegates alphabetically rather than in annual conference delegations.

7. Encourage a variety of ways in which possible candidates are identified, while remembering that it should be possible for one who is not a "declared" or "endorsed" candidate to be elected.

It would be best for the identification of possible candidates for election to take place at the General Conference itself. It should not be necessary for there to be a great deal of formal political activity prior to the conference, since a major purpose of the conference would be the election of bishops. At the same time, it is desirable that there be ways for elected delegates to have a chance to meet and come to know possible candidates either formally or informally, but many able persons are unwilling to participate in the overt political process that now characterizes episcopal elections. The requisite self-promotion is distasteful to many who might be excellent bishops. The danger is that only those who are willing to engage in aggressive political activity can be elected. This limits the range and diversity of those available for episcopal office. Bishops tend to be alike because most have taken the same path to get elected. Running for bishop can become an all-consuming passion. Once elected some may not know what to do, since they no longer have to campaign, but do not know any other way to function. The current process is not well-suited to the demands of the office and the qualifications necessary to meet those demands. The question needs to be asked, "Does this person have vision informed by God's Word, the Christian tradition, and the church community for the future of the church; and can that vision be communicated and implemented?"

8. Recognize that the council of bishops has need for persons of diverse backgrounds, age, ethnic identity, gender, and experience, but also that episcopal office is too important for a person to learn "on the job."

The church needs to give attention to persons who have some proven experience (a specific track record) at doing the kinds of things a bishop must do, and this does not mean only as a pastor or district superintendent. In the past two decades, while gender and ethnic diversity has been improved, there has been a narrowing of the backgrounds of bishops. More have had experience only as pastors and fewer have served in the connectional ministries or educational or social institutions, the publishing house, or boards and agencies. But the latter persons often have the kinds of experience actually needed in the annual conference, given what bishops must do in regard to personnel and financial management. Having persons of diverse experience can help the council of bishops in dealing with the crucial ministries of the United Methodist Church, with institutions, in the public sector, and with theological thought.

These eight suggestions are intended to stimulate change in the process of electing bishops for the United Methodist Church. At a time when leadership is so crucial, these ideas, or some combination of them, might assist the church to move toward a more satisfactory procedure.

What Style of Leadership Will Our Bishops Embody and Model?

Judith E. Smith

Introduction

The Duke Divinity School Project on United Methodism and American Culture brought together scholars and leaders from across the church. Throughout the project, in conversations among participants, the issue of leadership arose. And when it did, the frequent implication was that we do not have the kind of strong leadership that we need at this point in our history. "Bishops and cabinets search for persons who can give effective leadership to congregations that face challenges in vast array. Local church members yearn for [leaders] with integrity and vision who can share their pilgrimage and offer communal guidance toward more faithful discipleship. At every point within the connection, there is a cry for leaders who can help reinterpret God's call in the face of current reality and redesign the system that unites and nurtures a people in ministry."[1]

The issue is not a simple one. We proclaim with certainty that we need visionary, creative leadership, but we are less certain what that kind of leadership looks like. The church wrestles with many complex questions. What does it mean to give strong leadership in a global and multicultural church? How do effective leaders handle issues of authority and control?

What are the generational differences in the way that leaders lead? Are the concerns of the younger generation of leaders the same as those of the older generation? How is leadership shared across generations? What would a leadership style look like that would involve letting go of control and allowing diverse groups to share control? Where are the leaders who can help us talk with one another across increasingly angry divisions?

These questions apply to leadership in every part of the church's life. In local congregations much discussion about the need for leadership focuses on pastors. Concerns about the competence and effectiveness of clergy have raised serious questions about the itinerant system and whether it can continue as it now is. More and more questions are being raised about guaranteed appointments. An increasing number of people believe that the appointive system protects its clergy far more than it serves its local congregations. The pastor's salary and seniority may often influence the cabinet's appointments more than the gifts of clergy and the needs of local congregations. Few people believe that the call system works much better, but most remain convinced that we are in need of some kind of major change.

The current system often seems to reward clergy more for being good managers than for being dynamic leaders. Clergy are too often seen as program directors whose lack of leadership allows the church to fragment along the same lines that fragment our society. As one participant said, "We chase each new trend, embrace everyone else's agenda as our own, and substitute success for mission."

District superintendents are cast in the role of middle managers. They are rewarded for their ability to manage the institution in their geographical area, and they spend the majority of their time making appointments (i.e., managing the itinerant system) and confronting issues of incompetence and misconduct (i.e., managing the personnel system).

Questions of effective leadership also abound when we talk about our episcopal leaders. We are unclear about the purpose and function of the episcopacy, and consequently about the kind of leadership that we need most. The role of bishops as general superintendents and particularly are teachers, not only in the annual conference but also in the church as a whole, often seem incompatible with the task of appointment making. Which roles take precedence? How consuming are management tasks? If their effectiveness at those tasks played a major part in their election, then perhaps the management role is not only the role most requested but also the role that is most comfortable.

The next critical issue affecting leadership at all of these levels is that of the identification and training of leaders. Who is calling forth strong leaders, both lay and clergy? How are they identified, nurtured, encouraged? Not well, it seems to many. Do questions about competence and effectiveness arise not only because of inadequate preparation of clergy but also because of the capacities of the persons that we are calling forth as leaders? What can people be taught to do, and what capacities must they bring with them? If the system rewards good managers above all, how can we expect it to identify and nurture creative and visionary leaders? What is the role of the seminaries in all of this?

Inevitably we must ask whether the nature of our institutional structures contributes to this issue. Is our preoccupation with institutional survival affecting the quality of our leadership? We often talk about institutional survival at the general church level, but it may be as critical an issue in annual conference structures and in local congregations. The jurisdictional system has enormous impact on the choice and deployment of leadership. Is it serving us well? What would happen if it were abolished?

These urgent and perplexing questions are here focused on the episcopal leadership of our denomination. My research methodology for this chapter was very simple. I asked a wide number of people across the church: If you were to select four or five bishops that you consider to be creative, visionary leaders and ask them to reflect on their leadership role, with whom would you want to talk? Many of the responses clearly reflected regional experience, but several names kept surfacing in a variety of regions. Out of these conversations, I selected five persons. The group, in spite of its small size, was regionally, ethnically, and gender diverse. I asked each of the bishops to spend a couple of hours with me reflecting on their understandings of their leadership role and the ways in which they carry it out. I also asked what nurtures their leadership and what blocks it. All of these conversations were off the record. I made a commitment that in exchange for their openness and honesty I would not reveal their names. All five of the people I asked agreed to talk with me.

I provided them with a list of questions to stimulate their thinking in advance. The conversations themselves were not tied too closely to the list of questions but instead flowed rather freely. I did attempt to be sure that all of the major issues were covered in the conversation, and they were responsive to my consistent pushing for clarification or further detail.

I entered this process trying to be as objective as possible, knowing all the while that I have strong biases about the nature of effective leadership. I found the conversations to be not only stimulating but also deeply moving. The commitment of each of the bishops and the seriousness with which they wrestle continuously with these issues was impressive. I did not, of course, agree with all of their understandings of leadership, but I found them thoughtful and articulate about their own leadership and their understandings of the church. They have all thought deeply about these isues and are very intentional about the way in which they lead. It is important to remember that these five people were identified with some consensus as being "among the most creative and visionary" of our bishops. It was not a random group.

Nevertheless, I ended the study with a greater sense of hope about the episcopal leadership of our denomination.

What follows is a combination of my report of those conversations and my reflection on them. I have merged the conversations in an effort to keep faith with my commitment that my conversation partners would remain anonymous. These thoughts are offered not as statistically based conclusions or carefully researched facts, but rather as personal impressions and reflections on the nature of episcopal leadership in our church at the present time.

Setting the Context

In spite of the self-confidence of many who attempt to analyze the leadership of bishops in our denomination, it is difficult for those who are outside that office to understand all of its complexities. In an effort to set the context, I would like to quote excerpts adapted from an address given by Bishop Neil L. Irons to a joint meeting of bishops and college/university presidents in January 1995.

> The world in which the bishops serve is marked by incredible tensions—some ecclesial, some general. Of all the offices in the church, the one carrying the primary responsibility for faithfully passing on the apostolic faith is that of bishop. Christianity is both a historical faith and a faith grounded in history. The central truths given to, and conveyed by, the apostles are to be transmitted from generation to generation without error. However, every time and place demands that ancient truths be translated to each generation in ways whereby the apostolic faith can be understood and believed. The bishop, therefore, is both a teacher and a preacher. As such, the office has a certain conservatism (I am not speaking politically) built into it. For those of us educated in a liberal mode, the apologetic work of the office sometimes occasions in us real tension. Although we know better, there are persons who assume that all a bishop says and writes is meant to be taken as infallible. The freedom to explore new frontiers of meaning and faith is somewhat qualified by the necessity of "defending the faith." Thinking out loud can have unintended and troublesome results. Although we reserve unto ourselves the freedom of thought and inquiry, we are never far from the weighty theological and doctrinal responsibilities that go with leading the church.
>
> Nowhere does the day-to-day tension occur more often than in matters related to the institutional expression of the church, including but not confined to the United Methodist Church. United Methodist bishops live in a series of councils or conferences. Membership is held in the council of bishops, which is global in character. Bishops have presidential authority in annual conferences. The pastors receive their appointments from the bishop, who, along with the district superintendents, is responsible for the well-being of all the pastors and churches. In an increasingly litigious

society, bishops are often involved in processing and adjudicating potentially volatile personal situations. They preside over church trials and are themselves subject to grievances and trials.

The General Conference, which is the supreme legislative body for the denomination, is presided over by bishops, who otherwise are not allowed to speak on the major issues before the church, except through a single episcopal address. Yet each bishop is expected to carry out the directives of the General Conference without question.

The fourth conference/council is the jurisdictional conference, which is regionally formed, and in which bishops are elected and appointed. Here, also, the bishops have presidential authority.

Each episcopal leader becomes a part of a general agency in which s/he will serve in a subsidiary role to the general secretary of the agency, as well as serving on committees under the direction of both lay and clergy persons. Rather than overseeing all the church, one works at trying to understand a large institution within the greater institution of the denomination. Only a minority of bishops ever serve these agencies in a presidential way. Thus, leadership is shared within the denomination.

In many respects the results of this organizational structure are healthy, but the outward appearance is misleading. For many of us, these interwoven areas of responsibility prove to be sources of exhaustion, for each part of our institution expects to have our undivided attention and loyalty. Perspective needed for general leadership does not easily present itself.

Add to all of the above the ecumenical councils of churches and religion (some are involved with Jewish and Muslim communities), which are currently in some crisis and transition themselves. When things are going smoothly, judicatory heads can rely on leadership from others in these areas. But when financial crisis looms, the heads of church, synagogue, and mosque must give unstinting leadership, or the ecumenical commitment to society will wither. Finally, bishops sit as trustees on the boards of universities, colleges, schools, hospitals, homes for the elderly and youth, and social agencies.

Trained as pastors, teachers, and theologians, it is not uncommon for some of us to struggle within the maze of institutional duties to which we are bound. Understaffed and overextended describe where many of us live today.

This summary of episcopal responsibilities was articulated in various ways, but with great consistency by those I interviewed. I encountered a sense of continual overload among all of the bishops with whom I talked. And yet, in the midst of all their various responsibilities, the dominant attitude toward their work was one of hope and enthusiasm. They know that many of their constituents are critical of their work, but that seems to result in greater clarity about why they are acting in particular ways and a commitment to act in spite of criticism.

If anything, the bishops I spoke with erred on the side of optimism about the current and future state of the church. And none of them expressed any sense of powerlessness in having an impact on their episcopal area. Their understandings and their experiences follow in much the way that I heard them.

The Shape of Creative, Visionary Episcopal Leadership

Leaders must find ways to hold together being stewards of the vision and managers of the organization. That tension was articulated more frequently than any other, and in all cases shaping and keeping the vision is intended to be the top priority. The tensions arise when management demands first place. To provide visionary leadership requires participating in the creation of a vision. In most cases, that vision was seen as a vision for the annual conference(s) in which the bishop works, but it originates in the local congregations that make up that annual conference. In all of the conversations, three themes were continuously articulated.

1. *The vision is not created alone.* All of the bishops with whom I spoke are clear that it is not their task to create the vision alone, but to help an authentic vision grow out of the community. Effective leadership cannot happen without followers. Little attention has been paid in most of the literature on leadership to the role of followers, but their active involvement is the key to effective leadership. The power of the leader resides in being able to call forth the other person's power. Management, on the other hand, can be provocative but not very evocative. It is effective leadership that evokes the gifts of others in the creation of the vision for the community.

One person talked about this as the responsibility of the bishop to bring his or her gifts into participation with a community in discerning a vision. It cannot be the leader's vision alone, but the leader helps the community discern the vision and contributes to it. A faithful discernment process begins by acknowledging that the vision is not self-generated but is received, which requires attentiveness to the Spirit of God and God's purposes in the world as the starting place. The community participates together in discerning and articulating that vision and the leader then motivates, encourages, and organizes the community to live out that vision.

2. *The vision grows out of both past and future.* In order to discern and create a vision and make it live for the coming generation, the community must understand both past and future. The bishops are particularly sensitive to this tension since they have responsibility, on the one hand, for articulating the apostolic faith and, on the other hand,

for leading the church into the future. To focus too much on one without the other creates imbalance. One bishop spoke of a rope in a tug-of-war, with the two ends being the maintenance of the past and the creation of a new future. It is easy for members of the community to focus too much on one or the other. Part of the leader's task is to be a bridge between those who are running into the future without paying attention to the past and those who are entrenched in the past. To understand that the Christian community and its members are sent forth by God into the world implies both a "to" and a "from." "Leaders must work to balance where we are going and where we are coming from so that the community remains grounded and does not run first one direction and then the other," said one bishop.

To live in this tension, of course, endears you to no one. For many who want to move ahead quickly, it is difficult to remember that the vision not only comes out of the future but also is shaped and formed by the tradition. The classic and historic role of bishops is to be responsible for the unity of the church and the truth of the gospel. Vision relates to both of those. The tradition informs how the vision is being discerned. Creating a new future out of that vision is the task to which God calls the church. If past and future are not held in tension, the vision will inevitably be lopsided.

3.   *The vision can only be realized by the community not by the leader.* All agreed that it is more difficult to turn the vision into reality than to discern the vision initially. The task of the leader in this process is to be an energizer, a role quite different from that of visioner. Where a bishop places priorities and energies will have a profound impact on the life of the annual conference and will influence where others place their energy as well. "Energy draws out energy. People come forward and want to become a part of what is going on," said one bishop who believes that the annual conference is moving in positive directions. The danger, of course, is that the leader will forget that this kind of energy is not limitless and will risk burnout in the face of all the demands. That possibility is one that seems to surface often in the struggle to balance the diversity of tasks.

The way that bishops lead toward that corporate vision includes the way they do cabinet meetings, preside at annual conference, relate to conflict, make decisions, relate to persons at all levels. Leading toward a vision is not some ethereal undertaking but the way one lives and leads within the heart of the problems. Others in the community face the reality of making real the vision in their own arena day by day. Creative leadership is that which models for them that difficult task, including understanding and naming the current reality and then moving from that to the vision. That is the only way to help the organization achieve its intended purpose or mission. Some of the bishops I interviewed felt confident about how to be that model for the community, while others were more tentative.

In all of the conversations, the interviewees talked about the critical role that relationships play in this kind of leadership. Building a climate in which the vision can be discerned and realized and building relationships with others in the community are what make the leader an effective connector within the organization. It was apparent that some bishops are better at setting the context and keeping the "big picture" before the organization all of the time. They are comfortable thinking theologically and theoretically. Others are better at building relationships—teaching, coaching, stimulating, inspiring, and motivating others, asking them to engage with the vision and mission. The exceptional leader is the one who values both and is able to do them effectively.

The bishops frequently articulated the connection between the leadership issues they face and those faced in local congregations. They believe that their understandings of leadership apply to local congregations as well as to the episcopacy. One bishop indicated that one of the most important things is finding ways to heighten the understanding of clergy as persons who equip the saints for ministry, who turn the laity loose to do ministry. Throughout the denomination the ratio between laity and clergy continues to drop. Some say that is the result of a lack of evangelistic passion, but one bishop articulated the conviction that it is really the result of a controlling model of clergy leadership. "Our forebears delivered services through classes where people help one another whereas many of the clergy today are quite controlling." All of the bishops articulated their conviction that effective leadership is shared at every level, though some were clear that they would not be viewed in that way.

Leaders must understand the difference between power and authority. The bishops not only articulated this difference themselves, but several believe that it is also important to articulate this difference in leadership groups and all kinds of settings. One of the bishops pointed out that the consecration service speaks of authority but says nothing about power. The distinction is not always clear; so when bishops talk about the authority that they are given liturgically by the church, they must be able to help people discern the difference between that authority and power. Not all of their constituents would agree that they truly understand the distinction between the two.

The bishops also saw their authority as broader than their office. While the role of bishop is directly connected to authority, their authority did not begin with the consecration service. Bishops are chosen because people see in them authority, and so they bring to their leadership role personal as well as position-related authority. One bishop indicated that the process of discerning who bishops should be at this time and place in our denomination should have at its core a quest for the discernment of personal authority.

Another bishop feels strongly that episcopal authority does not come from the position or office, nor does it come from the individual. Instead, episcopal authority comes from God. The role of bishop gives visibility to the person in a way that allows God's leading to be seen and acted upon. All of those in the community must be careful that their assumptions and mental models do not block them from seeing God's authority.

In a poignant conversation, one bishop indicated the strong desire to lead in a nonhierarchical and collegial way—and, in fact, had a history of leading in that way prior to election as a bishop. However, people insisted on labeling the bishop as authoritarian because their preconceived understandings of the role prevented them from seeing the way in which this particular person was acting. The bishop's wistful conclusion: "One of the greatest gifts the church could give me is to take me out of the box they have put me in."

In several of the conversations there was discussion of the episcopal election process. Because of the way the election process takes place, persons who are creative, visionary leaders may not emerge. Too often those who take risks and act courageously may not be elected to the delegation or endorsed as candidates. And those who begin as courageous risk-takers may find their energies diminished as the pressures of institutional life increase.

In the end, one bishop said, "What is amazing is that in spite of the strictures of time and human energy limitations, we manage to break through that and catch an insight and announce it in a way that catches other people. It happens in a moment, sometimes carefully prepared and sometimes in an offhand moment, when one of God's visions/insights breaks through and takes life in other people. That is leadership for me."

What Supports This Kind of Leadership?

In responses to a question about the sources of support for leadership, the individual differences in the bishops' personalities were evident. For some who are more introverted, their energy was sustained more by internal resources while others received more strength from their interactions with others. While the emphasis was somewhat different, all of them spoke of the following four critical areas from which they gained support.

(1) *Attentiveness to God.* Without exception, this group of bishops spoke about a regularity of life that has devotions, reading, and study time as the most important support for effective leadership. Also without exception they articulated the difficulty of maintaining this kind of regularity in the midst of the pressures of the office.

Effective leaders pay attention to matters of faith and spirituality, was their universal conclusion. Matters of personnel and program are important, but they must be kept in balance. The most important ingredient for any spiritual leaders, said one bishop, is to be on a spiritual journey and to live as a faithful disciple. This includes continuously growing, learning, seeking to be in relationship to God. You cannot do that without prayer and Scripture reflection being your first time commitment and top priority. Effective spiritual leaders live in a way that honors that.

One of the bishops said, "I think I became a leader when I shifted from living out of other people's expectations to living out of the leading and direction of God and God's grace. That was a fundamental shift for me. What pulls me into the future is not what everyone wants from me, but what I believe God is asking of the church. I made a shift from living only in justifying grace to living in sanctifying grace—that is a characteristic of leadership. All of this spiritually has something to do with where your home is. If your home is with God, you can lead in a different way."

Most of the interviewees expressed strong feelings about coming into the office with misgivings about their own capacity to be a bishop but a strong sense that God gives us what we need in each situation. One bishop spoke of the importance of Hildegaard of Bingen's image of being a feather on the breath of God. In spite of not having all that it takes to do this job, it is important to pay attention to the ways in which God is calling forth the gifts of leadership.

(2) *Authenticity.* Leadership is more related to authenticity and vision than it is to role. One bishop said that there is something about knowing that life is *one*—not two or three or five. All is included. If your life is compartmentalized and you cannot live out of a singular vision yourself, you cannot help the organization live holistically. That kind of authenticity is essential to effective leadership.

Most of the bishops talked about experiencing resistance to their leadership at various times. They understood this as one of the inevitable consequences of their position. They did not resent the resistance but tried to understand it and respond to it. One person spoke of attempting to understand as engagement what some people might experience as resistance. This grew out of a strong conviction that people have a right to wonder why the bishop does certain things and ask those questions directly. "I say clearly that as long as you treat my office with respect (I am a steward of the office of bishop) there isn't anything you cannot say to me. Then we can honestly deal with things. I try continually to remember that my office and my person are different. Any deference comes to the office and not to me personally. But I am a person in this office, and I believe that people should treat the office with respect." This ability to see the difference between the person and the office makes possible an authenticity within the institutional structure.

(3) Relationships. The bishops spoke of supportive relationships in two different ways. The first is to be able to be a part of a team that is working together. The creative leader is called to create that team and build community, to evoke synergy, to help the community live together in such a way that through the sharing of every person's contribution they discover something larger than any one individual.

The most important team for the bishop is the cabinet. The interviewees had a variety of experiences with cabinets, and these experiences differed dramatically not only from one bishop to another, but even for the same bishop in two different conferences. Annual conference cabinets have their own ways of being, and all bishops come into a cabinet that is already established. The differences in these experiences can be significant. In some situations the cabinet never did become any kind of community; in other situations it provided great support for the bishop and the other members. The geographic makeup of the annual conference and the past patterns of relationships contribute to these differences.

The second kind of relationships that are critical are personal relationships. Spouse and family members become more and more important as other personal relationships seem to decline. Most of the bishops spoke of the difficulty of having open and honest relationships with persons in the annual conference because their role interferes. The time and energy limitations make it difficult to develop close personal relationships with persons who are not related to the church. Some of the bishops received their most important personal support from other bishops. There is a kind of "instant community" that grows out of the shared struggles and experiences. However, this group is together only twice each year for a brief period, and so family and other personal relationships bear an extra-heavy burden in providing support.

One of the bishops who is concerned about what is happening to clergy discovered that some research done on midcareer clergy who are at the point of burnout indicates that there is a difference between stress and burnout. Stress has to do with calendar management; burnout has to do with breaking human relationships. When important human relationships remain intact, fatigue and even exhaustion may set in; but serious burnout with its related depression rarely occurs. This is an important learning for bishops as well as other clergy. This may be one factor influencing the significant number of clergy leaving the ministry or choosing to retire early. More bishops are also considering early retirement, perhaps influenced by the struggle to find the necessary support relationships. It is very difficult, this bishop indicated, to develop support relationships in an annual conference where people are accountable to you or want something from you.

(4) Life experiences. Interestingly, the women bishops spoke most clearly about the way in which life experiences have contributed to their role as leaders. They believe that they were honed by the barriers that they had to overcome and the resistance that they faced as clergywomen. They had to learn to deal with those things or they would not have made it to the place they now occupy. One of them indicated that she saw a sign at a river saying that 2,000 years from now this spot would look entirely different because of the rocks that would reshape the earth around them. And so she learned to ask what are the rocks in the cauldron of her life, what are the things that have shaped and are shaping her.

Being a woman not only offered barriers to overcome and resistance to face but also presented opportunities at a time when the church in many places was trying to open its doors to women. Consequently, these women were given rich opportunities and were pushed into places that helped them grow. One of them said that women are freer to do some of the more creative and innovative things and, perhaps because they aren't afraid to fail and try again, are willing to risk more. Women traditionally tend to relationships that are not neat and manageable, and so they may be better able to deal with ambiguity and disorder.

One of the bishops said that women are countercultural just by walking in the room. Their leadership style is often more collaborative and collegial in systems that have not experienced that. It may be difficult for people unaccustomed to that style to take it seriously. When men do the same thing, it is accepted more quickly, whereas women are too easily discounted. She believes that both women and men who seek more collegial styles must work together to bring about real change.

The male bishops also talked about the way in which their life experiences prepared them for leadership. Most of them had grown up within the church, where they were nurtured and encouraged as leaders. During the early years of their ministry, they were put in places where they could grow and were mentored by other leaders within the annual conference. Most of them had significant leaders who were role models for them and whose leadership styles they have tried to emulate in their own leadership. One said that he watched bishops who were theologians and consequently tried to be a theologian himself. Their experiences in communities of faith that loved them unconditionally and taught them and helped them to develop their skills and their leadership were important factors for all of the bishops, male and female.

What Are the Roadblocks to This Kind of Leadership?

Resistance to a collegial style of leadership. Almost all of the bishops interviewed expressed a desire to function collegially, and many felt that they had been successful at that prior to their election. But since being elected, almost all of them have experienced an unwillingness on the part of others to cooperate with them in creating a collegial environment. This is particularly interesting because they are also aware that people talk frequently about wanting a more collegial style of leadership and criticize what they perceive as authoritarianism. They spoke of wanting to draw large numbers of people into decision-making circles but of encountering resistance when they tried. One bishop talked about constantly needing to bridge between different groups of clergy with differing perspectives and finding it almost impossible to create a collegial environment.

One bishop said that creative visioning always necessitates a larger community, but it was difficult to get people to talk back to the bishop. "When I talk, it shuts the discussion down. My episcopacy committee has been a flop because they won't talk back. The authority of the bishop always has the last word. That is not very helpful to my leadership—it shuts down my creative processes." This bishop did indicate that over time the cabinet had learned to talk back, but that was the only place where it happened effectively.

This same issue appeared in other ways. One bishop said that traditionally people see the bishop as proclaiming rather than exploring. It is difficult to talk about anything in a tentative, exploring way because people will hear it as a proclamation. Another said that people want bishops to wave their magic wand and fix it all—an attitude that prevents creative, mutual work. Deference to the office was also mentioned as a block to open communication, but one bishop indicated that passive-aggressive behavior is more common than deference. In every case, the bishops I interviewed longed for open, honest, and mutual communication and found it very difficult to achieve, in spite of the success they had experienced in doing so before being elected.

Spiritual malaise and other cultural factors. One of the bishops said that spiritual malaise is the ultimate barrier to the vision. The culture has co-opted the church. Our roots are on the surface, and there is cynicism, doubt, and mistrust even among those who call themselves faithful disciples. Too often they cannot even see beyond their own perspective. The radical individualism of the culture is diametrically opposed to what Christians are called to be, but it is so influential that sometime the primary question for leadership even in the church is: What is in it for me? It is the consumer question and must be guarded against all the time.

Most of the bishops also spoke about the lack of cultural credibility that pastors experience. In many cases, they feel beaten up by parishioners who do not take them seriously. One person indicated that the conservative swing of the country causes pastors and parishioners to be pitted against each other rather than joining together in the search for truth. The other side of this issue was also voiced. The church may actually be freer from cultural pressures when the culture is less affirming. It is our own insecurities that make us turn to the larger culture.

One bishop said that in order to move into the future, the church must go through a radical transition. "When I was elected I didn't really realize the fullness of the radical nature of that change, and I didn't know how difficult it would be to move an organization. And so my question has become, 'What does it mean to live in in-between times?' That is what I have given my life to—leadership in the in-between times."

Organizational inertia prevents the church from moving toward the next century. There is confusion, and there is resistance to change, transformation, the new. One bishop said, "There are folks who line up and knee jerk at every opportunity. But we go on! I am so clear that my life cannot be taken from me, even if I were killed. I just have to move and bring the folks along that want to come—and even if they don't go, I am still going to go. This is what God requires of me, and there is no negotiation about that. We can negotiate about how, but the fact of doing it has been laid on me and I must continue."

Another way of speaking about this organizational inertia was to talk about the limited institutional authority that the bishop actually has. One person was surprised, having always assumed that there were more possibilities for changing the organization, to discover that the bishop really has limited authority except in appointments and in ordaining clergy after the board of ordained ministry has decided.

In all of these areas, the bishops indicated, the culture and the institution made creative, visionary leadership very difficult.

Demands on time and energy. Of all the roadblocks that the bishops face in providing leadership for the church, the demands of the area were the most significant. The large number of "have-tos" absolutely saps the energy of leaders, not only bishops but also of district superintendents and council staff. "I have done terrible preaching because there is no time," said one bishop. "The demands of paperwork are monumental, and people are crying for some sort of personal, intimate connection." The suggestion was made that no district superintendent should oversee more than forty churches, whereas some have 100 churches and never have time really to be leaders. One bishop proposed that we extend the work of the conference council office to do some of the tasks of superintendents so that they could attend to the care of pastors.

Both bishops and district superintendents often come out of the pastorate, a place where they have had some regularity and steadiness of life. They no longer have imposed upon them the disciplines of weekly study and preaching, and they have to give up the thing that most feeds them—intimate pastoral care. They don't relate to people in the wholeness of life but only segmentally. In addition, they are often relating primarily to those clergy who are in trouble. "The ten percent of pastors in my area who are in trouble take ninety percent of the time. It would be energizing to do the opposite, but there is no time to be with the creative, energized pastors."

All of the interviewees agreed that the role and function of the district superintendent must change. In recent years it has been seen primarily as a middle management/administrative role. One bishop suggested that the district superintendent should be seen as the extension of the leadership of the bishop in such a way that he or she becomes the teaching elder working with clergy, present within every covenant and support group. Some episcopal areas are working intentionally to move certain tasks away from the superintendent by shifting administrative responsibilities elsewhere. Several of the bishops are working actively to change the role of district superintendent from being primarily maintainers of the institutions to being developers of leaders and Christian communities. Since these interviews, changes in the disciplinary paragraphs relating to district superintendents have attempted to redefine that office with greater priority on spiritual leadership and pastoral nurture. But these bishops are all clear that it will take a great deal of intentional conversation to know just what changes should take place. It is possible to move superintendents away from board and agency responsibilities, but it is much more difficult to deal with the amount of time required to address clergy misconduct and other legal issues.

That concern led each of the bishops to talk about the litigious atmosphere in which we live, and the ways it affects our common life. An increasing number of delicate legal matters must be dealt with by the bishop and cabinet. One bishop talked about spending more time on legal issues than on theological issues, but also expressed the hope that this will change. "In part this is because there are long-neglected situations that must be addressed. Perhaps ten years from now things will be quite different, and this will not be so all-consuming."

The Itinerant System

In spite of frustrations with the functioning of the itinerant system, none of the bishops interviewed was ready to give up on it. And even those who strongly advocate longer pastorates believe that a variety of experiences keeps pastors creative and that ministry is richer and broader when the pastor has served in several different places. Most of them are concerned about an entrenchment and ongoing inertia within the existing systems for both laity and clergy. It is difficult to intervene in lethargy. Appointments, salaries, and professional identity all contribute to a big investment in the status quo. This is true not only for clergy but also for laity. One bishop spoke about "a class of professional laity who are often leaders in the annual conference and are on general boards. They compete with clergy for power, have learned how to invest themselves in power, and have developed systems of self-protection. You always need laity involved in governance, but in this model of leadership, institutional governance takes precedence over the ministry of the laity in the world. We don't have a strong view of what it means for laity to be led by both clergy and laity. Instead they spend time in power games and budget battles."

In talking about what would contribute to revitalizing the itinerant system, two things were mentioned. The first is a renewed covenant among the clergy. It is talked about in relation to the itinerancy, but it is also critical for other reasons. With the increase in local pastors, who do not itinerate in the same way that ordained elders do, the clergy covenant must be redefined so that it will function at the district or cluster level in support and accountability. Currently there is not an effective covenant among clergy leadership.

In the opinion of one bishop, appointment-making is getting harder because the bishops have not only allowed but also contributed to a climate of careerism, and they need to work at changing that. In one area, the bishop is working hard at a spiritual discernment model of appointment making. The cabinet has experienced a different response from many clergy when they have been genuinely able to tell the person that they were led to him or her.

The second needed change in the system is to find a way for clergy to move in and out of the appointive system without judgment. This would allow people to set down the itinerancy for awhile and then come back and pick it up. To do this would require some financial way to sustain that person so the church could say, "Given all of your other life issues and what you need for you to flourish, we think you ought to step aside for awhile, and later you can come back." This would also help deal with ineffectiveness in the system that eats away at the whole system. "Even the most effective are affected by the ineffective," said one bishop.

The Role of the Council of Bishops in Leading the Church

In discussing the role of the council of bishops in leading the church, there are clear differences of opinion. Some believe that the council has become a reactor to multiple requests for agenda time, functioning in many ways like a reference committee that handles outside requests instead of being inner-directed. "We are a denomination without a center or an ethos. We must figure out a way to answer the question, 'What does it mean for the bishops to lead the church at this time?'" But others believe that over the last twenty years the council has become much stronger and has led the church in some important ways. *In Defense of Creation* and the ministry study were cited as examples.

The bishops all agreed on the need to affirm each other's leadership but differed sharply on whether one bishop should be selected for an office such as presiding bishop. One of the interviewees, who supports such an office, said, "The council of bishops has developed an almost neurotic concern for equality. The council cannot let one or two or three bishops have leadership in a constructive way over a long period of time. We have had some giants in the council of bishops, and they have been stifled because we can't let one person have leadership. We do not know how to affirm each other's leadership." Some feel that a "presiding bishop" would limit the freedom and creativity that are so important to the life of each annual conference. Others do not see such an office as limiting their role. Those who support this concept believe that we sacrifice a great deal by not having such a person, but most agree that there is too much resistance for it to happen any time soon.

The interviewees agreed that it is important for the council of bishops to move from a collection of individual conference leaders to becoming a corporate body in order to give effective leadership to the church. The council is working toward that goal in a variety of ways, and several of the bishops believe that the new leadership coming each quadrennium is helping to enable that.

How Do We Identify, Call Forth, Nurture, and Train Future Leaders?

In addressing the issue of future leadership, most of the bishops interviewed began by reflecting on their own nurture. Their families and their congregations asked vocational questions and then created an environment that helped them answer faithfully. They had encouragement and support and strong mentoring during their formative years. Because of the importance of this in their own lives, some of them are working intentionally to encourage others to become mentors and encouragers. "I have asked the lay members of the conference to enter into a covenant with their pastors to discern who are the people whom God is calling. I tell them that they have a special role as lay people and ask if they, as representatives of the annual conference, will see it as their responsibility to discern who has the gifts for ministry." One bishop spoke with sadness about encountering parents who discourage children who want to enter the ordained ministry.

"Raising spiritual leaders," said one bishop, "is the most important task in the annual conference." Congregations are not intentional about calling forth the brightest and best and need encouragement to do so. In addition, district committees and boards of ordained ministry need to improve the credentialing process. One of the major changes needed is to identify the right mentors for candidates, mentors with skills for discerning and evoking the gifts of others. In many conferences, probationary period requirements are getting stronger, and the new three-year probationary period with its use of mentors may improve that even more. And then, suggests one bishop, we need to gather classes of clergy at points along the way (five and ten years) to see where they are in their journey and to signal that we are all in this together. The annual conference is the place where systemic change can take place because this is the place where the covenant is spelled out most clearly.

Several of the bishops commented on the struggle to find strong leadership for ethnic churches, in large part because the leadership has been skimmed off the top for the episcopacy and for boards and agencies. Unfortunately, sometimes entrenched racial/ethnic minority clergy resist bringing in new leadership.

If our future leaders are to be effective, we need to change what we reward, said several bishops. We tend to reward management more than we mean to. Management deals with such things as attendance, membership, finances—things we can quantify. Even when they are seen as faith issues, they are dealt with in a managerial style. "Management," said one bishop, "generally supports a clear, closed canon view of truth and never opens it up. Management has a preconceived goal, knows what the end goal is, and must be orthodox." The current system has a tendency to call forth leaders who have learned how to lead by reacting, by learning the system, rather than leaders who not only can see the dynamics of the system but move beyond it in vision. "I wish we could find ways to spend time with clergy talking 'leadership talk' and not 'management talk,' to get the necessary accountability stuff done so the time we spent together was focused on who we are as God's servant leaders, what God is doing in our lives and in the world, and how we relate to that."

Another way of addressing this issue is to focus more on vocation than career. Clarity about vocation and strong connection, support, and accountability are the things needed most. "One of the biggest frustrations," said one bishop, "is isolated clergy. That is everyone's fault and everyone's responsibility."

One of the bishops interviewed said, "One of my mentor bishops told me that my greatest gift as a bishop would be the ability to see someone with the capacity for leadership and then have the authority to put those people in places where they can grow. He told me that he was so glad he had the opportunity to do that with me. So it is the responsibility of all of us to discern who can be the leaders."

Are you hopeful about future leadership? In responding to this final question in the interview, each bishop was not only hopeful but also enthusiastic. They talked about clergy who are giving more attention to personal spiritual care, clergy who are more collegial in their leadership, and fewer clergy who function as lone rangers. They said that seminaries are doing a better job of nurturing spiritual life and that the Preaching Academy and the Academy for Spiritual Formation are contributing to the spiritual life of clergy. The younger generation seems less competitive and more open to the leading of the spirit in healthy ways.

As the bishops talked about the ordinands of recent years they used words like *strong* and *visionary*. However, they also expressed concerns. One indicated that there seems to be a lot of specializing going on. These ordinands are aware of their own individual identity and are supportive of diversity, but they are less well equipped to bring unity. Another bishop said, "I worry about what will happen to them over the next ten years. Some of them are saying clearly, 'I don't want to become like those I see who have been in ministry ten or twenty years.' We have not been intentional about giving them real support. We give them continuing education money and let them do what they want, but we do not help them find their community with one another." That bishop is developing covenant groups and learning plans among the clergy in the area so that they can feed and nurture each other and become a learning community together.

In all of these conversations, I rarely heard the word *competent* in talking about leaders for the future. One of the bishops told of a pastor who said that when he goes to a local church their first question is, "Is God real to this person?" It is a question of faith and spirituality. Their next question is, "Does this person love us and want to be with us, or is he/she preoccupied with other people and things?" Only after those two questions are answered do the people even wonder, "Is this person competent?"

Conclusion

In reflecting on my conversations with the five bishops, I was left with several overarching impressions. The first is that the issues and concerns these leaders are addressing are closely related to the issues and concerns articulated in the many conversations across the church regarding the need for creative and visionary leadership. The bishops speak with some confidence about what they are doing to address these issues, while many of the other conversations sound as if these issues are not being dealt with at all. Why the discrepancy? Perhaps it is primarily because I sought out bishops who are perceived as some of the most visionary and creative leaders. Perhaps they are addressing these issues more effectively than some of their colleagues. On the other hand, perhaps the perceptions and the realities do not really coincide.

Leadership style is one of those issues. In many places we hear complaints about bishops who are too autocratic and authoritarian, implying that those persons want leaders who are more collegial. The bishops interviewed all talked about working intentionally at being collegial, and yet they often feel that others will not allow them to work in this way. Are these discrepancies related to the ambivalence we seem to have about strong leaders? On the one hand we long for people of vision who can be outstanding leaders, and on the other hand we resist their leadership and want everyone to have an equal say. Then when we are offered the opportunity to help shape the vision, we sometimes discover that we really want a bishop who has answers, not questions, and who will make decisions for us. Is our ambivalence about the role of leaders in our lives responsible for our inability to allow our leaders the freedom to lead? Or are the bishops' perceptions different from the reality they are living?

My second impression is that while these bishops are deeply committed to leading the church in response to the call of God, it takes enormous ongoing work to remain truly open and attentive to that call. They believe that their vision for the church comes from God, and yet they run into resistance at many turns. They are clear that there are tensions between their visions for the future and what already exists. They know that they must work to overcome obstacles in order to make the vision a reality. Several of them are very clear that God is calling them to provide leadership in moving the church in new directions. This clarity is often energizing and compelling, enabling their followers to move enthusiastically with them. But this assurance of God's leading may make it difficult for persons who disagree to challenge or question without appearing to be working against God.

How do effective spiritual leaders remain attentive to God, knowing that God is the source of their ability to lead, without seeing themselves as infallible or allowing others to see them in that way? There are no easy answers to that question, but it does seem clear that regular reflection and feedback from others are necessary in order to be certain that the concerns and visions of others who may understand God's call differently are invited.

My third impression is that there is a tension between the desire to call forth strong leaders for the future and the ongoing concern for equality. This was most evident in the bishops' discussion of the council of bishops, especially in what one bishop called the "almost neurotic concern for equality." On the one hand there was conversation about the need to mentor future leaders—to encourage their gifts and help to develop their leadership abilities—and on the other hand ongoing discussion of a climate that promotes equality. This mentoring was talked about in relation to clergy within the annual conference and also the mentoring of younger bishops by older bishops. In an atmosphere that does not allow leaders to rise above the crowd, how do you mentor people for the future? In an earlier time, some bishops became outstanding national leaders with visibility far beyond their local area. In current times the mood seems to work against the cultivation of such leaders. And yet the conversations still focus around the hunger for strong spiritual leaders. Wherever this discussion takes place, ambivalence abounds.

My final impression is that the bishops I interviewed are unanimously hopeful about the future of the church. They have not lost faith in the itinerant system, and they believe that they can make major changes in the institution. None of them is a "lone ranger" in the way that they go about seeking that change, and all of them believe that others help discern that vision and bring it to reality. The changes they talk about are challenging and risky, and coupled with their commitment to the church, one wonders whether they can accomplish the change they seek while still holding on to the institution they love. Some of them seem cognizant of the enormous upheaval these changes may bring about, while others see the needed changes as less disruptive. But all of them have a deep love for the church and have invested their personal and professional lives in its future. How then could they not be hopeful?

PART THREE
How Will United Methodism Express Its Connectional Nature?

What Is the Common Discipline for Local Churches?

Thomas Edward Frank

As the turn of the century approaches, United Methodism finds itself "between the times" in its polity of the local church. The 1996 General Conference, among the most radical in American Methodism's two-hundred-year history, has removed much of the common discipline providing a structure of authority and decision making in the churches. In its place is a functionalism that, while opening the way to broad diversity in organizational and leadership styles, leaves many churches confused about how to authorize and organize their mission. Most critically, churches in the United Methodist tradition now have even fewer concrete ways to share a common polity and disciplined purpose in the "connection."

From Structure to Function in Local Church Discipline

The movement from structure to function has been fomenting for some time. In part it might be viewed as an inevitable outcome of United Methodism's eclectic local church ecclesiology. One need only consider the introductory numbered paragraphs[1] of the local church chapter in the 1996 *Book of Discipline* (pars. 201–4). Here the local church is described successively as:

- "a community of true believers . . . the redemptive fellowship in which the Word of God is preached by persons divinely called and the sacraments are duly administered"—the rhetoric of classical Protestantism that is foundational to Methodism but not specific to it;
- "a strategic base from which Christians move out to the structures of society"—the rhetoric of social activism (which the *Discipline* unhappily does not connect with Methodist traditions of holiness);
- "a connectional society of persons who have professed their faith in Christ"—the rhetoric of class meetings and the General Rules, now little known or practiced per se in United Methodist churches;
- a place of "definite evangelistic, nurture, and witness responsibility for its members and the surrounding area and a missional outreach

responsibility"—the rhetoric of contemporary church revitalization programs.

To these already complex expectations the 1996 General Conference added a preface, oddly without paragraph numbering and thus with ambiguous status as legislation, that places "disciple-making" foremost among the church's purposes. "In order to be truly alive," the *Discipline* now declares, "we embrace Jesus' mandate to make disciples of all peoples"—the rhetoric of current church growth literature (pp. 114–15).

With such an array of competing demands placed upon the local church, it is perhaps not surprising that the *Discipline* increasingly would offer, not a structural framework, but a functional process for synthesizing them. Thus the "disciple-making" preface concludes with a systems understanding of the church as a flow from proclaiming the gospel, to nurturing persons in faith, to sending them into the world "as servants of Christ," to gathering them back again for further strengthening of commitment.

This systems understanding of church, advocated for several quadrennia by the General Board of Discipleship, is reinforced in legislative paragraphs as well. Here the "primary task" of the local church is described as a process of "reaching out and receiving," then inviting people to commitment, offering them opportunities for "growth in spiritual formation," and sending them into the world to live as disciples (par. 245).

The 1996 General Conference took the next logical step in functionalism, which was to remove much of the legislation either mandating or making normative certain structures of administration and program in the local church. Paragraphs detailing the powers and responsibilities of the administrative board, council on ministries, and program work areas—a structure in place since 1968—were simply deleted. In their place are permissive paragraphs describing a "church council" and three basic functions of local churches: nurture, outreach, and witness (par. 254).

The 1996 editorial decision to remove virtually all capitalization of administrative or programmatic church units—in annual conferences as well as local churches—reinforced the functionalist trend. The reader of the current *Discipline* has difficulty discerning whether titles such as church council refer to actual constituted entities existing by that name or only to functions to be attended to by one body or another, depending on whatever structures a particular local church decides to create.

The flexibility introduced by this organizational model was strongly advocated by several networks of church leaders organized to draft legislation and lobby for its passage in 1996. Arguing that the 1968 structure was too rigid and that local churches did not want specific program mandates imposed upon them, the reformers spurred General Conference to adopt paragraphs giving each local church freedom to organize for mission in its own way. The church council is described in general terms, but its nature as more of a suggestion than a mandate is made clear in the phrase, "if a church chooses to have a church council"—for anything is possible, including the continuation of the administrative board and council on ministries, or the administrative council, models from earlier *Disciplines* (pars. 254.4, 246.2).

Two fundamental problems emerge from this state of affairs. First, the ambiguity in United Methodism about what really constitutes a local church is more evident than ever in recent trends. The current legislation has further complicated already diverse understandings of church. Second, the legislation as it stands severely undermines congregational discipline as it has been traditionally understood in connectional polities, particularly the structures of authority in a local church. This situation creates the conditions of confusion and disorder in the local church as well as the connection.[2]

Sources of a Common Discipline

The eclecticism of local church polity, certain to become even more pronounced under the current permissive legislation, has deep roots in the ecclesiological synthesis of Wesley and Methodism. Steeped in his native Anglicanism, Wesley considered the Church of England "the best constituted national church in the world." He was particularly devoted to the *Book of Common Prayer* and viewed the disciplines of the Christian life, distilled in Methodism's General Rules, as ordered to the means of grace, particularly the sacrament of the Lord's Supper.

At the same time, Wesley was a full participant in the evangelical revival of his day, including the radical innovation of preaching outdoors. His declaration that "the world is my parish" was a protest against the limitations of geographic parish boundaries. His preaching literally outside the buildings was also more figuratively a refusal to let himself be bound by the authority of priests within their parish lines.

Thus he allowed competing criteria of ecclesial authority to emerge: the continuity of catholic sacramental practice "duly administered" by an ordained priesthood, and the spontaneity of preaching authenticated by the preacher's call and the hearers' response. The bridge between these was the class meeting in which those who responded to the preaching could pursue disciplined growth in the knowledge and love of God, practicing the means of grace—including most centrally the Lord's Supper normally received in one's parish church.

American Methodism inherited Wesley's synthetic ecclesiology without the national church to give it coherence. Consequently no one element of authority has ever gained sway over the others, and no one expression of the synthesis itself has ever proved lasting or compelling.

A. Rites and Ritual

Wesley's devotion to the Church of England, together with the English heritage of so many American Methodists, would seem to have offered an ecclesiological foundation in sacramental theology. Clearly Wesley assumed that the Americans would adopt his condensed and edited rites and ritual for their Sunday service, as well as his reduced version of the Articles of Religion. Indeed the Americans did and still do protect the latter under the Constitution's Restrictive Rules (par. 16), but the status of the ritual has been more ambiguous.

One could adduce various reasons for the failure of ritual itself to provide an ecclesiological axis for American Methodism. In the early days few preachers were ordained to administer the Lord's Supper. The unsettled conditions of a frontier society were not conducive to formal sacramental order. Parts of the Wesleyan family, particularly people of German and African heritage, shared the practices of piety without the traditions derived from the *Book of Common Prayer*. The spirit of camp meetings and quarterly conferences was spontaneous and effervescent, sometimes even actively derisive of ritual order and ordination.

But the truth is, of course, that Methodism had always privileged preaching as a central practice. Ordination came after one's election to the conference of preachers as a kind of added legitimation. Preachers were understood to have great latitude in leading worship and preaching, so long as they stayed loyal to the enduring themes of Wesley's teaching.

Consequently, American Methodism developed little in the way of ritual until well along in the nineteenth century. Books of discipline had chapters on "worship and ritual," but for many years retained a simple, lyrical sentence: "Let the morning service consist of singing, prayers, the reading of a lesson from the Old Testament, and another from the New, and preaching." In the twentieth century, ritual was increasingly elaborated and diversified, a reflection of liturgical renewal in the ecumenical church.

When United Methodism organized in 1968, the rituals were not printed in the *Discipline*. The new church's constitution authorized General Conference "to provide and revise the hymnal and ritual of the

Church and to regulate all matters relating to the form and mode of worship" (par. 15.6). But General Conferences have enabled this constitutional power mainly by authorizing hymnals and a book of worship that contain a wide variety of service orders and rituals. While these books are named in par. 1112.3, their legislative status remains ambiguous to most UM pastors and people.

Today's *Discipline* itself contains little that could be called canon law governing worship. Other than the declarations in the Articles of Religion that infant baptism "is to be retained" (XVII) and that the laity should receive both bread and cup in communion (XIX); the legislative specification that baptisms are to be administered in the name of the Father, Son and Holy Spirit (par. 215.1, though this is part of the section declared unconstitutional by Judicial Council Decision No. 811 in 1997); and the ban on "ceremonies that celebrate homosexual unions" added in 1996 to the Social Principles (par. 65.C); the *Discipline* gives little specific direction for worship. In fact, one of the ironies of singling out homosexual unions is that typically so little has been either prescribed or proscribed in United Methodist worship. Some UM churches celebrate the Lord's Supper once a month, some not at all; some require baptismal training and preparation, some none at all. One should not be surprised in visiting various UM churches to see an infant baptism performed with only one or two questions asked of the parents, or the communion elements served without so much as the words of institution being spoken, or service orders lacking a Psalm, creed, gloria, or any of the ancient forms of worship. One may expect to see clergy in academic gowns and hoods, in simple albs and stoles, in business suits, or even in jeans and pullover shirts.

In short, the rites and ritual of the church may be said to be a constitutive element of UM local church discipline only in the most general sense of providing widely—but unevenly—shared practices of song and prayer. From an ecclesiological standpoint the UMC continues to lack a consistent sacramental center that would provide a common ground comparable, for example, to the role of the *Book of Common Prayer* in churches of the Anglican communion. The widespread use of the services of word and table in the 1989 *Hymnal*—which has sold in the millions—is certainly a countervailing, centripetal force. But it seems unlikely that the UMC would undertake to enforce the use of the *Hymnal* in all local churches as a measure of congregational discipline.

B. A Preaching Ministry

Methodism began as a preaching movement. Its first conferences were gatherings of the preachers "in connexion" with John Wesley. Its first buildings were "preaching houses" designed around proclamation from the pulpit. Its "circuits" were planned as routes for traveling preachers, and its "stations" as points where preachers could take up residence. Its ordinations were inductions into a missionary order of preachers comprising those who covenanted to go where sent.

One could certainly argue that what common discipline United Methodism has for its local churches derives most basically from their status as preaching points. This is most evident in the endurance of the charge conference as the organizing body of the local church. The name "charge" itself refers to a pastoral appointment—"one or more churches . . . to which an ordained or licensed minister is or may be duly appointed" (par. 205.1). All major decisions of a local church, including the election of lay officers, the adoption of building plans, the approval of candidates for ministry, and the establishment of a pastoral salary, must be made in a charge conference authorized and presided over by a representative of the missionary order of preachers, a superintendent of the connection (or his/her designate).

What many Christian congregations would consider their most basic decision—who should be the pastor—is also finally in the hands of the superintendency. While UM local churches have a consultative role, only the bishop has the power to appoint pastors to their charges. Even UM church buildings, which some might consider the real "bottom line" of local church identity, in a sense travel with the connection. UM local church property is defined as a place to which a bishop appoints a UM pastor. That is, property deeds should state that the property is held "in trust" for the UMC; but even if those words are not in the deed, the property of a congregation that has been accepting a pastor under appointment from a bishop is considered part of the connection (par. 2503).

The term "congregation" has been flourishing in UM documents and discourse in recent years. It has found its way into numerous passages in the local church chapter of the *Discipline* and elsewhere in legislation. But from the standpoint of the preaching connection, in no sense can UM local churches be considered as self-constituted entities or as "congregational" in polity.

One could ask, of course, whether this backbone of Methodist tradition is strong enough to hold local church discipline together. The itinerant preaching ministry has been under severe strain for generations, but particularly in the latter half of the twentieth century.

Dual career marriages, increasing numbers of women in ministry, clergy couples, ethnic diversity among the clergy under a mandate of open itinerancy, and divorce rates comparable to the rest of society are among the many factors that have made the appointment system more complex to manage. Meanwhile, as personnel bureaucracies of employment, insurance, and pensions grow, many annual conferences have come to resemble regional business corporations or state merit systems as much as they do missionary orders of preachers.

Yet most United Methodists seem to know, if only by instinct, that to tamper with the itinerancy and all that devolves from it is to touch something essential to Methodism's identity. Perhaps one could argue that the reason General Conference has continually tinkered with local church program for the last twenty-five years is that the connectional polity exemplified in the charge conference cannot be altered without reforming the itinerant system of ministry. Conversely, any fundamental change in the itinerancy would have enormous implications for local church polity.

C. Disciplines of Holy Living

The disciplines practiced by the class meetings and ordered to growth in the knowledge and love of God were John Wesley's bridge between sacramental and evangelical ecclesiologies. In small groups of mutual accountability, Methodist people were encouraged in prayer, searching of Scripture, fasting or abstinence, and worship through word and sacrament. The General Rules of the Methodist societies admonished participants to avoid "evil of every kind, especially that which is most generally practiced," and to do good "of every possible sort." The class leader was the instrument of accountability, visiting "each person in his class once a week at least . . . to inquire how their souls prosper" (par. 62).

These rules and the structures for carrying them out were constitutive of Methodist "societies" for much of the nineteenth century. Even today the General Rules are printed in the *Discipline* and protected from facile changes by a Restrictive Rule (par. 19). But one must ask whether a sense of shared practices of the Christian life provides much common discipline among UM local churches today.

The kind of searching examination typical of early class meetings faded quickly in the American culture of private individualism. It was soon considered invasive and impolite for one lay person to ask another about the state of the other's soul. Class meetings gave way to the school model of church education, specialized by age level, in which one might learn about the faith. Catechism gave way to confirmation as the means by which adolescents could claim their growing adult beliefs. By the turn of the twentieth century the *Discipline's* mandate of a probationary period for church membership was waived in favor of local church options.

In today's UM churches the standards and expectations of membership vary greatly. Some local churches expect new members to attend an orientation class; others simply and poignantly announce after the sermon that "the doors of the church are open" to any who would come into the fellowship. Some conduct rigorous campaigns to make sure that all members make a financial pledge or choose not to; others simply announce financial needs and pray for the Spirit to stir response. Some call on members who have been consistently absent from worship; others leave such matters to individual discretion and make pastoral services available mainly to those who request them.

Local churches offer many formats to encourage growth in faith, from connectionally organized programs such as the Disciple Bible studies, to parachurch movements such as the Walk to Emmaus, to local efforts at prayer, Bible study, and volunteerism. One might even suggest that there is a kind of minimum standard of moral behavior that proscribes substance abuse, illegal activities, or forms of behavior abusive toward others. But it is debatable whether this standard could be differentiated from the ethos of acceptable behavior in the wider community.

One of the more striking changes in *Disciplines* over the course of the century is the migration of "membership" paragraphs from a free-standing section into a chapter entitled "the local church." In earlier days, when one became a "member" one was joining the movement of spiritual discipline and mission called by various names of Methodist. One joined the connection and then participated in a particular local class meeting or society. By midcentury, the *Discipline* made it clear that membership is held in a particular local church with the subsequent declaration that one is also "a member of the global United Methodist connection and a member of the church universal" (par. 216). This reversal of understanding reflected both a "localizing" of UM ministry and mission, and a dilution of consensus around a common discipline of life binding all Methodists together.

Today's *Discipline* provides relatively little guidance for the ministry of the laity. The promising and eloquent text in Part IV on "the ministry of all Christians" comprises only a couple of pages. Paragraphs added in 1996 to advocate "servant leadership" in the church, while unobjectionable in their ideals for "the forming of Christian disciples in the covenant community of the congregation," greatly muddy the distinctive ministries of laity and clergy (pars. 101–16). Only five pithy paragraphs in the local church chapter interpret "the meaning of membership" in general terms (1992, pars. 211–18). They would make a useful teaching document (though they lack any reference to the General Rules or to the text of Part IV).

The UM understanding of church membership, however, will have to be clarified by the 2000 General Conference. The 1996 legislators adopted new definitions of baptized and professing members in keeping with ecumenical ecclesiology and resonating with the earlier Methodist sense of a movement. But the assembly tried to expand the status of baptized Christians as members of the church without examining either the constitutionality of the new membership plan or its implications for other local church legislation. Reformers will have to distinguish more carefully between the rights and responsibilities of baptized and professing members if the distinction is to stand. Are both included, for example, in the qualifications of charge conference members, specifically that they must be "members of the local church" (p. 138)?

D. Mission

A fourth grounding of UM local church ecclesiology rests in the perennial mission activism of the UMC and its predecessor bodies. From the beginning Methodism has been a mission movement, taking as its mandate the first societies' charge, "to reform the nation, particularly the Church, and to spread scriptural holiness over the land" (p. 43). Mission projects in the service of others often galvanize UM people. In the 1980s, just when many voices were saying that denominational mission was moribund, Africa University arose to capture the imagination of many local churches. A small program that began modestly about the same time has blossomed into a Volunteers in Mission effort that has sent thousands of UM people into situations of human need. Mission energies run so high that a second mission society unrelated to the General Board of Global Ministries (and often in tension with it) has enjoyed an abundance of financial and volunteer support from United Methodists.

Mission has often been the rallying point of unity in a church divided over other issues. When Methodist arguments have broken out over the years, dissension in the conference could be quelled or at least postponed by the singing of "Marching to Zion" and the taking of an offering for mission.

On the other hand, mission has often created tension as well, particularly when it has been incorporated as an expression of congregational discipline. The programmatic scheme for the local church adopted and elaborated in the 1960s and '70s, and deleted in 1996, was essentially a plan for organizing local church mission. Its genius was in encouraging local church units for particular dimensions of mission—evangelism, religion and race, Christian unity, and so forth—that would have parallel units in districts, annual conferences, and the general church. This system would create a mutual account-ability and communication remarkable in its capacity for spreading information and for enabling 37,000 local churches to respond to common challenges.

Yet while many local churches found this plan a useful way to involve greater numbers of laity in ministries that were specialized in focus, many others found it burdensome. Many considered the specialization unwarranted and inappropriate for their local context. Organizational charts interpreting the relationship of local church units, together with charge conference report forms detailing the expected church offices, made every local church look like a little bureaucracy of ministry and mission.

Much of the impetus in 1996 for removing paragraphs detailing these ministry "work areas" was driven by a desire for local church initiative. If each local church were free to organize in its own way, then it could respond more decisively to its particular context and best utilize the gifts of its membership. The tradeoff, of course, was that this autonomy dispersed the connectional insistence on certain emphases that might challenge local assumptions. The Constitution retained the mandate of inclusiveness, for example, with its uncompromising declaration that "all persons, without regard to race, color, national origin, status, or economic condition, shall be eligible . . . to be admitted into . . . membership in any local church in the connection" (par. 4). But the 1996 *Discipline* reduced the earlier local church commission or work area on "religion and race" to a mere mention without any definition of duties at all (pars. 254.2.*b*; 256).

The current *Discipline* replaces the scheme of specialized units with a more generalized mandate for the church's mission "to make disciples of Jesus Christ" (p. 114). This statement, which now constitutes a kind of preamble to the local church chapter of legislation, is a rewriting of an earlier mission statement that formerly was placed among the theological documents of the church. Its removal to the local church chapter demonstrates the continuing localization of UM mission initiative. Its emphasis on "disciple-making" instead of the earlier statement's predominant theme of grace demonstrates a striking shift in metaphor, from grace as what God does "for us" that the church witnesses and proclaims to the world, to "making" as a form of production by the church as an organization. Whether the metaphor of "making" will prove compelling to a church whose eclectic ecclesiology also invites metaphors of grace and sacramental substance remains to be seen.

Challenges for General Conferences in 2000 and Beyond

Each of the four sources of common discipline, deeply rooted in Wesleyan and Methodist traditions and practices, contributes something to a shared sense of church. Each is a constitutive element of United Methodist ecclesiology. Yet one could certainly ask whether these four sources are being adequately taught to new generations, or whether their essential contribution to polity is adequately reflected in the current *Book of Discipline.*

Certainly there is fear abroad in the church that coherent discipline is lacking. One response is to advocate a new, more definitive confession of faith to which United Methodist people presumably would declare their allegiance. But United Methodism and the heritages that comprise it have not happily undertaken such doctrinal declarations. In fact, one of Methodism's strengths has been its historic reliance on the Articles of Religion as a kind of confession already made and at hand, leaving the movement free to engage in its distinctive practices of preaching and piety. Some would argue that the Articles are little known and that a contemporary confession of faith is necessary. But surely a compelling counterargument is the inevitable divisiveness of trying to compose words on which such a diverse community of believers would agree.

The church would do better to focus its attention on the practices that compose a common discipline. A lively Christian conversation about practices of worship, prayer, study, and service would bear fruit in a fresh sense of what is expected of church members. One might read the widespread acceptance of the 1989 *Hymnal,* the proliferation of Bible studies, and the thriving interest in small groups as signs of such vitality.

At the same time, the church must attend to the common forms that organize local churches for ministry and mission. The current local church chapter introduces myriad problems of authority and governance. Not only is there inconsistency between local churches and thus a dispersal of connectionalism, but there is now less structure for decision making to which a particular local church may turn for help in resolving internal conflicts.

Three problems come immediately to the forefront, but many others could be named. First, the General Conference has created an anomalous situation for many local churches by forcing them to turn to old *Books of Discipline* for authorization of structures. The administrative board and council on ministries are still optional bodies for local churches, but the *Discipline* now contains no description of them. By tradition and church law, each *Discipline* supersedes the ones before it and the earlier versions are no longer in effect. But many local churches must now turn to earlier *Disciplines* to find out how their governing bodies are to be constituted.

Some church leaders say glibly that each local church has to devise its own structures anyway, so if some use the 1992 *Discipline* as a blueprint it doesn't really matter. The impact of such claims, however, is to force each local church to devise its own by-laws for structures of authority and governance. The next step after that is for each local church to write its own constitution. The next step after that (and it would be a small step at that point) is for United Methodism (or some successor church) to move fully into a congregational polity.

Consider, for example, the 1992 paragraphs elaborating the duties and powers of a council on ministries. Here the process for authorization of new ministries was spelled out—consultation with finance and staff-parish committees, reporting to the administrative board, and so forth (1992, par. 258). The 1996 *Discipline* entirely lacks any such steps, leaving a local church wanting to use a council on ministries or administrative council structure either to rely on the 1992 rules or write its own.

Second, the legislation for the church council is fundamentally ambiguous and inconsistent. In one sentence the *Discipline* declares that the church council is "the executive agency of the charge conference" (par. 254.1). In another sentence is the phrase "if a church chooses to have a church council" (par. 254.4). How can a body be an executive agency if its existence is optional? Or is it really, since another paragraph states that "the basic organizational plan for the local church shall include provision for . . . a church council" (par. 246)?

Moreover, membership in the church council is remarkably fuzzy for such a key body. Unlike the 1992 *Discipline,* the current paragraph does not name as members the presidents of United Methodist Women, Men, or Youth. "Representatives of the nurturing, outreach, and witness ministries of the church" are included, but no offices (such as "chairperson") are named. Nor is it specified whether professional program staff, home missionaries, diaconal ministers, or other persons in designated ministries are to be members (cf. 1992, par. 255).

In place of such specifics is the permissive statement that membership may include "such other persons as the charge conference may determine." Once again, the local church is left largely to its own devices in resolving who has standing or office to serve on its governing council.

Third, the *Discipline* mandates a range of ministry and mission of the local church under the rubrics of nurture, outreach, and witness. Such terms as stewardship, global ministries, health and welfare, Christian unity and interreligious concerns, and communications appear in the text. But in its reforming zeal the General Conference deleted all paragraphs explaining the content to which any of these terms refers.

Thus there is no place to which a local church can turn to discover what these dimensions of ministry entail. They must either rely on old *Disciplines* or look to church publications for explanations. This situation puts the General Board of Discipleship, charged with writing guidelines for local church ministries, in the anomalous position of describing work that the *Discipline* does not specifically authorize. It also greatly increases the burden of the general church agencies that parallel these local church emphases to interpret their mission and communicate the resources they have available to enhance local church work.

In conclusion, one must hope that future General Conferences will take up the task of clarifying these matters. But above all, the UMC must face up to the greatest teaching challenge in its history. Generations of UM folk have dined on a rich, eclectic stew of varied understandings of church that together made for a distinctive ecclesiology. Today's United Methodists must learn the recipe well and teach it to their children, so that generations to come may be welcomed and fed at the table of "the people called Methodist."

Are the Local Church and Denominational Bureaucracy "Twins"?

Russell E. Richey

Interesting proposals for reform of United Methodism have surfaced recently, proposals that would free the local church from the perceived burden of remote, inflexible, centralized, hierarchical rule by boards and agencies; from the obligation to render up apportionments to this Caesar; from the yoke of mandated denominational structure.

This essay responds by suggesting that such analyses and antidotes are insufficient. Specifically, it proposes:

- that such analyses and antidotes only go halfway with treatment;
- that the local church and national denominational bureaucracy are twins, both generated out of the organizational revolution;
- that recovery of Wesleyan connectionalism at the local level requires as much sustained criticism of "the local church" as of bureaucracy;
- that such recovery or renewal is already well underway and pointing toward a new connectionalism normed on neither the corporate state nor congregationalism; and
- that a renewed connectionalism at the local level can help us reclaim some of the long-lost potential of our polity and our ecclesiology.

The Local Mission: A Retrospective

Early American Methodism knew what congregations and parishes were. The one epitomized church for New England Puritanism, the other typified Southern Anglicanism and much of western Christendom. Methodism opposed both, took a different form, and committed itself constitutionally to a more radical vision of church. It had no congregations and certainly no parishes. To be sure, it built or purchased preaching houses from its earliest days. But they were just that, houses for preaching. Except in rare (urban) instances, these small chapels did not center the movement at the local level; circumscribe the range of Methodist life, service, and mission; or command the services of a single preacher, even for his tenure in that locale. Preaching houses were just that, houses for preaching. And they had no monopoly on that.

232

Much of Methodist life, including the preaching, went on in houses for living. In homes, Methodists baptized, prayed, met, married, educated, and conducted funerals. Much of the early preaching as well went on in the houses in which converts lived. And the chapels not only resembled the houses amongst which they nestled but often took their name from the family chiefly responsible for erecting them—as Asbury's notation of their names indicates. When the crowd exceeded what a home or chapel would hold, preachers took the assemblage outside or to another denomination's facilities or to a public building. Such large gatherings—akin to today's Sunday worship—occurred infrequently, typically for quarterly meetings or camp meetings, which were often one and the same. On those occasions, presiding elders, preachers, local preachers, and exhorters would conduct the business of the circuit, hold love feasts, preach frequently, celebrate the Lord's Supper, and sometimes conduct memorial services. Methodist life did not center itself in its little buildings but rather was decentered and diffused across the Methodist landscape and was temporally rather than spatially centered in the weekly class, regular preaching, and liturgically rich quarterly conferences.

If Methodism did not locate itself in its buildings, it also did not confine itself in congregations or societies. The basic local unit of Methodist life, the unit to which one belonged, was not the society, but the class. And the next recognized unit of Methodist life, recognized by the *Discipline,* was not the society but the quarterly conference. To be sure, classes might, indeed did, associate into societies, but the unit most closely resembling the official definition of church—where the Word was preached, sacraments administered, and discipline exercised—was the quarterly conference, a regional affair, typically embracing multiple societies.

The following chart from the 1820s depicts Methodism as an array of orbits within orbits, the spin of one affecting and being affected by that of all others. The picture displays the interrelatedness of connectional life. For present purposes, it also makes a powerful statement by a signal omission. It simply omits anything resembling the local church, congregation or, for that matter, society. Methodism orbits from class to circuit, without housing itself, so to speak, in building or society. Methodism imaged itself, after the vision of Ezekiel, as intact, complete, integrated, whole, perfect—without the congregation.

Figure 1

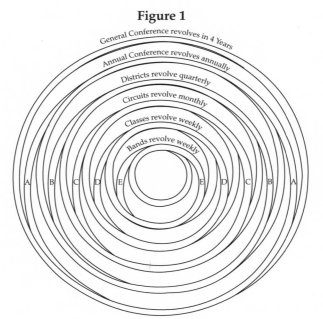

The point is not to deny the prevalence of societies, to suggest that early Methodists lacked a rich local life, or to attribute its strength to the preachers rather than those who gathered. Quite the contrary, it is to assert that Methodist life was too dynamic, lay-centered, and cooperative to be cooped up within congregations. Missional, flexible, adaptive, expansive, pluraform, decentralized, Methodism conducted its mission there, its education yonder, its baptisms and funerals here, its preaching over there, and so forth. And such a decentralized movement could and did embrace black and white, rich and poor, male and female, English- and German-speaking.

Should Methodism Emulate the Calvinists?

Some thought that this pattern of local connectionalism explained Methodist success and urged the church to maintain its simple, open, itinerant, camping style. Others, including Nathan Bangs, who as theoretician of the first phase of Methodism's organizational revolution and Methodism's first great historian, thought that Methodism ought to build churches so as "to occupy the young and thriving villages which were rising into being by the hand of industry." He asserted:

> In these countries the Methodist preachers were the gospel pioneers, and for many years, in various places, the people had no other preachers who

"cared for their souls." They were accustomed to go among them in their lonely retreats, preach in their log huts, hold their quarterly meetings in barns or in the woods, and they seemed to have been so long accustomed to this mode of preaching and living, that they almost forgot, in many instances, to provide themselves with better accommodations; and before they were aware of it, other denominations came, took possession of the villages, erected houses of worship, and thus drew the weightier part of population around them.[1]

Following Bangs's counsel, Methodism did increasingly orient itself toward the weightier and wealthier. In towns and cities, it abandoned what Kenneth Rowe has termed "its side street" chapels for proper "main street" churches. In the period before and after the Civil War, Methodism erected elegant, often Gothic, cathedrals. Such ventures lay beyond the capacity of the simpler, cellular class structure of earlier Methodism and were the expression of a new "congregational" style. Real *congregations* emerged, claimed the growing numbers of Methodists "on the make," demanded and got a stationed, more educated clergy, and kept clergy longer. And a stationed clergy increasingly took over the roles previously played by the class leaders and local preachers. Neither disappeared overnight, but throughout the middle decades of the nineteenth century various appeals to reclaim the class system document its peril. Some of the advocates of that older Methodism—a Methodism of class, quarterly meeting, camp meeting, and perfection—raised the holiness banner and took a separatist course. The mainstream of Methodism, however, moved, gradually at first, then more rapidly, to constitute itself like its competition—in congregations.

National Structures

Consolidation into congregations not only meant de-emphasizing Wesleyan classes. It also entailed coming to terms with voluntary societies. Bangs had led Methodism into creating missionary societies and an effective communication system through *Advocates,* the *Methodist Quarterly Review,* and more sophisticated employment of Sunday schools. At the local level, the missionary and reform societies—men's and women's—and the Sunday schools offered new roles for the laity and an array of purposive gatherings not well integrated into the local connectional system. With such institutions and roles, as with the class, the settled pastor and the stable congregation experienced problems—of accountability, control, authority. Such problems and issues derived from the fact that the new dynamic entities did not mesh with or report to the existing authority structure and from the fact that the existing authority structure remained the old quarterly meeting. In 1852 the MEC dealt with part of the problem by providing a seat for "male superintendents of our Sunday schools . . . in the Quarterly Conferences . . . with the right to speak and vote on questions relating to Sunday schools, and on such questions only."[2] In 1864, the northern church made the superintendent a full member and granted the Quarterly Conference "supervision of all the Sunday-schools and Sunday-school societies within its bounds."[3]

Such problems in accountability ran up and down the connectional structure, and in 1872 the MEC moved to attack them at a national level by bringing its five major benevolent societies—the Missionary Society, the Church Extension Society, the Board of Education, the Sunday-School Union and the Tract Society—"under the control of the General Conference." It did so by seeking necessary legal and legislative measures that would change each entity's charter and provide for General Conference election of its trustees or managers. This was the key maneuver in the organizational revolution by which Methodism achieved modern boards and agencies.[4] Three General Conferences later, the church effected the comparable revolution at the local level. It authorized quarterly conferences to "organize, and continue during its pleasure, an Official Board, to be composed of all the members of the Quarterly Conference," to be "presided over by the preacher in charge," to discharge many of the duties of the Leaders and Stewards' Meeting, and to "keep a record of its proceedings."[5] The creation of the official board brought to the local church what incorporation, consolidation, efficiency, bureaucratization, and professionalization brought to the church as a whole and, indeed, to American society, that is, corporate principles of finance, procedure, order, integration, governance, and cohesion. Bureaucratization at the top and business efficiency in the local church went together. Indeed, they were twins.

Institutional Churches

The fruits of this development at the local level emerged a decade later during the social gospel epoch in what were termed "institutional churches" (and were called "central halls" in Britain). These were large-scale church complexes, resembling the typical suburban or urban congregation of today, with sanctuary, educational wing, community service accommodations, kitchens, child-care facilities, and the like, and with a strong weekday as well as weekend program. Methodist life had fully moved from houses for living into houses for worship. Here was "the local church" we know today:

- a complex religious matrix incorporated or recognized as a single entity,
- functioning with a parish-like orientation to its geographical surroundings,
- channeling through its life the local mission efforts of the denomination,
- covering with its umbrella and governing structures a great variety of groups, missionary associations, benevolent causes, and educational endeavors (especially Sunday school),
- featuring one or more assemblies for weekly worship,
- owning or holding effective control over a building or buildings capable of housing the variety of weekly gatherings for worship, educational, service, and outreach ministries,
- understanding itself as a corporate religious body capable of, and perhaps charged with, exercising communal leadership,
- channeling through its budget(s) the monies raised locally for its own purposes and services and those of denominational and ecumenical boards, and
- existing under the guidance of lay and clergy leaders who share accountability for these local efforts under Methodist mandate.

The turn-of-the-century "institutional church" consolidated and incorporated the distinguishable, diverse, sometimes discrete expressions of local religion. And the prevalence of this form of the church today, reinforced by the American predilection for local rule and by principled congregationalism, makes the congregation as intellectual construct seem to be *the*, and *the only*, modality of local religiosity. Today, it just seems natural that local religious functions will center in a single "congregation."

Unease in Zion

All during this period of developing congregationalism, bishops and other leaders complained of the compromise of itinerancy and the appointive system. In 1912, for instance, in their episcopal address the bishops noted how congregational interests distorted the Methodist understanding of ministry. They argued, "The Christian ministry is not a profession," and therefore its should not be upheld "on the secular basis of compensation," that is salary.

> Methodist preachers are "supported," not hired. The difference is vital. A "support" is the sum estimated, *for a pastor already appointed*, by an authorized committee after consultation with the pastor, as sufficient to furnish himself and family a comfortable livelihood. Under this plan

consecration is not compromised, and the preacher's message may weigh
its full gospel value.

"Salary," on the other hand, implies a stated stipend proposed as
compensation for services to be rendered, fixed before the service begins
and as a condition to its beginning at all.

The "contract is not with the Official Board or Quarterly Conference. It
is an altar covenant with God alone." They complained of
"negotiations," asked "What yet remains of the system?" and
denounced the commercialization of pulpit service:

> Thus is pulpit service commercialized, and thus in time every prominent
> preacher is practically appraised, and not always by the gospel standard of
> success. His "rank" or appoint availability in cabinet is determined—
> himself, alas! too often consenting, by lay valuation in dollars and
> prospects.[6]

The bishops concerned themselves with the terms of the contract, the
monetary assessment of clergy, rather than the structural reality—the
congregationalism—that interposed a contracting entity into the
Methodism economy. Congregationalism and the official board rather
than the contracting spirit might have been a more effective target.

Instead, the bishops accepted "the local church" and the power
thereof as part of Methodist parlance and as much a given as its twin,
the national boards and agencies, with which they also contended. The
term "local church" crept into Methodist talk and became a touchstone
for judging Methodist work, integrity, purpose. Nowhere was its new
value better expressed than in the 1928 episcopal address (MEC). The
bishops recognized the new norm for Methodism—the local
church—by organizing their speech around it. They entitled the first
long section: "The Local Church and What It May Ask of General
Methodism." They affirmed:

> The local church is taken as the unit in our study of denominational
> progress, for it is there that we are to test the value of our organization and
> polity. It is the point of Methodism's contact with humanity. It is our
> recruiting office for the King's service. It is for us the institute of religious
> technology, our workshop, our training camp, our spiritual hospital, our
> home.[7]

Here, rhetorically and theologically, the bishops completed the long
process of redefining local Methodism. Methodism would be at home
not with its people and in their homes but "at home" in its buildings, its
congregations, its fortresses. Fittingly, they employed military language
to describe local Methodism's institutionalization ("training camp,"

"recruiting office," "point of contact," "service") and these nuanced the other terms ("hospital," "workshop," "technology") with military force.

The bishops devoted major subsections to the church building, members (of all ages), finances, the office, the pastor and pastoral office, laity, and educational institutions (within which they discussed the whole range of Methodist schools and colleges, not just local or intra-church education). In the next major section, the bishops explored "What the Local Church Owes to General Methodism," only then turning to "What World-Wide Methodism Asks of the World" and "What World-Wide Methodism Owes to the World." In the first two sections, the bishops had embraced Methodism within the local church; in the latter two, the bishops revisited major issues in relation to national bureaucracy. Rhetorically, the bishops had recognized the twins of the organizational revolution.

Adjusting the Discipline

Such episcopal statements played a vital role in the long process of obliterating the connectional principle that had once knit Methodism into a series of gatherings—band, class, quarterly conference, annual conference, and general conference—and replacing it with a series of corporate structures—local church, district office, conference staff and agencies, (jurisdictional staff?), and national boards and agencies. The *Discipline* gradually recognized the linguistic changes and institutional realities. For instance, in 1920, the church quietly interred the quarterly conference with a constitutional amendment changing "quarterly" to "local."[8] And in 1940, as one of the first acts of the newly jurisdictioned and united Methodism, the General Conference authorized the incorporation into one section of the *Discipline* all the various references to local Methodism that had been described under the many rubrics and aspects of Methodism's work:

> Motion of Alfred F. Hughes (West Wisconsin), duly seconded, prevailed that the Editors of the *Discipline* be instructed to bring together in one Section of the *Discipline* legislation referring specifically to the Organization and Administration of the local Church.

A subsequent motion (referred to the Committee on Publishing Interests) asked the editors to "consider publishing an inexpensive edition of said *Discipline* containing only those assembled Sections referring to the Local Church."[9]

The church achieved such salience for that part of the *Discipline* without dropping everything else out. With the 1944 *Discipline*, "The Local Church" became Part II of the Discipline, immediately following

"The Constitution" and preceding Part III, "The Ministry," and Part IV, "The Conferences." In the 1968 *Discipline,* "The Local Church" stood first, embracing even calendar, thus incorporating Methodist time into a congregational orbit. And in 1976 that section expanded to include the discussion of ministry, a symbolical reframing of Wesleyan horizons; Wesley had spoken of the world as his parish; now Methodism indeed made parish its world. Was this the end to which Wesley intended itinerancy or just the end of itinerancy?

The church appropriately recognizes the new norm—congregationalism—by construing local church as *the* primary form of ministry and construing anything and everything else with a new, now technical, phrase, "appointments beyond the local church." This trend produced the episcopal pastoral, *Vital Congregations—Faithful Disciples.* It culminates in the recent proposals to give the local church control over apportionments and appointments, effectively collapsing the connectional into the congregation.

Implications

It would be in the spirit of the recent proposals concerning the local church to move in the 2000 General Conference: (1) that the local church rather than the annual conference constitutes the basic unit of the church, and (2) that—to rephrase the motion of 1944—"we publish **as the** . . . *Discipline* . . . only those . . . Sections referring to the Local Church." Such motions would complete, constitutionally, the collapse of connectionalism into institutionalized congregationalism. This would be a mistake, as, I believe, are a variety of equally congregational but less dramatic recent proposals.

Methodism deserves better, both for its local mission and its wider witness. The question is not what is to be done at local level, nor really where money might be spent. The issue has to do with agency, control, limits, horizon, permission, expansiveness. Fundamental is housing. Where will Methodism be "at home"? Will it be at home only in its buildings, under corporate management, controlled by pastors, programmed only from one center, hemmed in by local bureaucratic procedure, preoccupied with accountability? Or will Methodism re-enter the homes of its people, and more important, the people who need to hear its message? Will it move out of its buildings into its neighborhoods? Will it become again too dynamic, lay-centered, and cooperative to be cooped up within a congregation? Will it reclaim its missional, flexible, adaptive, expansive, pluraform, decentralized, ecclesial principle?

Fortunately, we see signs that the answer is "Yes." That Wesleyan spirit we can see clearly at work in a variety of new efforts that work vitally at local levels but reconnect us nationally in new dynamic forms of gathering and witness. Such reconceiving and reanchoring the connection can be seen in the Disciple Bible Study, Emmaus Walk, Covenant Discipleship, the Academy for Spiritual Formation, Chrysalis, Volunteers in Mission, Good News, and the several caucuses, Reconciling Congregations, and a variety of efforts, particularly in urban ministry, some specifically Methodist, others ecumenical. Many would think of these as essentially local. Each has connectional leadership as well as powerful local expression. Each moves beyond the walls of our buildings to find "new homes" for religious expression. Each draws in and equips fresh leadership. Each beckons the whole of Methodism to a new spirit and to renewal.

A Methodism that moves out of "the local church" will, I believe, recover its reforming and evangelistic style. The local church "killed" one of our main engines of evangelism and outreach, the local preacher. It "killed" the office by bottling up within the congregation and making accountable to a congregational "official board" an office and persons that had been deployed regionally and on the circuit. Ironically, now it is the Southern Baptists who are rediscovering the office (now termed bivocationality), who are creating house churches and putting ministers on circuit to apartment gatherings. Methodism can also reclaim its evangelical heritage if it also reclaims its proper, Wesleyan notion of home and connection. Doing so does not mean abandoning existing buildings or congregations. Far from it. These constitute resources for local mission. The question is whether we will ask about that local mission, about where it calls us to be, about what it calls us to do. Will we put the same hard questions to "the local church" that we are now putting to boards and agencies? They are, after all, twins.

How Do Caucuses Contribute to Connection?

Kenneth E. Rowe

When United Methodists gathered for their first General Conference in Atlanta in 1972, they found themselves struggling to understand what it meant to be a pluralistic as well as a united church. The large number of persons wearing badges and buttons, handing out newsletters and buttonholing delegates startled many, including one bishop with whom I had breakfast in the middle of the first week. "Caucuses, quotas, and politics—how new, how un-Methodist" he fussed as we chatted about conference goings-on. The casual conversation that morning led me to two decades of reflection the matter of dissent and reform in the Methodist tradition—everything from gentle persuasion to the religious equivalent of civil disobedience.

Methodism was born as a caucus within the Evangelical Revival in the eighteenth century. The British wing of the revival early split into parties—Arminian and Calvinist. Despite shared assumptions about the primacy of Scripture, the need for personal conversion and holy living, each caucus concocted its own version of evangelicalism and set forth its own plan to renew persons and revive churches. Wesley's party platform, hammered out by trial and error over many years, aimed to train converts in the ancient spiritual arts and to connect them to each other and to him in a network of religious societies.

Methodism spawned caucuses as soon as it became an establishment at the end of the eighteenth century. Following Wesley's death, on both sides of the Atlantic, Methodism split into two rival parties, the denomination or church party, which stressed authority and wanted to close down the reforms, and the revival party, which stressed the charismatic gifts and wanted to continue the reforms. The church has been burdened or blessed by caucuses ever since—Methodist mavericks, square-peg EUB, untied Methodists. Caucus fever continues to infect large numbers of United Methodists, as the most recent history attests. Except in the Victorian era, when the principal caucuses were welcomed into the family and even written into the *Book of Discipline,* caucus-types and establishment-types have been at odds. At any given moment in our history the several caucuses have lived together under an uneasy truce. The tension between independence

242

and authority, between renewalist and immobilist, led to much trouble and several schisms.

There is something of Wesley in the caucus strain. It was Wesley's own stubborn commitment to Christian principle that led him to tinker with the structures of the Church of England and fashion fresh models of evangelism and Christian nurture. It was Wesley's impatient sense of missional emergency that led him to license lay women and men to preach and then to ordain some of them to administer the sacraments among his scattered flock in the North American colonies. Wesley was a nuisance to all bureaucrats, bishops, and complacent institutionalists who value structure over spirit, order over life, protocol over piety. Although by nature conservative and reluctant to change institutions, he nevertheless—and with accelerating power—changed inherited patterns of church life to fit the changing needs under the gospel. The spirit of independence carried over into many of his spiritual children. However not all possessed as much of his discipline as they did of his independence.

There is something of Otterbein in the caucus strain. Like Wesley, Otterbein felt compelled to alter inherited patterns of piety of the German Reformed Church in the interest of renewed lives and revived churches, first in Ockersdorf in his native Germany, then in Lancaster, and finally and fully in Baltimore. When, on the eve of the Revolution, his concern for the churchless Germans in the rural areas of Pennsylvania and Maryland drove him to travel out to preach in their barns and in their fields, he got "in Dutch" with his ministerial colleagues—Reformed and Lutheran, Moravian, and Mennonite. A few years later, when Asbury pushed Methodist-style organization on the "brethren" who united around him, Otterbein balked. He preferred to allow the preachers and people as much individual prerogative and initiative as possible. Horror of hierarchy was a hallmark of his United Brethren well into this century.

There is little of Asbury in the caucus strain. Methodism's founding bishop may have looked like a caucus-type when he insisted on being elected bishop by his colleagues at the Christmas Conference despite the fact that Wesley named him to the post. But once in office he quickly fashioned an imperial approach to episcopacy. Under his leadership the *Book of Discipline* rapidly expanded from a thirty-five page appendix to a much larger book in 1785 (Wesley's *Prayer Book*) to almost 250 pages in 1792, a gain of more than two hundred pages of rules and regulations in eight short years! All of this legislation was vigorously enforced by Asbury with military precision. Once the rules were set in print and in motion, talk of change was barely tolerated. Caucus types headed for their closets.

With that much as, I hope, a tantalizing introduction, my essay unfolds under five headings:

1. Inventing Methodism in the Age of Revolution (1760–1808): Caucuses Appear
2. Defending Methodism in the Early Republic (1808–1866): Caucuses Exit
3. Reforming Methodism at the Centennial (1866–1900): Caucuses Welcomed
4. Celebrating Methodism in a New Century (1900–1968): Caucuses Closeted
5. Lamenting Methodism at the Bicentennial (1968–): Caucus Fever

1. Inventing Methodism in the Age of Revolution (1760–1808): Caucuses Appear

Caucuses by definition have to do with policies, policies have to do with politic, and politics have to do with power. The new church in the new nation had no clearly defined or well-established power centers or system of governance. Two power centers emerged early and competed for power—the bishops and the conferences of preachers. The precise role of bishops was not spelled out, and their relationship to the conference was unclear. Did legislative power reside in the conference of preachers, and executive power in the episcopacy? Were the bishops amenable to the conference, or were they an equal and coordinate authority?

The preachers in America met annually in conference since 1773. As the church followed the frontier, those nearest to the site of the conference predominated in decision making. To respond to this situation several conferences, not just one, were established until at any one time there were more than a half dozen regional (later annual) conferences held each year. Parliamentarily this meant that for any action to be binding on the whole church, it had to be endorsed by every regional conference. This concurrent conference plan continued until 1792 among the Methodists, until 1815 among the United Brethren, and until 1816 among the Evangelicals, when a pattern of quadrennial General Conferences was established.

The conflict between bishops and conferences was particularly intense among the Methodists. The matter came to a head in 1789 when Bishop Asbury proposed that a council of presiding elders chaired by him should handle all matters of doctrine and discipline for the whole church. The defects for freedom-loving Americans—preachers and layfolk—were obvious. Since the presiding elders were appointed by Asbury, they were not representatives of the rank and file. The composition and control of the proposed council would be solely in Asbury's hands. After much hew and cry Asbury bowed to pressure and agreed to call a general conference of preachers in the fall of 1792 to resolve the dilemma of who was in charge.

All of the traveling preachers were invited to attend and vote on all matters of doctrine and discipline. The chief architect of this new plan was not Asbury but James O'Kelly. In the years immediately following the Christmas Conference, O'Kelly was Asbury's chief lieutenant in the southern states. Increasingly O'Kelly felt that unless the power of Asbury to manage the conferences and to appoint the preachers was curtailed, some of the best preachers and lay people would be lost. He and other like-minded colleagues, especially William Hammett of Charleston, argued for the right of clergy to appeal their appointment, for an elective versus appointive presiding eldership, and for conference rights for "local," i.e., lay, pastors.

When the preachers gathered in Baltimore for Methodism's first General Conference in November of 1792, the O'Kelly caucus and the Asbury caucus were ready for a show-down fight. The O'Kelly forces won round one when Asbury's council plan was soundly defeated. But when O'Kelly's motion to ease the absolute appointive power of the bishop lost, the O'Kelly caucus and the Hammett caucus walked out and formed independent churches. Not surprisingly, the O'Kelly-ites called their new church the *Republican* Methodist Church, while the Hammett-ites called their church the *Primitive* Methodist Church. No lone mavericks, O'Kelly and Hammett took with them significant numbers of clergy and lay members, especially in Virginia and the Carolinas, where they were revered. A pamphlet war between "Republican" and "Primitive" Methodists and "Episcopal" Methodists waged for a decade. To calm things down Asbury published *Causes, Evils, and Cures of Heart and Church Divisions*, extracted from British divines Richard Baxter and Jeremiah Burroughs.[1]

Four more General Conferences were held between 1792 and 1808. But this plan of governance also had problems. From the preachers' point of view, General Conference membership was unequal and unfair, since preachers close to the conference site predominated. From the bishops' point of view it was unsafe. The chief features of Methodist polity—episcopacy, itinerancy, and the appointive power, etc.—were vulnerable. A simple majority vote at any one time could profoundly alter the governance pattern of the new church. There was, from Asbury's point of view, no *safe* power center.

By 1808, when the preachers gathered for a General Conference in Baltimore, the inoperability of the previous experiment in governance was obvious and forced the naming of the church's first governance study committee. A committee of fourteen was appointed on the first day to draft a "constitution" for the church. Their report, much debated but finally adopted, significantly altered the two principal authority centers in the church. For the first time there was a clear delineation of powers in a formal constitution. Bishops were to have presidential, executive, and administrative duties. Legislative powers were vested in a delegated quadrennial General Conference. Most important of all for our study of the caucus strain, "restrictive rules" were added to safeguard the heart of the system.

In essence, Methodism's polity canon closed in 1808. Only two major changes have been made to the church's basic constitution in the next century and three-quarters—lay representation beginning in 1866 (MECS) and 1872 (MEC), and jurisdictional conferences in 1939. A hefty book of discipline complete with a constitution protected by "restrictive rules" made it almost impossible to make any fundamental changes in the church's doctrine and discipline. The future of the caucus tradition seemed dim. But, as we shall see, almost as quickly as the conservatives adopted the constitution, caucus-types rose up to challenge the system.

The development of power centers proceeded more slowly and along different lines among the United Brethren. Although the final shape was similar to the Methodist plan—leadership by bishops and policy by conferences—the spirit was different, more voluntary than mandatory, more room for local and lay initiative.

Formal organization of the "Albright people" came quickly. Four years after Albright's followers declared themselves an independent religious society, the 1807 conference asked ailing Albright to prepare a book of discipline. Albright, who admired Methodism's discipline and Asbury's style, did not live to complete the task. His successor, George Miller, proposed to the 1808 annual conference an Asbury-sponsored German translation of the Methodist discipline published in Lancaster earlier that year. With minor adjustments, Albright's preachers adopted it and ordered its publication to guide their life together. Although published in 1808, the Asbury-sponsored German discipline was the 1804 version, so the Evangelicals did not inherit the Methodist restrictive rules.

2. Defending Methodism in the Early Republic (1808–1866): Caucuses Exit

By 1808 the Methodists, and to a lesser extent the Evangelicals and United Brethren, had become establishments. Almost unconsciously they had become immobilist in temper and procedure, heavy on discipline and harsh on dissenters. And this was justified by the stable conviction of the leaders of each of the three churches that any change would be for the worse; since "the system" as it stood was so nearly perfect, it needed no radical reformation. "Guard against innovation," Asbury counseled junior bishop and heir apparent McKendree in 1813. "Alas for us if our excellent constitution and order of things be changed or corrupted."[2] Besides, Francis Asbury and Nathan Bangs were having enough trouble beating off attacks from without—from Congregationalists, Presbyterians, Baptists, and Episcopalians in particular—to tolerate any from within.

Caucuses were not absent in this period, especially among the Methodists. So inflexible were the sons and daughters of Asbury that in almost every decade between 1810 and the Civil War they had a full-blown church fight that led to schism. The decade of the 1810s saw the rise of three independent black Methodist denominations. Peter Spencer's Baltimore-based African Union Methodist Church pulled out first in 1813. Richard Allen's Philadelphia-based African Methodist Episcopal Church exited in 1816, after a long and bitter battle over control of black church property and failure to ordain black elders. James Varick's New York-based African Methodist Episcopal Zion Church did the same by the end of the decade, although ordinations were delayed until 1822. In each case governance issues were mixed with racial issues.

Both the beginning and the end of the same decade—the 1810s—were marked by schism on the Euro-American side as well. Anti-slavery, antiwar, anticonnectional Methodists in upstate New York and New England, led by Elijah Bailey, organized the Reformed Methodist Church in 1814, and the Stillwell brothers, Samuel and William, led anticonnectional Methodists in New York City out of the fold by in the early 1820s. By 1825 the new church (called simply the Methodist Society) numbered 864 members in New York City and claimed over 2,000 members in the whole denomination, which had spread to Long Island, Connecticut, and New Jersey.[3] They were relatively minor schisms compared to the larger ones that were brewing in Baltimore, Pittsburgh, and Raleigh.

Asbury's death in 1816 signaled to Methodist caucus-types that they might now get a better hearing, so out of the closets they came.

The next General Conference (1820) literally met over Asbury's dead body. He was then buried under the pulpit of Eutaw Street M.E. Church, Baltimore, where the General Conference gathered that year. The reform caucus rallied around three issues during that conference and kept them on the agendas of cabinets and conferences for the rest of the decade—an elective presiding eldership, conference rights for local pastors (who by that time outnumbered itinerant elders three to one), and—most explosive of all—lay representation in the clergy-dominated conferences. The reform caucus gained a momentary victory in 1820 when the General Conference voted in favor of electing presiding elders. However, when the propriety and constitutionality of the legislation was questioned by bishop-elect Soule (chief drafter of the constitution of 1808), the conference declined to implement its new plan and the bishop-elect went unconsecrated. The matter was reconsidered at the next General Conference (1824), but the reformers lost by a close vote and Soule was at last consecrated a bishop. In the quadrennium that followed, the establishment responded to the challenge with gag rules, punitive appointments, and church trials. When the third General Conference of the decade (1828) refused to reform the episcopal office or to admit the principle of lay representation, the reformers withdrew in large numbers and formed the Methodist Protestant Church—with no bishops but conference presidents elected annually, appointment of pastors by a committee of clergy, and equal numbers of lay and clergy representatives in all of their governing conferences.

During the 1830s slavery and constitutional questions became intertwined in an increasingly bitter decade, which would erupt into schism twice in the following decade. Methodists bent on abolishing slavery as well as bishops exited to form the Wesleyan Methodist Church in 1842. Two years later, a major explosion occurred when Methodists north and south divided over the twin issues of slavery and episcopacy.

In the 1850s compromises on the issue of slavery, the reemergence of the lay liberation lobby, and debate over the Wesleyan doctrine of perfect love conspired to raise still more church fights. At the end of the decade (1860), the charismatic leader of an expelled band of mavericks, Benjamin T. Roberts, formed the Free Methodist Church, which proclaimed freedom for blacks as well as freedom from bishops and promised free pews as well as free grace.

3. *Reforming Methodism at the Centennial (1866–1900):*
Caucuses Welcomed

Midcentury Methodists, Evangelicals, and United Brethren could not relax and savor their success. Although each was big and getting bigger, many agreed, established ways of doing things needed to change if the churches were to attract growing numbers of upwardly mobile Americans. This time mother Methodism could afford to listen and even to bend. The church of Bishop Asbury and Editor Bangs faded away; the church of Bishop Simpson, Educator Vincent, and Administrator Kynett was taking shape.

Methodists celebrated not one but two centennials in the years following the Civil War—1866 and 1884. In the intervening twenty years the Methodist family of churches took steps to reform themselves with the help of several energetic caucuses. No caucus was more visible and vocal in the post–Civil War churches than women. Public participation in the abolition movement before the war led women to press for increased participation in their churches after the war. Methodist, Evangelical, and United Brethren women mapped strategy to battle their male-dominated churches on two fronts: the struggle for laity rights (the right to vote and to hold any lay office in the church) and the struggle for clergy rights (the right to a theological education, to ordination, to a parish or missionary appointment, and to hold any clergy office from pastor to bishop).

As the first half of the century ran its course, women grew impatient with their sharply curtailed role in missions. Concerned about the degrading state of their own sex among "the heathen," women wanted to have a say in the management of the church's missionary enterprise and to be sent as missionaries. After raising missionary money for fifty years for the men to spend, in the spring of 1869 Methodist Episcopal women organized a Woman's Foreign Missionary Society, the first of eight independent women's home and foreign missionary societies in the Methodist, Evangelical, and United Brethren family of churches organized between 1869 and 1890. The formation of each one of them sent shivers up and down the spines of male bishops and bureaucrats who fared the loss of power and financial boycott. Within a few years of their founding, however, each of these new societies was adopted by a male-dominated conferences and made a part of each denomination's structure, required in each local church.

As America's cities grew under the impact of industry and immigration, urban churches became islands surrounded by a sea of strangers. Women saw the usefulness of home missionary societies and even a religious order of women trained to serve the physical and spiritual needs of the new urban population. Once Methodist, Evangelical, and United Brethren women accepted the logic of their own reasoning, they approached the hierarchy with their plans for home missionary societies and Deaconess orders. After failing to get a hearing at the 1880 General Conference, Methodist Episcopal women, without authorization, organized a Woman's Home Missionary Society and recruited the first lady of the land, Mrs. Rutherford B. Hayes, to be their first president. When the General Conference met again in 1884, it made the WHMS part of the church's growing family of general agencies with local church units. The pattern was repeated in other branches of the family over the next few years.

Women were less successful on other fronts. When the battle for lay representation in the General Conference was finally won by the Methodists (1866 for the MECS and 1872 for the MEC) women were disqualified as lay delegates. Beginning in the 1860s a growing number of Methodist women held local preacher's licenses, the first step to ordained ministry. By 1880 two women (Anna Oliver and Anna Howard Shaw) had graduated from one of the church's new theological seminaries. In an immobilist mood the 1880 General Conference of the MEC declared these licenses invalid and told its women they were not eligible for ordination. During these years only the Methodist Protestant and the United Brethren opened their seminaries and their pulpits to women.

Organizations for men also became a fixture of Victorian Methodist church life, but not without the efforts of several energetic men's caucuses. Precise origins of the men's "brotherhood" movement are elusive. Half a dozen "brotherhoods" sprang up among the Methodists during the centennial decade (1880s). The Wesley Brotherhood appears to be the oldest, having been founded in Philadelphia in the early 1880's by a pastor, later bishop, Thomas B. Neely. As the decade wore on, the number of rival brotherhoods grew. Largest of all by the turn of the century was the Brotherhood of St. Paul, founded in Little Falls, NY, by a pastor, later bishop, Frederick D. Leete. A cross between the Masons and the men's Bible class, each brotherhood tried to outdo the other with snazzy regalia, inspiring rituals, and snappy mottoes. The Wesley Brotherhood gets the prize, I think, for the snappiest motto: "Methodist Men Making the Mind of the Master their Main Motive and Mission."

At the turn of the century, the competing brotherhoods increasingly felt the need to form one churchwide brotherhood. A convention to bury the hatchet met appropriately in Union M.E. Church, Philadelphia in 1898, and where a single brotherhood was established. Proposals to the General Conference to adopt the organization and incorporate it into the church's official structure were not successful until 1908. By that time the hierarchy realized the men were serious and that their energy needed to be channeled and controlled. So another caucus was adopted by the establishment. The ME General Conference in Buffalo that year, 1908, made the thousand-chapter Methodist Brotherhood official, and a paragraph was added to the *Book of Discipline* making mandatory the formation of a chapter in each local church. An Otterbein Brotherhood for United Brethren men was organized the next year, 1909. The Evangelical Church delayed organizing its Albright Brotherhood until 1930.

Young people were another energy center in the Victorian era eager to work in and for their church. In 1884 John Vincent, of Sunday-school and Chautauqua fame, later a bishop, organized a national youth ministry organization modeled on Wesley's Holy Club. The goals of Vincent's Oxford League were to promote biblical and literary study, to build religious and moral character, and to train middle-class teenagers in the arts of "mercy and help." In 1889 in Cleveland the Oxford League merged with several other competing Methodist youth organizations to form the Epworth League. A year later the M.E. Church, South organized its own Epworth League along similar lines. By 1896 over 20,00 local chapters had been established in local churches. The Evangelical Association formed a Young People's Alliance in 1891, and the United Brethren formed a Young People's Union two years later—in each case, not without the pressure of an organized youth-ministry caucus.

Methodism's campus ministry organization, the Wesley Foundation movement, was begun at the University of Illinois, Urbana, in 1913, the brainchild of two pastors, James C. Baker and Elmer A. Leslie. The program as developed vested the care of Methodist students enrolled in a state school with the Foundation and made its financial support the responsibility, not of the church in the university center alone, but of the annual conference of the state in which the university was located. The Urbana idea grew and in comparatively short time became a pattern for student work among other churches. The first Wesley foundation in the MECS was established at Austin, Texas, in 1922. The Methodist Student Movement came along in 1937.

Campus ministry, youth groups, men's brotherhoods, women's societies, and deaconesses all began as independent caucuses in Victorian churches and ended up as fixtures of the system, something latter-day caucuses dream about. Each caucus as it came along was well received by Victorian Methodist, Evangelical, and United Brethren.

Why? Growing numbers of youth, women, and men were committed and ready to serve the denomination and its mission. In order to tap that energy, to channel it in the interest of the mission of the denominations as a whole, and perhaps also to control it, the late Victorian family of Methodist denominations reorganized themselves around these new energy centers. Bishops and bureaucrats wisely saw that the new national program boards with local units would provide an ideal way to strengthen the commitment of the laity to work for the church. They promoted connectional consciousness by providing denominationwide programs that enabled local congregations to make these concerns a part of their own ministry. This is the only instance I know about in the Methodist tradition when the churches restructured themselves around selected caucuses.

At the same time other caucuses were less well received. The leaven of lay rights reform, dormant for decades after the Methodist Protestant pull-out, barely got a hearing, even in the less tense years after the Civil War. Following a successful churchwide referendum on the matter, the 1872 General Conference of the MEC implemented a compromise plan: lay delegates would be seated in the general but not the annual conference, and only two delegates per conference rather than in numbers equal to the number of clergy delegates, as the caucus insisted. Women, who voted in large numbers for the change in church policy, were excluded until well into the new century. The plan of 1872 was a caucus victory, to be sure, but only the thin edge of the wedge pierced the church's armor-plated *Book of Discipline.*

Northern Methodists began to draw the color line in their churches and in their conferences immediately after the Civil War. Separate black annual conferences were formed beginning in 1864. In the next decade, newly freed black Methodists in the south were organized by their white patrons into an independent Colored (later Christian) Methodist Episcopal Church. Following a decade of debate over the proper interpretation of the Wesleyan doctrine of perfect love, holiness advocates "went out" in the 1890s to form the Church of the Nazarene and a whole family of holiness churches.

It was only in the later years of the nineteenth century that United Brethren and Evangelicals experienced wrenching schisms. United Brethren reformers, who had been pressing their church to update its doctrinal standards and overhaul its discipline, successfully promoted a whole new constitution for the church plus a fresh confession of faith at the General Conference of 1889. A small minority refused to accept the changes and withdrew to form the Church of the United Brethren in Christ (Old Constitution). This is another instance in the Methodist tradition where the renewalists outnumbered and outvoted the immobilists.

A decade later in the 1890s the Evangelicals experienced their one and only schism. A bitter battle raged between the Philadelphia-based progressive minority who favored English language, a curtailed episcopacy, and openness to new theological developments (i.e. biblical criticism and theological liberalism) and the Indianapolis-based majority who favored German language, strong bishops, and a conservative theological stance. For a quadrennium, until the courts settled the matter, there were two Evangelical associations, each claiming to be the whole. In 1894, however, the renewalist minority organized the United Evangelical Church, while the conservative majority continued as the Evangelical Association.

4. Celebrating Methodism in a New Century (1900–1968): Caucuses Closeted

The recently reformed churches were a smash hit. They flourished in the crowded religious marketplace of middle America. There were more Methodist churches than post offices. In sheer numbers, no other church bodies even came close. If I were to talk of a "Methodist Age" in American church history, it wouldn't be the early republic but the first three-quarters of the twentieth century.

The "system" got refined along the way: in leadership, administration was by resident bishops in episcopal areas and presiding elders became district superintendents in the northern church in 1908 (middle managers, program pushers); in finance, apportionments were collected (one year ahead of federal income tax!) and duplex envelopes were employed. Symbolic for me of this era are the crusades (later "quadrennial emphases") we used to pull off every four years. The first one, the Crusade for a New World Order, was a doozy! The "United Crusade" of the Evangelical Church 1954–58 brought in $5 million.

Ecumenism was a new word in the new century. From the beginning in 1910 Methodists took leadership in the national and world councils of churches and cooperated with other denominations in a wide range of missions and movements. But it was family-style ecumenism that Methodists majored in during this period. Four big reunions occurred during the first seventy-five years of the twentieth century, but little reform. These beginnings in 1922, 1939, 1946 and 1968, inspiring as they were, appear in retrospect more as grand pageants marking the merging of similar bodies than as the creation of something new. What differences there were between the parties were always resolved in favor of the traditional (majority) pattern. All of the older Evangelical principles were continued in 1922 when dissident Evangelicals merged with the Evangelical Association. In 1939 Methodist Protestants gave up dearly held and hard won principles— term episcopacy, peer appointment of pastors, and women clergy. In that same union, northern Methodists gave in to southern (racist) pressure and agreed to segregate black members into a non-geographical Central Jurisdiction. In 1946 the United Brethren quietly gave up the practice of ordaining women at the insistence of the more conservative Evangelicals. In 1968 the Evangelical and United Brethren pattern of term bishops and elected superintendents, long advocated by Methodist reformers from O'Kelly and Hammett in the 1790s to Methodists for Church Renewal in the 1960s, were given up under pressure from the Methodist triumphalists.

Merger mafias stressed agreements and suppressed differences. Caucuses who saw reunions as occasions for reform and renewal were muzzled. Plans of union called for no strenuous adjustments in the newly united churches. Methodism's twentieth-century unions were rather like the remarriage of two middle-aged old pros—relatively painless, little change in lifestyle, few new commitments.

In the first sixty years of the new century program boards proliferated and gained power and influence at the expense of bishops, clergy, and layfolk. Programs developed by the boards were adopted by general and annual conferences and passed on to the people by obedient bishops, superintendents, and clergy. Pray, pay, and obey was the only way. The church's oldest caucus (the Methodist Federation for Social Action, formed in 1907) was marginalized as it pressed for economic and social justice. Temperance and Prohibition became the church's preoccupation (if not obsession) as they sought to monitor the nation's conscience throughout these years. The "Red Scare" of the 1930s and the "Pink Fringe" allegations of the 1950s kept MFSA under a cloud. A tamer, safer Board of Christian Social Relations was formed in 1952. During these same years the church's black caucus celebrated no victories. After 1939 black Methodists endured a segregated church as well as a segregated social order.

5. Lamenting Methodism at the Bicentennial (1968–): Caucus Fever

Through all of this triumphal activity Methodists still seemed to be big and getting bigger. Actually the family was big but already getting smaller, although no one noticed. Methodism's percentage of the U.S. population peaked in 1932, and we have been on a downward slide ever since. Aggregate numbers continued to climb, so no one noticed.

The turbulent sixties marked the coming of age of Methodism's caucus tradition. The long-standing tension in the denomination between authoritarian and democratic tendencies heightened as similar tensions tore apart the social order. The rise of racial/ethnic feeling indicated a renewed search for identity as well as a search for power. By the end of the decade a growing family of caucuses emerged. Four racial ethnic caucuses—Black Methodists for Church Renewal (BMCR) 1968, Native American International Caucus (NAIC) 1970, National Fellowship of Asian American United Methodists (NFAAUM) 1971, and Methodists Associated Representing the Caucus of Hispanic Americans (MARCHA) 1971—took their place alongside the newly energized women and youth caucuses (NYMO). The sixty-year old Methodist Federation for Social Action (MFSA) roused to action and to respectability by the civil rights and antiwar movements was joined on the other side by the Forum for Scriptural Christianity (Good News), the caucus of conservative Evangelicals in 1966. Charismatic Methodists as well as liturgical Methodists (The Order of St. Luke, founded 1946) also competed for attention. By the middle 1970s a gay and lesbian caucus (Affirmation) had been organized. The time had come, each said in its own way, to redress the balance and rediscover the rich diversity of the Methodist family. The caucus spirit, dormant for decades, burst out all across the church.

The ruling principle of the commission that worked out the 1968 merger between Methodist and EUB was—unite now, settle the differences later. Issues such as ministry and episcopacy, doctrinal standards and social principles, the number of seminaries, and an unbelievably complicated cluster of national program boards had to be addressed. The uniting conference wisely established a pattern of quadrennial study commissions to tackle them one by one. Twenty-five years later few of the issues have been settled. It remains to be seen whether the breakthroughs—doctrinal standards and hymnal in 1988 and book of worship in 1992—will be long-standing.

The 1972 General Conference in Atlanta was a major turning point. But the highly centralized remodeling of 1972 with four super boards (Global Ministries, Higher Education and Ministry, Discipleship, and Church and Society) and three councils (GCOM, GCFA, and Bishops) made matters worse. Methodists overcentralized at a time when folks back home, and in society at large, longed for decentralization, if not dismantling of what were perceived as overgrown and unresponsive bureaucracies. The highly refined system that marked Methodism's heyday from the late-nineteenth century through the Eisenhower years no longer worked as advertised. Bureaucrats as well as bishops had become suspect rather than revered, let alone obeyed. The push from the grass-roots for participation and the call for sunshine politics and accountability, meant, I think, that fundamental alienation had already occurred between Methodism's top and bottom. No wonder caucus fever hit the Methodists like an epidemic during the late 1960s and early 1970s. Since then our history has been studded with one caucus after another—more than twenty in my latest count—as group after group set new agendas and plotted new paths.

Since 1968 the quota system for electing members created new and uncertain boards, but youth, women, and minority representatives gained articulation, and middle-aged white male clergy learned the consequences of sharing power. Required consultation in clergy appointments was at last written into the *Book of Discipline* in 1976. Newly created general commissions on religion and race and on the status and role of women indicated that the church was serious about combatting racism and sexism, although at General Conference 1988, GCOSROW narrowly escaped being closed down!

Concluding Unscientific Postscript

For three centuries in a row Methodism has been in disarray at century's end. The last two times (in the 1780s and 1880s), Methodists reformed themselves and confidently moved in the new century. This time around it is just taking a little more time. Caucuses had a lot to do with the major transformations last time around, and I assume they will have a crucial role to play this time too. Caucuses, quotas, and church politics are neither new nor un-Methodist—nor are they bad per se. Consensus historiography and the bias of surviving documents (favoring winners rather than losers) has simply hidden this part of our tradition.

In spite of imperial bishops and bossy bureaucrats, parliamentary maneuvers, and merger mafias, the caucus strain found its way into the heart of the Methodist tradition, and there is every evidence that it is still alive and well. In the wake of the "Re-Imagining" conference of 1992 there should be little doubt of that.

Have we been burdened or blessed by the caucus tradition? As for the records I care for (and occasionally read) in the denomination's attic, they generally see caucuses as a curse. Few bishops from Asbury to those most recently elected have celebrated the presence of caucuses among us. Historians from Jesse Lee to William Warren Sweet wrote them out of the story. To my mind, caucuses provide necessary balance to connectional authority. On more than one occasion they enriched our understanding of the gospel, refocused our mission, and redistributed our power. And how much spice have they added to an otherwise bland story! Every generation of Methodist, Evangelical, and United Brethren has had its independent characters and cantankerous caucuses, who would not be put down by episcopal authority or by majority vote. Many of the issues they championed required an extended campaign before the church bowed to reform. The fact that occasionally such conduct smacked more of the eccentric than the responsible should not obscure the importance of the caucus strain in Methodism. Long live caucus Methodism!

Is United Methodism a World Church?

Janice Love

In a world of remarkable challenges and changes, efforts to understand the future organization of the United Methodist Church (UMC) raise important questions about how we understand our church, our world, and our faith. In this chapter I hope to pinpoint a few questions and offer insights that provide something of a "reality check" to recent reports and discussions on the global nature of the UMC. In particular, three general questions provide the framework for exploring matters central to United Methodism: concepts of international affairs, recent world history, and the demography of the UMC.

Is Globalization an Appropriate Organizing Concept for the United Methodist Church?

Building on a similar report to the 1992 General Conference, the council of bishops invoked the concept of globalization in their 1996 "Report on the Global Nature of the United Methodist Church." This term has broad popular currency in the United States and in many other parts of the world. Asserting its significance, the bishops state:

> The context of mission is a world that is increasingly being drawn into a global community by irresistible globalizing forces, such as: increased global travel, global communication, the universalizing of human rights, the globalizing of the free market economy, the universal character and influence of science and technology, the increasing awareness that the one earth in the one universe is our home, and preserving it and being at home in it are a common global responsibility, etc. Can mission be less than global in a global context? If the world becomes a global community must the Church be left behind?[1]

Since its introduction in the early 1980s and its popularization in the early 1990s, the term "globalization" has generated numerous articles and books as well as a fierce debate on what, if anything, this concept means. One introductory text in world politics sympathetic to the use of the term defines it as follows:

> . . . globalization refers to processes whereby social relations acquire relatively distanceless and borderless qualities, so that human lives are

increasingly played out in the world as a single place. Social relations—that is, the countless and complex ways that people interact with and affect each other—are more and more being conducted and organized on the basis of a planetary unit. By the same token country locations, and in particular the boundaries between territorial states, are in some important senses becoming less central to our lives, although they do remain significant. Globalization is thus an ongoing trend whereby the world has—in many respects and at a generally accelerating rate—become one relatively borderless social sphere.[2]

Terms and phrases that echo similar sentiments, not always sympathetically, are: interdependence, integration, economic liberalism, the end of history (Fukuyama),[3] the end of geography, global village (McLuhan),[4] global pillage, McWorld (Barber),[5] videology, cultural homogenization, and modernization. Some equate globalization with capitalism, just as some equate it with colonialism. Some point to how globalization draws people more closely together, while others demonstrate how globalization leads to the further exclusion of the poor and marginalized. Some point to the wide availability of consumer goods in defining globalization, while other see it as ever-expanding environmental destruction. Clearly the term does not always have a positive or life-affirming connotation. In its many and sometimes contending definitions, it can also evoke negative meanings or, on occasion, benign ones.

Virtually all analysts agree that the term emerged to distinguish somewhat new and more intense processes of interaction across the world from those that traditionally have been called international. Internationalization implies connections among national domains. Although globalization and internationalization both exist, they are different. The textbook states: "To put the difference in a nutshell, the international realm is a patchwork of bordered countries, while the global sphere is a web of transborder networks . . . (and) in this sense supraterritorial."[6] Analysts also agree, however, that this "web of transborder networks" is unevenly disbursed, being concentrated in North America, the Pacific Rim, and Europe. Most prominently missing from these connections, in particular, are sub-Saharan Africa and Central Asia.

This chapter is not the place to debate the meaning of this recently developed term or to discuss in detail the processes it entails. Rather, we must ask if this popular but unclear concept should be the basis on which we organize our church. In embracing the term, obviously, the council of bishops understands it in a positive way. Yet in their fairly brief document, the bishops do not fully examine the concept.

If globalization means a "web of transborder networks," churches have always been such, beginning with the activities of Christians enumerated in the New Testament. In the late-twentieth century, Christian organizations demonstrate a number of models of transborder networks. A preliminary, nonexhaustive list based on geography and confession can be characterized as follows:

1. *Global confessional model:* This model is distinguished by vast geographic reach and genuinely global organization. Members are located in virtually all regions of the world. Furthermore, these organizations draw together Christians on the basis of historic articulations of a particular doctrine. The Roman Catholic Church (RCC) provides an excellent illustration. No one region or country dominates in terms of RCC membership. The Ecumenical Patriarch of Constantinople, one of the largest Orthodox churches with members in most regions of the world, is another example. The world confessional bodies like the World Methodist Council (WMC), the Lutheran World Federation, and the World Alliance of Reformed Churches also fit in this category. Another confessional group, the Anglicans, have two organizations of this type: the Anglican Consultative Council (much like the WMC) and the Lambeth Conference (where bishops gather without other clergy or lay participants).

2. *Global interconfessional:* These Christian organizations stretch across all regions and most countries of the world and put Christians of many different doctrinal identities together in one organization. The most prominent illustration of this category is the World Council of Churches, with membership of over 300 churches in more than a hundred countries from virtually all the Protestant and Orthodox traditions as well as the Old Catholic Church. Another example, the World Evangelical Fellowship, has membership based in about 60 national evangelical fellowships (e.g., the National Association of Evangelicals in the U.S.) across the world.

3. *Extended-national confessional:* This model provides for a particular doctrinal tradition embodied in members primarily in one country, with additional churches in a few other nations or regions (hence the characterization as extended-national rather than global). Some illustrations include the Episcopal Church in the U.S. as well as U.S. Methodist churches, both the historic black churches and the UMC. For example, UMC membership resides primarily in the United States, but UMC bodies also exist in Africa, Europe, and the Philippines. Other examples of this model are a number of Orthodox churches such as the Bulgarian, Ethiopian, and Romanian Orthodox churches, all of which have churches in North America as well as their home countries.

4. *Regional confessional:* Here churches of a particular doctrinal identity can be found in a number of countries in a concentrated geographic area. The Kimbanguist Church in Central Africa provides a good illustration. Its members reside in the Democratic Republic of the Congo (formerly Zaire), the Republic of the Congo (Brazzaville), the Central African Republic, Angola, and Burundi.

5. *Regional interconfessional:* This model demonstrates Christian organizations concentrated in a particular geographic region, but the churches within the body stretch across a range of doctrinal traditions. Illustrations are the regional ecumenical organizations, such as the All African Conference of Churches, the Conference of European Churches, and the Christian Conference of Asia.

If we compare this list of models to the report of the UMC council of bishops, a number of questions arise. When they call for a global church, do the bishops mean that they want the UMC to move from being extended-national as in model 3, to being truly global as in model 1? Do the bishops aspire for the UMC to be more like the Roman Catholic Church? the World Methodist Council? If so, what does this imply for non-UMC Methodists all over the world and for the World Methodist Council itself?

Just as important as the models, however, are the questions about the use of the concept globalization itself. What if the term does not carry a benign or positive connotation like "web of transborder networks?" What if, instead, many people understand globalization to mean domination (as in the International Monetary Fund's control over financing of many countries' economies), exclusion (as in the poor having little access to many communications networks), or cookie-cutter culture (as in products like Coca Cola or McDonald's hamburgers, which taste the same no matter where one buys them)? With these less positive kinds of definitions, what would the globalization of the UMC mean?

How Does the History of the United Methodist Church Relate to World History?

World events shape churches, just as, on occasion, churches shape world events. An interesting exercise for contemplating the organizational future of the United Methodist Church is to reexamine its institutional history and the relationship of this history to world events. How did we come to have the particular form of organization we now hold? How is it different from or similar to that of other Protestant churches? How does our institutional history follow or depart from trends in the world around us?

Just as the American colonies broke free from Great Britain beginning in 1776, the Methodist Episcopal Church in the United States established itself independently of the British Methodists in 1784. John Wesley gave his blessings to this organizational separation of these national churches even though a few years earlier he had opposed the American Revolution.

In the next century, like other Protestant and Catholic churches, Methodists in both Britain and the United States took advantage of world events to spread the gospel. Missionaries accompanied the European and the U.S. colonial conquests of Africa, Asia and other parts of the globe in what many analysts call "the age of imperialism," that era in the nineteenth century when most of the world came under the direct control of the Western industrial powers. Two powers, the British and U.S., cooperated to ensure U.S. informal control over (as distinct from colonial occupation of) Latin America. Considerable literature exists on the consequences of converting people to Christianity through conquest and domination, but this is not the place to explore these issues. Clearly the relationship between missions and colonialism was complex: some missions cooperated fully with colonial authorities whereas others resisted them. For brevity's sake, the point here is quite simple: the geographic spread of Western colonialism and industrial domination meant the geographic spread of Christian churches. Just as nations acquired colonial territories, Western churches acquired mission churches. Just as the Western governments somewhat amicably divided up continents so as not to fight over acquiring remote territories, churches reached "acts of comity" assigning particular churches certain geographic areas in which to establish missions. In the case of United States Methodists, the clearest examples are the Methodist churches established in the Philippines and Liberia, two American colonies, as well as those founded in Latin America, regionally dominated by the U.S.

During this period of the mid- to late-1800s, Britain became the hegemonic economic, military, and political power in the world, holding more colonies than any other Western power and dominating world finance, trade, and shipping routes. This era of Pax Britannia began waning in earlier years but was decidedly finished with World War I. The era of Pax Americana began after World War II, when the United States took up the mantle of world leadership in the face of European economic and political devastation, a strong and expanding U.S. economy, and concern by U.S. policy makers that the former Soviet Union held aggressive intentions toward much of the world. In contrast to Britain, the U.S. held direct political control over few colonial territories, but very much like the period of Pax Britannia, America exercised hegemony in finance, trade, military matters, transportation, and in the newly formed intergovernmental organizations of the United Nations and Bretton Woods (the International Monetary Fund and the World Bank). In the 1970s, Pax Americana gave way to Pax G-3 (Group of Three), wherein the large industrial and postindustrial nations of Europe, Japan and the U.S. (also called the Group of Seven after the individual nations involved) guide world economic affairs. The collapse of the Soviet Union in 1989–91, further centralized economic control in this group and facilitated their expanded political and military coordination.

In other parts of the world, the end of World War II witnessed the rise of independence movements in colonial territories. Domestically, the British in particular began wrestling with the meaning of being a great power in decline, and except for a few cases, the British government peacefully negotiated the end of its formal colonial empire within two decades. Also with a few exceptions, the United States fairly quickly shed its formal role as a colonial power. In contrast to Britain's decline, however, the American people began to wrestle domestically with the meaning of being a great power in ascendancy, including fighting or abetting wars in distant places.

As the second half of the twentieth century progressed, meanwhile, former colonial territories learned that political independence did not bring with it economic independence. Although a few countries cleverly manipulated the global political economy to their benefit to become the "newly industrializing nations," most so-called third world or southern countries found themselves very much at the mercy of the international political economy and, for some decades, at the mercy of superpower rivalry as well. With a few exceptions, dictatorships took hold in most southern countries, supported by one superpower or the other. Ordinary people in Africa, Asia, Latin America, the Middle East, and the Pacific found themselves with little control over the political systems of their countries and with little or no control over distant economic and military forces that profoundly affected their lives. In general, significant political change (not always for the better) only became possible in the 1980s, with the demise of superpower rivalry and, in many countries, the strengthening of domestic forces for change, some of which had operated more or less clandestinely for decades.

I retell this admittedly broad sweep of familiar history because these trends are, I believe, relevant to the institutional histories of various Methodist and other Protestant churches around the world.

Just as colonial territories became independent nation states, the mission churches of most Protestant "parent" churches in Europe and the U.S. became organizationally independent and self-governing. This includes Anglicans, Baptists, Congregationalists, Lutherans, Presbyterians as well as other Reformed Churches, and most Methodists. Furthermore, to overcome denominational factionalism inherited from their parent churches and their small size, some of these former mission churches joined together to form larger Protestant bodies. (For example, Presbyterians, Congregationalists, Anglicans, and British Methodists joined to form the Church of South India. The Church of North India has a somewhat similar history, but on the whole, Lutherans, Baptists and U.S. Methodists in India formally remained outside these unions.)

Many Methodist churches followed this pattern of establishing their own national organizational identity. This includes those of British descent all over the world and Latin American Methodist churches begun by predecessor bodies of the UMC (as well as some Evangelical United Brethren Church churches elsewhere). Institutionally these Methodist churches exist independently of their former parent church. A few churches established in Africa, Europe, and the Philippines by predecessor bodies of the UMC, however, chose to stay organizationally tied to their parent churches. And the parent church has not urged them to become independent.

Examined together, this secular and church history raises important questions. Why did UM churches in Africa, Europe, and the Philippines not follow the pattern set by UM-related Methodists in Latin America and by other Protestants all over the world? Did the secular history of the United States' substantial political and economic domination of Latin America (which many call neocolonialism) make Latin American Methodists eager to end their organizational ties to and dependence on the UMC in the U.S.? If so, what explains the case of the Philippine UMC remaining in the fold of the larger UMC, in a place where the U.S. government held a formal colony and remained dominant thereafter? What has become of the concerted efforts over many years by large numbers of Philippine UMCs to become organizationally separate from the U.S. UMC?

For small Methodist churches in Europe and Africa, does the ascendancy of Pax Americana and Pax G-3 make formal integration with a powerful, rich church in a powerful, rich country all the more inviting, especially since no formal colonial ties exist between the countries where these churches exist? Is this a more compelling and attractive option than being one of many (and perhaps one of the smaller) independent churches with a national or regional base?

Does formal organizational separation for Latin American Methodists and other Protestant churches in the so-called third world end their dependence on their former parent churches? Or, alternatively do ties between nominally independent churches in the north and south follow dependency patterns that exists between countries and businesses in the North and South? Does being a nationally or regionally based church in the so-called third world offer more options for relating as a full partner in more equitable relationships with Western churches like the U.S. UMC? With other churches in the same country? Or does organizational independence matter little in establishing equitable partnerships?

Are U.S. UMC members eager to accept the secular mantle of Pax Americana and Pax G-3 in our civic life, and are they similarly eager to emulate benevolently this model by institutionally integrating Methodists in other countries into the UMC? Does the global hegemony of the United States as a nation push us as churches in this direction, making UMC global domination among all Methodists an easy, natural option? Is this what we mean by the globalization of the church?

A great deal of attention has been focused on declining membership and eroding budgets for so-called mainline churches in the United States, including the UMC. Are U.S. UMC members tired of institutional decline within our country and thus eager for institution-building in others? If we cannot attract more members in the United States, should we compensate by attracting more members for the UMC outside our country? Do we need for mission and evangelism to result in the growth of the UMC? Or, are there other equally significant forms of evangelism and mission?

If the UMC is to retain its present extended-national structure, what does this imply for relating to non-UMC Methodists in various parts of the world (including in some of the same countries where the UMC exists)? For example, how does the UMC in Zimbabwe relate to the considerably larger Methodist Church of Zimbabwe (of British origins)?

What does the present UMC structure imply for ecumenical relations among churches in particular nations? For example, should the extended-national structure of the UMC (i.e. delegates from both the U.S. and non-U.S. constituencies) be represented in the UMC delegation to the National Council of Churches of Christ in the USA? to the Zimbabwe Council of Churches? to the National Council of Churches in the Philippines? On a more technical matter (of which there are many), what would equality among bishops mean: paying

UMC bishops outside the U.S. the same salaries as their U.S. counterparts, or a salary comparable to bishops of other denominations inside their countries?

What does an extended-national structure mean for ecumenical relations with the World Council of Churches and the World Methodist Council, both of which are premised primarily on a national institutional church structure?

What Are the Political, Economic, Demographic, and Cultural Realities of Transnational UMC Membership?

The Table of Countries with United Methodist Members (see below) compares a number of characteristics of the countries where the UM churches are located. It also compares membership and other statistics by region for the whole church. The data show two important realities: in sheer size, the number of UMs in the United States overwhelms the number of UMs in other parts of the world; and the life circumstances, material wealth, and culture of U.Ms. in the United States, even among the poorest of U.S. UMs, far exceed those of most UMs in other parts of the world.

The table displays countries of widely varying size in population, geography, and economy. Stark differences also exist in types of economic activity prominent in Africa and the Philippines, on the one hand, and Europe and the United States on the other hand. Rural life and agriculture are much more important to Africa and the Philippines, while urban life, industry, and services characterize Europe and the U.S. As expected, the figures demonstrate that the U.S. and European countries possess tremendous material wealth and human services, as indicated not only by gross national product figures, but also by the human development index, life expectancy at birth and adult literacy rates. The same kinds of statistics show that Africa and the Philippines are materially poor. A similar sharp contrast exists in communications capabilities—for example, in the availability of newspapers and televisions, indicators that begin to tap into cultural differences. On the whole, for example, United Methodists in the United States live in the information age. United Methodists in Angola and Mozambique do not.

Statistics on membership and number of organized churches display the obvious as well: 86 percent of UMs in the world live in the United States, just as the U.S. is home to 85 percent of the organized UM churches. Africans make up 12.5 percent of all UMs, Europeans 0.8 percent, and Philippines 0.7 percent.

None of these statistics reveals anything about the determination of these churches and parishioners to minister and witness to the people

around them, to spread the gospel, or to build on and renew their
Methodist traditions. Christians rich in spirit may or may not be poor in
material goods. Therefore, this data is not intended to imply how well
or how poorly equipped each church in each place may be to fulfill its
mission in Christ's kingdom.

These contrasts, nonetheless, raise important questions. With such
an imbalance in membership, will the UMC *in the near future* be a
genuinely global church as outlined in model 1 above, where no one
region dominates? Will the UMC remain an extended-national church
(as in model 3) with aspirations to be, but no concrete chance of
becoming, a global confessional institution (model 1)? The Connectional
Process Team, commissioned by the 1996 General Conference to bring
proposals on the global nature of the UMC to the General Conference
in 2000, may find a brilliant design for ensuring the best possible
partnership for equalizing relations among the different geographic
regions of the UMC. Are the best intentions and best design *ever* likely
to be sufficient to counteract the realities of the United States global
presence, size, history, wealth, and culture—no matter if all regions of
the UMC remain within the same organization or if those in Africa,
Asia, and Europe separate from the U.S. UMC? If not, how does the
whole of the UMC grapple with this reality? What does this reality
imply for the UMs relating as partners to Latin American, Indian, or
other non-UMC Methodists or other non-UMC Christians?

Unfortunately, the bishops do not give a great deal of guidance for
addressing these kinds of questions. Their report states:

> If [the United Methodist Church] does not take this step of becoming a
> global church, it will most likely face the danger of becoming fragmented
> into autonomous churches in various nations of the world, with the
> American segment becoming merely that—an *American* fragment of the
> once future global United Methodist Church! . . .
>
> It would be considered odd at this time—to say the least—for a church
> with a national identity or label (for example: *American* United Methodist,
> *Korean* Presbyterian, etc.) to be doing mission in another country for the
> purpose of planting itself there. This problem, however, would not arise for
> a global Church because it is already in almost every country, and it will
> not bear the label or identity of a nation! In a post-colonial world, mission
> cannot be another form of neo-colonialism.[7]

This paragraph raises an number of questions related to the
demographic characteristics of the UMC as well as its mission. Almost
200 countries exist in the world. Do the bishops understand that UM
presence in approximately twenty-six countries to be the same as a
presence in "almost every country?"

Furthermore, is church planting always the goal of mission? Is church-planting the most appropriate form of mission in most countries, particularly those where substantial numbers of churches already exist? How does church planting enhance or hinder ecumenical relationships? If UM mission work in a particular place results happily in an increase in the number of Christians in that area, do we as United Methodists care whether they become attached to a local Baptist, Presbyterian, Lutheran, Orthodox, or Catholic church, as opposed to a United Methodist church? If we do, what does our belief in the "one holy catholic church" mean?

Is neocolonialism confined to relations among national churches? Or, could neocolonialism be the mode of operation for a global institution as well (as, for a secular example, in the International Monetary Fund)? Examined as a whole and with the characteristics described above, will (in the foreseeable future) the UMC ever be considered *anything other than* a United States church (an *"American* fragment," as the bishops pejoratively state)? If not, is its mission work destined to be characterized by neocolonialism?

Conclusion

Many of the questions raised here are profoundly theological, but space does not permit a full theological exploration of issues embedded in the UM Church's presence across the world. Theology exists within historical, social, political, economic, and cultural contexts, however, and my hope is that this chapter helps to ground the discussions on "the global nature of the UMC" in a fuller understanding of these concrete realities. The future of the church—its structure as well as it local, national, and international witness—will attain more credibility and authenticity if undergirded by a keen awareness of who we are and where we have been.

Table of Countries with United Methodist Members

Country	UMC Number Members	UMC Number Churches	Land Area (1000 square km)	Population (millions)	GNP (US$ billions)	Urban population (as % of total)	News papers (per 100 people)	TVs (per 100 people)	Human Development Index	Life Expectancy at Birth (years)	Adult Literacy Rate (%)
Angola		1247	10.5	N/A	32	1	3	0.335	47.2	42.5	
Burundi		28	5.9	0.9	7	N/A	1	0.247	43.5	34.6	
Congo (Zaire)			2344	43.9	N/A	29	N/A	N/A	0.381	52.2	76.4
Liberia		111	2.2	N/A	44	1	2		55.4	35.4	
Mozambique			802	16.6	1.3	33	1	N/A	0.281	46.0	39.5
Nigeria		924	108.5	30	39	2	4	0.393	51.0	55.6	
Sierra Leone			72	4.1	0.7	35	N/A	1	0.176	33.6	30.3
Tanzania			945	29.2	N/A	24	1	N/A	0.357	50.3	66.8
Zimbabwe			391	11	5.4	31	2	3	0.513	49	84.7
(Africa Total)	1,239,722	4,585									
Austria		84	8	198	56	47	48	0.932	76.6	99.0	
Bulgaria		111	9	10	70	21	26	0.780	71.1	93.0	
Czech Rep			79	10	33	65	22	38	0.882	72.2	99.0
Slovakia		49	5	12	58	26	28	0.873	70.8	99.0	
Denmark			43	5	145	85	36	54	0.927	75.2	99.0
Estonia		45	2	4	73	24	36	0.776	69.2	99.0	
Finland		338	5	96	63	47	50	0.940	76.3	99.0	
Germany			357	81	2076	86	32	55	0.924	76.3	99.0
Hungary			93	10	39	64	23	52	0.857	68.8	99.0
Macedonia			26	2	2	59	2	16	0.748	71.7	94.0

Country	UMC Number Members	UMC Number Churches	Land Area (1000 square km)	Population (millions)	GNP (US$ billions)	Urban population (as % of total)	News papers (per 100 people)	TVs (per 100 people)	Human Development Index	Life Expectancy at Birth (years)	Adult Literacy Rate (%)
Norway		324	4	114	73	61	43	0.943	77.5	99.0	
Poland		313	39	95	64	14	30	0.834	71.2	99.0	
Russian Federation		17,075	149	393	76	27	38	0.792	65.7	98.7	
Sweden		450	9	206	83	48	47	0.936	78.3	99.0	
Switzerland			41	7	265	61	41	40	0.930	78.1	99.0
(Europe Total)	81,180	1,117									
Philippines	66,901	605	300	66.4	63.3	30	7	12	0.672	67.0	94.4
United States	8,456,986	36,170	9573	265	6737	76	23	78	0.942	76.2	99.0

Sources:

The United Methodist Church, *General Minutes* 1996 and 1997; New Internationalist, *The World Guide 1997/8* (Instituto del Tercer Mundo, 1997); The World Bank, *World Development Report 1997* (New York: Oxford University Press, 1997); United National Development Program, *Human Development Report 1997* (New York: Oxford University Press, 1997); United National Development Program, *Human Development Report 1995* (New York: Oxford University Press, 1995).

Notes:

1. The statistics on UMC members and churches are given by region for Africa and Europe because individual country data is not always available.

2. The data on all the indicators (except those for the UMC) are the most recent available, usually from 1994 or 1995, as published in the above sources.

3. A composite index, the Human Development Index contains three variables: life expectancy, educational attainment and real Gross Domestic Product per capita. One is the highest value and zero is the lowest.

Will Homosexuality Split the Church?

Daniel M. Bell Jr.

Few issues in the church today are as explosive as the question of the church's stance towards homosexuality. Few issues can match this one in terms of the intensity of feeling that it generates; few are as passion-laden. Over the past several decades the church's effort to engage the issue of the presence and participation of homosexual persons in its life has evolved under the tremendous weight of this concern. The intensity of this concern should be unsurprising. After all, few issues intersect with such a vast array of the most vital and significant areas of our daily lives, touching as it does on marriage and the family, on a person's sense of dignity and self-worth before God, on the primacy of Scripture and centrality of charity in the Christian life. Likewise, the result of the church's efforts should be unsurprising. The church appears to be polarized into two camps, separated, as a delegate at the recent General Conference suggested, by a continental divide. Something as imposing as a continental divide would appear to be an apt metaphor for the divisions that traverse the body of the United Methodist Church: there appears to be no middle ground; everything flows to one side or the other.

But, as the cliché goes, appearances can be deceiving. After teaching and discussing this issue in a variety of contexts, I am convinced that between the camps mustering their forces and attracting the limelight exists the vast body of the church, a body for whom the metaphor of the continental divide is inappropriate. A body consisting of the majority of the clergy and laity who, although perhaps inclined to one camp or the other, nevertheless long for a new way to talk about this issue, one that generates more light and less heat. A body whose features resemble not a continental divide, with its powerful forces flowing in opposite directions, but an archipelago, a cluster of islands covering a theological spectrum that nevertheless remain intimately related to one another—sharing the same pews, shedding tears over the same losses, celebrating the same joys, studying the same Scripture.

What follows is one attempt at articulating a theological framework that might serve as the springboard for a process of discernment by those who do not find themselves fully persuaded by the dominant positions. Whereas claims about the nature and limits of homosexual persons' participation in the life of the church are advanced, I hope that the real strength of this effort lies less in its particular conclusions than in the nature of the theological conversation that it engenders. In other words, what I hope to contribute are signposts for a theological conversation that may advance in directions beyond the tentative steps I take here, but that most certainly progresses beyond the current modes of (non)conversation in the church.

The Study as a Start

The effort to articulate a theological framework for a process of discernment does not, however, have to begin from scratch. A theological framework has been percolating ever since 1972, when the newly fashioned Social Principles included under the heading of "Human Sexuality" a statement that declared homosexuals "persons of sacred worth," although recognizing that the church does not condone the practice of homosexuality and considers it "incompatible with Christian teaching." The intricacies of this history need not detain us; suffice it to say that the discussion quickly moved beyond "human sexuality" to embrace questions concerning ordination, civil rights, the funding of advocacy, and what constitutes a "self-avowed practicing" homosexual. It was only sixteen years into this debate that the church formed a committee to study the matter. The report of this committee was received by the church and is available as *The Church Studies Homosexuality*.[1] The strength of this study lay in the recognition that the discussion of homosexuality needs to be couched in an explicitly theological context. That is, the study contributes to the church's process of discernment by relocating the debate, by raising the issue of homosexuality as a theological issue worthy of discussion in its own right, apart from the particular polity concerns that have tended to capture and constrict discussion in recent years. Moreover, the study is laudable for its attempt spell out the theological context in accord with United Methodist commitments to Scripture, tradition, experience, and reason.

This repositioning of the discussion in terms of an explicitly theological context and the seriousness with which it takes United Methodist commitments to the quadrilateral certainly do not exhaust all that is commendable in the study. However, these two points provide a valuable basis for the constructive proposal that follows. These two strengths serve not only by indicating the direction we need to move, but also by exemplifying the weaknesses of current discussions. In other words, the study's strengths are also its weaknesses. Let me explain.

First, although it acknowledges the primacy of Scripture in United Methodist theological deliberation, as the study unfolds it displays a certain confusion in this regard. For example, in several instances the study dismisses Scripture out of hand for the sake of avoiding a "scriptural absolutism" or in the name of recognizing its "cultural boundedness."[2] Likewise, the study expresses a heavy reliance on experience, particularly in its scientific manifestations, stating that the committee was "hopeful that science could provide definitive answers" and "settle our debates, once for all."[3] Hence, we are left with a sense that Scripture was taken seriously, but its primacy is left in some doubt.

Second, although the study rightly acknowledges the need to anchor the discussion of homosexuality in a distinctly theological context, its effort to spell out that context in terms of "human sexuality" leaves much to be desired. After acknowledging that sexuality is a gift of God to all persons that nevertheless can be misused, the study offers the following statement that appears to summarize the Christian contribution to a sexual ethic: "While human sexual expression exists at different levels in the rich interplay of social relationships, a serious moral case can be made for reserving sexual intercourse for permanent covenantal unions between persons who are exclusively pledged to one another. In such unions, the depth of unqualified love offered by each to each can become a human manifestation of that grace by which we are made whole."[4] Both the general framework of "human sexuality" and this statement present several difficulties. For example, exactly what sort of moral force is the statement attempting to generate when it says a "serious moral case can be made" for limiting sexual intercourse to a permanent covenantal unions? How serious a case is it? Is it one case among several equally serious cases? Furthermore, what are (or are there any) institutional preconditions for these covenants? Can two people enter this covenant, say, alone by the seashore one day? Are such unions really primarily about love and are such unions necessary for wholeness? Is a permanent covenantal union the same thing as marriage? As Christian marriage?

These sorts of ambiguities effectively undermine any theological traction the committee might have hoped to provide. The question of the relation between these unions and Christian marriage, furthermore, raises the question of the framework of "human sexuality." Why does a theological account of human sexuality serve as the foundation for discussion instead of a theological account of Christian marriage? After all, as a very charitable reading of the statement indicates, when

Christians talk about sex they are talking about Christian marriage, which suggests that the logical place to begin a theological discussion of homosexuality would be with the nature and ends of Christian marriage. In what follows, the long tradition of theological reflection on Christian marriage will provide the theological context for the discussion of homosexuality. Before engaging that tradition, however, we need to look at Scripture.

Scripture Is Primary

As United Methodists, we confess that Scripture should not just be taken seriously, but that it holds primacy in our theological deliberations. Hence, the scriptural witness needs to be engaged up front, while avoiding several common errors. First, because Scripture is primary we should not dismiss troublesome passages as culture bound.[5] Second, we should read the texts closely in order to discern what is being addressed and not assume anachronistically that something called "homosexuality" has always been the same everywhere.[6] Third, the recognition that those practices addressed by Scripture may not be identical to same-sex sexual practices today does not mean that Scripture is irrelevant. Confessing the primacy of Scripture means acknowledging that its moral authority extends beyond the situations it explicitly addresses.

As we turn to the texts most frequently used in the discussion of homosexuality, it is clear that every reference to homosexual practices in Scripture is negative. The texts merit scrutiny, nevertheless, in order to ascertain what is being addressed.

Genesis 1:26-28. This passage does not address homosexuality, but it is often invoked in defense of normative claims for heterosexual unions. Whereas it would be a mistake to equate gender and reproduction—traits shared with many creatures—with the image of God in humanity, this account does link gender differentiation with procreation, a point that will prove pivotal as my argument unfolds.

Genesis 2:24. Also frequently cited as grounds for the sole legitimacy of heterosexual marriage, this passage is more faithfully read as an explanation of why a man leaves his kin and joins a woman sexually. It is not a command about either monogamy or marriage. Indeed, polygamy, concubinage, and even males' use of prostitutes were accepted practices among ancient Jews. Nor does the witness of Scripture read this passage exclusively as a reference to marriage. Even as Jesus makes reference to this passage in a discussion of marriage (Mark 10; Matt. 19), Paul alludes to it with reference to prostitution (1 Cor. 6). Furthermore, were this an exhortation concerning heterosexual coupling, we would be left wondering where this leaves those mentally and physically incapable of such couplings, as well as the celibate, in God's order of creation.

Recently, the creation accounts of Genesis 1 and 2 have been used not as an explicit command to enter heterosexual marriage but as the basis for appeals to male-female complimentarity. Certainly creation as male-female is a paradigmatic example of human sociality, but such a paradigm does not preclude the legitimacy of other modes of human sociality. A person called to celibacy, for instance, follows a different paradigm. Traditionally, male-female complimentarity has been understood in terms of procreation. As Aquinas says, in classic patriarchal style, "We are told that woman was made to help man. But she was not fitted to help man except in generation, because another man would have proved a more effective help in anything else."[7] In other words, complimentarity has been a matter of procreation and not simply of how parts fit together. What the tradition has labeled unnatural were all sex acts (hetero, homo, or solitary) that were non-procreative. Moreover, accounts of complimentarity premised on the biological fit of male and female overlook the fact that Christians claim it is the marriage bond that creates complimentarity and not the sex act itself. Christians do not believe that any heterosexual coupling creates the God-ordained complimentarity; only in marriage is such complimentarity produced.[8]

Genesis 19:1-29. The story of Sodom and Gomorrah is a clear condemnation of homosexual rape. The multiple references to Sodom and Gomorrah in Scripture tend to denounce those towns for a variety of sins, from general wickedness to inhospitality.[9]

Leviticus 18:22 and 20:13. These passages stand as categorical prohibitions of homosexual practices. Opponents of this prohibition often circumvent it by invoking a ritual/moral distinction, claiming the prohibitions are part of a ritual or ceremonial purity code that does not constitute an enduring moral norm, or by dismissing the prohibition as the rather arbitrary effect of an effort to establish Israelite identity by setting them apart from surrounding peoples. Proponents of the ban invoke similar distinctions to explain their selective application of Leviticus, dismissing, for example, the dietary codes and economic regulations. The problem with these ritual/moral distinctions is that they are foreign to the text. Such distinctions amount to an alien imposition on a people who envisioned their lives much more holistically. For the ancient Israelite, there simply was no clear division between morality and ritual.

So what is a Christian to do with Leviticus? As United Methodists, we should resonate with Leviticus' call to holiness, a call repeated by Jesus and John Wesley. Scripture, however, is clear that with Jesus' advent, God's holy order has changed—extended in some ways and in other ways made more rigorous. Hence, eunuchs and Gentiles are embraced and dietary laws are abolished. But nonretaliation is enjoined and the grounds for divorce are narrowed. The question, then, before us is "has God amended God's holy order with regard to homosexual practice?" Nowhere does Scripture state that God's order has been broadened with regard to homosexual practice. Yet the theological space for that *possibility* is created when we consider the logic of the prohibitions in light of Christ's advent, something the church father Augustine does in a discussion of celibacy.[10] Augustine argues that with the advent of Christ celibacy becomes a faithful possibility for Christians, whereas prior to the birth of Christ the command was to procreate. At the time of Leviticus, God's holy order required that persons procreate so that the Messiah might be born, but with the birth of Christ celibacy becomes a faithful possibility. Thus Augustine shows how faithful changes in the sexual ethic of Leviticus *might* be made on theological grounds. But we still have the New Testament witness to consider.

1 Corinthians 6:9 and 1 Timothy 1:10. The interpretation of "malakoi" and "arsenokoitai" remains hotly contested. Some connect "arseno-koitai" with the prohibition of Leviticus. Recently, however, strong evidence has been presented that "arsenokoitai" is a reference to some sort of sexual practice associated with economic exploitation and not a reinforcement of the categorical prohibition of Leviticus.[11] If the meaning of "arsenokoitai" remains elusive, "malakoi" does not. It refers essentially to men who were effeminate—too soft morally or otherwise.[12]

Romans 1:18-32. Two common errors attend the reading of this passage. The first error asserts that Paul was addressing heterosexual persons who "switched" and engaged in homosexual practice. The problem with this reading is that it imposes on Paul our modern belief in two distinct forms of sexual desire, whereas Paul held that there is but a single sexual desire. Consequently, Paul is rejecting not heterosexuals who "switched," but the excess of a single desire that results in homosexual practice. The second error asserts that Paul is offering an analysis of humanity in general and that consequently his rejection of homosexual practice is a categorical rejection on par with the general prohibitions of Leviticus. The problem with this reading is that it defies the logic of Paul's argument in the first chapters of

Romans. In this passage, Paul is not condemning humanity in general, but the Gentiles and their idolatry in particular. What difference does this make? Paul is not condemning homosexual practice in general but homosexual practice that is an excess of desire and rooted in pagan idolatry.

What conclusions can be drawn from this overview? Scripture does not condone any form of homosexual practice and it prohibits several particular forms of homosexual practice, although there may be good reason for extending what Scripture says about particular homosexual practices to other practices that it does not address. The only text that offers a categorical prohibition is Leviticus, and there *may* be theological grounds for understanding that this prohibition is not currently in effect. What resources do we have for discerning whether either God's holy order or the prohibitions have been extended?

A Theology of Marriage

Christianity has supplemented the scriptural witness with a rich tradition of theological reflection on marriage, and it is to this tradition that we turn for guidance in our process of discernment. Because United Methodists assert that Christians are called to "celibacy in singleness and fidelity in marriage," the church's reflection on marriage provides the proper theological context for the discussion of homosexual practice. Until recently the western Christian tradition of reflection on marriage has followed Augustine in describing marriage in terms of a calling to three ends, identified as the procreative, the unitive, and the sacramental.[13]

The tradition's reflection on marriage begins with the claim that marriage is a calling, a vocation. It is an *officium,* a societal duty, a particular office in the service of the church and the kingdom of God. A marriage that would not serve God by embodying the three ends is a marriage that cannot rightly be called a Christian marriage. Not every couple that comes before the church ought to receive the church's blessing. In other words, the three ends define the calling to Christian marriage.

The first end is the procreative end. Christian marriage must be open to children. Marriage is a matter of raising children in and for the kingdom of God. The second end is the unitive. The couple learns fidelity to one another, and in so doing they witness to the world of the fidelity of God to the people of God. The third end is the sacramental end. As it developed, this end was associated with holiness. Marriage is understood as a remedy for sin. In the Wesleyan tradition we might refer to marriage as a means of grace, whereby God through the gracious oversight of the church aids the married in overcoming sin and growing in sanctification.[14]

The question before us, then, is whether or not some Christian homosexual couples evidence a calling to marriage no less than some Christian heterosexual couples. Another way of putting this is, can a Christian homosexual couple embody the three ends of Christian marriage? I see no particular impediment to the possibility of Christian homosexual couples entering into a union that embodies the unitive and sacramental ends.[15] The procreative end would seem to offer the gravest difficulties to the recognition of homosexual unions as Christian marriages. Yet, I believe there are theologically legitimate ways in which a homosexual couple might embody the procreative end of marriage. This possibility hinges on severing the procreative end from biological reproduction, a severing that both happens in the church in a various ways—the principal one being adoption—and finds ample support in the Christian tradition. Let three examples suffice. First, Augustine himself does not hold that the biological inability to reproduce necessarily forecloses on a union being blessed as a Christian marriage.[16] Indeed, he explicitly distances Christianity from blood ties when he writes, "What else was [Jesus] teaching us except to prefer our spiritual kinship to carnal affinity, and that men are not blessed by being connected with just and holy people through blood relationship, but by being united to them through obedience to their teaching and imitation of their life?"[17] Second, Paul, in Rom. 9:8—a passage that finds support throughout the Gospels—suggests that the children of God are not those born "of the flesh" but those born "of the promise."[18] Third, baptism suggests that being open to children is a matter not of biology but of water and the Spirit; that is, in the church, parenting is established not as the result of biology but of baptism, of the pledge we make to assist in raising the church's children.[19]

* * *

The witness of Scripture and the rich tradition of Christian reflection on marriage provide the parameters for the church's process of discernment concerning homosexual practices. Scripture teaches that some homosexual practices, no less than some heterosexual practices, are clearly and unequivocally prohibited. The Christian tradition builds on that witness as it firmly positions faithful sexual practice within the context of marriage. In other words, Christian marriage is the proper theological context for the evaluation of homosexual practices; the church's process of discernment is best guided by theological reflection on the nature and ends of Christian marriage.

Theological reflection on Christian marriage, however, provides no simple answer to the question of homosexual practices. It provides neither a categorical affirmation nor a categorical rejection of homosexual practices. Rather, it guides the church's discernment; it indicates what questions we ought to be asking instead of waiting for science or dissecting Scripture in search of a transcultural essence. Two people present themselves to the church and seek the church's blessing of their marriage. In each case the church must faithfully discern: Does this couple manifest the call of God to Christian marriage? Are they committed to learning fidelity? Are they subject to the support and discipline of the church? Are they open to children?

This discernment is not easy; the answers are not self-evident. Hence, repositioning the discussion in terms of the nature and ends of Christian marriage does not promise to be a "magic bullet" that will suddenly heal all our divisions. Indeed, such a repositioning should start new conversations over exactly what constitutes the nature and ends of Christian marriage and over whether and how Christian homosexual couples can embody God's call to marriage as manifest in those ends. Nevertheless, if we can begin to discuss these matters, then we will have begun to make progress. At the very least, the church would benefit from serious theological reflection on its practice of marriage; at best, such a theological framework might provide the common ground for a path beyond the turbulence of the continental divide and into the calmer regions where most of us reside, struggling together to discern where the Spirit is moving.[20]

Is There a Crisis in Church Finance?

Vivian A. Bull

For more than thirty years I have served on United Methodist Church finance, investment, equitable salaries, and other such committees at the local, regional, and national levels, and in recent years, at the international level.[1] During that time, the church has continued to expand its programs, both locally and in the world. It has carried on this work with a declining membership and in some cases with declining financial resources, in spite of being in a time where there has been the greatest aggregate personal affluence that the western world has ever experienced. The church has not become affluent; indeed, many of our local churches and denominational programs are struggling to meet their financial needs.

In years past, many of our churches worked to pledge the budget, and though falling short, were able to generate a surplus by year's end and, more important, to meet a number of new economic challenges, such as the United Methodist Commission on Relief (UMCOR) might present during the course of the year. Within the congregation, there was a commitment to meet the needs, whether through personal giving or running fund raising events. In the small Swedish Methodist church in which I was raised, the local community depended upon the Grace Ladies to bake and sell Cornish pasties on Thursday and doughnuts on the weekend. And those pasties and doughnuts paid many of the bills for that small congregation. But we are living in different times, and I fear that we may not have fully understood how we, too, have to change our institutions in order to restore vitality and energy in the areas of finance and stewardship.

The importance of these issues has been addressed in a number of recent studies based on several of the mainline denominations, but we can draw information from them applicable to the United Methodist Church. John and Sylvia Ronsvalle, in *Behind the Stained Glass Windows,* report on what church members and leaders are thinking concerning money and the role it plays in church dynamics. Following World War II there was a resurgence of the mainline denominations as soldiers returned from the war. Work patterns were changing as more women remained in the workforce, but there was an effort to return to some semblance of "normalcy" in the communities. Church and community participation were part of the norm that was sought.

Membership began to sag in the mid-1960s and the churches sought new programs to attract people, hoping to meet the changing needs within society. There was increased emphasis upon day care centers, soup kitchens, shelters, and activities for all ages, with perhaps a decreased emphasis upon spiritual growth and missions.[2] During the following decades, people were becoming more affluent and more involved as community and school activities increased in number. Individuals and families saw themselves as being more self-reliant and yet, overcommitted. Sunday became a day of rest and increasingly did not include attendance at church. Overall support for the churches declined, and the aging of the congregation and the sources of future funding became a concern.

The Ronsvalles' study focused on mission giving and traced the changes that were taking place. As children, many of us remember the visits of the missionaries to the local congregations and the exciting stories about "far away places." Today many people have the opportunity to travel widely or participate in foreign experiences vicariously through television specials, which are more dynamic than thumbing through the encyclopedias or *National Geographic* magazines. The Ronsvalles found a general ambivalence toward past missionary activity, and this caused a weakening of support at the congregational level.[3] As colonial powers have given former colonies independence, indigenous churches have developed. Support of these has replaced the support given to missionaries. In recent years, congregations have turned to funding projects at the local level, often projects in which the members can be actively involved.

Some of the more successful overseas projects are conducted by Volunteers in Mission, where people travel and provide their personal services for a church-related project. The key to the success of these projects is good on-site supervision. Local populations often question whether the money could be better spent if the participants would just send cash instead of funding traveling and related expenses. These work opportunities are important, for they not only provide personal experience and gratification but also prepare spokespersons for future projects and activities, thus encouraging wider support and participation.

In the Methodist church, women were traditionally the mission educators and promoters within the congregations. Methodist women were also leaders in the establishment of mission projects around the world. As more women are in the workforce today, there are fewer dedicating their time and energies to this field. In fact, in the last half century, trained Methodist women often found greater areas of service open to them overseas than in the United States, particularly in education and medicine. I recall a woman missionary, who spent her working career in a teaching hospital in India, expressing concern that the pool of western women available for mission work was considerably smaller because there were so many job opportunities in their own countries. Her fear was that this would negatively impact the work in the mission field and thus the personal interest of the sending churches.

At a time when the leadership and interest level in the area of missions have changed, one can expect the funding to be reduced until new ways of involving greater personal participation can be identified. During this same time, the mission field itself has changed, for the call often now comes from the receiving entity, rather than the missionary being sent forth from the sending community.

In a study entitled *Money Matters: Personal Giving in American Churches,* Dean Hoge and others report on the factors influencing church giving in America. Interviews were conducted with some 625 churches in five representative denominations. The authors formed some interesting conclusions. Personal giving was highly correlated with active involvement in the church. Evangelical theology helped to generate support for outreach ministries, such as "aid to the needy and support (for) people seeking a more meaningful life in Jesus Christ."[4] Pledging as a way of planning one's giving and commitment for the year was important. Participatory decision making within the church and high standards of fiscal accountability are also important to encourage and sustain high levels of giving.[5]

When looking to the future, discussions with both pastors and parishioners most often turned to the baby boomers, those between the ages of thirty-five and fifty. That is the age group that might now be expected to provide leadership and financial support within the church.[6] The findings are somewhat disheartening. This generation has less denominational identity and loyalty than their elders. More often, they are highly mobile and have not established a long-term relationship within a single church or denomination. They tend to switch denominations easily.

Hoge suggests that this age group will respond to high quality programs. Those churches with good programs for many interests will attract them. The baby boomers were described as "consumer-oriented, meaning that they approach churches almost as they approach retail stores—seeking to buy something without expecting to get involved."[7]

This would seem to indicate that large churches with a variety of programs would have an advantage, but size may work against another interest of this group, that is to have hands-on involvement.

Baby boomers are reported to be more responsive in giving to special projects than to a general program. They tend to fund those causes in which they are interested. And they tend to have local loyalties and share in the nationwide trend of distrusting large institutions or bureaucracies.[8] This would help explain the success of UMCOR in the local churches when a call comes to fund a specific project or meet the needs created by a particular disaster. Often these events have been covered by television news, thus allowing people better to understand and respond to a particular problem. But this type of designated giving will not always be available to fund the budget or cover the cost of maintenance and repairs of the church plant.

If it is clear that we cannot depend upon the baby boomers to support the church in the traditional way, what can we expect from future churchgoers, those who are currently in college or new to the work force? The generation of students in their late teens and twenties is having a very different religious experience. Many of them have not grown up in the church or been regular in their attendance. They find themselves living in a more racially and ethnically diverse world, and they are more comfortable with cultural expressions of diversity. This also includes their understanding of religious pluralism.

In a recent article in the *Chronicle of Higher Education* (16 January 1998), Diane Winston discussed "Campuses Are a Bellwether for Society's Religious Revival." She tells of a student who, when asked about her religious preferences, responded "Methodist, Taoist, Native American, Quaker, Russian Orthodox, and Jew." Winston goes on to say that though this sounds confusing and contradictory, the student is faithful in her own fashion. "She works for world peace, practices yoga and meditation, attends a Methodist church, regularly participates in American Indian ceremonies and shares a group house with others who combine various spiritual practices."[9] As we are living in a more pluralistic society with persons of many different faiths and religions, we are learning about beliefs and behaviors that once seemed unusual but are now more appreciated and, in some cases, incorporated into the religious practices of our younger folks. "Religion—or, in the more popular term, 'spirituality'—is thriving among undergraduates (on the campuses) as it is in the country at large."[10] This trend is true across the country, from state institutions, to historic black colleges, to small liberal arts colleges, to the Catholic universities.

Students are sincere in their seeking and learning and in their practice of new traditions, beliefs, and customs. In discussions, many of them question the importance of the traditional church, when the way to serve is to be out among the people. Nontraditional services and activities, community gathering places, outdoor experiences (perhaps recreating the camp experience of earlier years) all are found to be more attractive as places for the expression of one's religious beliefs. As the children of the baby boomers, they express some of the same interests and concerns of their parents. Young people today are very service oriented, but they wish to be involved with people and projects, not supporting others to do the work.

This trend must raise some questions for us. If the baby boomers are not responding to the institutional church in traditional ways, their children, this next generation, is even less likely to do so. The students of today will be living and working in a vastly multicultural world, and even now, there are areas of the United States where Anglos are in the minority. Demographic changes in the culture will affect religious life not only at the colleges and universities but in society at large. The financing and funding of our traditional institutions and programs will not be accomplished unless we learn to respond proactively to our changing culture. Winston concludes her discussion by writing, "Now, as in the past, young people are exploring new ways of believing and behaving in their search for a richer, more meaningful way of being in the world. Rather than dismiss their attempts, we should try to learn along with them."

In a paper entitled "Methodists on the Margins: 'Self-Authoring' Religious Identity" Penny Long Marler and C. Kirk Hadaway support the thesis that "the conditions of late modernity pose particular epistemological and practical problems for the nature and shape of religious self-identity—and that these problems have reciprocal effects on religious institutions and may explain, for instance, declining church membership and attendance" and probably, also declining financial support.[11] The authors suggest that this is a time of "great unsettlement." In the present era, we are somewhere in between the traditional community and some kind of new community: "some (people are) adrift and at the mercy of the sea; some (are) clinging desperately to once-friendly shores resisting the force and lure of 'the beyond'; some (are) anchored obstinately at the harbor's mouth arguing over what to do or whether to go; and some (are) intentionally setting out in search of whatever may be just over the horizon."[12]

A time of "great unsettlement" can be a time of enormous opportunity. As we look to the financing of the church in the next century, we will have to develop new approaches and understandings based on what we are observing today. We must empower the local churches and find ways of reducing a bureaucracy that does not relate directly to those who are called into the churches. We must develop new systems that will provide leadership at many levels, that call upon churchgoers to be doers. We need to find new ways to reach the people, new ways to work with members and potential members. Marler and Hadaway suggest that we need to know what is going on in the minds and lives of people, what cultural resources people are drawing on, what strategies or actions they are building.[13]

We must develop new methods to promote stewardship. In the United States, everyone is bombarded with sophisticated marketing materials to encourage contributions to a large number of worthy causes and organizations, some of which were originally funded by government, many of which are new opportunities in our changing culture. We must develop appropriate, energetic campaigns for stewardship within the church. The Ronsvalles discuss several points of consensus arrived at by the Stewardship Project National Advisory Committee in 1995, which include: the church needs a positive agenda for the great affluence in our society and healthy churches produce generous people.[14] The focus on stewardship must be as a whole life response to the gift of life.

There is no direct translation for the word stewardship in Spanish. The Catholic Pastoral uses the word *coresponsibilidad*, which "implies that stewardship involves a person in shared response with other Christians, with those in need, and with God Almighty. . . . Coresponsibility points toward a partnership in the mission and vision of God's plan."[15] What a powerful image this creates! Perhaps we should incorporate the concept of *coresponsibilidad* into the core of our understanding of good stewardship.

A time of "great unsettlement" must be a time for change. In the past we have drawn upon our historic Methodist traditions. We must do so as never before and empower those who will help to educate and focus our work, to build a secure future, to find new ways for a traditional institution to serve and grow and find its authentic place in an increasingly nontraditional world. Marler and Hadaway correctly state that "it is no longer a case of telling persons what to believe and what to do but helping them figure out in the face of a dizzying array of options how to choose their beliefs and live authentically."[16]

When the church is vital in the hearts and lives of our people, when we have defined new ways to reach out, when we have developed new ways of expressing who we are as United Methodists in this time of "great unsettlement," then there *will* be the financial resources to meet the needs of the church. But there is much work to be done!

What Defines Clergy Compensation: Mission or Market?

William B. Lawrence and Meghan Froehlich

United Methodist preachers do not take vows of poverty. They expect to be, and are, compensated. But how is the amount of their compensation determined? Does "mission" or the "market" control the process? What is the relationship between the money pastors receive and the ministerial services they provide?

Salary figures from the denomination's statistical tables provide partial answers for these and other questions. The emerging patterns suggest that "market" in fact controls clergy salaries, and that United Methodist compensation mirrors American society—with very high and growing salaries for a very few at the top (media elite, corporate chief executives, celebrity sports figures, medical specialists, and others), and a growing gap separating those few from the mass of white-collar and blue-collar individuals in the rest of their work force. What we have found is a large and growing gap between the compensation received by the vast majority of United Methodist pastors and a small minority of preachers at the top of the compensation scale. We have also found significant differences among the annual conferences. This situation has serious implications for clergy morale and itinerancy. But there are some options available to the church.

In one episode of his 1896 novel *The Damnation of Theron Ware*, Harold Frederic pictures a young Methodist preacher learning some facts of parish life from an astute, itinerant revivalist named Sister Soulsby. "Why, man alive, do you know what I've done for you?" she asks. "I got around on the Presiding Elder's blind side, I captured old Pierce, I wound Winch right around my little finger, I worked two or three of the class leaders—all on your account. The result was you went through as if you'd had your ears pinned back, and been greased all over. You've got an extra hundred dollars added to your salary—do you hear?"[1]

During an ensuing board meeting he learned a few more facts of parish life: his church's income might be lower than pledged; and there were doubts about meeting the increased payroll. A motion to approve the budget, including the hundred-dollar raise for the preacher, was offered. The pastor, as chair of the meeting, put the motion before the board for decision. Each member declared an "Aye" or "Nay" individually. The final vote was offered orally by an adversary of the pastor: "I vote No, and it's a tie. It rests with the chairman now to cast the deciding vote, and say whether this interesting arrangement shall go through or not." The pastor, "with a cool self-control," responded "Me? Oh, I vote Aye."[2]

Every fall, in their church and charge conferences, United Methodists set the rate of compensation that their pastors will receive for the ensuing year. These decisions do not occur in a vacuum. Based on the recommendations of an annual conference "Commission on Equitable Compensation" (see *The [1992] Book of Discipline,* par. 722.3) a "schedule of minimum base compensation for all full-time pastors or those clergy members of the annual conference appointed less than full time to a local church" is adopted in each conference. A pastoral charge is then obliged to "provide," and each pastor is entitled "to receive," no less than the scheduled minimum compensation (see paragraph 441). However, a pastor's actual level of compensation is the result of a local decision made at the Charge Conference after consultation by the Committee on Pastor-Parish Relations and with the District Superintendent (see par. 270.2*f*[4]).

The local process that leads to a final decision varies widely.

At one extreme, it may simply be the perfunctory approval of the minimum rate fixed by the annual conference for full-time service. At the other, it may be a complex series of deliberations and consultations, both formal and informal, which could include a performance evaluation, a cost-of-living factor, a range of adjustments based on "merit," an assessment of current clergy compensation compared with other professionals in the community, some comparisons with remuneration paid to other clergy in similar congregations within and outside the denomination, and a direct negotiation in which the pastor and the church officers agree upon a package of benefit and compensation items.

While there are variations in procedure, the structure of the process clearly lodges decision-making authority at the local church level. Laity in congregations that are accustomed to paying the conference minimum often complain that they "do not decide" how much to pay the preacher, and insist that they "are told" what the salary must be. Yet the church or charge actually does decide whether it wishes to receive, and thereby support, full-time pastoral service. (And, of course, the church or charge elects a lay member of the annual conference where the minimum is set.) Laity in congregations that are able and/or willing to pay the pastor above the minimum tend to view this local authority as vital to their interests: an effective pastor can be rewarded, and an ineffective one not rewarded, with increases in pay; a salary decision sends a signal to the cabinet about the type of pastor it expects to receive when a pastoral change occurs; and the higher the salary, the greater degree a local church has influence in the appointing of a new pastor. Clergy tend to see this local authority as vital to their interests as well: "the system is designed to reward the pastor who is effective in persuading the congregation to raise the salary," wrote Lyle Schaller.[3]

This local authority to decide on compensation has been part of our structure for so long that we can forget it was not always the case. For Methodism's first hundred years or so, in Britain and America, preachers received an "allowance" or "support" that was designed to cover the expenses of traveling, but little more. That the amounts were quaint and meager ($64 a year in 1792, raised to $80 in 1800 and to $100 in 1816) is not so important as the structure of the compensation: it was not in any sense a fee for services rendered, but rather a basic stipend to sustain an individual's survival and to cover the costs of itinerating; it was deemed to be the level needed to support one person, which meant that a preacher's spouse received an equal amount for support and that graduated amounts were fixed for children of various ages; and, it was an equal level of support for all preachers, regardless of the circuits through which they traveled. Funds were collected quarterly from the circuits, but they were distributed equally according to need for support, rather than proportionately according to church revenues collected. A preacher who had other means of support (like Freeborn Garrettson, who came from a wealthy family) received no stipend.[4] The General Conference of 1804 determined that a preacher who had other resources available would receive something less than a full conference share.[5] Moreover, support was provided not only to active, traveling preachers but also to "worn-out" preachers and itinerants' widows.

Asbury believed that this compensation structure was essential to the itinerant system. It assured unity, mobility, and covenantal account-ability. Whether the current pattern of congregational accountability is compatible with the itinerancy continues to be an episcopal concern: "The impact of salary differential on the appointive system has been debated for years. . . . But we face a situation in some annual conferences where the setting of pastoral salaries is being used as a way to step out of the appointive system. Although the authority to set salary rests with the charge conference, the danger of a rampant congregationalism here must be recognized."[6]

In any case, the current system has hardly burst upon us suddenly. It has gradually evolved over a very long time, perhaps more than a hundred and fifty years. Michael Nickerson says that the connectional salary system was in its final stages in the 1840s.[7] Donald Messer points out that in 1860 the General Conference of the Methodist Episcopal Church gave each quarterly conference the authority to set pastors' salaries. Parallel bodies made similar moves not long afterward. "By 1915, the system in place today had already evolved."[8]

These developments in setting compensation were not unrelated to larger transitions in Methodism. The movement was redefining itself as a network of settled congregations. The church was reestablishing itself to appeal to the emerging middle class. The lay leadership of the church tended increasingly to come from the rising class of leaders in business and the professions. The values of business, where success and incentive and reward could be measured in dollars, found expression in local church decisions to offer their pastors salary increases for services rendered.

Attempts to alter the system have failed. The option of establishing a basic salary plan within an annual conference has been withdrawn.[9] An appropriate compensation level tends to be determined by contemporary professional and consumer criteria rather than by notions of personal "support." The General Conference does indeed legislate a mechanism for setting minimum levels of compensation. But there are no prospects for creating a similar mechanism to set maximums. Most important, local churches of every size and at every level of compensation cherish their authority to decide what their pastors shall be paid.

How has this system served the church? What has it achieved? How well does it help us fulfill our mission and ministry as a denomination?

In an attempt to develop answers for these and other questions, we have been examining recent statistical tables for each of the annual conferences of the United Methodist Church in the United States. Specifically, we have looked at the reported figures for salaries paid to pastors across the church during the period from 1982 to 1992. In addition to using a denominational average compensation, we have looked at the figures for each annual conference. That allowed us to identify any significant differences in minimums, and also to assess any differences in the range from minimum to maximum from one conference to another.

Other boundaries helped define the scope of our study. To assure consistency, we have limited the bottom level of compensation studied to the minimum set by each annual conference in each year for ordained elders in full connection. Associate members, probationary members, full-time local pastors, and ordained ministers from other denominations tend to have lower minimums in each annual conference, but we did not attempt to calculate the differences in compensation or the numbers of pastors in those categories who are affected. (Though obvious, it should simply be noted that there are pastors serving full-time and receiving less compensation than the amount we have used as a minimum figure for an annual conference in a given year.) Further, we *have not included* the modifications that individual conferences may allow for additional years of service, advanced education beyond the master of divinity degree, family size, or other considerations. We *have not included* any persons who are appointed beyond the local church. We *have included* only cash compensation, not travel allowance, housing allowance, or other benefits. We *have included* those pastors serving in station appointments and those in multichurch charges; however, we *have not included* those persons who are appointed as associate pastors because of the way that the statistical tables aggregate the salaries of all associate appointees on a church staff. Our purpose was to learn as much as possible about the patterns of clergy compensation and the impact that local decisions about salary may have on the connection.

One preliminary point should be made about the annual conference minimums. In the initial year of our study (1982), the lowest of them was $8000, and the highest was $15,029. In the final year of our study (1992), the lowest conference minimum was $10,000, and the highest was $25,650. Thus, measured in whole dollars, the *difference* between the conferences with the lowest and highest minimums more than doubled in ten years: from $7029 in 1982 to $15,650 in 1992.

The evidence for the years 1982–92 leads to several conclusions, among them the following:

- There is a growing gap between the compensation received by clergy at the lower levels of the scale (where 75 percent of the salaries hover) and the 25 percent at the top of the scale, becoming most dramatic between the top 1 percent and the other 99 percent.
- The rate at which the gap grows is increasing.
- There is no apparent correlation between changes in compensation level and the cost of living.
- Each annual conference manifests these trends differently, and not all fit a single pattern.

Figure 1 illustrates the salary data for all of the annual conferences during the period under study. By using quartiles of the total clergy population, we can see the clustered compensation levels of those in the lowest 25 percent, the lowest 50 percent, and the lowest 75 percent. Moreover, by illustrating the 99th percentile, we can mark the difference separating the top 1 percent from the rest.

Figure 1
United Methodist Clergy Compensation 1982–92

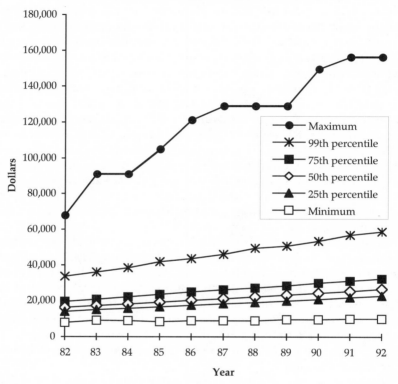

In 1992, 75 percent of United Methodist pastors were receiving $32,136 per year or less. We can see how closely those 75 percent track with the minimum compensation in each year. Indeed, it appears that up to 99 percent of United Methodist pastors are compensated on a similar track. One possible explanation is that three-fourths (and perhaps as many as 99 percent) of the local churches that set their pastors' compensation at some level above the minimum tend to use about the same rate of increase as the scheduled rise in the minimum for an annual conference. But less than one-fourth of the pastors (and perhaps as few as one percent) are appointed to churches that use other means of determining compensation.

The top line of the graph indicates the maximum compensation that was paid in each year, with the space between the top line and the 99th percentile showing the range of compensation covered by the upper 1 percent. One can readily see that most of the gapping increase occurs in the top 1 percent.

It might seem simple to explain this pattern in terms of congregational size: the bigger the church, the higher the salary. And it is certainly true that the higher levels of compensation tend to occur in the local churches with the largest worship attendance. However, a closer comparison of size and salary forecloses all but the broadest generalizations. For instance, in 1989, a church at the 75th percentile in compensation had a larger worship attendance than a church at the 99th percentile in compensation. In 1991, a church at the 50th percentile had a larger attendance than a church at the 75th. And in 1986, a church at the 25th percentile in compensation had a larger worship attendance than churches at the 50th and 75th salary percentiles.

To reiterate, this graph illustrates the range of compensation received by those pastors who are serving full-time and who are being compensated at or above the annual conference base for elders in full connection.

In his study of clergy compensation, Michael Nickerson focused on the period just prior to the decade that we are examining. He compared the difference between the *median* and the *maximum* salaries for 1912 and again for 1976, and he concluded that the difference between the lowest and the highest salaries in the church "has actually diminished."[10]

Our conclusions are just the opposite—perhaps because the situation changed dramatically in the decade following 1982. In that year, the median was $16,100, and in 1992 the median was $26,264. However, it is clear that compensation levels for the top 1 percent of United Methodist clergy soared in the period from 1982 to 1992. The maximum compensation received by any pastor in 1982 was $68,000, while in 1992 that number had risen to $156,200—an increase of about 130 percent. The difference between the median and the maximum in 1982 ($51,900), when compared with the difference between median and maximum in 1992 ($129,936), reveals a gap that has more than doubled. And the rate at which the gap grows is increasing.

Figure 2 uses the same data, but measures them against the changes in the cost of living. One consideration here involves the role played by housing in calculating the living costs, since most United

Methodist pastors live in church-owned parsonages and are not directly affected by fluctuations in mortgage rates, fuel costs, hazard insurance premiums, or maintenance expenses. A small percentage of the denomination's pastors receive housing allowances, and as homeowners or renters they are directly affected. However, we have determined that the cost of living rose at an average annual rate of 3.82 percent from 1982 to 1992, and that housing costs were a consistent part of that increase through the period.[11] In other words, it was not necessary to extract housing before calculating the changes in the cost of living.

Figure 2
Cost of Living and Clergy Compensation

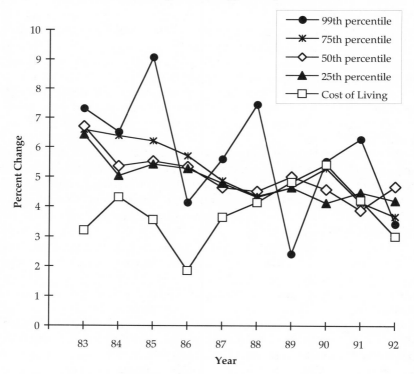

What this graph demonstrates is the lack of any coherent relationship between changes in the cost of living and changes in pastors' compensation. Generally, it appears that from 1982 through 1989, United Methodist clergy compensation grew at a rate higher than changes in the cost of living; but compensation for the top 1 percent rose much faster than the cost of living in every year except 1989. We can measure this by using the Consumer Price Index, which fixes the number 100 as the index for living costs in a base period (1982–84). In 1992, the CPI was 140.3,[12] meaning that it took 40.3 percent more dollars in 1992 than in the base period to live comparably.

In 1983, which is the middle of the base period and the calendar year with a CPI closest to 100, clergy at the 25th percentile were paid $14,900. In 1992, at that same level, the compensation was $22,505, an increase of 51 percent; thus the rise exceeded the cost of living increase. At the 50th percentile, clergy in 1983 received $17,180 and in 1992 they were paid $26,264; this was an increase of 53 percent. At the 75th percentile, the 1983 compensation was $20,680; in 1992, it was $32,136, an increase of 55 percent.

This suggests that changes in the Consumer Price Index do not directly correlate with changes in the compensation of United Methodist pastors. At all levels, increases in compensation appear to have exceeded the cost of living; and the higher the compensation level, the greater the rate increases, which further increases the dollar gap. Factors other than a desire to keep pace with inflation seem to be driving compensation decisions. For the top 1 percent of clergy, those other factors are substantially increasing pastors' net incomes.

Figure 3 is actually a set of graphs that indicate the importance of looking at individual annual conferences whenever one studies United Methodist clergy salaries. The three conferences selected for this illustration include neither the lowest minimum nor the highest maximum level of pastoral compensation during the decade under review. In one respect, they have nothing in common. They come from different jurisdictions: Central Texas is in the South Central Jurisdiction; Rocky Mountain is in the Denver Area of the Western Jurisdiction; and Wyoming is part of the Albany Area in the Northeast. They are of differing size geographically and statistically. And they have a different blend of congregations with larger and smaller membership. Yet, in another respect they exemplify the common character of our denomination with regard to clergy compensation: a polity in which annual conferences set the minimum and expect local churches to meet it; and the local freedom to decide how much to pay the preacher.

Figure 3a
Wyoming Conference

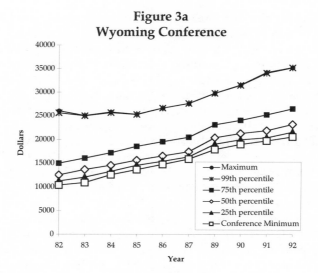

Figure 3b
Central Texas Conference

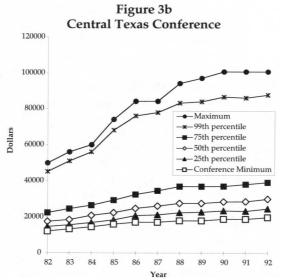

Figure 3c
Rocky Mountain Conference

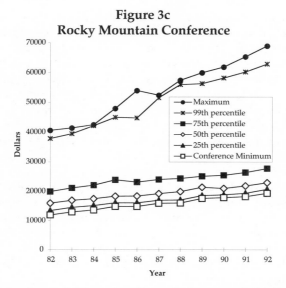

What this shows is that the Central Texas and Rocky Mountain Conferences have followed almost exactly the same track with regard to their minimums—from $12,000 in each case in 1982 to $19,685 and $19,373 respectively in 1992. Wyoming had a much lower minimum in 1982 ($10,375) than either of the others, but by 1992 it had set the highest minimum of the three ($20,560)—almost double! Whereas the Consumer Price Index rose 40.3 percent, the Wyoming minimum rose 89 percent between 1983 and 1992. For the same period, the Central Texas and Rocky Mountain minimums rose 49 percent.

The real differences, of course, are at the upper income levels. In Wyoming, the gap between minimum and maximum salaries actually *decreased* between 1982 and 1992. In Central Texas, the gap was $38,000 in 1982 and $81,000 in 1992. In Rocky Mountain, the gap was less than $28,000 in 1982 and almost $50,000 in 1992. At the 75th percentile, Rocky Mountain rose 31 percent, Central Texas rose 60 percent, and Wyoming rose 66 percent.

One could argue that Wyoming has, in effect, created something very close to a basic salary plan by local church decisions about compensation while increasing the minimum substantially. This result has not occurred as the consequence of some conference strategy, but (based on our knowledge of the conference) simply as a development that reflects congregational size, community salary patterns, and other local factors.

One could also argue that what really matters is the percentage of a congregation's budget that it commits to pastoral compensation. But in smaller congregations, the pastor may be the entire program staff, and it is likely that a larger share of the church's budget will be spent on salary and benefits for the pastor. And in larger congregations, it seems arbitrary to offer the pastor a share of the church budget. If the budget grows from one million dollars to two million dollars, should the pastor's compensation double?

Hypothetical arguments aside, there are two fundamental issues to be addressed. One has to do with clergy **morale**: the sense that one is fulfilling one's call to the ordained ministry, the belief that one is joined in a covenant of service with others who are similarly called, the feeling that one is serving effectively, the conviction that one's pastoral practice has value and purpose. The other issue has to do with **itinerancy**: the authority of a bishop to make appointments, and the freedom and willingness of pastors to move where they are appointed.

Morale is a quality that should be assessed both in its individual and corporate dimensions.

An individual pastor who feels unfulfilled in the practice of ministry will not find the ministry any more fulfilling for twice as much income. And a pastor who finds the practice of ministry spiritually fulfilling will not feel any more spiritually fulfilled with an increase in compensation. Both those who find satisfaction in their ministries, and those who do not, may feel trapped by an economic system that limits everything from the form of their children's education to the quality of their family's health care to their opportunities for study and travel. An unhappy pastor may therefore devise ways to stay in the pastoral ministry and pursue rising levels of compensation in search of substitute satisfaction. A happy pastor may feel obliged to move merely because the money is better.

Within the corporate life of an annual conference, morale is significantly affected by disparities in compensation. So imbedded are we in the culture of upward mobility that clergy tend to feel themselves more in competition than in covenant with one another. Preachers assume that an appointment "ladder" will take them to larger congregations with higher levels of compensation through their careers. But the data do not confirm that a "ladder" exists. Only 1 percent of the appointments seem to offer compensation that significantly exceeds the cost of living. In other words, up to 99 percent of United Methodist clergy will find themselves not on a ladder but on a gently sloping floor. The others are riding escalators: the current system offers a potentially perverse incentive to get on if one can.

It takes as much time to prepare a sermon for 50 people as it does for 1500, but the hourly rate at which the preacher is compensated for preparation time will probably be vastly different in our current system. It takes as much pastoral competence to counsel a family whose six year-old was struck by a drunk driver whether the pastor providing the counseling is paid $90,000 a year or $25,000. It is as important to articulate a vision for ministry in an area of urban blight as it is in an area of suburban subdivisions. Should the compensation for the pastor in each of those settings be what the congregation can pay or what supporting a pastor in each setting requires? Should the size of the market be the sole factor in determining the value of the sermon preparation time?

We impair the corporate morale of a conference when we use only congregational market factors to decide the level of compensation for ministry in each locale.

Itinerancy lies at the center of these matters. Bishops, superintendents, pastors, spouses of pastors, and members of pastor-parish relations committees know that compensation is one of the dominant issues in making pastoral appointments. Compensation levels have veto power when cabinets are considering appointments: a good match of pastoral "gifts" and community "needs" will be set aside because the salary is not "right." Local church committees may negotiate with superintendents to find a salary level that will secure for them a specific (or a specific type of) preacher, or they may recommend substantial raises for their beloved incumbent pastors so that no one will be tempted to make a change. Pastors may negotiate higher salaries in their current appointments so that they can remain under consideration for still higher levels of compensation in a future appointment. Critical goals, like open itinerancy, can be deferred because of such factors.

Three proposals for modifying the compensation system merit discussion:
- define the clergy as "employees" of an annual conference;
- have the conference structure all clergy compensation as "basic support" for mission and "goals" for mission; and
- make appointments on the basis of gifts and graces for mission and ministry, rather than on considerations about salary.

The first proposal takes into consideration the current effort by the Internal Revenue Service to deny "self-employment" status to United Methodist clergy. Our current compensation system was in place early in the twentieth century before the federal income tax was established. It may now be time to reclaim the original Wesleyan plan and to recognize that our polity is best accommodated to the IRS by identifying pastors as employees of the annual conference: only the conference can "hire" or "dismiss"; only the conference can determine the location of one's service; only the conference evaluates performance. So it makes sense, within our polity, to symbolize the common covenant contractually and to treat the clergy members of the annual conference as employees of the conference.

The second proposal would have the annual conference set a "basic support" level rather than a "minimum" compensation level. This "support" would be an amount judged by the conference to be sufficient for enabling a preacher to serve full-time in an appointment. Then as part of the consultation regarding a new or continuing appointment, the superintendent, the pastor, and the charge committee would set goals for the charge—for example, to establish a shelter for the homeless in the community; to train twenty Bible study leaders and church school teachers; to equip thirty laity for evangelism; to increase worship attendance by twenty-five percent; to support one full-time urban missioner; and so forth. Periodically the rate of success in achieving these goals would be determined by consultation, and supplemental compensation would be provided by the conference on the basis of the goals for mission and ministry that had been achieved. The annual conference would request and receive from pastoral charges revenues for this "goals" fund, and the amount distributed would depend on the total amount received by the conference.

The third would be made possible because the salary structure for all pastors would be the same within an annual conference. Consultation about an appointment could focus exclusively on matters of mission and ministry, on the gifts a pastor would bring to a situation, on the goals for that setting, and on the nonmonetary impact of the move upon the pastor's family. Itinerancy would not be impeded by concerns about the affordability of a move.

The uniqueness of United Methodism lies in its historic merger of mission and ministry through an itinerant, connectional system. Not only is our present system of compensating clergy inconsistent with our history, theology, and polity, but it inhibits effectiveness and morale. We need a new method that supports persons who are called into ministry and enhances the effectiveness of their service.

What Difference Do the Size, Site, and Style of the Annual Conference Make?

Dennis M. Campbell and Russell E. Richey

In the course of the last decade we have visited many sessions of United Methodist annual conferences across the United States. During these visits to preach, speak, bring greetings, or simply to attend, we have come to think that attention urgently needs to be given to the question, "What difference do the size, site, and style of the annual conference make?" Research on this question as part of our United Methodism and American Culture Project leads to several policy recommendations that conferences might consider.

Many clergy and laity can still recall an era when the style of gathering differed greatly from the present pattern. It was common for sessions to be convened in churches and for members to be housed in nearby Methodist homes. The congregational setting provided a worshipful atmosphere for meeting, a physical referent for the conference's mission, and working space that linked means and ends. It also brought Methodist connectionalism into the communal and individual lives of the city or town where it met. Conscious of this connection-promoting aspect of its meeting, conferences made a point of moving around. And conferences monitored their size with a view to making it feasible to hold their sessions in a variety of communities.

Today most annual conferences meet in settings far removed from the context of the church. Dennis has preached ordination sermons at annual conference meetings in college gymnasiums, in university theaters, in college auditoriums, in vast civic centers, in hotel ballrooms, and even in a Holiday Inn Holidome. Once in a while an annual conference will still meet in a church (First Church, Houston, comes to mind), or a college or university chapel (like West Virginia Wesleyan). Several meet in church conference centers, such as Lake Junaluska, North Carolina, or Lakeside, Ohio, but many conferences are now housed in large secular civic centers or institutions that, the week before, might have housed a play, circus, wrestling match, or political fund-raising dinner.

Why the change? The driving factors for the siting of conferences now seem to be convenience for the delegates and the size of the assemblage. The argument for a college or university campus is that in one setting delegates can be housed (in student dormitories), fed (in student dining rooms), and accommodated for meetings in a gymnasium, auditorium, or theater. Convenience, and especially adjacent parking, is sometimes used to advocate using a civic center, hotel, and shopping mall combination. It was recently argued on the floor of one annual conference that adjacency to a shopping mall would increase attendance. The plea for the vast civic centers, however, is usually size alone. Some annual conferences have grown so big that only a civic center will accommodate all of their members.

The size of an annual conference must, of course, govern where it meets. Members must be accommodated. Space must be made for committee meetings, operations, the press, and visitors. The sessions and other important activities must be accessible to persons with disabilities. Location within the conference, access by car, parking, costs, all count in the siting of a conference. However, size and these related factors are not fixed. They are variables determined:
• by how jurisdictional conferences draw boundaries;
• by how conferences and bishops wish to configure their work and undertake their mission;
• by what local churches and conferences expect in the way of services and staffing; and
• by what the church generally thinks are the ideal membership and geographical contours for effective appointment-making.
Indeed, conference size constitutes a statement about the church and its mission, about the nature of the conference covenant, about how this basic body of the church will do its work.

It is appropriate, therefore, to ask some questions about size and site. Why have annual conferences grown so large? Should size be thought about in instrumental and programmatic terms? How has size affected style? What difference does or might the meeting place have? What might conferences do differently were they smaller or larger? What might they be if they were of a different size?

A Retrospective

Size, site, and style certainly have changed. Jesse Lee observed the 1782 annual conference at Ellis' Chapel, in Sussex County, Va., a gathering of about thirty preachers. Attending all its sessions save the examination of character, he wrote:

> The union and brotherly love which I saw among the preachers, exceeded every thing I had ever seen before, and caused me to wish that I was worthy to have a place amongst them. When they took leave of each other,

I observed that they embraced each other in their arms, and wept as though they never expected to meet again. Had the heathens been there, they might have well said, "see how the Christians love one another!" By reason of what I saw and heard during the four days that the conference sat, I found my heart truly humbled in the dust, and my desires greatly increased to love and serve God more perfectly than I had ever done before.[1]

John Kobler reported similarly:

April 20 [1791] our Conference began in Petersburgh. The ministers from all the circuits around attended. We also had Bishop Coke from Europe to sit at the head of conference. Here we continued three days and it was a great time of God's power both in publick and in private.[2]

For earlier Methodism, such intense spirituality defined conference, and conference spirituality defined Methodist life. Early Methodists 'did' church, conducted business, shaped themselves in a gracious, conferencing fashion. Ends and means were tightly linked. Methodist structure was what it purposed: it was gracious. Conferences indeed revived, as a careful reading of the record will show. They lived up to Wesley's expectations of conference.

Conference as a Means of Grace

Wesley had spoken of Christian conference as one of the instituted means of grace. By that he had referred, not to formal governing structures, but to the form of engagement of Christians with one another that he expected in band, class, and society—Christian conversation that opened to others the working of God in the self and that by such intense, authentic self-disclosure (witness) opened other selves to God's workings. Though Wesley may not have so fully intended it, the small annual conferences became Christian conference. Wesley's Christian engagement and conversation went on through the formal governing organization of conference—general, annual, quarterly—and through its local counterpart, the class. Although Wesley may not have put it this way, to speak, as he did, of Christian conference as one of the instituted means of grace, to surround it with other instituted gracious means, to identify additional prudential means clearly evocative of Wesleyan structure, to call his governing gatherings "conference," and to conduct his business in a conferencing mode was to say something very profound, not about form, but about *style*.

Well into the nineteenth century annual conferences were intimate "brotherhoods" that cared for the spiritual health of each member, of the whole fraternity, and, of course, of the people called Methodists. Their small size made such care possible, care of one another, but also care for the connection. They provided, of course, for public preaching during their sitting. Taking advantage of the assemblage of talent, they farmed out the gathered preachers to the churches of the immediate and neighboring communities, Methodist and non-Methodist. Frequently, they met in conjunction with a camp meeting so as to structure that communal and revivalistic outreach.

Most important, conferences nurtured the spiritual potential of their own gatherings. They attended to the religious character and journey of one another, undertaking serious review of ministerial character in closed but plenary session. Conferences, because of their intimate size, permitted probing and frankness. Confidences were protected by closed doors because all annual conferences included only full ministerial members. And conferences provided, as did the Western Conference in 1805, time for witness: "The conference spent a few hours, this evening, in speaking of the work of God in their souls and Circuits." In the 1807 New England Conference, "Mr. Asbury read several letters he had rec'd from the preachers, giving an account of the work of God."[3] Later in the same conference, "Mr. Asbury read a letter from br. Chandler giving an acc't of the great revival in Delaware District—also a letter from br. Stith Mead giving an acc't of the work of God in Richmond District, Virginia." That conference then devoted time and attention to their own spiritual estate: "To close the present sitting an hour or two was spent in conversing on the state of the Lord's work among the people under our charge, and in our own souls." For one of his conferences and as late as 1859 Bishop Janes reported:

> We had an unusually pleasant session of the Cincinnati Conference. It was characterized by a high degree of spiritual interest. When I examined the candidates for admission into full connection, I requested several of the senior members of the Conference to give a relation of their ministerial experience—especially of their call and early ministry. We spent nearly two hours in these exercises and prayer. Sunday was a most gracious day. I preached at half past ten o'clock with considerable liberty and more unction than God has often granted me. Deep impressions were made. Bishop Simpson preached in the afternoon. God was with his servant and in his word. The evening meeting was a precious one. Several professed religion and joined the Church. Among those who joined during the Conference were a son and son-in-law of ex-Governor Trimble.[4]

The spiritual self-care of the small conference empowered it to render comparable care for the whole connection. The Western Conference in 1805 made overtures to the other conferences calling for collective fasting and prayer. They heeded their own mandate: "We have this day covenanted to pray for our brethren in the succeeding Conferences; especially in the time of their sitting." The special, intimate, class-like quality of early conferences drew much remark, in retrospect, from those looking back from a later day and recalling with nostalgia the conferences of their youth. Peter Cartwright, for instance, remembered the effect of such sessions of the Western conference:

> These early Conferences were often seasons of refreshing showers of Divine grace, and of the gracious outpouring of the Holy Ghost. Sinners were convicted and converted to the Lord Jesus. The conference business had not become so great as to require the time now occupied by an Annual Conference.[5]

Such intense, seemingly spontaneous spiritual exercises seemed requisite for those who believed that "God's design in raising up the Preachers called Methodists," was to "reform the Continent, and to spread scriptural Holiness over these Lands." Conference spirituality was essential to spreading it more broadly and reforming the continent.

Policies of Division versus Policies of Aggregation

In the early-nineteenth century, United Methodist predecessor churches, by policy and/or practice, kept annual conferences small. Annual conferences sought their own division when growth made them unwieldy, and General Conferences kept boundary committees at work making sure that missional purposes were served by conference divisions. When division of the Baltimore Conference was being considered in the mid-nineteenth century, letters to the *Christian Advocate* enumerated a variety of reasons why smaller size was beneficial. One correspondent cited nine reasons, another four, the latter including the point:

> The conference would not be too large to be held in any of our principal towns. This would be greatly to our advantage, increasing our influence as a Church, and making our people better acquainted with our chief ministers, and our general plan of operations.[6]

The compelling rationale, policies, and practices reversed in the twentieth century. Conferences grew, and grew dramatically. These once face-to-face "fraternities" became, through the unifications of 1939 and 1968, faceless gatherings that, of necessity, broke into groups and eventually caucuses.

Why? Perhaps the chief reasons had to do with the phenomenal growth of Methodism, *the hesitancy to alter long-established boundaries, and most important the myriad effects of the 1939 merger.* Throughout the nineteenth century, and into the twentieth, Methodism grew rapidly. This growth increased the number of preachers, and thus caused some growth in conference size. The growth can be visualized through the opening roll calls[7] of two of the older conferences of the Methodist Episcopal Church:

| | Baltimore | | Philadelphia | |
	Clergy	Laity	Clergy	Laity
1860	73	0		
1870	115	0	118	0
1880	146	0	155	0
1890	144	0	156	0
1900	160	0	240	0
1910	178	0	215	0
1920	217	0	254	0
1930	202	0	217	0

The large conferences of today are not explained by these glacial patterns of growth but instead by the 1939 merger, which equalized clergy and lay membership and brought together into single conferences ministerial and lay delegates from the Methodist Episcopal Church, the Methodist Episcopal Church, South, and the Methodist Protestant Church. That merger established the large conferences of the twentieth century. The 1939 conference mergers produced bodies so large as to make difficult, if not impossible, the kinds of personal bonds of each with all that once characterized relationships among Methodist ministers. And 1939 only set the stage for a series of other mergers, even more dramatic growth in the size of annual conferences and *the expectation that conference needs might be met through consolidation rather than through division.*

The 1939 growth in size escaped, and continues to escape, extensive remark by historians and commentators for various reasons, but particularly because other adjustments claimed immediate attention. These included adjustment:

• to the merger itself,
• to the new jurisdictional system,
• to the new faces (the strangers now "brothers"; the sisters came a decade and a half later),
• to different ways of doing business requiring harmonization,
• to new leadership,
• to a new class of membership (the laity for the MEC), and

- to a new identity as a conference of the Methodist Church, and, of course, to the regimens and austerities of yet another World War, a war that brought massive numbers of women into the work force and made their presence in conference hardly remarkable.[8]

Even for rather large conferences like Philadelphia and Baltimore unification represented change. Both *doubled* just by the admission of laity into what were already quite large bodies:

	Baltimore		Philadelphia	
	Clergy	Laity	Clergy	Laity
1940	294	233	258	232

Only former Methodist Episcopal Church conferences experienced doubling merely through the admission of laity. From its inception, the Methodist Protestant Church had accorded laity parity and full membership. Conferences of the Methodist Episcopal Church, South, were used to lay members but not in equal numbers. Members from these churches found themselves in much larger conferences, particularly in border areas. Many of the Methodist Protestant conferences had been small, and the MECS, as noted, had not accorded the laity parity. Further, many conferences from these two traditions felt the change in scale from being put together with conferences of the other two churches. The Virginia Conference of the new church grew dramatically over its primary predecessor body. In 1939, the MECS conference had convened with 269 ministers and 127 laity in attendance. The new Methodist Church conference that same year experienced difficulty in opening because it had problems in determining its new membership from the lists of the three predecessor bodies. The first episcopal ballot revealed its new size, 401 clergy and 276 laity. The next year (1940) the roll call was answered by 477 clergy and 179 laity. In future years the laity would turn out in better proportions. Like Baltimore and Philadelphia, it was twice the size of its largest predecessor body.

The new West Virginia Conference of the Methodist Church grew even more remarkably. It brought together the West Virginia conferences of the three churches and drew also from Baltimore and Holston. In its first meeting, in 1939, the leadership apparently despaired of straightening out membership and attempted no roll call. The first ballot for General Conference elections showed 353 clergy and 224 laity in session. The next year a roll call indicated 415 clergy and 286 laity. The predecessor conferences had been nowhere near that large. In the 1938 Methodist Episcopal Church conference, 156 ministers (plus 23 supplies) had answered roll call. In the 1938 Methodist Episcopal

Church, South conference 109 clergy and 44 laity answered. The Methodist Protestant Church was of roughly the same size, with equal numbers of clergy and laity (69 and 69). Fraternities of 150 had suddenly through merger become an institution of roughly 700. Roll calls for such a crowd were too time consuming and difficult. Not surprisingly, many conferences that had not already done so abandoned yet another fraternal ritual and resorted to registration cards. Clergy complained about the impersonality of conference size.

Some conferences remained small. In the Northeastern Jurisdiction, in fact, only West Virginia and Baltimore were of such large scale. New York East, Newark, Philadelphia, New Jersey, Central Pennsylvania, and Pittsburgh had ministerial memberships of 200 or so. Two New England conferences, New Hampshire and Vermont, were under 100. In the Western Jurisdiction, Southern California had 285 ministers in effective relation and California had 225; the jurisdiction's other conferences, including the Japanese, Hawaiian, and Latin American, were quite small.

A Policy of Growth?

Still, smallness was no longer prized, and a new pattern of conference unifications was set, reversing what had been the nineteenth century policy of dividing conferences when they grew. Over the next decades bishops and clergy actively sought to enlarge conferences. Some clergy argued that this allowed for an increase of appointment opportunities for ministers. They liked having a larger geographic area open to them. The bishops wanted to reduce the number of conferences over which they had to preside. Arguments for merger and growth also cited efficiency of conference staff, programs, and finance. A larger conference might provide a better financial base for pension and health care programs. Staff efficiencies could be achieved. Larger numbers might allow for better programming

By 1970, when yet another merger had taken place (with the Evangelical United Brethren Church, in 1968) conference size came as a shock to former members of the small EUB conferences. The *ministerial membership* (in full connection) of the Baltimore Conference had reached 662, of Eastern Pennsylvania 559, of West Virginia 541, and of Virginia 887. Texas was by then 657, Southern California-Arizona 828, East Ohio 799, Iowa 813, West Ohio 1,190, Western North Carolina 834, and Florida 854. With roughly equal numbers of laity present, such conferences were outgrowing the sanctuaries, and even the college chapels, in which they had often met and resorting to gymnasiums and civic centers.

Growth also came because of the dissolution of the Central Jurisdiction conferences. Increasingly Methodists objected to dividing out conferences by language and race, a pattern practiced and sanctioned for over a century in the interest of the older (European) ethnic groups within Methodism (for instance Swedes, Danes, and Germans), but problematic when imposed because of race. The Central Jurisdiction became Methodism's public scandal. The issue, of course, was that it was not freely chosen by black members. Among the results of the abolition of the Central Jurisdiction conferences was that aversion to division and distinction by conference became a principle. So when, in the 1970s and '80s, Americans again found ethnicity essential and when some United Methodists again thought a measure of group identity and self-determination requisite for ministry, the church resisted according ethnic minorities "conference" status. Lacking conference as a vehicle for connection, revival, and order, Koreans, other Asian Americans, Hispanics, Native Americans, African Americans, women, and gays have experimented with other forms of community. The alternative to conference as face-to-face community was the caucus.

Despite such efforts at "smaller" conference, the tendency toward growth through merger continues today, as in Kentucky, Mississippi, and New England, and with discussions in Michigan, Illinois, and Tennessee. Rarely, if ever, is the question asked about whether a conference should be divided because it is too large, or for other missional purposes. One might at least ask such a question about Florida, Virginia, or West Ohio. Koreans in the U.S. are asking the question about a Korean Conference.

A Matter of Style

The size and site of the annual conference affect, if they do not determine, style. The huge, impersonal civic centers or gymnasiums cannot allow for the feeling that is achieved in a church or college chapel. One of the most successful sites we have visited is Wesley Chapel at West Virginia Wesleyan College, where the West Virginia Conference meets. The Chapel is a beautiful, warm setting for the annual conference. Worship, and particularly, ordination benefit, but so do scale and relationship. The sense of community evident at the West Virginia Conference is in part related to its place and style of meeting. Church conference centers are certainly better than the civic convention centers (which are among the worst sites) because they are church facilities, and they tend to encourage family attendance. One of the great losses in recent decades has been the absence of families at annual conference meetings. Perhaps the worst sites are the gymnasiums, because they are noisy, ugly, and inappropriate for a business session, let alone the high moments of worship, and especially ordination.

Size and site have made the annual conference feel more like a convention for business than a family gathering. Laity and clergy consistently say that what they like most about annual conference is the people, relationships among friends and colleagues in the ministry of the church, and the sense of community in worship and celebration. The perfunctory style of business that accompanies the changes we have noted does nothing to build up the church. It promotes the wrong images and impressions and kills inspiration. When was the last time anyone was converted at an annual conference session?

We are aware that this chapter could be read as simply nostalgia, looking back to a time when things seemed better. We do not mean it to be so. We are also aware that size alone is not the issue. It is perfectly possible for a small annual conference session to function primarily as a business meeting, and for a large gathering to attempt to act out its life with specific reference to theological norms. We know of small conferences whose life is defined more by politics and business than by theology and worship. We are also aware of the fact that if the style of the annual conference were refashioned along the lines of "revival" and "renewal of the connection," it might actually need a larger site to accommodate visitors, guests, and families of conference members. We need to encourage attendance from a greater diversity of persons, including younger people, many of whom are unable to attend for more than a day, or even part of a day.

Let us be clear that we do not think size alone determines style. Nevertheless, the two are related. Conferences, and the church as a whole, should be reflecting on the issues of substance and scale suggested by our research, because these issues will have an impact on the vitality of the church in the coming decades. Also, we are aware that serious efforts are being made to deal with the style of annual conference. Bishop Ken Carder, of the Nashville Episcopal Area, for instance, has addressed this issue and made efforts to change both substance and style in the two conferences over which he presides. Other bishops and annual conferences have done the same. Even so, changing the culture of an annual conference session is difficult, and that difficulty is aggravated by size, because size helps to determine site. There is no simple answer, because the issues of size, site, and style are more complex than they first appear.

What practical suggestions does this research offer?

1.   *Should fresh examination be made of the size of annual conferences?* We cannot and should not return to the small intimate gatherings of the early nineteenth century. The inclusion of women, laity, diaconal ministers and now deacons has been of enormous good to the church. However, we should not assume that larger is better, and that merger is automatically to be preferred. Some evidence suggests the opposite. Conference size should not be set with consideration primarily to clergy careers, cabinet convenience in making appointments, or episcopal preference not to itinerate, legitimate though those factors are. With each of these considerations, there may be other solutions. Nothing, for instance, would prohibit two or more conferences from sharing an office, staff, print and electronic resources, and joint publications. Appointments across conference lines might be reconsidered, for a variety of reasons, as we have suggested in other of these essays. Two small conferences carved from one too large do divide the bishop's attention and represent considerably more work, but they oblige a bishop to no larger an area or larger a flock or number of appointments. We suggest that when an annual conference outgrows the seating capacity of its largest congregations or approaches the size of General Conference (1000) it is time to consider new conferences.

2.   *Should more exploration be given to forming conferences for particular missional needs, and should appointments of ministerial members cease to be arbitrarily limited to conference bounds?* The Korean initiative is interesting for this reason and may be the occasion for discussion of these matters. The idea that appointments are almost invariably made within the bounds of an annual conference requires serious reconsideration given the needs of the church, especially with ethnic minority congregations, but also where particular needs of churches require special leadership.

3.   *Should the style of the annual conference session be determined by theological conversation, not by parliamentary conversation?* We need to set aside portions of each day for nonparliamentary activities such as prayer, preaching, discussion, and nonlegislative debate and sharing. We now do too much voting and not enough sharing about the major issues facing the church and the society. We ought to spend at least as many hours in such endeavors as in the usual business.

4.   *Should the principal meeting space of the annual conference be large enough to seat all members comfortably, but not so cavernous as to be alienating?* Every effort should be made to avoid impersonal civic centers, or gymnasiums, and to use facilities appropriate to the kind of meeting a church conference represents. One alternative would be to have the annual conference session in a city where several church buildings (perhaps not even United Methodist facilities) are close

together. This would allow for multiple, and even expanded, gatherings at which numerous persons, both from within and without the annual conference, could be invited to preach, lead Bible study, conduct prayer meetings, and gather groups who want to share particular concerns (seminary or church college groups, for instance).

5.   *Should serious effort be made to have major worship services, and especially ordination, in a church or chapel?* Not only is that a proper setting for conference, but also the scale of our sanctuaries, and the seating afforded therein, speak graphically of what we believe to be the right size of church gatherings.

6.   *Should families of clergy and laity who are members of the annual conference, as well as members from churches across the conference be encouraged to come for all or part of the annual conference session?* In addition to worship, some provision for common meals and other informal gathering opportunities should be made so that persons can feel connected in ways other than business sessions. One dramatic idea would be for the annual conference to undertake a joint service project that could be accomplished during the time of the session in the community of meeting.

7.   *Might housing in a conference center, college dorms, or a hotel where members can informally gather be explored?* Is it impossible to reconsider housing in the homes of local Methodists? Relationships are key to the theological meaning of connection.

8.   *Should the bishop and leaders of the annual conference do everything possible to lessen the feeling of a business meeting or political convention and increase the feeling of the community of God's people, the body of Christ, gathered to review and plan mission and ministry?*

Connectionalism: End or New Beginning?

Russell E. Richey

Connectionalism constitutes one of the fundamentals of Methodism, a tradition since Wesley,[1] a central feature of our practice, an essential in our identity. Connectionalism has in recent years expressed itself powerfully and graphically in our board and commission administrative order. Through general agencies and their counterparts on jurisdictional, conference, and congregational levels, United Methodists have done their work, made their witness, carried on their mission, undertaken ministry. Agency structures—the elaborate grammar of organizational life that prescribed for all levels "councils" or "chairs" of ministry, church and society, higher education and campus ministry, missions, religion and race, and Christian unity and inter-religious concerns—knit United Methodism into a giant communication and programmatic empire.

Denominational initiatives and program came from above, from the center, from the national level—whether as a Sunday school module, missional emphasis, or exercise in discipleship. Agencies led. The church followed. Agencies undertook national, indeed global, tasks; drew board membership from across the entire church (the positions were avidly sought as a distinction and recognition); appointed high profile and able staff; worked with significant proportions of the denominational budget; enjoyed clear lines of access to their counterparts on conference and congregational level and open channels to the United Methodist media; and truly *connected* United Methodists in life and work.

Or so it was for a at least the century from 1872 to 1972. But now, like Oliver Wendell Holmes's "Wonderful One-Hoss Shay," general agency connectionalism seems to be disintegrating. And what won't self-destruct, critics seem intent on destroying. Agencies seem unable to lead; the church will not follow; the connection is voiceless.[2] Rather than being emblems of the best of Methodism, agencies become scapegoats; they are held up as what's wrong with the church. Protesting board policies, individuals and congregations withhold apportionments. Reformers and even bishops bash board practices, events, expenditures, values, and personnel. Some wonder whether we need a General Council on Ministries. Critics on the right have set up shadow agencies, the Missionary Society being only the most prominent. And the General Conference resolves, in punitive "Vietnam" fashion, to save the General Board of Global Ministries by destroying it.[3]

Connection and Congregation

Equally erosive of confidence in agency connectionalism are the new norms that United Methodist leadership hold up, norms of decentralization, local initiative and structuring, parish ministry, vital congregations. In fashioning a "vision for the church," the council of bishops located "vitality" not on an agency level, but on the congregational. "The central, focal expression of ministry and mission in the name of Christ," they say, "is found in the local church congregation." The ignoring of that fact, they hold up for criticism:

> Too often as a denomination we do not treat congregations as unique. We develop regional or national programs and goals, and hope they will trickle down to be "applied" in congregations. We emphasize congregational performance on institutional scales of membership and money. Our appointive system has sometimes encouraged pastors to think that all congregations are basically alike and can be ministered with in more or less the same way. . . .

The document mostly ignores the conference, episcopal, and agency structures that have connected Methodism but occasionally remarks upon "the increasing financial load our congregations are carrying." "Our Confession as a People of Faith," calls us to no-holds-barred prophetic self-incrimination:

> The United Methodist Church is the one on the stretcher (Mark 2). We are paralyzed by the loss of our culture's support. We have let our institutional structures become a burden to us.

In recounting the Methodist story, as part of the larger Christian story, the bishops accent class and congregation, slighting the translocal, collective, and connectional revivalism of quarterly conference, camp meeting, conference, a moving people, and an itinerant ministry. They insist on a connectionalism of common discipline and holiness and affirm: "Not so much our institutional ties or our financial support, as our mutual commitment and constant prayers for one another, constitute the connection." Instead, the connection, in its vitality and its mission, comes to expression locally:

A new imagination for tomorrow's church will arise by God's grace from the creativity and vitality of congregations who find their life in Christ. The local church truly is the church through whose ministries the reign of God must be made known if we expect that reign to be known anywhere. Worshiping, witnessing, serving communities of faithful disciples are Christ's living body in the world. United in one Spirit, bound together in a connectional covenant of mission, they are instruments of God's world-encompassing work.

The bishops expect little from trickle-down religiosity.[4]

The "Foundation Document" is a wonderful and powerful vision. I lift occasional statements only to illustrate what are now Methodist commonplaces. Congregation and parish are now our talk. Clergy routinely speak of themselves as in parish ministry. The Discipline, which only came to recognize "the local church" after 1940,[5] now defines ministry in that local fashion and construes other ministry, by contrast, as "extension ministries" or "appointments beyond the local church." The phrases now serve as self-identification. Ministers wear the acronym, ABLC, for what were once special appointments. Parish has become norm (has the parish of Wesley's Church of England triumphed over his connectionalism and itinerancy?).[6]

Connectionalism at Risk?

Similarly, we subvert our connectional/communication grammar by experimenting with new, nonconnecting, structures on local and congregational levels. Though inspired by desires to reclaim the tradition and to serve United Methodist ends, such efforts produce new organizational patterns and new, renamed conference or church commissions no longer mesh with the agencies at the top. And this process, under way before the 1996 General Conference, now enjoys *Disciplinary* warrant. The disengagement of parts of the connection from other parts threatens to worsen as budget-cutting and down-sizing oblige the church to decentralize and delegate what had once been done centrally.

Is connectionalism dying or being killed? Do the attacks on boards and agencies, criticisms of that style of decision-making, objections to agency expenditures for travel and meetings, and efforts to decentralize and take initiative at regional and local levels mean the end of Methodist connectionalism as we know it?[7] As we know it, maybe. An end of Methodist connectionalism? Not necessarily. Revived and renewed connectionalism can come through radical agency down-sizing, considerable decentralization, and new patterns of mission, ministry, program, and witness.

A number of major studies of our denomination were conducted during the last quadrennium—seven if our Lilly project is included[8]—and several, especially the General Council on Ministries "Connectional Issues Study," concerned themselves with a new vision of our connectional structure. That latter study continues under slightly different auspices and with new leadership, with vision still among its concerns. A new vision might be helped by a little hindsight, and particularly by a glimpse of a Methodist connectionalism not defined by boards and agencies. These have been with us for a long time, a century, in fact, but they have constituted our primary centralizing, unifying and connecting force only since 1939. Prior to that Methodism connected itself together quite effectively through other instrumentalities.

Connectionalism Historically Considered

How did American Methodism connect itself, of what did its connectionalism consist, in earlier periods?[9] Until 1816, Francis Asbury did much of the connecting. A fuller statement would be that Methodism connected itself through an itinerant general superintendent (and specifically Asbury), annual and general conferences, and a nationally itinerant traveling ministry. Asbury deployed itinerants and presiding elders across conference lines and on a national basis, reinforcing the itinerant general superintendency with an itinerant general ministry. The ministry, the episcopacy, and the conferences constituted a particularly important and underappreciated connective voice. Methodism hung together in hearing a common Arminian gospel. While that continued after Asbury's death, itineration increasingly occurred within conferences. Multiple bishops, though still itinerating, lacked the cohesive and connective power that had been Asbury's, and the bishops soon began specializing by region. And General Conferences met only every four years.

Who or what would connect, day-to-day, week-to-week, as had Asbury? How would Methodism hear a common word? The General Conference of 1816 answered that less with its episcopal selections than in electing Joshua Soule book agent/editor. Soule and particularly his successor, Nathan Bangs, made the book concern, *The Methodist Magazine*, and the *Christian Advocate* the connecting force in Methodist life. Connection came through paper, tract, hymn book, discipline, and Bible. Every itinerant peddled for the book concern. Regional *Advocates*, their editors also elected by the General Conference, came eventually to nuance Methodism's written word for our many audiences. And regional slanting played its role, along with issues of democracy and later slavery, in dividing Methodism into warring parties. For a time, Methodism seemed to connect itself by its partisanship.

In the middle decades of the nineteenth century, even while Methodism warred with itself and went to civil war with Americans generally, two more programmatic interests came to have great connective power within the divided church. They were the Sunday school and missions. Both channeled Methodist lay imagination and energies into the building of great networks of loosely-related societies, male and female, zealously committed to evangelization of youth and the "heathen." Methodists still connected with oral testimony and the written word but increasingly channeled their witness through societies with a missional or programmatic purpose.

By the 1870s, such societies—then including the Missionary Society, the Church Extension Society, the Board of Education, the Sunday-School Union and the Tract Society, as well as the more loosely related Freemen's Aid Society and Book Concern, not to mention temperance organizations, preachers' aid societies, and various others—had become too successful, General Conferences thought, to be allowed to run themselves. And so in 1872 and 1874, the MEC and MECS took action to make the boards elective and thereby accountable to General Conference, thus turning voluntary societies into national, corporate denominational boards. Connectionalism had, at last, a denomina-tional-structural expression. Agencies proved remarkable connectional delivery systems, as we noted initially. However, until 1939 or so, they were surrounded with other bodies, also active on a national level, that bound the connection together. These included, of course, the college or board of bishops, General Conferences and other national organizations (women's, youth, reform, etc.), national papers, clergy magazines, the seminaries (particularly Boston for the north and Vanderbilt in the south), and the publishing houses.

Ironically, the union of 1939, in an endeavor to create a more national church, tore up much of the connectional fabric—dropping power and authority into jurisdictional conferences, including particularly the power to elect; making bishops regional, not general, superintendents;[10] bloating General Conference by intention, and regionalizing seminaries and other teaching agencies by accident; consolidating boards into even more significant bureaucracies and empowering those boards to select their professional staff. The net effect of these changes was to leave the agencies as *the* connecting power nationally *and* to undo the accountability that 1872 had achieved. In 1939 rather than in 1968 lie many of the concerns that trouble agency critics. Other problems in agency governance are not Methodist-specific but characterize other denominations, large scale business enterprise, and government at all levels. Americans have apparently tired of working in, under, and through corporate, bureaucratic structures and protest them in various ways—tax-payer revolts, rebellions against headquarters, voting the rascals out. And organizations respond by downsizing, aping Japanese management, adopting total quality management, and resorting to new measures of influence—regulation, grant-making, franchising, consulting, credentialing—tactics that by intrusion and manipulation further undercut goodwill towards corporate structures.[11]

Disquiet over United Methodist agencies, then, belongs within the larger cultural quest for new modalities of community, cooperation, labor and governance. In finding such new modalities of connection, United Methodists can and should lead. It's our specialty. And we are doing so. All around are experiments in connection—in the caucuses, in media ministries, in new and old efforts at discipleship, in listening groups, in council of bishops initiatives. Such experiments cannot, probably, reconnect us without forcing us to end the connectional monopoly that the *Discipline* now accords agencies.

Thinking the Unthinkable

In thinking the unthinkable, here are some questions that might help us. They presume that a church that has "connected" itself in non-bureaucratic form in the past can imagine new connections now.

1. Can we not end the financial scandal induced by accountability? Can we not spend fewer denominational dollars on board meetings and travel thereunto and devote more to missions, to works of mercy, to evangelism, to new church starts, to spirituality?

2. To that end can we sacrifice the principle—viable when we were a church of only six conferences but hardly now—of achieving representation by guaranteeing every conference a seat on major committees and boards? Could we do our work, provide representation and expertise, and achieve appropriate inclusivity with really small boards of thirty or less, with representation worked out by careful nominations? And might the (small) full board meet rarely, perhaps only during General Conference?

3. Would we be willing to make agencies really accountable by returning to General Conference the power to elect staff *and* board members, a power that belongs with oversight and responsibility?[12]

4. With agencies already delegated to regions by their spacing around the country (somewhat), would we be willing to trust the month-to-month supervision of staff and the detailing of policy, now achieved

through costly board meetings, to a small executive committee composed of a few bishops, local laity, and clergy (the practice up through 1872)? And when full board assent must be sought, can it be achieved more frequently via the information highway and by other electronic-, media-, or tele-hookups?

5. In such oversight by delegation, might we also trust the bishops, if truly itinerating general superintendents, to provide the national vision and viewpoint?

6. And by reinvigorating our traditional connectional bodies—by optimizing the connectional capacities of General Conference and the bishops—might we open up other connective opportunities? Might we invite our leaders out of their parish fortresses into expansive mission to American society and the world? Might we unleash Methodist creativity anew into some new Sunday-school-like venture? Might local experiments in disciplined holiness again claim connectional recognition? Might we be open to multiple-connections? And can we then give less-grudging status to new national United Methodist ventures? Might we even establish our own venture capital?

7. Should not United Methodist connection feature first-class overtures to our society/ies with the best in modern media, perhaps inviting the United Methodist Publishing House to follow its recent successes and, reclaiming the mantle of Soule and Bangs, to make every pastor once again an agent for the Methodist word?

Contributors

Daniel M. Bell Jr. is a Ph.D. candidate in Religion at Duke University; his dissertation is titled "The Refusal to Cease Suffering: The Crucified of History and the Poetics of Forgiveness." He is an instructor at Truman State University, Kirksville, Missouri, and an ordained deacon in the Florida Conference of the United Methodist Church.

Thomas E. Boomershine is Professor of New Testament at United Theological Seminary, Dayton, Ohio. An ordained United Methodist elder in the West Ohio Conference, he is the author of the book *Story Journey* and an executive producer of *Out of the Tombs,* an award-winning video and multimedia story of the healing of the Gerasene demoniac. Dr. Boomershine founded the Network of Biblical Storytellers and GoTell Communications.

Vivian A. Bull is President of Linfield College, McMinnville, Oregon. She is an international economist, author of *The West Bank: Is It Viable?* and coauthor of *Survey of the Educational Potential of the West Bank.* Dr. Bull has served the United Methodist Church on the Connectional Process Team, the General Board of Higher Education and Ministry, and the Commission on Institutional Review. She has held various corporate and nonprofit directorships.

M. Garlinda Burton is Editor of *Interpreter,* a magazine for laity and clergy in local United Methodist congregations. Burton is also Founder and President of Challenges & Possibilities, a training company that helps schools and businesses address issues of racial and gender equality. She resides in Nashville, Tennessee.

Jackson W. Carroll is the Ruth W. and A. Morris Williams Jr., Professor of Religion and Society and Director of the J. M. Ormond Center of Duke Divinity School, Durham, North Carolina. He is known for using sociological methods to aid the church's understanding of its relation to society. Dr. Carroll is the author of several books, including *As One With Authority, Women of the Cloth, Carriers in Faith: Lessons from Congregational Studies,* and *Handbook of Congregational Studies.*

Thomas Edward Frank is Associate Professor of Church Administration and Congregational Life and Director of Methodist Studies at the Candler School of Theology, Emory University, Atlanta. His most recent book is *Polity, Practice, and the Mission of the United Methodist Church.* He also authored *Theology, Ethics, and the Nineteenth Century American College Ideal: Conserving a Rational World.*

Meghan Froehlich is a graduate of Duke Divinity School, Durham, North Carolina, and a candidate for the priesthood in the Episcopal Church. She is a former business consultant.

S T Kimbrough Jr. is Associate General Secretary for Mission Evangelism at the General Board of Global Ministries of the United Methodist Church, New York, N.Y. He is a distinguished musical performer and scholar. For a number of years he was the leading baritone of Germany's Bonn Opera. Kimbrough is the author of *Methodism in Russian and the Baltic States: History and Renewal* and the editor *of Sweet Singer: Hymns of Charles Wesley.* He is President of the Charles Wesley Society, Editor of the *Proceedings of the Charles Wesley Society,* and General Editor of the series of facsimile reprints of Charles Wesley publications.

Sarah Sloan Kreutziger is Director of the Center for Life-Long Learning at the School of Social Work, Tulane University, New Orleans, Louisiana. Her research foci include social policy and community development, women's history, and spiritual values and social work. Recent publications include chapters entitled "Wesley's Legacy of Social Holiness: The Methodist Settlements," in *Connectionalism: Ecclesiology, Mission, and Identity* (Abingdon, 1997), and "Social Work's Legacy: The Methodist Settlement Movement," in *Christianity and Social Work* (NACSW Press, 1998). Dr. Kreutziger holds degrees from Columbia College, the University of Tennessee, and Tulane University.

Thomas A. Langford served as Dean and as Professor of Theology and Methodist Studies at Duke Divinity School, Durham, North Carolina. He is an elder in the Western North Carolina Conference of the United Methodist Church. His books include *Philosophy of Religion; Intellect and Hope; Prayer and the Common Life; Practical Divinity, Volume 1: Theology in the Wesleyan Tradition;* and *Volume 2: Readings in Wesleyan Theology; Christian Wholeness.*

Janice Love is Associate Professor of Government and International Studies at the University of South Carolina, Columbia, South Carolina. She is the author of two books, *The U.S. Anti-Apartheid Movement: Local Activism and Global Politics* (1985) and *Globalization and Regionalism in Southern Africa* (forthcoming). In addition, she has a long record of service with the World Council of Churches; she currently serves on the organization's Central Committee. Dr. Love received her Ph.D. from Ohio State University.

William B. McClain is Professor of Preaching and Worship at Wesley Theological Seminary in Washington, D.C. His areas of interest are Western studies in homiletics, African American church history, and Wesleyan studies. Dr. McClain is the author of *Come Sunday: The Liturgy of Zion,* a liturgical companion to religious songs from the African American tradition, and *Black People in the United Methodist Church.* He also coedited *Heritage and Hope: The African American Presence in Methodism.*

Priscilla Pope-Levison, Assistant Professor of the Practice of Evangelism at Duke Divinity School, Durham, North Carolina, focuses in her research both on liberation evangelism and the history of women evangelists. Her book, *Evangelism from a Liberation Perspective,* was selected as one of fifteen outstanding books for mission studies in 1991. Dr. Pope-Levison cochairs the Evangelical Theology Group of the American Academy of Religion.

William K. Quick served as Senior Minister at Metropolitan United Methodist Church, Detroit, Michigan, for 24 years, and also served as Pastor of Trinity United Methodist Church, Durham, North Carolina. He is the author of *Signs of Our Times: A Vision for the Church.*

Kenneth E. Rowe is Methodist Research Librarian and Professor of Church History at Drew University, Madison, New Jersey. He holds degrees from Drew, Yale, and Rutgers Universities. He is Editor of *United Methodist Studies,* the *Methodist Union Catalog,* and the American Theological Library Association Monograph Series. He is coauthor of *The Methodists, United Methodism in America: A Compact History,* and the two-volume *The Methodist Experience in America.*

Roy I. Sano is Bishop of the Los Angeles Area of the United Methodist Church. He served in various pastoral roles for 19 years and has taught at Mills College and the Graduate Theological Union/Pacific School of Religion. He has represented the denomination at three Assemblies of the World Council of Churches and has participated in five sessions of the Oxford Institute on Wesleyan Studies. Bishop Sano is the author of *From Every Nation Without Number: Racial and Ethnic Diversity in United Methodism.*

Judith E. Smith is Director of Special Projects and Church and Public Relations, the United Methodist Publishing House. Until recently she was Associate General Secretary of the Board of Higher Education and Ministry of the United Methodist Church, Nashville, Tennessee. Her research focus has been leadership of the church at general agency and episcopal levels. She holds degrees from the University of Puget Sound, the School of Theology at Claremont, and Vanderbilt University, and she is a member of the Oregon-Idaho Conference.

Editors

William B. Lawrence is Senior Pastor of Metropolitan Memorial United Methodist Church in Washington, D.C. He formerly taught at The Divinity School, Duke University, and served as the project associate for this study of United Methodism and American Culture. His recent publications include *Sundays in New York: Pulpit Theology at the Crest of the Protestant Mainstream, 1930–1955.* A graduate of Duke, Union Theological Seminary in New York, and Drew, he served as a United Methodist pastor and district superintendent prior to teaching at Duke.

Dennis M. Campbell was Dean of The Divinity School and Professor of Theology, Duke University and served as President of the Association of United Methodist Theological Schools. He is now headmaster of Woodberry Forest School, Woodberry, Virginia. Dr. Campbell is the author of *Who Will Go For Us? An Invitation to Ordained Ministry* and *The Yoke of Obedience,* and he is codirector of United Methodism and American Culture.

Russell E. Richey is Professor of Church History at The Divinity School, Duke University, in Durham, North Carolina. Dr. Richey is a member of the Historical Society of the United Methodist Church and the American Society of Church History. He is the author of *The Methodist Conference in America* and coauthor with James Kirby and Kenneth Rowe of *The Methodists.* Dr. Richey is codirector of United Methodism and American Culture.

Notes

Notes to "Introduction"

1. Nathan Bangs, *The Present State, Prospects, and Responsibilities of the Methodist Episcopal Church* (New York: Lane & Scott, 1850).

2. Ibid., 16. Much of this he attributed to the Millerite delusion.

3. The resultant volume was entitled *Proceedings, Sermon, Essays, and Addresses of the Centennial Methodist Conference,* ed. H. K. Carroll, W. P. Harrison, and J. H. Bayliss (Cincinnati: Cranston and Stowe; New York: Phillips and Hunt, 1885).

Notes to "Does Methodism Have a Future in American Culture?"

1. Christopher Dawson, *The Historic Reality of Christian Culture* (New York and Evanston: Harper Torchbooks, 1960), 70.

2. See Russell E. Richey, *Early American Methodism* (Bloomington: Indiana University Press, 1991).

3. George M. Marsden, *Religion and American Culture* (San Diego: Harcourt Brace Jovanovich, 1990), 101.

4. E. Digby Baltzell, *The Protestant Establishment: Aristocracy and Caste in America* (New Haven: Yale University Press, 1987), 15.

5. Marsden, 101.

6. Paul Johnson, *A History of Christianity* (New York: Atheneum, 1977), 516–17.

7. Kosmin is quoted in "Portrait of Religion in U.S. Holds Dozens of Surprises," by Ari L. Goldman, *The New York Times,* April 10, 1991, sect. A, p. 1.

8. Johnson, *History,* 513–14.

Notes to "Is a Holistic Evangelism Possible?"

1. Materials for this essay were published previously in the following articles by the author: "Evangelism and Liberation: Perspectives from Latin America" *Catalyst* 15 (April, 1989), 3, 5, and "Is Evangelization Liberation?" *United Theological Seminary Journal of Theology* (1993), 4–22.

2. Norman E. Thomas, "Evangelism and Liberation Theology," *Missiology* 9 (October 1981), 483.

3. The word "theologies" is plural to denote the existence of various liberation theologies and feminist theologies. See our discussion, Priscilla Pope-Levison and John R. Levison, *Jesus in Global Contexts* (Louisville: Westminster/John Knox, 1992), chaps. 2 and 5.

4. Orlando Costas, *El Protestantismo en América Latina Hoy: Ensayos del Camino (1972–1974)* (Publicaciones INDEF, 1975), 121–122.

5. In Jesus' ministry the table was the place for social reintegration to happen. Jesus seemed always to be accused of eating with "tax collectors and sinners" and even commended an unnamed woman who caressed his feet while he was at table. Even his vision of the future is encapsulated in the image of the heavenly festive table: "And people will come from east and west, and from north and south, and sit table in the kingdom of God. And behold, some are last who will be first, and some are first who will be last" (Luke 13:29-30).

6. Mortimer Arias, "Ministries of Hope in Latin America," *International Review of Mission* 71 (January 1982), 7.

7. Valerie Saiving, "The Human Situation: A Feminine View," in *Womanspirit Rising*, ed. Carol Christ and Judith Plaskow (San Francisco: Harper & Row, 1979), 35.

8. Ibid., 37.

9. Anne Carr, *Transforming Grace: Christian Tradition and Women's Experience* (San Francisco: Harper & Row, 1990), 186.

10. Emilio Castro, *Hacia una Pastoral Latinoamericana*, Coleccion "Iglesia y Mision," no. 2 (San José: INDEF, 1974), 88.

11. Leonardo Boff, *Jesus Christ Liberator: A Critical Christology for Our Time* (Maryknoll, N.Y.: Orbis, 1978), 287.

12. Emilio Castro, *Freedom in Mission: An Ecumenical Inquiry* (Geneva: WCC, 1985), 267.

13. Juan Luis Segundo, *The Historical Jesus of the Synoptics* (Maryknoll, N.Y.: Orbis, 1985), 141.

14. Ibid., 131.

15. Orlando Costas, *Christ Outside the Gate: Mission Beyond Christendom* (Maryknoll, N.Y.: Orbis, 1982), 37.

16. Edwina Gateley, *Psalms of a Laywoman* (Trabuco Canyon, Calif.: Source Books, 1992), 96–97.

Note to "What Is the Character of Methodist Theology?"

1. No one is without received perspectives, whether assumed or carefully worked out. Self-criticism is always necessary in any assessment of the gospel message of the regnant intellectual persuasion, yet it is hard to come by.

Notes to "Can United Methodist Theology Be Contextual?"

1. This paper was written for the Contextual Theology Working Group of the Tenth Oxford Institute of Methodist Theological Studies on the theme "Trinity, Community, Power." It is dedicated in loving memory to the late Jung Young Lee,

the most erudite, original, and productive Asian North American theologian. His book, *The Trinity in Asian Perspective* (Nashville: Abingdon, 1996), traces the contributions of Taoism for our understanding of the triune God. It represents the culmination of a caring, courageous, and creative ministry.

2. Contributing to the diversity is that many national ancestry groups have their largest U.S. population in Southern California. They include Armenians, Mexicans, Central Americans, Chinese, Taiwanese, Indo-Chinese (Vietnamese, Cambodians, Laotians), Malaysians, Indonesians, Filipinos, Koreans, Japanese, and Pacific Islanders (Samoans and Tongans).

3. The Kenyan struggle, like others against classical European colonialism, illustrates the parallels with the history of salvation. They first rallied people to [1] *uhuru*, liberation. After independence, they called for [2] *harambe*, unity or community, and for [3] nation building. Reordering the two stories of salvation is as foundational as the Reformation reversing the sequence within the Medieval order of salvation that moved from sanctification to justification. It is no exaggeration to say that theological retrenchment in postmodern "Christendom" is making the reordering as wrenching as the retrenchment against the Reformation reversals that prompted religious wars. Incorporating the new theological contributions could heal rifts in the church and societies.

4. The dye was cast in the formulation of the question at the Sixth Institute, as is evident in the papers from the gathering. See *Sanctification and Liberation: Liberation Theologies in Light of the Wesleyan Tradition,* ed. Theodore Runyon (Nashville: Abingdon, 1981).

5. According to the Bible, participation in both stories promotes holiness and evangelism (Ezekiel 36:23). Our preoccupation with our holiness has become indulgently humanistic. Scriptural holiness finally has to do with the sanctity and vindication of the divine name. That kind of scriptural holiness spreads as more and more people come to know Yahweh through both stories (Exodus 6:7; 7:5; Isa. 11:9; Jer. 31:34; Ezekiel 36:23). Not surprisingly, we see church growth in societies that have gone through new versions of the history of salvation in Africa, Asia, Latin America, and more recently in Eastern Europe. In the U.S., we experienced the same growth in the decades following the Revolutionary War, which our forebears supported.

6. Since Asian and Pacific peoples in the U.S. are generally overlooked on these basic issues, I mention the recent documentation in *Civil Rights Issues Facing Asian American in the 1990's* (U.S. Commission on Civil Rights, February 1992) and in *Policy Issue to the Year 2020: The State of Asian Pacific America: A Public Policy Report* (LEAP Asian Pacific American Public Policy Institute and UCLA Asian American Studies Center, 1993).

7. The Holy Spirit anointed the consistently marginalized Judges to liberate their people from the oppression of sin and evil (Judg. 3:10; 6:34; 11:29; 15:14). The Spirit does lead us through the *ordo salutis*, but also empowers us to launch the history of salvation as well.

Notes to "Will the City Lose the Church?"

1. Merton S. Rice, Letter to the congregation of North Woodward Methodist Episcopal (later Metropolitan Methodist) Church, 1916.

2. Robert W. Fox, "The World's Urban Explosion," *National Geographic* 166, No. 2 (August 1984); 179–85.

3. *The Detroit Free Press* (December 15, 1997), C2.

Notes to "Does United Methodism Have a Future in an Electronic Age?"

1. Richard B. Wilke, *And Are We Yet Alive?* (Nashville: Abingdon, 1986), 12. The enrollments in the church school programs of the UMC fell from 7.9 million in 1960 to 4.15 million in 1984, a drop approaching 4 million.

2. Russell E. Richey, "Introduction," in *Connectionalism: Ecclesiology, Mission, and Identity,* United Methodism and American Culture 1 (Nashville: Abingdon, 1997), 9.

3. James Penn Pilkington, *The Methodist Publishing House, Vol. 1: Beginnings to 1870* (Nashville: Abingdon, 1968), 58. This history contains a long series of great stories about the formation and development of the Book Concern.

4. Ibid., 80. The finances of the Book Concern and the Dickens family were so closely intertwined that when Dickens died during the plague of yellow fever in 1798, it took years to settle the estate. Asbury continued to look after the Dickens family after John's death. And in his will, Asbury left $2000 to the Book Concern and an income of $80 a year to Betsy.

5. Ibid., 165. John Emory, after whom Emory University was named, was appointed the book agent at an early age and declined to be elected as bishop at the age of 35. He was elected as bishop at the next General Conference and served as a bishop in the Southern Church until his death. Throughout his life, he was warmly honored by the connection for having gotten the Book Concern out of debt in his years as book agent.

6. Richey, 16.

7. Pilkington, 181.

8. Ibid., 240

9. Mark Noll, "The Evangelical Enlightenment and Theological Education," in *Communication and Change in American Religious History*, ed. Leonard I. Sweet (Grand Rapids: Eerdmans, 1993), 275.

10. Ibid., 273.

11. Ibid., 288. This development in theology was mirrored in the development of historical criticism in the study of the Bible. Indeed, scientific study of the "book of revelation" was the source for the doctrines that theology systematized.

12. See David Paul Nord, *The Evangelical Origins of Mass Media in America, 1815–1835*, Journalism Monographs, 88 (Columbia, S.C.: Association for Education in

Journalism and Mass Communications, 1984); also "Systematic Benevolence: Religious Publishing and the Marketplace in Early Nineteenth-Century America," in *Communication and Change in American Religious History,* ed. Leonard I. Sweet (Grand Rapids: Eerdmans, 1993), 239–69.

13. Edwin H. Maynard, *Keeping Up with a Revolution: The Story of United Methodist Communications, 1940–1990* (Nashville: United Methodist Communications, 1990), 18.

14. Ibid., 20.

15. Ibid., 37.

16. See Maynard, 155–56. As he observes, "The hoped-for network has yet to develop." The responsibility for this failure lies equally with UMCom and the community of United Methodist scholars.

Notes to "Is Division a New Threat to the Denomination?"

1. This chapter was presented at Harvard Divinity School for the Lilly Endowment-sponsored project "Protestantism and Cultural Change in American History." It appeared with a different title than that used here in *Quarterly Review* 18 (Spring 1998), 3–17 and is used here with permission.

2. On the mainline problematic, see Milton J Coalter, John M. Mulder and Louis B. Weeks, *The Reforming Tradition: Presbyterians and Mainstream Protestantism* (Louisville: Westminster/John Knox, 1992), the seventh culminating, synthetic volume in the series "The Presbyterian Presence: The Twentieth Century Experience."

3. On the timing of "dis-establishment" and its consequences, see William R. Hutchison, *Between the Times: The Travail of the Protestant Establishment in America, 1900–1960* (Cambridge and New York: Cambridge University Press, 1989).

4. See Robert Wuthnow, *The Restructuring of American Religion* (Princeton: Princeton University Press, 1988) and *The Struggle for America's Soul* (Grand Rapids: Eerdmans, 1989).

5. Commentators employing "liberal and evangelical" as rubrics include Richard J. Coleman, *Issues of Theological Conflict: Evangelicals and Liberals* (Grand Rapids: Eerdmans, 1972); James Davison Hunter, *American Evangelicalism: Conservative Religion and the Quandary of Modernity* (New Brunswick: Rutgers University Press, 1983); Richard Quebedeaux, *The Worldly Evangelicals* (San Francisco: Harper & Row, 1978); and R. Stephen Warner, *New Wine in Old Wineskins: Evangelicals and Liberals in a Small-Town Church* (Berkeley: University of California Press, 1988).

6. The contrast that James Davison Hunter employs in *Culture Wars* (New York: Basic Books, 1991) is "progressive and orthodox."

The "public and private" formulation of the two-party division for twentieth-century Protestantism was by Jean Miller Schmidt, accessible now in the published version of her dissertation, *Souls or the Social Order: The Two-Party System in American Protestantism* (Brooklyn: Carlson, 1991), and by Martin E. Marty in *Righteous Empire*

(New York: Dial, 1970). See also Dean R. Hoge, *Division in the Protestant House* (Philadelphia: Westminster, 1976).

A contrast of this worldly and other-worldly is drawn by David A. Roozen, William McKinney, and Jackson W. Carroll in *Varieties of Religious Presence* (New York: Pilgrim, 1984). Richard J. Mouw ("New Alignments: Hartford and the Future of Evangelicalism," in *Against the World For the World*, ed. Peter L. Berger and Richard John Neuhaus [New York: Seabury, 1976]) contrasts the two parties as "ecumenical and evangelical."

7. On the end to denominationalism, see Robert Wuthnow, *The Restructuring of American Religion* (Princeton: Princeton University Press, 1988) and especially *The Struggle for America's Soul* (Grand Rapids: Eerdmans, 1989), 72–94. See also Wade Clark Roof and William McKinney, *American Mainline Religion* (New Brunswick: Rutgers University Press, 1987).

8. The easiest way to access such judgments with respect to the Creech trial is through the updated entries by United Methodist New Service at http://www.umc.org/umns.

9. Niebuhr had earlier affirmed, "The evil of denominationalism lies in the conditions which makes the rise of sects desirable and necessary: in the failure of the churches to transcend the social conditions which fashion them into caste-organizations, to sublimate their loyalties to standards and institutions only remotely relevant if not contrary to the Christian ideal, to resist the temptation of making their own self-preservation and extension the primary object of their endeavor" (H. Richard Niebuhr, *The Social Sources of Denominationalism* [New York: Living Age/Meridian, 1957; first published in 1929], 21, 25).

10. See, for instance, *Yearbook of American & Canadian Churches 1966*, ed. Kenneth B. Bedell (Nashville: Abingdon, 1996).

11. "The American Religious Depression, 1925–1935," *Church History* 29 (March 1960), 3–16, and in John M. Mulder and John F. Wilson, *Religion in American History* (Englewood Cliffs: Prentice Hall, 1978), 431–44.

12. To speak as though denominationalism were a living creature is only to grant the religious historian the license of the economist who treats the market in similar fashion. The analogy, I would suggest, is a close one.

13. Richard P. Heitzenrater, *Wesley and the People Called Methodists* (Nashville: Abingdon, 1995), esp. 207–8, 218–19, 232–33, 237, 256, 269, 284, 293–96, 304–5.

14. "Minutes of Conference from the year 1774 to the year 1779 [from minutes kept by Philip Gatch]," *Western Christian Advocate* 4/5 (May 26, 1837), 18–19: Minutes of a Conference held at Roger Thomson's in Fluvanna County, Va., May 18, 1779.

15. Quest. 8. *Why was the Delaware conference held?*
Ans. For the convenience of the preachers in the northern stations, that we all might have an opportunity of meeting in conference; it being unadvisable for bother Asbury and brother Ruff, with some others, to attend in Virginia; it is con-

sidered also as preparatory to the conference in Virginia" ("Minutes of Some Conversations between the Preachers in Connexion with the Reverend Mr. John Wesley," *Minutes of the Methodist Conferences Annually Held in America; From 1773 to 1813, Inclusive* [New York: Daniel Hitt and Thomas Ware for the Methodist Connexion, 1813], 19).

16. Ibid., 19.

17. Ibid., 25–26.

18. *Minutes of Several Conversations . . . Composing a Form of Discipline* (Philadelphia 1785). Convenient access to the first *Discipline* can be had in Jno. J. Tigert, *A Constitutional History of American Methodism*, 3d ed. (Nashville: Publishing House of the Methodist Episcopal Church, South, 1908), 534.

19. See Carol V. R. George, *Segregated Sabbaths: Richard Allen and the Rise of Independent Black Churches, 1760–1840* (New York: Oxford University Press, 1973); *The Life Experience and Gospel Labors of the Rt. Rev. Richard Allen* (2d ed., New York: Abingdon, 1960); Will B. Gravely, "African Methodisms and the Rise of Black Denominationalism," *Rethinking Methodist History*, ed. Russell E. Richey and Kenneth E. Rowe (Nashville: Kingswood Books, 1985), 111–24; and *Perspectives on American Methodism*, ed. Russell E. Richey, Kenneth E. Rowe, and Jean Miller Schmidt (Nashville: Kingswood Books, 1993), 108–26.

20. For a firsthand treatment, see Jesse Lee, *A Short History of the Methodists in the United States of America* (Baltimore: Magill and Clime, 1810), 178–80.

21. See on the latter Neil Semple, *The Lord's Dominion: The History of Canadian Methodism* (Montreal: McGill-Queen's University Press, 1996).

22. See Melvin E. Dieter, *The Holiness Revival of the Nineteenth Century* (Metuchen: Scarecrow, 1980).

23. C. C. Goen, *Broken Churches, Broken Nation: Denominational Schisms and the Coming of the Civil War* (Macon: Mercer University Press, 1985).

24. Reginald F. Hildebrand, *The Times Were Strange and Stirring: Methodist Preachers and the Crisis of Emancipation* (Durham: Duke University Press, 1995); Katharine L. Dvorak, *An African-American Exodus: The Segregation of the Southern Churches* (Brooklyn: Carlson, 1991).

25. See Clarence E. Walker, *A Rock in a Weary Land: The African Methodist Episcopal Church During the Civil War and Reconstruction* (Baton Rouge: Louisiana State University Press, 1982).

Notes to "Is There a New Role for Lay Leadership?"

1. I thank Dr. John Winn, the Rev. Leslie Aikin, and other Louisiana Conference Council on Ministries members who previewed this chapter and offered helpful suggestions.

2. Michael Barone, "The Age of the Creditors," *U.S. News & World Report* (August 15, 1994), 38.

3. Peter M. Senge, "Leading Learning Organizations: The Bold, the Powerful, and the Invisible," ed. Frances Hesselbein, Marshall Goldsmith, and Richard Beckhard, *The Leader of the Future* (San Francisco: Jossey-Bass Publishers, 1996), 54.

4. Mary Lunn, "The Model Deaconess as Superintendent of a Home," *The Message and the Deaconess Advocate* (June 19, 1895), 5; *The Deaconess Advocate* (October, 1901), 5; *The Message* (May, 1889), 1; Alice Cobb, *Yes, Lord, I'll Do It: Scarritt's Century of Service* (Nashville: Scarritt College, 1987), 20.

5. Rosemary Radford Ruether and Rosemary Skinner Keller, eds., *Women and Religion in America: A Documentary History*, Vol. III (San Francisco: Harper & Row, 1986), xx.

6. Jane M. Bancroft, *Deaconesses in Europe and Their Lessons for America* (New York: Hunt & Eaton, 1889), 9–17; Isabelle Horton, *High Adventure: Life of Lucy Rider Meyer* (New York: The Methodist Book Concern, 1928), 44–49; and Mrs. R. W. MacDonell, *Belle Harris Bennett: Her Life Work* (Nashville: Board of Missions, Methodist Episcopal Church, South, 1928), 36–47.

7. Isabelle Horton, *High Adventure: Life of Lucy Rider Meyer* (New York: The Methodist Book Concern, 1928), 187.

8. Carol Gilligan, *In a Different Voice: Psychological Theory and Women's Development* (Cambridge: Harvard University Press, 1982), 129.

9. Richard Hofstadter, *The Age of Reform* (New York: Knopf, 1955), 182–86.

10. Carolyn De Swarte Gifford, ed., "Introduction," to "The American Deaconess Movement in the Early Twentieth Century" in *Women in American Protestant Religion 1800–1930* (New York: Garland, 1987), 2.

11. Carol E. Becker, *Leading Women* (Nashville, Abingdon, 1996), 171.

12. Becker, *Leading Women*, 20; Loughlan Sofield and Donald H. Kuhn, *The Collaborative Leader: Listening to the Wisdom of God's People* (Notre Dame: Ave Maria, 1995), 36–40; Lovett H. Weems Jr., *Church Leadership* (Nashville: Abingdon, 1993), 70.

13. Jean Baker Miller, "The Development of Women's Sense of Self," in *Women's Growth in Connection: Writings from the Stone Center,* by Judith V. Jordan et al. (New York: Gilford, 1991), 16.

14. Gilligan, *In a Different Voice*, 73, 129; Jordan et al., "Introduction," *Women's Growth in Connection*, 1.

15. Janet L. Surrey, "The Self-in-Relation: A Theory of Women's Development," in Jordan et al., *Women's Growth in Connection,* 61.

16. C. William Pollard, "The Leader Who Serves," in Hesselbein, Goldsmith and Beckhard, *The Leader of the Future*, 245.

17. Mrs. R. W. MacDonell, *Belle Harris Bennett: Her Life Work* (Nashville: Board of Missions, Methodist Episcopal Church, South, 1928), 248.

18. Ibid., 282.

19. Horton, *High Adventure*, 190–97; Women's Home Mission Society, "The Early History of Deaconess Work and Training Schools for Women in American Methodism," (n.p.: The Methodist Episcopal Church, South, 1911), 6–22.

20. Horton, *High Adventure*, 182–86.

21. Ibid., 186–91.

22. Leander E. Keck, *The Church Confident* (Nashville: Abingdon, 1993), 65; Weems, *Church Leadership*, 48.

23. Loren B. Mead, *The Once and Future Church: Reinventing the Congregation for a New Mission Frontier* (New York: The Alban Institute, 1991), 8–29.

24. Ibid., 46.

25. William H. Willimon and Robert L. Wilson, *Rekindling the Flame: Strategies for a Vital United Methodism* (Nashville: Abingdon, 1987), 44.

26. See Charles M. Olsen, *Transforming Church Boards into Communities of Spiritual Leaders* (New York: The Alban Institute, 1995), for a fuller explanation of "story weaving" between the organizational stories and Scripture (the master story).

27. Mead, *The Once and Future Church*, 46–47.

28. Thomas Moore, *Care of the Soul: A Guide for Cultivating Depth and Sacredness in Everyday Life* (New York: HarperCollins, 1992), 226.

29. David J. Lawson, "Study of the Ministry," *Circuit Rider* (March 1996), 12.

30. Betty J. Letzig, "The Deaconess in the United Methodist Church," a Presentation to the Committee to Study the Ministry of the Council of Bishops, December 14, 1993, 17.

31. Mead, *The Once and Future Church*, 57.

Notes to "Clergy Leaders: Who Will They Be? How Will They Emerge? To What Will They Lead Us?"

1. *The United Methodist Book of Worship* (Nashville: The United Methodist Publishing House, 1992), no. 544.

2. Quoted in *Leadership*, vol. III, no. 2 (Kansas City: St. Paul School of Theology, January 1993), 3.

3. Ibid.

4. A brief bibliography might include Kennon L. Callahan, *Effective Church Leadership* (San Francisco: Harper and Row, 1990); Jackson W. Carroll, *As One With Authority* (Louisville: Westminster/John Knox, 1991); Peter F. Drucker, *Managing the Non-Profit Corporation* (New York: HarperCollins, 1990); Edwin H. Freedman, *Generation to Generation: Family Process in Church and Synagogue* (New York: Guilford, 1985); and Lovett H. Weems, *Church Leadership: Vision Team Culture Integrity* (Nashville: Abingdon, 1993).

5. Paragraphs 604.4 and 605.6, *The Book of Discipline of The United Methodist Church 1996* (Nashville: The United Methodist Publishing House, 1996) provide

the basis for the first question asked at the clergy (executive) session of the annual conference: "Are all the clergy members of the conference blameless in their life and official administration?"

6. Gal. 3:28, Rom. 10:12, 1 Cor. 12:13, and Col. 3:11 are among the texts that emphasize the unity and equality of all in Christ.

7. Rom. 12, 1 Cor. 12–14, and Eph. 4.

8. Freedman, *Generation to Generation,* chap. 9, 220–249.

9. Circuit riders once moved to new appointments every three months. Later, the pattern of an annual appointment developed. Until the middle of the twentieth century, four years in one place was generally deemed a maximum. Currently, five to seven years in a pastoral appointment are thought to be ideal.

10. Marjorie Procter-Smith, *In Her Own Rite: Constructing Feminist Liturgical Tradition* (Nashville: Abingdon, 1990), 34; Christine M. Smith, *Weaving the Sermon: Preaching in a Feminist Perspective* (Louisville: Westminster/John Knox, 1989), 23.

11. *The Book of Discipline 1996,* par. 433.5a.

Notes to "Leading Small Congregations: Persistence or Change?"

1. Nancy Ammerman, *Congregation and Community* (New Brunswick, N.J.: Rutgers University Press, 1997).

2. Ibid., 326.

3. Ibid., 327.

4. The term "adaptive work" is from Ronald A. Heifetz, *Leadership Without Easy Answers* (Cambridge, Mass.: Belknap, 1994), 30–35.

5. Carl Dudley, *Making the Small Church Effective* (Nashville: Abingdon, 1977), 71–74.

6. Heifetz, *Leadership Without Easy Answers,* 104–5.

7. Quoted as part of an interview by Celia Allison Hahn with Rabbi Edwin Friedman, "A Family Systems Expert Talks About Congregational Leadership," in *Alban Institute Action Information,* vol. xi, no. 3, 2.

8. Steve Burt, *Activating Leadership in the Small Church: Clergy and Laity Working Together* (Valley Forge, Pa.: Judson, 1988), 32–33.

Notes to "Has Our Theology of Ordained Ministry Changed?"

1. In January of 1997, instructors of United Methodist polity gathered in Atlanta for a meeting organized by the Division of Ordained Ministry of the Board of Higher Education and Ministry. It was intended to orient participants to all of the significant changes wrought in our church by the 1996 General Conference, but the core of the conversation concerned ordained ministry. One of the participants was Susan Henry-Crowe, the chaplain at Emory University and a member

of the judicial council. She offered the opinion that the 1996 General Conference "was the most radical conference in two hundred years in terms of ministry."

2. Thomas Edward Frank, *Polity, Practice, and the Mission of The United Methodist Church* (Nashville: Abingdon, 1997), 175, 178.

3. They could, of course, return to school, pursue a theological education, relinquish their permanent status as Associate Members (but not their deacon's orders), apply for Probationary Membership, and hope at some point after reaching age forty to be elected to full membership as well as elder's orders. Or, before the end of the year 2000, those who were Associate Members before January 1, 1997, can simply ask the Board of Ordained Ministry for a recommendation to full membership. If recommended, if they have met certain educational requirements, and if two-thirds of the full members approve it, they become full members eligible for ordination as elders, without relinquishing their Associate Membership or becoming Probationary Members. See *The Book of Discipline of The United Methodist Church 1996*, par. 365.2.

4. Normally, that limit is six years, but it may be extended for as many as three additional years if three-fourths of the full members vote to grant it. See *Discipline* (1996) par. 318.

5. The Western Pennsylvania Conference, for instance, apparently decided at its 1997 session that all candidates for ministry (even those already certified and enrolled in theological school) will be treated according to the legislation in the 1996 *Discipline*.

6. "The Constitution," Division Two, Section II, Article IV (*Discipline*, 1996, par. 15, p. 25).

7. See, for example, decisions numbered 243 and 358.

8. David L. Bartlett, *Ministry in the New Testament* (Minneapolis: Augsburg Fortress, 1993), 23.

9. Lyman Edwyn Davis, *Democratic Methodism in America: A Topical Survey of the Methodist Protestant Church* (New York: Revell, 1921), 64.

10. See pars. 310–314.

Notes to "Has United Methodist Preaching Changed?"

1. Nolan B. Harmon Jr., "Methodist Worship: Practices and Ideals," in *Methodism: A Summary of Basic Information Concerning the Methodist Church,* ed. William K. Anderson (Nashville: The Methodist Publishing House, 1946), 229.

2. There is some small comfort that Clyde Fant and William Pinson include at least seven American Methodist preachers in their vast 12-volume edition, *20 Centuries of Great Preaching: An Encyclopedia of Preaching* (Waco, Tex.: Word, 1971). Those included, as far as I can tell, are: Sam Jones, Samuel Parkes Codman, E. Stanley Jones, Halford Luccock, Ralph Sockman, and Gerald Kennedy. But this can hardly substitute for a more comprehensive and discerning history of Methodist

preaching. They had a different purpose. Besides, there would be many others included in a specialized work devoted to Methodist preaching. Examples abound among some great and legendary African American Methodists of whom they would not necessarily be aware of, e.g., Charles Albert Tindley, Alexander P. Shaw, Joshua O. Williams, John Wesley Golden, Lorenzo H. King, Harry B. Gibson Sr., W. D. Lester, W. L. Turner, George Outen, Frank L. Williams—to name but a few.

3. Pius Parsh, *The Church's Year of Grace* (Collegeville, Minn.: Liturgical Press, 1964–65), 5 vols.

4. James F. White, *Introduction to Christian Worship* (Nashville: Abingdon, 1980), 60.

5. Nolan B. Harmon Jr., "Methodist Worship: Practices and Ideals," 234.

6. White, *Introduction to Christian Worship,* 137.

Notes to "Are Extension Ministries an Opportunity to Reclaim a Wesleyan Understanding of Mission?"

1. *The Book of Discipline of The United Methodist Church 1996* (Nashville: The United Methodist Publishing House, 1996), 206.

2. *Minutes of the Methodist Conferences, Annually Held in America; From 1773 to 1813, Inclusive* (New York: Daniel Hitt and Thomas Ware, 1813), 1799, 226; 1801, 259. For the intervening year for some reason, the *Minutes* reverted to the earlier form.

3. On the evolution of the office and especially the role of John Dickins, in or around 1783 made publisher, see James P. Pilkington, *The Methodist Publishing House,* I (Nashville: Abingdon, 1968), 43–116.

4. *Minutes,* 1802, 278. For similar earlier treatment see *Minutes,* 1789, 82–83; 1790, 93; 1791, 104; 1792, 113, 116; 1793, 129; 1794, 144; 1795, 157–62; 1796, 182; 1797.

5. *Minutes,* 1803, 297, 300.

6. *Minutes,* 1804, 322.

7. *Minutes,* 1809, 459, 458, 454–55, 460.

8. *Minutes,* 1809, 459.

9. *Journals of the General Conference of the Methodist Episcopal Church,* I (1796), 17.

10. *Minutes,* 1797, 198–99.

11. "Journal of a Conference Held in New York, Tuesday 12th June 1804," (Typescript, Drew University), 22/52.

12. *Minutes of . . . the Philadelphia Conference of the Methodist Episcopal Church,* 1862, 22–26.

13. *Minutes of the . . . Philadelphia Conference of the Methodist Episcopal Church,* 1865.

14. *Minutes of the . . . Philadelphia Conference of the Methodist Episcopal Church*, 1886, 39.

15. William Phoebus, *Memoirs of the Rev. Richard Whatcoat, Late Bishop of the Methodist Episcopal Church* (New York: Joseph Allen, 1828), 30.

16. Ibid., 37.

17. Ibid., 39.

18. This is a point that I cover in *The Methodist Conference in America: A History* (Nashville: Kingswood Books, 1996). See especially chaps. 6 and 8. The assertions in the preceding and following paragraphs derive also from that volume.

19. Abel Stevens, *The Centenary of American Methodism: A Sketch of its History, Theology, Practical System, and Success*. With a statement of the plan of the Centenary Celebration of 1866 by John M'Clintock, D.D. (New York: Carlton & Porter, 1865), 180, 185–87.

20. This was the fourth of Warren's seven points. Here is the list:
1. Each is officially placed under the direct supervision of the bishops of the Methodist Episcopal Church.
2. No professor can be appointed to any chair in either of the three institutions without the concurrence of the bishops.
3. In at least two of them no professor can take his chair until, in the presence of the Board of Trust, he have signed a solemn declaration, to the effect that so long as he occupies the same he will teach nothing inconsistent with the doctrines and discipline of the Methodist Episcopal Church.
4. At the Annual Conference examination of character, every professor—save one who chances to be a layman—is each year liable to arrest if even a rumor of heterodoxy is abroad against him.
5. Each institution is inspected, and its pupils annually examined as to what they have been taught, by visitors delegated from adjacent annual conferences.
6. Each has ecclesiastical qualifications affecting the appointment of trustees.
7. Each is required to report to every General Conference.
William F. Warren, "Ministerial Education in Our Church," *Methodist Quarterly Review*, 54 (April 1872), 246–67, 260.

Note to "What Style of Leadership Will Our Bishops Embody and Model?"

1. Gordon Goodgame, address delivered to the General Council on Ministries of the UMC, November 1995. Dr. Goodgame is Executive Director, Southeastern Jurisdiction Administrative Council.

Notes to "What Is the Common Discipline for Local Churches?"

1. Unless otherwise indicated, paragraph references are to *The Book of Discipline of The United Methodist Church 1996*.

2. For further discussion of the issues raised in this essay, see Thomas Edward Frank, *Polity, Practice, and the Mission of the United Methodist Church* (Nashville: Abingdon, 1997) and "Harmonic Convergences: Constituting a Church for a New

Century," *Quarterly Review* (Spring 1998); and, with William Johnson Everett, "Constitutional Order in United Methodism and American Culture," in *Connectionalism: Ecclesiology, Mission, and Identity*, ed. Russell E. Richey et al. (Nashville: Abingdon, 1997), 41–73.

Notes to "Are the Local Church and Denominational Bureaucracy 'Twins'?"

1. Nathan Bangs, *A History of the Methodist Episcopal Church*, 4 vols. (New York: Carlton & Porter, 1860; first publ. 1838–41), II, 293–94.

2. *Journal of the General Conference of the Methodist Episcopal Church* [henceforth: *JGC-MEC*], 1852, 116.

3. *JGC-MEC*, 1864, 261, 404–5.

4. *JGC-MEC*, 1872, 295–98.

5. *JGC-MEC*, 1884, 337.

6. *JGC-MEC*, 1912, 178–82.

7. *JGC-MEC*, 1928, 152–74.

8. *JGC-MEC*, 1920. The action amended Division III, Chapter, I, Article II, par. 35 to read, "A Local Conference shall be organized in each Pastoral Charge, and be composed of such persons and have such powers as the General Conference may direct." In the floor action and debate, the original language of the legislation which had spoken of "Church conference" was so amended (1457, 424–25).

The MECS had, of course, recognized "Church Conferences" really from 1870.

9. *JGC-MEC*, 1940, 236–38.

Notes to "How Do Caucuses Contribute to Connection?"

1. *Causes, Evils and Cures of Heart and Church Divisions, Extracted from the works of Mr. Richard Baxter and Mr. Jeremiah Burroughs* [by Francis Asbury]. Philadelphia: Printed by Parry Hall and sold by John Dickins, 1792. The General Conference of 1792 added—in section XVIII of the *Book of Discipline:* "Of the Necessity of Union among ourselves"—a directive to ministers and members to read Asbury's *Causes, Evils & Cures.* The book was reissued in times of stress in the denomination until 1897. The second edition was published the year after Asbury died. For publishing record, see K. E. Rowe, *Methodist Union Catalog*, I:279.

2. J. Manning Potts, ed., *The Journal and Letters of Francis Asbury*, 3 vols. (London: Epworth; Nashville: Abingdon, 1958), "A Valedictory Address," III, 475–92, 488.

3. Emory S. Bucke, ed., *The History of American Methodism*, 3 vols. (New York and Nashville: Abingdon, 1964), I, 629.

Notes to "Is United Methodism a World Church?"

1. "Conferences: A Report on the Global Nature of The United Methodist Church, by the Council of Bishops of The United Methodist Church," The General Conference of The United Methodist Church (1996), *Daily Christian Advocate Advance Edition* (Petition No.: 21718-CO-NonDis-O$; COB), 169.

2. John Baylis and Steve Smith, eds., *The Globalization of World Politics: An Introduction to International Relations* (New York: Oxford University Press, 1997), 14–15.

3. Francis Fukuyama, "The End of History," *The National Interest* 16 (1989).

4. Marshall McLuhan, *Understanding Media* (London: Routledge and Kegan Paul, 1960).

5. Benjamin R. Barber, *Jihad vs. McWorld: How Globalism and Tribalism Are Reshaping the World* (New York: Ballentine, 1995).

6. Baylis and Smith, *Globalication of World Politics,* 15.

7. "Conferences: A Report on the Global Nature of The United Methodist Church," 169.

Notes to "Will Homosexuality Split the Church?"

1. *The Church Studies Homosexuality* (Nashville: Cokesbury, 1994).

2. See, for example, comments to this effect on 17–8, 19, 20, 21, 32, 33, 35. Incidentally, this move did not appear to be limited to either "conservatives" or "liberals" (see 20).

3. Page 25. The force of comments overshadows the brief and rather ambiguous acknowledgment that "science cannot be used to 'prove' moral conclusions" (25).

4. *The Church Studies Homosexuality,* 23.

5. Stephen E. Fowl and L. Gregory Jones provide a wonderful account of the issues surrounding the faithful reading Scripture in their book entitled, *Reading in Communion: Scripture and Ethics in Christian Life* (Grand Rapids: Eerdmans, 1991).

6. For a detailed historical survey of homosexual practices, see David Greenberg, *The Construction of Homosexuality* (Chicago: University of Chicago Press, 1988).

7. Thomas Aquinas, *Summa Theologica,* trans. Fathers of the English Dominican Province (Westminster, Md.: Christian Classics, 1981), I.92.8.

8. I owe this insight to David Matzko, "Homosexuality and the Practices of Marriage," *Modern Theology* (forthcoming).

9. The single association of Sodom with sexual sin is found in Jude 7, where lusting after the alien flesh of angels is condemned. Some translations of the Old Testament make several references to "sodomites," a term that refers to temple prostitutes.

10. Augustine, *The Good of Marriage,* chaps. 15, 22.

11. Dale Martin, "*Arsenokoitēs* and *Malakos*: Meaning and Consequences," in *Biblical Ethics and Homosexuality: Listening to Scripture*, ed. Robert L. Brawley (Louisville: Westminster/John Knox, 1996), 117–36.

12. See ibid., 124–28.

13. The three ends were explicitly articulated in the service for the solemnization of marriage John Wesley sent to America in 1784. For reasons that remain elusive, the exhortation containing the three ends was dropped in the course of the revisions initiated in 1792.

14. It is worth noting that "love" is absent. The Christian tradition has held that marriage is one context where love grows, but that love is not a precondition for marriage. Historically, the primacy of love in marriage emerged with the arrival of modernity and the elevation of third end.

15. Some have argued that homosexual couples could not fulfill the unitive end because their bodies cannot replicate the complimentarity of a heterosexual union. Such an argument falters, however, in light of what we know about gender complimentarity in the Christian tradition. Such complimentarity is not created by the parts fitting together in a particular way, but by marriage itself.

16. In *The Good of Marriage* Augustine recognizes the legitimacy of marriage in three separate cases where the union did not biologically produce children (see chaps. 3, 5, 15).

17. Augustine, *Holy Virginity*, trans. John McQuade, in *Saint Augustine: Treatises on Marriage and Other Subjects* (Washington, D.C.: The Catholic University of America Press, 1955), chap. 3. See also chaps. 10 and 12. In chap. 10 Augustine distinguishes between the blessing of nature (related to the biological act of birth) and the blessing of marriage, which he unpacks in chap. 12 where he writes, "Let spouses have their blessing, not because they beget children, but because they beget them honorably and lawfully and chastely and for society, and bring up their offspring rightly, wholesomely, and with perseverance. . . ."

18. See also Matt. 12:46–50; Mark 3:31–35; Luke 8:19–21; Matt. 3:9; Luke 3:8; John 3:3–6.

19. I mention baptism only to highlight that, for the Christian, procreation is not tied to biology. One might respond by suggesting that it is irrelevant to the issue of homosexual marriages because baptism entails all persons in the church being open to children in a general way, whereas the calling to marriage involves a more specific call, and it is this more specific call that is in question. Certainly fulfilling the baptismal commitment to nurture new Christians is not sufficient to meet the procreative end of marriage. Hence, any couple discerning the call to marriage needs to explore how their union will embody this end in a way that is qualitatively different from baptism's general call to parenting. I appeal to baptism only to show how separating procreation from biology is not novel.

20. I wish to express my gratitude to David Jenkins, William Lawrence, and D. Stephen Long for the ways in which they have encouraged me to develop this essay.

Notes to "Is There a Crisis in Church Finance?"

1. All references are to the church in the United States, with particular reference to the United Methodist Church.

2. John and Sylvia Ronsvalle, *Behind the Stained Glass Windows* (Grand Rapids: Baker, 1996), 299ff.

3. Ibid., 266f.

4. Dean R. Hoge, Charles Zech, Patrick McNamara, and Michael J. Donahue, *Money Matters: Personal Giving in American Churches* (Louisville: Westminster/John Knox, 1996), 170.

5. Ibid., 171–72.

6. Ibid., 174–76.

7. Ibid., 174.

8. Ibid., 175.

9. Diane Winston, "Campuses Are a Bellwether for Society's Religious Revival," *The Chronicle of Higher Education*, January 16, 1998, A60.

10. Ibid.

11. Penny Long Marler and C. Kirk Hadaway, "Methodists on the Margins: 'Self-Authoring' Religious Identity," in *Connectionalism: Ecclesiology, Mission, and Identity,* ed. Richey et al. (Nashville: Abingdon, 1997), 290.

12. Ibid., 291.

13. Ibid., 310.

14. Ronsvalle and Ronsvalle, *Behind the Stained Glass Windows,* 293.

15. Ibid., 294.

16. Marler and Hadaway, "Methodists on the Margins," 311.

Notes to "What Defines Clergy Compensation: Mission or Market?"

1. Harold Frederic, *The Damnation of Theron Ware* or *Illumination*, vol. III, *The Harold Frederic Edition*, Committee on Scholarly Editions, Modern Language Association of America (Lincoln: University of Nebraska Press, 1985), 164–65.

2. Ibid., 168.

3. Lyle E. Schaller, "Who Is the Client? The Clergy or the Congregation?" in *Send Me? The Itineracy in Crisis,* ed. Donald E. Messer (Nashville: Abingdon, 1991), 90.

4. Michael Nickerson, "Historical Relationships of Itineracy and Salary," *Methodist History* (vol. XXI, number 1, October 1982), 45.

5. Ibid., 50.

6. "The Episcopal Address to the 1988 General Conference," *Daily Christian Advocate* VII, 2 (April 27, 1988), 82.

7. Nickerson, "Historical Relationships," 57.

8. Donald E. Messer, "Where Do We Go From Here?" in *Send Me? The Itineracy in Crisis,* ed. Donald E. Messer (Nashville: Abingdon, 1991), 164.

9. "The Episcopal Address to the 1988 General Conference."

10. Nickerson, "Historical Relationships."

11. We are grateful to Brian Balyeat of the Fuqua School of Business at Duke University for assisting us in this part of our research.

12. *The World Almanac and Book of Facts 1995* (Mahwah, N.J.: Funk and Wagnalls), 110.

Notes to "What Difference Do the Size, Site, and Style of the Annual Conference Make?"

1. Minton Thrift, *Memoir of the Rev. Jesse Lee. With Extracts from his Journals* (New York: N. Bangs and T. Mason for the Methodist Episcopal Church, 1823), 42.

2. John Kobler, *Journal and Sermons* (Lovely Lane), 77–78.

3. William W. Sweet, ed., *The Rise of Methodism in the West,* 107–8. *Minutes of the New England Conference* (typescript), 105, 110.

4. Henry B. Ridgaway, *The Life of Edmund S. Janes* (New York: Phillips & Hunt; Cincinnati: Walden & Stowe, 1882), 171–72.

5. Peter Cartwright, *Fifty Years as a Presiding Elder,* ed. W. S. Hooper (Cincinnati: Hitchcock and Walden; New York: Nelson and Phillips, 1871), 45.

6. The author also argued that the small size would make access easier, would contribute to "the better preservation of our conservative spirit, and the promotion of the peace, unity, and effectiveness of the Church in our territory," and accorded "with the wishes of a large majority of the laity" ("Division of Baltimore Conference," *Christian Advocate and Journal,* XXXI [December 18, 1856], 201).

7. For documentation and further illustrations of these patterns, see Russell E. Richey, *The Methodist Conference in America: A History* (Nashville: Kingswood, 1996).

8. Another reason that the new size escaped extensive comment, one might need to concede, was that the conferences in older areas of Methodist labors had been growing all along, reversing what had been the earlier practice of reducing the size of conferences through division whenever they became too large.

Notes to "Connectionalism: End or New Beginning?"

1. *Minutes of Some Conversations Between the Preachers in Connexion with The Reverend Mr. John Wesley.* So read the titles (with slight variations) of the early American conference minutes. On this topic see *Connectionalism: Ecclesiology, Mission, and Identity,* United Methodism and American Culture, I (Nashville: Abingdon, 1997).

2. In a paper for our Lilly Project, Andy Langford observed: "The present denominational structure of competing powers (a quadrennial General Conference, a weak council of bishops, remote general agencies, and ideological special interest groups among others) results in no one voice speaking to or for the church."

3. "It became necessary to destroy the town in order to save it," said an American officer of Ben Tre in February 1968.

4. The United Methodist Council of Bishops, *Vital Congregations—Faithful Disciples: Vision for the Church* (Nashville: Graded Press, 1990), 10, 9, 35, 66–69, 74, 21, 75.

5. On this point see in this volume the related essay "Are the Local Church and the Denominational Bureaucracy 'Twins'?" and Thomas E. Frank, *Polity, Practice and the Mission of the United Methodist Church* (Nashville: Abingdon, 1997), 155–73.

6. See the related essay on this topic.

7. The reader may note that this catalog of antiagency queries does not include questions framed in terms of the norms of parish ministry and vital congregations.

8. Connectional Issues Study (General Council on Ministries), Annual Conference Listening Project (General Council on Finance and Administration), Agenda 21 (Association of United Methodist Theological Schools), Annual Conference Dialogue (General Board of Global Ministries), Ministry Study (Council of Bishops), Global Nature of the Church (Council of Bishops), United Methodism and American Culture (Duke/Lilly Endowment).

9. For a fuller statement of the argument of this paragraph see "The Legacy of Francis Asbury: the Teaching Office in Episcopal Methodism," in *Quarterly Review* 15 (Summer 1995), 145–74. In another work, *The Methodist Conference in America* (Nashville: Kingswood Books, 1996), I attend more fully to Methodist Protestant and Evangelical United Brethren experience. Here, for sake of brevity, I focus on Methodist Episcopacy.

10. In very recent years the council of bishops has begun to take important leadership initiatives as a council, a point we treat elsewhere in this volume.

11. For discussion of changes in denominational life see *Reimagining Denominationalism: Interpretive Essays*, ed. Robert Bruce Mullin and Russell E. Richey (New York and Oxford: Oxford University Press, 1994), and especially Richey, "Denominations and Denominationalism: An American Morphology."

12. In another chapter, we put implicit and related questions: Would we be willing to abolish jurisdictions and elect bishops once again in General Conference? Can we make our bishops once again general superintendents, thus giving them individually as well as collectively a national circuit? Could we imagine a much smaller General Conference? Can we achieve representation with much smaller gatherings?